J. L. GIDDINGS

THE ARCHEOLOGY OF CAPE DENBIGH

BROWN UNIVERSITY PRESS

PROVIDENCE, RHODE ISLAND

1964

Library of Congress Catalog Card Number: 63-10231

MADE AND PRINTED IN DENMARK
BY ANDELSBOGTRYKKERIET I ODENSE

ACKNOWLEDGMENTS

This report was made possible through the sponsorship and generosity of the Arctic Institute of North America; the University of Alaska; the University Museum and the University of Pennsylvania, aided by a contract with the Office of Naval Research, Department of the Navy (NR160–903); the Wenner-Gren Foundation for Anthropological Research; and Brown University. The Wenner-Gren Foundation, in addition to its support of field work, has granted funds to the Brown University Press as a substantial aid to publication.

The planning and most frequent discussions of the field work were, as usual since our work together at Point Hope, with Drs. Froelich Rainey and Helge Larsen. The excavations at Cape Denbigh were quite directly an outgrowth of the 1939 discovery of the Ipiutak site at Point Hope.

Many archeologists have examined the Denbigh flints while they have been in my possession, and I am indebted to each for his interest and comments. In particular, I wish to acknowledge the helpful suggestions of Drs. Hallam Movius, Carleton Coon, and Ralph Solecki at the time I first looked into the Old World affinities of the Denbigh Flint technology. Dr. David M. Hopkins has studied the geology of the site and he and other members of the United States Geological Survey working in the Arctic have maintained an interest in the Denbigh stratigraphy, keeping me informed of the changing interpretations of post-Pleistocene events in Alaska. Dr. Henry Michael, while still a graduate student at the University of Pennsylvania, offered valuable assistance with the Russian archeological literature. Other associates at the University of Pennsylvania who were often willing to discuss the Cape Denbigh collections with me, or to offer technical help, include Drs. Loren Eiseley, Linton Satterthwaite, and J. Alden Mason, Mr. A. Erik Parkinson, Miss Frances Eyman, and Miss Geraldine Bruckner. I am most grateful, also, to Dr. James B. Griffin and Mr. Roscoe H. Wilmeth, Jr., for their analysis of the Iyatayet pottery, and to Dr. Daris R. Swindler for his description of the Iyatayet cranium.

I was especially fortunate in having the following people, while they were still students, work in the field with me at Cape Denbigh: Dr. and Mrs. Wendell Oswalt, Mr. Walter Arron, Dr. Gerald M. Henderson, Dr. Alex Ricciardelli, and Dr. James W. VanStone. And to Mr. Simon John Newcomb, who had earlier worked with me in Kobuk River excavations, I am grateful for the invitation to dig the sites at Cape Denbigh.

Those at Brown University who have been of particular help with the manuscript include Mrs. Judith Huntsman, Mr. Stephen Dyson, Mr. William S. Simmons, III, Mr. Douglas D. Anderson, and, especially, Mrs. Marjorie Tomas, whose critical and editorial judgment has improved each page.

The writing and illustrating of this report, spanning fourteen years, was done in the museums of those universities where I taught anthropology and pursued arctic studies. I photographed plates of Nukleet artifacts at the University of Alaska. The Nukleet section was concluded, and the Norton and Denbigh Flint complex plates were made, at the University Museum, Philadelphia, where I benefited from the superb photography of the late Reuben Goldberg. The remaining chapters and the drawings were completed at the Haffenreffer Museum of Brown University.

The descriptions and photography have generally preceded the cataloguing of artifacts, and no attempt is made here to identify specimens with their permanent housing. In fact, the Denbigh flints are still on loan to me from the two institutions between which they will soon be divided, and I am particularly grateful to Professor Ivar Skarland and the museum staff of the University of Alaska and to Dr. Froelich Rainey, Director of the University Museum, for permission to borrow the collection until analysis was complete.

CONTENTS

LIST OF PLATES

(at end of volume)

LIST OF FIGURES

LIST OF TABLES

I. NARRATIVE

More than a decade has gone by since a deposit of remarkable artifacts of flaked stone began to turn up at Cape Denbigh on the northern Bering Sea coast of Alaska (Fig. 1). Flints like many of these had not been seen before in America. The search that followed in many places across the Arctic brought to light various crossties, and now only a few of the individual artifact forms of oldest Cape Denbigh remain without close relatives; yet, as a unique association of stone tools lying isolated in the ground below the leavings of later peoples, the Denbigh Flint complex has lost none of its significance in a study of early camp sites in the region of Bering Strait.

The discoveries at Iyatayet—the oldest site—and elsewhere about Norton Bay between 1948 and 1952 show that some people hunted there at times when the climate was somewhat warmer than now, and that others having two distinct forms of culture, the latest like that of recent Eskimos, settled there in succession after the climate had become more like it is today. The earliest of the three cultural layers at Iyatayet contains little else than objects flaked of chert, obsidian, and other flinty stones. The later levels tell more about people because they hold objects of both stone and perishable material, and because they may be compared with "pure" sites of each of their aspects of culture on other parts of both Cape Denbigh and neighboring shores.

My choice of Cape Denbigh as a digging place stemmed from earlier work. I had already established a tree-ring chronology for the general region, and I wanted to extend this as well as to trace farther the archeology of peoples who had lived at the forest edge. In a plan submitted to the Arctic Institute of North America in 1947, I proposed a search of the coasts of Norton Bay and Norton Sound for sites in which both local timber and abundant driftwood deposits would provide the material for tree-ring studies. A tree-ring chronology nearly 1000 years long which had been worked out for the Kobuk River area, some 200 miles to the north, had made possible the accurate dating of five large sites of the inland Eskimo (Giddings, 1948; 1952), and two other chronologies found in the trees of different parts of the Yukon River had proven to be applicable to much of the driftwood in Eskimo sites of late periods on St. Lawrence Island and other localities along coasts of the Bering Sea and Arctic Sea (Giddings, 1941, 1952a). The northern Bering Sea coast seemed, for these reasons, to be a place where old Eskimo sites, if they existed, could be counted on for well-preserved artifacts and buried wood suitable for dating.

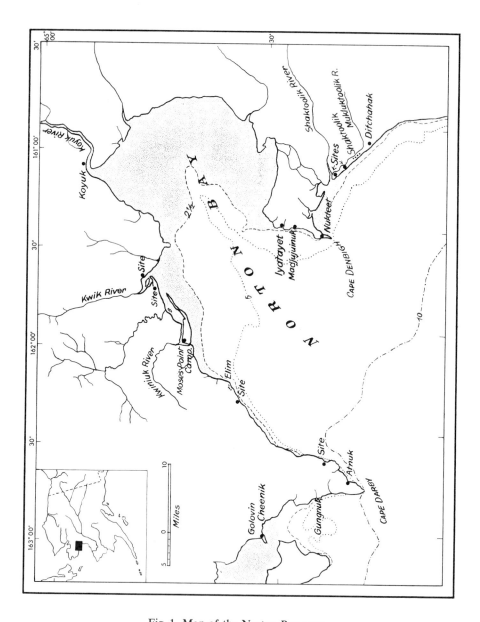

Fig. 1. Map of the Norton Bay area.

2

Field Work in 1948

Our first plans were to begin a reconnaissance at St. Michael, at the mouth of the Yukon River, and then to search for sites by travelling in a small boat around the coast to the north and west, proceeding to St. Lawrence Island later in the season. A letter received during the spring of 1948 changed these plans, however. Simon John Newcomb, who had worked with me in 1941 along the Kobuk River, wrote from Shaktoolik, where he and Mrs. Newcomb were teaching in the Alaska Native Service School, that he had visited legendary sites on nearby Cape Denbigh, finding that two of these sites were not only real, but extensive and well preserved. In a test pit in the site nearest to Shaktoolik, Newcomb had turned up potsherds with a curvilinear stamp and other objects that indicated the upper layers of the site to be as old as some of the oldest of the Kobuk River sites.

On the strength of this report I changed our plans somewhat. To save the time of a long reconnaissance for all of us, I asked Wendell Oswalt, who was already an experienced student field assistant, to examine the coast between the mouth of the Yukon River and Shaktoolik, while I went directly to Shaktoolik. Oswalt and Walter Arron, another University of Alaska student, decided that the funds needed to fly from Fairbanks to St. Michael could better be invested in building a boat and buying a motor with which to traverse the 1200 miles of the Yukon River below Fairbanks. They followed this plan, arriving at St. Michael about the middle of June.

Early in June, my wife and year-old son and I travelled by airplane to Shaktoolik. While we were guests of the Newcombs, we investigated sites around the village. One of these, an enormous site of about 100 deep house pits, called Difchahak, lay on old beach lines a mile or two south of Shaktoolik. This was a legendary site in no way associated by the local Eskimos with their own genealogical background. Two smaller sites to the north were known to have been occupied by Shaktoolik people in fairly recent times.

On the first clear, calm day, Lewis Nakarak, a Malemiut-speaking Eskimo, took Newcomb and me in his boat the fifteen miles to Cape Denbigh (Fig. 2). The large site on the southeast side of the Cape from which Newcomb had procured his samples is called Nukleet. This proved to be a rounded slope from 40 to 70 feet above sea level, fronted by steep cliffs. The mound is covered by a heavy growth of bunch grass, in contrast to surrounding thickets of alder and poplar. Only a few depressions seemed to mark former house locations, but test cuts down to the top of frost showed that the ground was rich in pottery and organic leavings of the last occupants. The contents of the frozen ground could be determined only by slowly thawing the mound.

Investigation of the other site took us seven miles to the northwest side

Fig. 2. Cape Denbigh from the north.

of the Cape, past cliffs 300 feet high. The narrow ledges of these cliffs were crowded with swarms of nesting birds—murres, puffins, cormorants, and gulls. Small beaches appeared at intervals, but we saw no suitable place for a village to be built until we came to the little bay called Iyatayet. In contrast to that of Nukleet, this site boasted a small but permanent stream. The steep slopes on both sides of the mouth of the stream were covered by the coat of bunch grass which often marks long-abandoned habitation sites. Elsewhere the slopes held a low jungle of alder and willow.

Nakarak told again the legends that had long been offered in explanation of the two sites on Cape Denbigh. They were new to me, although Newcomb had previously written out the various episodes of each tale. Briefly, the legend of Nukleet Village concerns the daughter of the "chief" and her singular child. By the time he was one year old, the boy had grown so big that one day he ate his mother, an act that led people to abandon the village forever. The other legend, of Iyatayet, deals with incidents in the rise to power of a dwarf not more than two feet tall, who held together two rival factions of his people. Iyatayet also fell into ruins when its people moved away to the north. We had reason to remember these stories later.

Sampling Iyatayet was difficult this early in the season. The solid tussocks of bunch grass, still frozen at the center, had not yet begun to turn green. In tests at the grass roots, however, we saw chips of flint. We had found none of these at Nukleet. This fact was also to become more significant later in the summer.

Nukleet appeared to be the more promising site upon which to spend

4

Fig. 3. Camp on the beach at the foot of Nukleet Site.

the time required for the slow thaw of a planned excavation. Our camp, finally established on the narrow, rocky beach below the site, resembled a village (Fig. 3). Four Eskimo helpers brought their families, and tents blossomed on every flat part of the beach above high tide line. The men built fish racks. Whitefish were plentiful and the season for salmon was not far away. Nukleet is a good sealing place, and the small white whales, or beluga, often forage just off the point. Before long, seal meat and whale skin hung drying on the racks. The Eskimo women showed my wife where to find various edible wild plants—rhubarb and onions, sour greens, and a number of leaves and herbs that substitute well for spinach and lettuce. Berries ripened later in the summer.

We laid out four test areas, two of them forming a six-foot-wide trench extending 180 feet from the upper edge of the mound to the cliff edge. Once stripped and cleaned to the top of frost, these cuts were taken down at the rate of daily thaw. The thaw, depending upon the sunshine and the nature of the deposit, varied from two to six inches a day.

By mid-July we knew a great deal about the people whose houses and refuse heaps made up Nukleet. Their houses had been rectangular and partly subterranean, with long entrance tunnels. The people had been primarily sealers and fishers, in the Eskimo tradition; yet, like other coast-dwelling Eskimos, they had stressed certain inland practices. The counts of animal bones in refuse heaps showed that they had hunted caribou extensively. They had also used birch bark vessels and beaver tooth knives.

Their pottery was coarse-tempered, thick, gray ware. The preservation of

5

organic materials in this permanently frozen deposit was such that house timbers, antler objects, wooden arrow shafts, bone needles, grass mats, and even bits of skin clothing came out looking quite as fresh as though they had been discarded only a few days before. A miniature animal head carved in ivory still had bits of quill decoration in small bored holes. Surprisingly, however, we did not find at Nukleet any of the flint chips like those in the tests at Iyatayet.

When we reached a maximum depth of seven feet in one spot and began to scrape bedrock in others, it became obvious that the flint at Iyatayet represented some development that we had not found at Nukleet. Consequently, we moved camp temporarily around Cape Denbigh to the more remote site and began a series of test cuts. The Eskimos were not averse to a move since the puffin and murre eggs that had been in the cliffs were now hatched and that source of food depleted. My wife in particular was delighted with the stream of clear water in camp, as she had tired of carrying buckets of drinking and laundry water down from tundra pools on top of the cliff at Nukleet. The Eskimo women spent most of their time at the new site gathering blueberries from the slopes, for each family wanted to fill at least one barrel for use during the coming winter.

The upper few feet of the deposits at Iyatayet were obviously related to those in which we had been digging at Nukleet. Scattered throughout these levels, on the other hand, were chips and artifacts of flinty materials such as we had not encountered at the first site. Some of the blades, points, and scrapers were of kinds known previously only from the Ipiutak site at Point Hope, and a few were of shapes that we had not seen before. These were diagonally flaked on both faces with almost microscopic precision. The immediate explanation of these miniature blades was offered by Naka-rak and his friend Sokpilak, who were of the opinion that they had been made by the legendary dwarf chief.

A less romantic explanation offered itself when we found that beneath the midden deposit containing organic material lay thawed clays enclosing mainly objects of stone. Apparently the more recent occupants of this dwelling site had dug their houses down into an older layer of culture, mixing the earlier artifacts into the upper layers. This culture level in the thawed clays had in it artifacts resembling those of the Point Hope Ipiutak culture. These included flints and other stone objects known from the more northerly site, but also new types, among which were a thin, hard, check-stamped form of pottery and triangular stone lamps. The finding of an Ipiutak-like site in stratigraphy in this area was cause for excitement, and we dug late into dusk each day as the August sunlight grew briefer and the big autumn storms threatened the high beach on which we camped.

Then, at the end of the season, we made an even more interesting disclosure. Below the Ipiutak-related levels we exposed sterile soil that held no

6

trace of occupation and, under that, a thin layer of pebbles on top of bedrock, revealing the source of the diagonal flaking and containing what appeared to be the earliest traces of man yet located on the Alaskan coast.

With this discovery, we decided to concentrate on the Cape Denbigh sites and forego our original plans for a wider reconnaissance. Fortunately, Oswalt and Arron had completed their survey of the coast, locating several sites that promised well for future work. When they arrived at Cape Denbigh in mid-July, I asked them to continue on to St. Lawrence Island to collect archeological timbers for dating. It is enough to say here that Oswalt and Arron secured passage to Nome, and then to St. Lawrence Island, and made valuable collections.

Field Work in 1949

A second grant from the Arctic Institute of North America made possible the continuation of work at Cape Denbigh in 1949. We knew by the end of the 1948 field season that the triple-stratum site of Iyatayet could unseal some previously unknown aspects of Alaskan archeology. Far to the south, in the Bristol Bay region, Helge Larsen's party had uncovered during the same summer three sites that related both to the Point Hope Ipiutak culture and to the middle Iyatayet horizon (Larsen, 1950). Our plans, therefore, concerned mainly the oldest find at Cape Denbigh. In order to secure additional information about the more recent periods, however, and to collect as much wood as possible for tree-ring dating, we planned to excavate both at Iyatayet, where wood in the latest levels was relatively scarce, and at Nukleet, where permanent frost in the ground offered excellent preservation of organic materials. Wendell Oswalt and his wife, Helen, camped at Nukleet and excavated a large, rectangular area adjoining the 1948 test cut.

Early in June I set up camp at Iyatayet with two Eskimo families. The season, like the latter half of the 1948 one, was wet and cold. During the period between mid-June and the end of August, we had only a few pleasant days. Protracted storms of wind and monotonous drizzle prevailed. The slowly thawing midden deposits often became flowing mud. Drying and storing organic materials became a major problem, and it was often hard to trace stratigraphy in the ground.

The greatest excavation problem at Iyatayet was avoiding the thick deposits of the later Eskimo materials (we were obtaining enough of these at Nukleet) while searching out relatively shallow areas where both the early Eskimo materials and the bottom level were undisturbed. This was solved by taking down test rectangles to bedrock at intervals along the site and expanding the favorable tests in directions where continuity was indicated. The Eskimos were employed in stripping sod and then in removing the late-period deposits in six-inch levels under my close supervision. I was careful to take over all excavations when they approached the sterile layer below which normally lay the "microlithic" level. By the end of the summer we had uncovered 400 square feet of the oldest level in place, in addition to nearly as much more footage of the site in which this level had been disturbed either by early erosion or by the activities of later occupants of the site. If there had been any doubt at the end of 1948 that the oldest cultural leavings were ancient, we knew now that a long time span must have separated the site components. The finding of a fluted point and many flint forms like those of both the Old World pre-Neolithic periods and the American "early man" sites showed us that Iyatayet had far-reaching significance.

During the same season, Helge Larsen, representing the University of Alaska and the National Museum of Denmark, was searching for sites of the Ipiutak culture along the north coast of Seward Peninsula. He and his party left the coast late in the season to investigate a series of limestone caves at Trail Creek, and found there stratified deposits that included both Ipiutak flints and, at lower levels, a few microlithic objects like some of those of the Denbigh Flint complex. At the end of this field season, we were all vitally interested in coordinating the search in order to piece together as much as possible of the prehistory of Alaska. Froelich Rainey, Director of the University Museum at Philadelphia, and Larsen that fall planned the finances and cooperative effort that would make it possible for the three of us to work in the field together for the first time since 1939.

Field Work in 1950

The Bering Strait Expedition of 1950 was financed by the Wenner-Gren Foundation for Anthropological Research, the University of Alaska, the Danish National Museum, and the University of Pennsylvania. My part of this cooperative effort was mainly to continue the work in the Norton Bay region.

While Larsen's party concentrated on an Ipiutak site at Deering and the Trail Creek caves, I began a reconnaissance of the Cape Darby Peninsula with Gerald M. Henderson and James W. VanStone, both of the University of Pennsylvania, and an Eskimo helper. Froelich Rainey spent a few days with us and then travelled westward to explore the Alaskan side of Bering Strait.

Cape Darby is the extension of land that forms the western side of Norton Bay, as Cape Denbigh forms the eastern. Here we located several archeological sites, but only one containing flints such as we had come to associate with the earlier cultures of the region. This site lies on the western side of Cape Darby. The Eskimos call the place Gungnuk, a name that we applied to the site. Surface finds and a single excavated house indicate Gungnuk to be a pure site of the Norton culture (as we designate the Ipiutak-related "middle" levels at Iyatayet). The artifacts from Gungnuk are thus valuable crossties with Norton culture deposits at Iyatayet, where stratigraphy in the later levels is often difficult.

After three weeks on Cape Darby, we crossed over to Cape Denbigh, where Henderson, VanStone, two Eskimo families, and I worked at Iyatayet for the remainder of the summer. Our accomplishments there were in part the uncovering of about 300 square feet of the Denbigh Flint complex in place, the excavation of a Norton culture house pit, and further work in the parts of the site where the earliest horizon had been disturbed by later occupants. The outstanding new contribution, however, was the tracing of geological aspects of the earlier levels. Fossil solifluction lobes were brought to light, along with buried soil profiles and other evidences of climatic change marked by separate occupations. We were fortunate in receiving a visit from David M. Hopkins, of the Alaska Terrain and Permafrost Section of the U. S. Geological Survey, at a time when these exposures were in progress. Hopkins's conclusions made possible a close correlation of archeologic and geologic events (Hopkins and Giddings, 1953).

A second site of Norton culture was discovered in the course of the summer only a few miles from Iyatayet. This site, which we call Madjujuinuk, after the local place name, was one of those rare ones located by deduction in the absence of outward signs that people had ever lived there. The site lies nearly 100 feet above sea level, at the top of the steep, sea-cut face of the northeastern side of Cape Denbigh. We decided to sink test holes under the dense alders on top of this bank because there appeared to be no other place for people to build near both a good seal-hunting point and a small stream. This site, together with Gungnuk, on Cape Darby, offers the means of narrowing down the range of artifacts that may be classed in Norton culture at Iyatayet.

Field Work in 1952

A fourth visit to Iyatayet was made after a reconnaissance of the Beaufort Sea coast in 1952 (Giddings, 1957a).[1] With Alex Ricciardelli, of the Uni-

[1] Aided by a contract between the Office of Naval Research, Department of the Navy, and the University of Pennsylvania (NR 160–903).

versity of Pennsylvania, I returned to Cape Denbigh to search for charcoal that might be used in dating the Denbigh Flint complex. Charred areas were again located, as in previous summers, and this time we carefully scraped up the mud of the old layer with its entire content of carbon flecks, hoping that it could be processed for dating (Giddings, 1955).

At the end of this fourth season we felt prepared to set forth in considerable detail and perspective three cultural horizons that had been established at widely separate times in the Norton Bay region.

II. NUKLEET

The Shaktoolik River Eskimos have a place name, which we call "Nukleet," to designate either the hilly portion of Cape Denbigh or the legendary village site on the southeast side of the Cape (Fig. 1). This dual application of the name perhaps accounts for Hrdlička's placement on his map (Hrdlička, 1930, p. 198) of a reported site called "Nuklit ... on the eastern shore of Norton Sound, immediately behind Cape Denbigh" (*Ibid.*, p. 199). The Shaktoolik people insist that they know of only one old village site bearing the name in question, and that this one is the subject of present consideration. The site was probably completely abandoned by the time of Cook's visit in 1778, for dwellings that he saw at this particular locality were "seated close to the beach" (Cook and King, 1784, vol. 2, p. 484), rather than high on a bluff. Henry B. Collins appears to have been the first anthropologist to recognize the Nukleet mound as an archeological site of importance.[1] Collins's party visited the site in 1929 and made such test excavations as time and ground frost would permit (Collins, 1930, p. 154). No further digging seems to have been done at the site until the time of our excavations.

Nukleet site is an accumulation of house and midden deposits sprawling over the top and sides of a rounded slope leading to a 40-foot limestone bluff at the sea edge (Fig. 4). These deposits reach a depth of seven feet near the edge of the bluff and tend to thin out laterally and uphill. The "mound" that seems to represent the most concentrated occupation of the site is thus some 200 feet in diameter, but tests show that a cultural deposit of some significance, and probably including house floors, extends at least 100 feet beyond the central area on either side.

Huge boulders stand above normal sea level directly in front of the site, at the base of the cliff, obscuring any low tide beach continuity. Eastward of this point, however, a narrow, rocky beach extends about the shores of a small bay. This beach (Fig. 3) is a favorite camping place for Shaktoolik Eskimos during the times of spring sealing, herring fishing, greens gathering, and egg hunting. No living person recalls having camped at the top of the bluff on the old village site, but the older people state that about a half-

---

[1] "Norton Sound, though in some ways less promising that the region to the south, should be investigated to determine the effects—physical, cultural, and linguistic—of the relatively recent intrusion of the Malemiut, an Eskimo group from the north. The only archeological site of any size in the Norton Bay area that I know of is one at Cape Denbigh, though others doubtless exist." (H. B. Collins, quoted from Flint, 1946, p. 51).

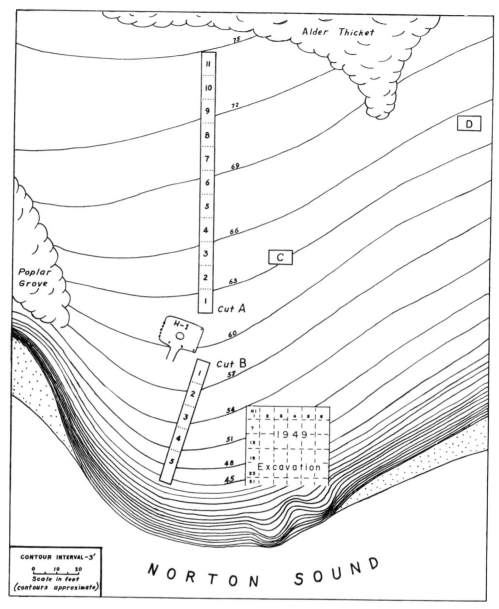

Fig. 4. Sketch map of Nukleet Site.

century ago one or two families built winter houses above the beach some-where in the general area of the small bay. At least two grass-marked pits of houses, apparently recent, were located about a mile east of Nu-kleet, and it seems likely that these are the building sites dimly remembered.

Nukleet itself does not seem to have been a permanent building site during the last two or three centuries. Only one house pit could be clearly discerned. This house, as it turned out, was built before European trade goods were available in quantity, and probably before the time of exten-sive dog traction. We found no evidence in even the uppermost artifacts at Nukleet of a close relationship with a mid-nineteenth-century site that I had test-excavated in 1940 at the mouth of the Koyuk River on Norton Bay, although a few objects found in the sod layer seem to have been dropped by temporary visitors to the site since the time of its last permanent occupation.

The entire site is covered with rather permanent vegetation. Over the deeper middens—that is, the center and sides of the rounded ridge—lies a mat of tough sod out of which grow tall grass and local tangles of berry bushes, willows, and low alders. The grass does not form large tussocks, as it does at Iyatayet. Encroaching on the uphill and eastern margins of the site are thickets of alder that become more continuous and dense on the cliff slope and northeastward up the hillsides. A small stand of spruce, in-cluding a few trees over two hundred years old, begins about 1000 feet from the site, on the north hillside above the little bay. On the western mar-gin of the mound is a grove of sturdy poplars, flanked on the uphill side by alders. Cultural deposits under the roots of the poplars show that this grove did not exist at the time of the last occupation of the site. Other than the tall grass, however, the present plant cover shows no more than a chance relationship to the organic soil contents of the midden.

Nukleet has no permanent summertime supply of drinking water. Water must be transported from tundra pools, or shallow "wells," far up the hill-side. This handicap is offset by many advantages, however. From the van-tage ground of the mound, one can see white whales and seals almost as easily when they are moving under the surface of a calm sea as when they are surfaced. Sea birds favor the protected bay at the foot of the cliff, and the sea mammals return to the deep water just off the rocky point with alacrity after each time that they are frightened away. Fish nets that are set close to the bank catch salmon in quantity during the seasonal runs, and herring habitually pass by in enormous schools. Rock cod and other fish can be caught with hook and line in the deep water. The various vegetable foods that make up an important part of the diet of Norton Bay peoples can be obtained in plenty along the protected slopes.

Another advantage of the site lies in the view it affords of many miles of sea and land. On a clear day, one can make out the houses of Shaktoolik, twelve miles across the bay, observe the boats of any travellers along this part of the coast and scan many square miles of the flat neck of Cape Denbigh, where caribou formerly roamed in herds.

When pressed for their reasons for avoiding the Nukleet mound as a camping place, the Eskimos explained that they like to be near their boats and nearer to a supply of driftwood. However, we detected an anxious attitude towards the site based on the legendary death and destruction that had taken place there. When the Oswalts decided to override the advice of their Eskimo companions in 1949 and place their tent on the site itself, they noted that within a few days the comments of the Eskimos became quickly more speculative than critical. Soon the entire camp was established happily on the mound, despite the need to carry driftwood for fuel up the difficult paths from the beach.

Excavations, 1948

The Nukleet site, upon our arrival in mid-June of 1948, was still brown with the dead grass of the previous season. The grass-covered, mound-like portion of this promontory that juts out into Norton Sound differed in appearance so sharply from the remainder of the alder- or moss-covered areas of the south side of Cape Denbigh that we could recognize it as an archeological site from several miles away, while crossing the water from Shaktoolik. The open, grassy area apparently encompasses the more abundant deposits of former residents of Nukleet. However, tests indicated that archeological materials are to be found in the ground at some distance from this central area, and alder and poplar growth is by no means a boundary marker to old occupied areas.

The choice of areas to be sampled, as shown in Fig. 4, was determined largely by the highest points of the mound along a low ridge of the promontory. In the absence of any indication other than topography as to where the thicker and older parts of the site were to be found, it seemed to us that we should have the best chance of sampling the whole site by trenching along the relatively dry and well-drained ridge.

Cut A was laid out as a series of eleven 6 by 10 foot sections, determining a trench 110 feet long. One of only two obvious house pits to be identified from the surface lay partly in line with the lower end of the trench. Allowing a space for this pit (House 1), we laid out Cut B at a slight angle to the line of Cut A. This angling of Cut B was partly to avoid a disturbed area near the brow of the hill where native curio hunters had possibly continued from time to time the test begun by Collins (1930, p. 154) on his brief visit to the site in 1929. Cut B was originally meant to include only four sections,

14

but drainage requirements caused us later to add a fifth section. This gave us a test trench 160 feet long, extending from the edge of the alders on the northwest to the steep brow of the promontory, broken only by the space left for the House 1 excavation. A narrow drainage ditch was later cut from Section 1 of Cut A into the back of the House 1 excavation to allow run-off through the tunnel of House 1.

Cuts C and D (Fig. 4) were laid out in further exploration of the site to the north. Cut C turned out largely a failure. Without provision for drainage, this pit collected water and was explored only to the three-foot level. Cut D was drier, but proved to be relatively shallow, containing a few artifacts in a poor state of preservation down to bedrock at a depth of about three feet.

The removal of sod was possible immediately, as frost had already dropped to the base of this dense mat of grass roots and peaty matter, a depth of six to ten inches. The sod was most easily rolled, like a carpet, by two or three men working together from shovel-cut margins. This sod was found to contain practically no artifacts, but to have grown immediately upon ground trodden by the last occupants of the site. The sod lifted naturally from this level, leaving stone artifacts and broken pottery exposed beneath it. Except at the upper end of Cut A, the ground was solidly frozen from the base of sod to the bottom of the cultural deposit. Perennially frozen ground seems to underlie most of the southeastern slopes of Cape Denbigh.

Once exposed, the dark soil and midden beneath the sod thawed rapidly enough to allow us to remove materials in six-inch levels without delay. We worked from section to section during a working day, taking out artifacts from the few inches of thaw, and commencing again the following morning to remove those from the previous night's thaw. During the first two weeks of our stay at Nukleet the sky remained clear and the air warm, and we made rapid progress. After this encouragement, however, storms blew in, and during the remainder of the summer, both at Nukleet and at Iyatayet, rain fell almost daily in the slow, driving drizzle characteristic of this region. Work suffered greatly from the rain. The trenches became mud-holes, determination of stratigraphy became extremely difficult, the sides of trenches tended to slough, and drainage remained a major problem.

By mid-July, in spite of the rains, we had completed work on Cut A and had finished all of Cut B except for a frozen area at the base of Sections 4 and 5. The 4000 artifacts and more than 2000 potsherds removed from the Nukleet tests of 1948 are the materials upon which is based the presentation of Nukleet culture in the following pages.

Stratigraphy of Cut A (Fig. 5)

The contents of Cut A, beneath the sod, consisted of a dark loam liberally imbedded with cultural materials in various stages of preservation (Fig. 6). Wood comprised a large part of the bulk of the deposit. Most of this had been driftwood—originally logs of cottonwood, spruce, birch, and poplar. Tree-ring analysis shows us that little of the spruce wood, at any rate, could have grown in the immediate vicinity. The driftwood had been used in the building of various structures, for firewood, and for the manufacture of implements and utensils. Chips and splinters of wood and local deposits of shavings indicated that the mound must have bulked larger at one time, until extensive decay set in. Most of the wood was badly decayed, especially near the surface, where little organic material of any kind had withstood the annual thaws of two or three centuries. The soundest logs lay deepest in the frozen ground, where the annual thaws of present times cannot penetrate even at the height of the summer season.

The best preservation lay in a few lenses where rubbish had apparently accumulated for some time in one place—as in an old house pit. Most of

Fig. 6. Nukleet Cut A
partly excavated.

the soil of Cut A retained a strong odor of decaying matter. The bottom of the cultural deposit was clearly marked by a dense, reddish clay immediately overlying a crumbly bedrock. In some parts of the cut, this soil appeared to have been walked on as an original surface, but a great deal of the bottom had been altered from time to time by the digging of house-builders.

When the rains began, the part of the cut that contained the least organic matter turned into flowing mud. One of our greatest difficulties lay in channelling the flow so that the downhill portions of the cut would not be silted in by sediments from above.

The more meaningful features of Cut A are shown in the section plans and profile of Fig. 5. Our interpretation of these features is as follows:

The base of Section 10 had formed a more or less level floor, the rear of which had been dug two feet into the clay and eroding bedrock. It is possible that Cut A ran through the house area at about center. In this case, the two steps in Sections 9 and 10 would have been the tunnel entrance to the house, and the posts and fallen timbers in Sections 8 and 9 may have been part of the tunnel construction. However, the latter appear to represent an edge of some construction later in age than the proposed house floor. The row of posts shown in Section 8 and the flooring of split planks over-lapping Sections 6 and 7 appear to have been the parts of a separate house or houses. If the flooring were to be considered as that of a tunnel, this might be seen as the central portion of a house facing downhill. However, we found no floor indications such as would definitely join the two features. The relation of the parallel rows of sturdy posts slanting across Section 5 to the features of the uphill sections is also unclear, but all of these could be the manifestations of a single, large house. The portion of Cut A extending from the middle of Section 5 to the lower end of Section 3 contained no large construction, although a few posts had been driven into the ground, failing to reach the lower levels.

The logs shown in the lower portion of Cut A are definitely those of a house structure. Cut A extends through the center of this house ruin, encompassing the upper end of the tunnel. The house concerned had been excavated to eroded bedrock during a middle period of the occupation of Nukleet. A tunnel (Fig. 7), partly floored with split planks and lined with poles held in place by stakes which were driftwood logs with the roots left on, led to a step-up over a retaining log and a fairly level earth-floored inner room. Both the tunnel floor and the house floor contained a matting of debris—mainly shavings and chips and the contained artifacts. No fireplace was found. A deposit of ash on the east side of the inner end of the tunnel probably is intrusive. The rear wall had been formed of heavy spruce logs laid horizontally. Three of these logs had been laboriously adz-grooved above to receive the log on top (Fig. 5, Sec. 3). The other logs that had probably been part of the roof construction also showed this feature. Preservation about the floors of this house was exceptionally good because of an insulating layer of rubbish which lay above. The house had probably fallen into ruins, leaving a depression into which generations of later occupants of the mound had discarded their rubbish. Stratigraphy in this part of Cut A was clear-cut, a comparable situation appearing only in the lower part of Cut B. However, the house in question, though shown by cultural materials lying on its floor and above to have been relatively early, nevertheless contained the kinds of artifacts and pottery that relate to an intermediate, rather than to the earliest, occupation of the site.

In summary, Cut A gives us a picture of the accumulations from a series of time periods when houses were built over a wide section of the site, but it does not include in recognizable form the remains of the early occupation of the site.

House 1

The depression in which lay remains of House 1 (Fig. 4) promised to relate to the latest period of occupation of Nukleet, if only because other surface

Fig. 7. Nukleet Cut A. Detail showing tunnel floor of Sections 1 and 2.

18

indications of houses were nearly lacking. This depression was about two feet deep at center, and, though oval in shape, it led downhill into a narrow and shallower depression that marked the position of a tunnel. These surface signs indicated to us the approximate location of the house walls and guided our sod-stripping. Even though late in relation to Nukleet as a whole, this house was very poorly preserved, and its floor contained so little solid organic material that we were unable to separate all of the artifacts which belonged to the house from the materials below. While at first we were able to remove the cultural materials from their loamy soil with some accuracy because of frost in the ground, the thaw quickly extended, leaving a working surface of quaking mud.

A fireplace appeared near the center of the house directly beneath sod, and an old earth floor could be traced out from the edges of this deposit of ash and small stones towards the walls. The ash, now a yellow mud, indicated that fires had been built over a long period of time. Wall uprights, though poorly preserved, gave the position of each of the walls, and two corner roof support posts and a pair of posts at the inner margin of the tunnel, just forward of wall construction, indicated this house to have been of the "four-post center" construction characteristic of the later Kobuk River periods (Giddings, 1952, pp. 32–4).

Although the floor of House 1 could not be determined so clearly as to separate the later materials from the earlier with certainty, we kept separate account of the artifacts recovered from the two feet of muddy deposit that overlay clay bottom. Most of this material correlates with that from the older parts of Cut B.

Stratigraphy of Cut B (Fig. 8)

The oldest materials isolated at Nukleet lay in a well-preserved midden overlapping the brow of the promontory in Cut B. Unlike the muddy deposit that characterized all but a few pockets of Cut A, this cut contained mainly the organic deposits of solidly frozen rubbish heaps. The middle and lower levels of this midden seemed not to have been thawed for hundreds of years. Wood, bones, artifacts of all kinds, and even bits of skin were removed from this area looking as though they had been discarded only recently. Many of them quickly darkened or cracked, however, upon exposure to the air.

The profile of Cut B, in Fig. 8, shows that clear-cut stratification occurred only in the lower four sections. Section 1 contained only the materials like those of Cut A. This section appeared to have been dug to bottom clay by some house-builders of the middle period of occupation at Nukleet, as shown by a row of posts (see the plan panels of Fig. 8). An old earth floor, with its deposits of charcoal-blackened earth and artifacts, lay at the bottom to

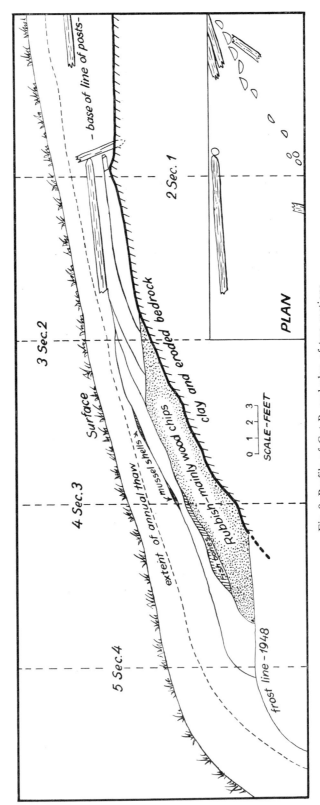

Fig. 8. Profile of Cut B, and plan of two sections.

PLAN

base of line of posts

2 Sec. 1

3 Sec. 2

4 Sec. 3

5 Sec. 4

Surface

extent of annual thaw

mussel shells

Fish bones

Rubbish—mainly wood chips

clay and eroded bedrock

frost line - 1948

SCALE-FEET
0 1 2 3

20

the east, and to the west of the posts was a nearly sterile deposit of rotten logs—perhaps part of a house or tunnel wall earlier than the row of posts. Over the well-preserved part of this section lay materials related to those of the upper part of most of Cut A.

The remainder of Cut B contained the usual amount of most recent materials near the sod layer. Below this was a relatively thin deposit of loam-enclosed artifacts and pottery like that of the lower sections of Cut A and Section 1 of Cut B. Under this, and marked off by a thin, but traceable, layer of mussel shells (center of profile, Fig. 8), lay the clean, hard-packed midden (Fig. 9) that outlined for us the earlier occupation of Nukleet.

This solid midden contained lenses and streaks of shells and fish bones at intervals that aided in separating related areas. This midden, in its later aspects, had been built up by successive deposits downhill. All of the shell- and fish-marked midden lay, in turn, over a rich deposit of wood-chips, bones, and artifacts. We separated artifacts by vertical depth below original surface, in six-inch levels, though notes were made of significant relations to shell lines and the wood-chip bottom deposit.

Fig. 9. Lower midden exposed in Cut B. Protruding sticks and bones, still frozen in the walls, made a sheer face impossible.

21

As to the origin of the oldest midden in Cut B, as much as seven feet below surface, we have no direct indication. Apparently the house sites, or camp sites, from which these deposits were derived had been out of range of our test cuts, or had been obliterated higher on the slope by later activity and construction. There seems little doubt, however, that the earliest occupation of the site was limited to the cliff edge. Otherwise, we should have found more of the oldest materials farther up the slope, within Cut A. It seems probable that at the time of the first occupation alder thickets had discouraged movements within most of the area now covered by grass.

The only traces of any cultural materials earlier than the wood-chip layer of Cut B were a number of chert chips and a side blade of chert, similar to those of Norton culture, on top of clay at the southwest corner of House 1.

As will be shown later, the abundant artifacts recovered from the stratified lower layers of Cut B are readily distinguishable in the main from those of the upper levels of Cut B, and from all of Cut A. Some of the materials from the bottom of the House 1 excavation also relate to the earlier period. Bow and arrowhead styles clearly show this basic distinction, and generally the cross-relationship between Nukleet and the earlier St. Lawrence Island cultures is seen in artifacts of the lower midden of Cut B.

Excavations, 1949

At the end of the 1948 season the Nukleet site still held some questions. For one thing, the lower end of Cut B had not been completed where it was possible that the oldest cultural material lay upon the brow of the cliff. I asked Wendell Oswalt to undertake the further excavations at the site in 1949, especially to try to learn the extent of the midden deposits left by the first occupants of the site. Rather than to work long test trenches back into the obviously more recent deposits of the higher parts of the once occupied slope, we decided to lay out a square region 36 feet to the side, east of Cut B, and extending across the brow of the cliff. Had the projected area been completed, this would have given a total of 36 six-foot squares, an over-ambitious goal for the short thawing season and small crew.

The whole area was designated by the letters NI, and the squares were numbered from uphill west to east, as is shown in Fig. 13. By the end of the season, 19 of the uppermost squares had been brought successfully to bedrock. Excavation progressed in six-inch levels, with depth to clay bottom ranging from six to six-and-a-half feet. Some further work was done in the lower part of Cut B, where frost had halted work in 1948, as well as along the west wall of House 1. By the end of the season, the site had yielded

22

2,410 artifacts and 2,395 potsherds. Upon examining these materials in the laboratory, we found some minor variations from the specimens collected during the previous year, but almost nothing to change the conclusions obtained from the test cuts. It was clear that all of the materials from the NI Cut, as far as completed, fitted into the time period of the middle and upper deposit of the previous season—that is, mainly corresponding to the materials in Cut A and the upper part of Cut B. Presumably the older midden, to correspond with the older sections of Cut B, is yet to be found under the unexcavated sections of the NI mapped area.

Although the Nukleet culture is defined in the following sections almost exclusively from the 1948 collections, the architectural structures of Cut NI are illustrated here in Figs. 10 to 16. Figures 10 and 11 show large, heavy stones directly under the sod in Section 4, and down to 24 inches in Sections 22–24. These stones, brought to the site late in its period of occupation, are not obviously related to buildings.

In Sections 1 and 2, at a depth of 18–24 inches (Fig. 12, left), was found the base of some kind of oval structure with grass lying on its top in the midst of a large deposit of ash. Directly beneath this feature, as shown in Fig. 12, middle, emerged, at a depth of 30–36 inches, the end of a tunnel outlined by upright posts. At a similar depth, and farther down the slope, were found thick deposits of fish bones from three to eight inches thick (Fig. 12, right).

The part of another tunnel, built during the last occupation of the site, ran diagonally across the mapped area shown in Fig. 13. At a maximum depth of only 32 inches these post bases disappeared, however, showing that the tunnel floor had been less deeply excavated. At a greater depth appeared the back wall of what seemed to be a small house (Fig. 14). The logs had been thoroughly burnt, and only about four inches of the bases of these logs stood upright. Within this line of upright posts lay some six inches of ash deposit, presumably the ash of a burned structure. The row of uprights similar to those of house walls appearing in the lower half of the same figure do not comprise an identifiable part of the same house.

The features shown in Fig. 15, at a depth of 48–54 inches in the lower part of the mapped area, probably make up the parts of another house structure. Grass fibers lay directly on top of the split logs showing in Section 26. Part of another house seems to have been represented in Fig. 16. The lower features were not thawed by the end of the season. The long, wooden tray indicated in the diagram may have lain near the back wall of a house outlined by the parallel rows of upright charred posts and the horizontal log fragments indicated in the upper margin. If so, the floor lies at a greater depth than these excavations.

Preservation of organic materials was very good in the middle and lower levels of Cut NI. Objects of bone, wood, and fiber were uncovered in excel-

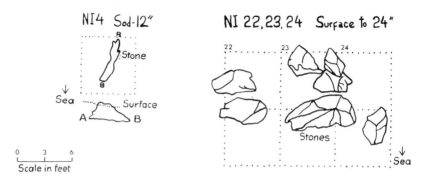

Fig. 10. Detail, Cut NI, Nukleet.

Fig. 11. Detail, Cut NI, Nukleet.

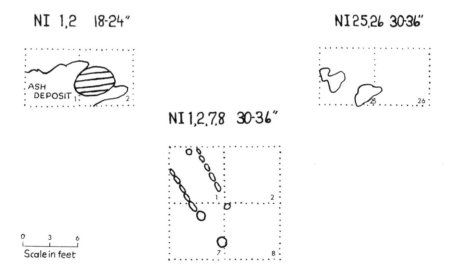

Fig. 12. Detail, Cut NI, Nukleet.

24

NI 1-19   12-30"

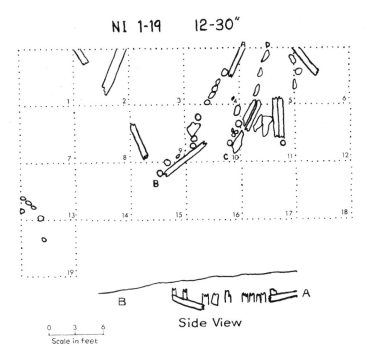

Side View

Scale in feet

Fig. 13. Detail, Cut NI, Nukleet.

NI 3-24   36-42"

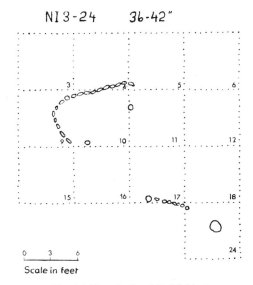

Scale in feet

Fig. 14. Detail, Cut NI, Nukleet.

25

NI 19-21,25-27,31-33   48-54"   NI 28-30,34-36   66-72"

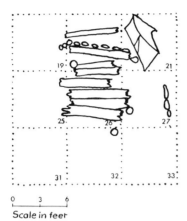

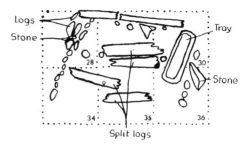

Fig. 16. Detail, Cut NI, Nukleet.

0   3   6
Scale in feet

Fig. 15. Detail, Cut NI, Nukleet.

lent condition. Two objects in particular are not represented in similar form in the earlier excavations. One of these is a long, wide, wooden runner, penetrated to receive stanchions, and presumably that of some form of sledge. It is unique in that it shows no sign of having had shoes of bone or other material attached. A whole coiled basket from earlier levels is similar to those recently made along the lower Yukon River, showing that the coiling technique is old in the region. Even older coiled basketry has been unearthed recently by Larsen farther south, in the paleo-Eskimo deposit at Platinum (Larsen, 1950, p. 184; Fig. 57, *1* and *2*). A quantity of woven matting was taken from the floors in Cut NI in good condition, also, often as whole pieces, suggesting rugs or serving mats.

The samples of many suitable building timbers were preserved for tree-ring dating.

For several reasons the second season's artifacts are not included in the analysis of Nukleet culture. First, upon examination of these materials, we found no reason to change our broader conclusions that were based upon the controlled test excavations of the previous season. Second, the stratigraphy here was not as easily defined as it was for the test cuts because of numerous house disturbances; hence, artifacts would have to be referred to the time scale already set up. Third, the oldest styles of Nukleet are represented but sparsely here, as indicated by such definitive characteristics as stems of arrowheads, harpoon heads, and the like. And, most importantly, the incorporation of this material with the rest would have demanded its costly shipment to the States for close analysis. Certain features within this large and valuable collection will merit further attention, and we hope this will lead to the completion of Cut NI.

26

Nukleet Collections, 1948

The artifacts removed from the Nukleet mound in 1948[1] are described in the following sections primarily under groupings of presumed function and only secondarily in terms of form. This approach is dictated largely by the nature of the artifacts, most of which are familiar to Eskimos now living in the area and are well documented in the ethnographic literature. The sections to follow embrace the broader fields of activity and enterprise about which there can be relatively little error in identification. They are:

1. Land hunting.
2. Sea hunting.
3. Fishing.
4. Tools and manufactures.
5. Food preparation and household.
6. Clothing, personal adornment, and ornamentation.
7. Travel and transportation.
8. Community.
9. Miscellaneous.

A section on "Pottery" is added to this list even though the subject might be included under "Food preparation" or "Manufactures."

Each of the sections is accompanied by a distribution list on which appears the artifact type, a reference to its text or plate illustration, and the levels of the test cuts at which it was found. These lists are reduced in bulk and made more readily intelligible by condensing two or three of the six-inch levels observed in the field into a single column. This treatment is found to bring together significantly large figures without seriously distorting the three recognized major style shifts represented in the site. Thus, the levels are numbered from the surface down and lumped together as follows: 1–2, 3–5, 6–8, 9–11, and 12–14. These columns concern only materials from Cuts A and B. Although some distortion is obtained from materials out of the deepest parts of Sections 1 and 2 of Cut A, which are not as old as are those of equivalent levels of Cut B, it is felt that a fairly true presentation of depth and time correlations is achieved in this form of diagram.

A break follows the lines representing levels, and below this break are entered three more horizontal rows, each of which presents the total count of artifacts for three additional excavation areas. Under "Miscellaneous" are included the materials from Cuts C and D and all objects for which collection data were lost or indecipherable in full. The next col-

---

[1] The Nukleet plates, *1–35*, made by the author before he left Alaska in 1949, include a few specimens from the 1948 excavations at Iyatayet, all of forms similar to those from Nukleet. The identity of these specimens is indicated in the plate legends and usually also in the text.

27

umn (H–1) includes Nukleet House 1 artifacts, without breakdown as to depth. The last column includes comparable materials from the neo-Eskimo cultural deposits at Iyatayet for 1948.

The descriptions of artifacts are limited to references to comparable, or nearly identical, forms previously reported for other Eskimo sites except where a local variation or an entirely new form is present. Further condensation of the text is made possible by referring to only one of several site reports where a single region is concerned, so long as no further distributional data are needed. For example, Holtved's (1944) comprehensive report is usually cited as reference for eastern Thule types, rather than the excellent basic Thule culture report of Mathiassen (1927) and the peripheral Thule reports of such investigators as Larsen (1934; 1938), Meldgaard, and Bandi (Bandi and Meldgaard, 1952), even though many of the references could be made to the latter works. The Holtved report makes available a more convenient relative time scale upon which to range types of artifacts than does the earlier, multi-site report of Mathiassen and is thus a more convenient source to the reader of the present report who may simply wish to turn to an illustration and relative time placement of the type in question.

The comparison of Nukleet types with those of other areas is confined largely to those types exhibiting close identity in method of elaboration rather than in basic function. Thus it is felt that little is to be gained by comparing whetstones of no particularly distinctive form, since these are to be found generally distributed throughout the Eskimo area. On the other hand, the treatment of stems of arrowheads promises to be very useful in indexing across wide areas and is, therefore, emphasized.

The sites of the Kobuk River (Giddings, 1952) are geographically, environmentally, and culturally close to Nukleet. The presence of forests in both regions has impressed a special stamp on culture. For these reasons, the most frequent references are to Kobuk River sites rather than to those of St. Lawrence Island or some other area for which printed reports exist.

The five major Kobuk River sites are dated in a tree-ring chronology. A brief recapitulation of these sites is as follows:

Ambler Island. (1700–1760 A. D.) A forest site of the upper river where emphasis lay on caribou hunting and seasonal fishing. Semi-nomadic existence; temporary winter pit-houses with indoor fireplace; sea-hunting artifacts lacking; dog traction.

Intermediate Kotzebue. (1500–1550 A. D.) A coastal site at the river mouth, with dependence divided between harbor sealing, fishing, and caribou hunting. Permanent winter pit-houses; built-up sledge, but no dog traction indicated. (See VanStone, 1953, for the Kotzebue sites.)

Old Kotzebue. (About 1400 A. D.) Same location as above, but close correlations with Tigara phase at Point Hope and later eastern Thule culture.

Ekseavik. (1380–1420 A. D.) Middle Kobuk River site, same cultural affiliations as above, but stronger Thule cast; some seasonal residence on the coast indicated in sealing apparatus, together with thorough exploitation of forest environment.

Ahteut. (1200–1250 A. D.) A site on the middle river of a rather permanent winter population. Pottery well fired, and often paddled, with curvilinear stamp, and textile-impressed inside. Full adaptation to forests indicated, but also sealing, as at Ekseavik. The culture period is that of western Thule at Point Hope. Harpoon heads like Early Punuk of St. Lawrence Island.

A typological cross-dating of Nukleet phases with the dated ones of the Kobuk affords a kind of orientation center from which to gauge directions and times of diffusion into and out of other areas.

Land Hunting (Table 1)

The resources of the forests, mountains, and rivers of the interior enriched Nukleet culture in all periods. Caribou must have furnished food and clothing, as they did the materials for fashioning a high proportion of the tools and weapons in daily use. The beaver, another animal of the inland forests, would have been prized for its meat and skin in addition to its teeth that we find at Nukleet. The beaver tooth, hafted both as a side blade and as an end blade to be drawn towards the user, has left its distinctive mark on a variety of wooden artifacts of all periods. This tool, largely supplanting slate in all kinds of whittling, especially of curved surfaces, is strong evidence of basic inland Eskimo affiliations.

Nukleet is a coastal site, however, and in the absence of known inland sites that may have been seasonally inhabited by the Nukleet people, our discussion of land hunting must be based largely upon the established Eskimo traits concerned with the taking of caribou, birds, and small land game. The components of bow and arrow hunting are exceptionally well represented in the Nukleet collections, and these have undergone at least one major transition that aids in cross-comparison with other sites on a temporal as well as a typological basis.

The change is partly in the form of arrowheads. The early specimens all have a rounded shoulder above the stem and this is replaced in late specimens by an angular shoulder. Larsen and Rainey have pointed out the much greater stability of styles of stem and shoulder than of blades of arrowheads and have illustrated these changes at Point Hope in terms of phases of culture (Larsen and Rainey, 1948, pp. 169–73). While only two of the major differences described for Point Hope arrowheads (Western Thule and Tigara) show up in the Nukleet materials, these are arranged in the same time order as at the Arctic Sea site. The change in shoulder form from round to angular made possible a firmer seating for the arrowhead in its shaft socket, and no doubt helped to eliminate bulky lashing. Most of the arrowheads below the sixth level in Cut B are of the earlier type, while most of those above and in nearly all of Cut A are of the sharp-shouldered variety.

Table 1. LAND

TYPE (PLATE)	Bow – Type A (4, 1)	Bow – Type B (4, 4, 5, 9)	Bow – Type C (4, 2, 6–8)	Bow ? – Type D (4, 13–14, 16)	Composite Bow (4, 10, 17)	Bow fragments (4, 15)	Sinew twister (3, 16–18)	Bow marline spike (3, 15)	Wrist guard (3, 13–14)	Arrowhead – 1 (1, 7)	Arrowhead – 2 (1, 2, 8, 10)	Arrowhead – 3 (1, 1, 3–4)	Arrowhead – 4 (1, 6)	Arrowhead – 5 (1, 15, 16)	Arrowhead – 6 (1, 13–14)	Arrowhead – 7 (1, 9, 20)	Arrowhead – 7A (1, 5, 11)
Levels 1–2	·	·	·	·	·	·	·	·	·	·	2	3	1	·	2	2	·
3–5	3	3	1	·	·	6	·	1	·	·	2	1	1	·	2	3	·
6–8	·	2	8	1	1	19	1	·	·	·	1	·	·	·	·	3	1
9–11	·	1	5	4	2	16	1	·	·	·	·	·	·	·	·	·	·
12–14	·	·	5	5	·	13	1	·	·	·	·	·	1	1	·	1	·
Miscellaneous	2	2	·	·	1	10	1	·	·	·	1	2	1	2	·	1	·
H–1	·	·	1	·	·	·	·	·	1	1	2	1	1	·	·	·	·
IY	·	·	·	·	·	·	·	·	1	·	1	·	2	·	·	·	·

Barbs in the earlier type range from one to three and are found on one or both edges—in the latter case, usually symmetrically placed. Barbing in the later type is various, ranging from a single large barb on one edge to multiple small barbs on one or both edges. Heads of the early type are shown in Pl. *2*. *2, 9–10,* have the type of stem best known from Jabbertown (Larsen and Rainey, 1948, *95, 7*), and *2, 12–13,* take the form of Ahteut heads (Giddings, 1952, XVI, 1, 7). Heads shown in Pl. *1* are of the later type. *1, 1, 3, 5–6,* are especially like Ekseavik heads (*Ibid.,* XXVII), while *1, 10, 13,* which have more cylindrical bases, are like heads from Intermediate Kotzebue (*Ibid.,* XXXVII).

All but six of the arrowheads are made of antler. These exceptions, executed in walrus ivory, are triangular in cross-section and closely resemble certain heads from Punuk phases on St. Lawrence Island (Collins, 1937, p. 222). Two of these, from the lower levels of Cut B, have undifferentiated shoulders (*2, 1*) while the others have sharp shoulders (*1, 19, 21*).

Only one arrowhead is end-slotted for receipt of a stone (probably polished slate) blade. This specimen, from House 1, is shown in *1, 7*. Another head, *1, 11* is partly decayed about the tip. The base of an end groove on one flattened face, however, indicates that it was designed for receipt of a flint blade—perhaps for such blades as those shown in *3, 10–12*. This type is known from Ekseavik (Giddings, 1952, XXVII, 4, 5).

Arrowhead – 8	Arrowhead – 9	Arrowhead – 10	Arrowhead – 11	Arrowhead – 12	Arrowhead – 13	Arrowhead – 14	Arrowhead – 15	Arrowhead – 16	Shaft straightener	Arrow shaft – 1	Arrow shaft – 2	Arrow shaft – 3	Arrow shaft – 4	Arrow shaft – 5	Blunt arrow shaft	Blunt arrowhead	Blunt arrowhead	Arrow point, chert	Bola weight	Bird spear, end prong	Bird spear, side prong	Throwing board	Throwing board peg	Blunt arrow ? shaft
1, 17	*1, 18, 19, 21*	*1, 12*	*2, 1*	*2, 2, 12, 13*	*2, 16*	*2, 3, 14, 17*	*2, 10, 11*	*2, 4, 9, 15*	*3, 19*	*3, 2, 9*	*3, 7*	*3, 5, 6, 8*	*3, 1, 4*	*3, 3*	*2, 6–8*	*2, 5*	*5, 2–6*	*3, 10–12*	*5, 17–19*	*5, 7–8, 12, 22*	*5, 10–11, 13–15, 20–21*	*5, 1, 16*	*5, 9; 8, 14*	*10, 8–12*
·	3	1	·	·	·	·	·	·	·	·	·	·	·	·	·	·	·	3	·	1	3	1	·	1
2	1	2	·	·	3	·	·	1	1	2	·	·	·	1	3	1	3	1	·	2	1	·	2	2
1	·	1	·	3	1	4	1	1	·	3	·	3	·	2	5	·	·	·	1	·	·	1	1	4
·	2	1	·	2	2	·	1	1	·	3	1	1	3	·	7	·	·	·	1	1	2	1	·	6
·	·	·	1	·	·	·	·	1	·	·	·	·	3	·	·	1	·	·	·	·	·	2	1	5
2	·	1	1	2	1	·	·	·	·	2	·	3	1	2	1	·	·	1	·	·	·	·	·	5
·	·	·	·	·	·	·	·	·	·	·	·	·	·	·	·	1	·	1	1	·	1	1	1	·
·	·	2	·	·	1	·	·	1	·	1	1	1	·	·	·	·	·	2	1	·	·	·	·	·

Arrow shafts of spruce wood from all levels have deep nocks, as shown in *3, 1–9*. 11 of a total of 29 shaft fragments in which the nock is intact are provided with shallow lashing grooves to strengthen the nock. Feathering is indicated by faint lashing stains in some cases, for which a feather setter does not appear to have been used. Three thin, fragile specimens appear to be parts of toy arrows. One of these, *3, 1*, is decorated with evenly spaced, broad bands of red pigment. Two of the large specimens were red painted, as were many of the miscellaneous shaft fragments. A rather thin specimen, *3, 4*, is provided with two opposite shallow vanes at right angles to the plane of the nock, evidently in imitation of feathering. *3, 3* is one of five specimens that are thicker than average; these are probably the nock ends of fish arrow shafts. Unclassified worked fragments of wood, of which 1,112 are preserved in the Nukleet collection, include a great many arrow shaft fragments, but these lack nocks or other aids to positive identification.

The parts of bow frames are usually well represented, especially in the lower levels of Cut B. In these fragments, some of which are illustrated in Pl. *4*, we have a significant change in style which appears to be correlated with the basic change in arrowhead shoulders. *4, 1* is a fragment of the type of bow, with broad cable groove, angular bends near each end, and squared nocks, which was prevalent at Ekseavik (Giddings, 1952, XXXV, 7). This specimen occurred at a depth of 1½ to 2 feet in Cut B. Five such bow tips are all from the more recent levels. Specimens below this all lack a cable groove, taper strongly towards the nock, and apparently lack the sharp bends associated with bow bracers. *4, 2* is a small bow fragment from under the floor of House 1 which illustrates the features of the early bow. It is constricted laterally and ridged inwardly to provide a hand grip, as is the larger fragment, *4, 15*. It flares towards the nock and then tapers to a rounded tip in which the lateral notches are cut. Variations of this type appear in *4, 4–9*. All but three of 29 specimens of this type in which the nock is intact are from below the fourth level of Cut B. Two others, probably from the same area, have lost their identification, and the third is from the fourth level of Cut C.

Since none of these earlier specimens shows signs of having been backed with sinew, a first conclusion is that sinew backing was not known when these bows were made. Three sinew twisters found in the lower levels of Cut B show, however, that sinew backing, in some form, must have been used. Two fragments of a compound bow, both from lower levels of Cut B (*4, 10, 17*) may represent a sinew-backed bow of Thule type. *4, 13, 14, 16* illustrate three of ten nock ends of what appears to be a hunting bow of another type. Examples of this type come from the oldest levels. Where the preceding type is rounded slightly on all surfaces, one or both faces of this bow are planed, thus offering the possibility of sinew backing.

With the exception of the late Nukleet bow, a style which was prevalent at Ekseavik as early as 1400 A. D. and has historic counterparts, comparative material is scarce. The unbacked Nukleet bow, however, agrees closely with Collins's tentative description of an Old Bering Sea bow: "From a number of fragments—and toys—it appears that the middle was constricted and thickened and the ends tapering" (Collins, 1937, p. 134). The Ipiutak bow may also have been of this type (Larsen and Rainey, 1948, p. 67). Although the unbacked bow seems to have been forgotten at about the time of change-over to sharp-shouldered arrowheads, it appears to have been co-existent with, and preferable to, the backed bow during the early periods at Nukleet.

The blunt arrow occurs in both composite and a one-piece form, the former only in more recent levels. Ten to eighteen tip fragments of the wooden blunt arrow in one piece (possibly toys) occur in lower levels of Cut B. The others are from respectable depths in Cuts A and C. Examples are shown in *2, 6, 8*. *2, 7* may also be a blunt arrow fragment, though its identification is less certain. This blunt arrow is one piece that appears to be unique. It is unlikely to be an imitation of a composite arrow or a toy because of the scarcity of composite blunt arrows in the levels where these are concentrated.

Blunt arrowheads of bone and antler total seven specimens, two of which are toys. The different types are shown in *5, 2–6*. All of these have fluted tips, but they were joined to the shaft in various ways. *5, 2,* of bone, had a bifurcate tang, one side of which is broken away. This type is known from the Kobuk River, where it first appears at Ekseavik (Giddings, 1952, p. 46). *5, 5* of antler, has a drilled socket and is identical with specimens from Intermediate Kotzebue (*Ibid.,* XXXVII, 17, 22, 23). Wedge tangs on blunt arrowheads, illustrated in *5, 3, 4,* of bone and antler respectively, were prevalent at Ekseavik (*Ibid.,* XXVII, 10–12). Two toy heads with wedge tangs—one illustrated (*5, 6*)—are of antler. The unusual specimen, *2, 5,* may also be a form of blunt arrowhead.

Shaft fragments that are adapted at the distal end for receipt of a bifurcate head or socket piece occurred commonly in the lower and middle levels (*10,* 8–12). Some of these may have accommodated blunt arrow tips such as *5, 2,* although, if this were the case, it is difficult to explain the scarcity of the tips in the same levels.

Sinew twisters include three of animal bone from the lower levels of Cut B (*3,* 17–18) and one of wood (*3,* 16), the location of which is unknown. *3,* 15 appears to be the upper half of a bow marline spike of animal rib, broken off at a central, drilled perforation. It is from the upper levels of Cut A. Another adjunct of archery is the antler wrist guard fragment from the sod level in front of House 1, illustrated as *3,* 13. *3,* 14 is an antler wrist guard from Iyatayet House 1.

An arrow shaft straightener, *3,* 19, from the fourth level of Cut B, has a rhomboid hole cut through a section of antler paddle and resembles a specimen from Ekseavik (Giddings, 1952, XLIV, 16).

Bola weights, for taking birds in flight over land, include two irregular ivory specimens from the lower levels of Cut B (*5,* 18) and a probable bola weight of antler from Cut A (*5,* 17). *5,* 19 is an ivory specimen from Iyatayet.

Another widespread method of capturing waterfowl is the Eskimo casting of bird spears by means of throwing boards from kayaks on ponds, streams, and bays. According to E. W. Nelson:

> Bird spears are generally cast overhand, so as to strike from above, but if the birds are shy and dive quickly, the spears are cast with an underhand throw so that they skim along the surface of the water. I have seen a hunter throwing a spear at waterfowl on the surface of a stream when small waves were running; the spear would tip the crests of the waves, sending up little jets of spray, and yet continue its course for 20 or 25 yards. This method is very confusing to the birds, as they are frequently struck by the spear before they seem to be aware of its approach. When throwing spears into flocks of partly fledged ducks or geese that are bunched together, two or even three are sometimes impaled at once upon the triple points.
>
> —Nelson, 1899, p. 153.

Bird spear side prongs range widely in form. The two late-period specimens, *5, 10, 13,* are both of antler and have barbs on either edge of the inner, curved surface as in specimens from Tigara burials (Larsen and

Rainey, 1948, *89,* 20) and Intermediate Kotzebue (Giddings, 1952, XXXVII, 20). Others all have a single row of barbs pointing inward. *5,* 11, of antler, is provided with lashing notch and lip. Two other antler specimens, *5,* 14, 21, have lashing notches on the convex face, and small barbs. Two ivory specimens, *5,* 15, 20, though their tips are missing, are alike in the shape of the stem and in having widely spaced, prominent barbs.

Bird spear end prongs, the identification of which is always somewhat questionable, are seen in *5,* 7, 8, 12, 22, and four specimens not illustrated. The two antler specimens with cut-in, conical stems may be arrowheads.

Throwing boards, used for hunting sea mammals as well as birds, are represented by the fragments of four boards, two ivory pegs (*5,* 9), and one possible specimen of antler (*8,* 14). The throwing board tip fragment, *5,* 1, and the ivory pegs are in conformity with throwing boards illustrated by Nelson (1899, Fig. 143), but the handle section from the earlier levels, *5,* 16, has a forefinger hole through the center of the shaft somewhat as do specimens of Birnirk culture (Mason, 1930, Pl. I; Geist and Rainey, 1936, *73,* 7).

Summary

The artifacts of Nukleet that are clearly concerned with land hunting fail to give a balanced picture of the land quest for game. They indicate in no appreciable way that communal enterprises existed for the driving and surrounding of seasonal herds of caribou; and yet we know from ethnographic accounts everywhere in the circumpolar region that such means of hunting provided the great majority of the animals taken throughout the year.[1] Cairns of piled-up stones in more or less straight lines near the bare tops of the hills on Cape Denbigh indicate that game drives formerly existed here as at other points throughout the Eskimo range. The people of Shaktoolik do not know the meaning of these cairns directly through experience. They are inclined to connect them to legends and interpret them as the piles of rocks heaped up by individual whalers to represent the numbers of whales killed during their lifetime. Regardless of whether or not these particular cairns have served the people of Nukleet in land hunting, we assume on ethnographic evidence that communal drives existed in the past and that snaring and trapping of both birds and animals accounted for a large part of the land game obtained. Snare pegs are seldom identifiable as such when found in middens, and snares and traps themselves are still less likely to be preserved.

The view of land hunting given by the Nukleet collections is mainly that of the individual hunting alone in the off-season, or of the stalker apart from his community at any season. In this respect, Nukleet differs not at all

---

[1] See note on p. 53 concerning the netting of beaver, otter, ptarmigan, and geese.

from excavated Eskimo sites in other areas. However, the number of artifacts concerned with land hunting probably does not give as accurate a measure of animals secured as does the table of bone counts. The amount of stalking by an individual hunter is likely to be reduced when his snaring efforts are more successful. Hence the diminution of numbers of bows and arrows in later Nukleet levels may simply indicate more success in community enterprise and snaring.

Changes through time are highly significant in the Nukleet collections, on the other hand. Basic changes in the stems of arrowheads and the forms of bows, and the far-reaching nature of these changes in terms of other sites, mark off the lower part of Cut B from all other areas of the test cuts. The change of arrowhead stem appears to have made possible a firmer seating for the head in the shaft, and this marks improvement in arrows that was not subsequently lost here or in any known area. Bows were consistently sinew-backed at Nukleet after the change in arrowhead stem. It seems quite likely that the combination of these two traits meant an appreciable improvement in hunting methods that would have made possible the taking of more animals at greater distances than before. These changes were by no means strictly local. They seem to have been general among the Western Eskimos. Conservatism thus gives way to innovation in the more important aspects of archery. We should like to know why the Nukleet people, in about the 14th century, were suddenly persuaded to believe that the sinew-backed bow, which they had known but not fully accepted, and the new way of hafting arrowheads were desirable features.

The distribution of blunt arrows indicates another trend that coincides with the changes mentioned above. The earlier blunt arrows were fashioned in one piece. Arrowheads with separate tips appear only in the upper levels of Cut B and in Cut A. The one-piece form in which a shaft widens at the distal end to take the place of a separate head is found only in the older sections of Cut B. Also mainly in this deposit appear the arrow shafts provided at the distal end with two grooves for the receipt of some kind of a tip with a bifurcate base—presumably a blunt arrowhead like an illustrated specimen from late levels (5, 2). This evidence seems to mean that the blunt arrow in one piece was preferred until the previously mentioned archery changes became accepted, after which all blunt arrows were capped by separate tips. The later blunt arrowheads were socketed or provided with either bifurcate or wedge-shaped stems.

No significant innovations appear in the land-hunting artifacts after the time of deposit of the older middens of cut B. Although the innovations seem to have added variety and greater efficiency to the practice of archery, it is to be noted that they coincide with a decrease in the relative numbers of caribou bones (p. 93). Three questions, as yet unanswered, are suggested by this distribution:

1. Did more efficient hunting methods cause a decline in the caribou herds?

2. Were better hunting methods originated or borrowed as a result of a slow, natural decline in the available herds?

3. Did a new people, whose land-hunting equipment was adequate and various, but whose food preference was sea mammals or fish, replace those who left the lower middens of Cut B?

Bird spears with side prongs and throwing boards are included under land hunting, although we understand from ethnographic evidence that they are primarily associated with boats and use over water. The bird spear was not designed to fall upon hard surfaces, but into the water, where its slender barbs could escape damage. The throwing board may also have been used with fish-spearing and seal-harpooning activities. No appreciable change is seen in these types—perhaps because of insufficient materials.

Those features of land hunting that appear to be unique at Nukleet, in light of other excavated sites in the Eskimo area, are: the Type D bow, the blunt arrow shaft in one piece, and, possibly, the arrow shaft (?) with a provision for attaching a head with a bifurcate stem (*10,* 8–12). All other manifestations are known in like form from areas other than Norton Bay.

Table 2. SEA

PLATE	6, 1–3, 5–7, 10–12, 16–19, 25	6, 8–9, 22	6, 14	6, 13, 20, 21	6, 28–29	6, 4	6, 15, 23–24, 33, 35–37	6, 30, 32	6, 27, 31, 34	6, 26	8, 9–11	7, 2, 7	7, 3	7, 4–5	7, 8, 10	7, 1, 9
TYPE	Harpoon head – 1	Harpoon head – 2	Harpoon head – 3	Harpoon head – 4	Harpoon head – 5	Harpoon head – 6	Harpoon head – 7	Harpoon head – 8	Harpoon head – 9	Harpoon head – 10	Harpoon foreshaft	Harpoon socket piece, tubular	Harpoon socket piece, socket each end	Dart socket piece	Dart socket piece	Composite socket piece
Levels 1–2	·	·	1	1	·	·	·	·	·	·	·	·	1	1	1	·
3–5	4	2	·	1	·	1	1	·	·	·	·	1	·	·	1	·
6–8	4	·	·	·	2	·	3	·	1	·	1	·	·	·	1	3
9–11	4	1	1	1	·	·	2	2	1	·	1	1	1	·	1	1
12–14	1	·	·	·	·	·	·	·	1	1	·	·	·	·	2	1
Miscellaneous	·	·	·	·	·	·	·	·	·	·	·	·	·	·	·	·
H–1	1	·	·	·	·	·	·	·	·	·	·	1	·	·	·	·
IY	·	·	·	·	·	·	·	·	·	·	·	·	·	·	1	·

36

Sea Hunting (Table 2)

The present Eskimos of Shaktoolik are hunters of seals and white whales. Large whales and walruses do not seem to have been important in recent times, and it is doubtful whether they ever were, because this part of Norton Sound is not in the mainstream of migration of those mammals. Bone counts show, however, a scattering of the bones of both large whales and walruses throughout the Nukleet midden (Table 9). Some of these may be the remains of stranded animals. Walrus ivory and baleen show up mainly towards the lower levels of Cut B, indicating either different hunting habits or more active trade in these materials during the earliest times.

Harpoon heads from Nukleet total 36, including one unfinished specimen and three small, but significant, fragments. The earlier heads are like those of other archeological sites at distant points, in both form and decoration. This seems a strong indication that sea hunting during early Nukleet times at Cape Denbigh followed patterns firmly entrenched in those places where sea mammals furnished the principal sources of livelihood, and that it was not until much later that innovations were made locally. The earliest harpoon heads can be duplicated, for the greater part, on St. Lawrence Island, and those of intermediate times are mainly like specimens from Kotzebue Sound and Point Hope sites of the 14th and 15th centuries. The latest heads, most of them closed-socketed and lacking inset blades, are

HUNTING

8, 1, 2, 4	8, 3	7, 6	8, 12-14	8, 19	7, 11-14	8, 20-32	10, 7	10, 2-6	33, 1-3	8, 17-18	8, 5-7	8, 8	8, 15-16						34, 3-5
Harpoon shaft	Dart shaft	Lance foreshaft ?	Finger rest	Kayak harpoon rest	Harpoon ice pick	Harpoon dart head	Dart socket piece, stepped scarf face	Dart shaft, stepped socket	Cord attacher	Wound plug	Float mouthpiece	Mending disk	Float toggle	Dragline handle	Harpoon blade, uniformly thin	Harpoon blade, concave base	Harpoon blade, thick	Harpoon blade, thick strong bevel	Snow goggles
·	·	·	·	·	·	3	·	·	2	·	·	·	·	·	5	·	1	·	·
2	1	·	1	1	1	4	·	1	·	1	·	·	3	·	10	·	3	1	·
3	1	1	1	·	1	3	·	2	·	1	1	·	·	·	5	·	·	·	1
2	2	·	·	·	1	4	·	2	·	·	1	·	·	·	1	·	1	·	2
2	1	·	·	·	·	1	·	·	·	1	·	1	1	·	4	·	·	·	·
·	2	·	·	·	2	1	·	·	·	1	·	·	·	·	2	·	1	·	·
·	·	·	·	·	2	2	·	·	·	·	1	·	1	·	4	·	·	1	·
·	·	·	·	·	2	1	1	·	1	·	·	·	·	·	7	3	3	·	·

plain and relatively crude, giving the impression of being local products uninfluenced by any widespread style.

Harpoon heads are readily divided into ten categories, mainly on the basis of socket form and blade, and described in terms of other areas as follows:

1. *Plain, closed-socket heads without barbs or inset blades.* These appear in all levels and differ most from widespread Thule types. Pl. *6, 1, 2* are antler heads with line grooves that are broad and flat-topped at the proximal end, as are end-bladed specimens from Intermediate Kotzebue. *6, 3* and *6, 18* are antler heads from early levels that show similar thinness, and curving of the outline, although these are thinned in opposite planes with respect to the line hole.

6, 5, 6 are small antler heads in which the line holes are near center. This position of the line hole is also to be seen in *6, 7, 10,* and *11* (which apparently was longer before its final sharpening), *6, 12* (remade into a sinew reel [?] by notching at the ends), and *6, 17* and *19* (also sharpened short). Although it is not possible to determine, in most cases, whether the original form of one of these heads was long, gradually becoming short as it was resharpened, all of these specimens appear to have an imbalance as compared with separately bladed or barbed heads, and to be set apart in this respect from harpoon heads commonly encountered about Bering Strait and across the northern Arctic. On the other hand, many heads of similar style from the Cook Inlet sites appear to have been subjected to repeated sharpening. The Nukleet antler head, *6, 10,* for example, shows close identity with de Laguna's (1934) Pl. *38, 1,* a head that falls in the Yukon Island III period.

6, 16 is a thin ivory head that has not been sharpened often, and may thus illustrate the original shape of some of the preceding specimens. *6, 25* is a very small head of the same shape, made of bird bone, and is possibly a toy.

2. *Barbed heads with closed socket.* These are forms characteristic of western Alaska in fairly late periods. *6, 8* has a pair of opposite barbs in the plane of the line hole. An almost identical specimen appeared at Intermediate Kotzebue (Giddings, 1952, XXXVIII, 4). Another head, *6, 22,* is similar, but its barbs lie at right angles to the line hole. This specimen has had the socket partly broken out and mended by grooving and lashing. Another form of barbed head appears in *6, 9.* This originally had two pairs of opposite barbs, and is known from Utkiavik (Collins, 1932, Fig. 45d) and Tigara Burials at Point Hope (Larsen and Rainey, 1948, *89, 7*) as well as from specimens purchased in 1940 at Kotzebue by the author for the University of Alaska. These are all made of antler.

3. *Closed-socket, bladed, plain harpoon head.* A single head of whale bone, *6, 14,* is set apart as a separate type because of a thin, sharp "fin" on both the dorsal and ventral surfaces. This head appears to be complete in its polished surface, drilled socket, and blade slit, but the line hole has not

been drilled. This late-period specimen is not identified with those of other areas, and may represent a local fashion.

4. *Closed-socket, bladed head with raised design.* The distinctive decorative ridges that form the simple designs on these antler heads (*6, 13, 20, 21*) afford a means of closely identifying them with specimens from Ekseavik (Giddings, 1952, Fig. 32, *2, 3*). *6, 21* is further marked by a design duplicated on other objects. This design is a pair of compass-drawn circles concentric about a dot, the outer circle with tick marks pendent. A probable cross-dating between the two areas is thus strongly indicated for the time of production of heads of this form. This would mean that by 1400 A. D. most of the levels below three feet in the B Cut were already laid down, and that the materials found in the A Cut were being deposited.

The thick, almost square, cross-section at the line hole in all heads of this type, as well as the general shape exclusive of decoration, recalls a class of Punuk heads found in St. Lawrence Island sites (Collins, 1937, *70, 20, 22, 23*). If such a connection is real, however, a considerable time lag is indicated for the Alaskan mainland specimens.

5. *Closed-socket heads with engraved lines and inset dots.* This is a form of harpoon head well known from the Punuk sites on St. Lawrence Island. Although only fragments are included here, the arrangement of lines (*6, 29*) and small cylindrical pits that have been filled with pigment (*6, 28*) show these to be closely similar to heads from Miyowagh (Collins, 1937, *26, 7, 9,*), Ievoghiyoq (*Ibid., 70, 21*) and Kukulik (Geist and Rainey, 1936, *68, 7–10*), the last from depths of 11 and 12 feet in the mound. The cross-identity of decorative style indicates strongly that the levels of the lower part of Cut B at Nukleet below 4 feet in depth were contemporary with Early Punuk developments on St. Lawrence Island, and that direct passage of objects or ideas was possible at the time.

6. *Plain head with open socket.* The one specimen of this type (*6, 4*) has a wide socket and appears to have been repeatedly resharpened in the manner of most of the Style 1 heads until it was no longer useful. This form is hardly distinctive enough for close comparison with specimens from other areas.

7. *Open-socket head with two opposite barbs.* This is the widespread Thule Type 2 (Mathiassen, 1927, II, pp. 15–18), which is here represented only in the middle and earlier levels. *6, 15* is a plain antler head that is probably the latest of this type represented at Nukleet. It appears somewhat foreshortened as compared with other specimens. *6, 23*, of antler, has an unusually long spur, even though this feature is accentuated in the photograph because the socket section is partly broken away. *6, 24* is an ivory specimen from Iyatayet that shows close identity with a head from Ahteut (Giddings, 1952, XVI, 9) and with another from Western Thule deposits at Point Hope (Larsen and Rainey, 1948, *88, 2*). The other heads in this group

are all broken or reworked about the barbed end, but all are closely identical with Western Thule heads such as were the style in the Point Hope-Kotzebue Sound area between 1100 and 1300 A. D. *6, 33* shows a vestigial point part-way along the spur that characterizes Jabbertown specimens (Larsen and Rainey, 1948, *95*, 1), and *6, 35–37* appear to be in the identical style with other Point Hope heads of the same period (*Ibid., 88, 2*).

8. *Open-socket head with blade.* The two heads representing this type, the broken specimen *6, 30*, and the whole specimen *6, 32*, are identical in shape and engraving with a class of harpoon heads from the Early Punuk materials on St. Lawrence Island. Heads of this type occurred at Kukulik at about the 10- to 11-foot levels (Geist and Rainey, 1936, *58*, D) and in the Miyowagh site at Gambell (Collins, 1937, *96*, 9, 11, 14). The two specimens at Nukleet were both in place in the ninth level of the B Cut and are, therefore, contemporary with most of the heads described as Type 5, above, which similarly cross-identify with St. Lawrence Island Early Punuk specimens.[1]

9. *Heads with a double spur.* The three heads considered in this class are placed together because of the peculiarity of a split spur rather than because they are otherwise alike. *6, 27* is an antler fragment of a closed-socket harpoon head from the middle levels of Cut B. Its split spur seems to be in the tradition of a long, closed-socketed, bladed head from the bottom of the deposit, *6, 31*. The latter specimen, also of antler, appears to be outside the tradition of other Eskimo heads of early periods and may be a local development. *6, 34*, on the other hand, was an open-socketed ivory head with paired barbs (broken off) that resembles other barbed heads from Nukleet except for the spur, which is split in the manner of many heads from Okvik to Birnirk times. This head comes also from the bottom of the oldest Nukleet section.

10. *Toy (?) harpoon head.* The tiny harpoon head of bird bone, *6, 26*, seems more likely to have been a toy or ceremonial model than an object meant for use, although it is conceivable that it was used as a fishing harpoon head.

Harpoon foreshafts are represented by only three specimens. One of these, an antler specimen from House 1 (*8, 9*), is of a widespread Thule type found in many sites north of Bering Sea. It is closely duplicated by a foreshaft from Ekseavik (Giddings, 1952, XXVIII, 21). Another antler specimen, *8, 10*, has a flattened, broad proximal end in which the line hole was drilled near one edge. This sort of foreshaft appears in the last two periods at Yukon Island at Cook Inlet (de Laguna, 1934, *41*, 1, 2) and is

---

[1] More recently this form has been identified as characteristic of Western Thule culture sites of the Kotzebue Sound region and western Alaska, and it seems to be a horizon style marker for not only Western Thule culture but for one aspect of Eastern Thule culture (Ford, 1959, pp. 83–6; Giddings, 1961, p. 169; Holtved, 1944, pp. 149–56; 1954, pp. 100–6).

rarely encountered in the more northerly regions. *8, 11* is a long ivory fore-shaft somewhat flattened towards the broken proximal end, the line hole of which is in a lateral position.

Most of the harpoon blades and fragments of ground slate are uniformly thin and nearly straight across the base, but three blades, all from Iyatayet, have strongly concave bases, and nine blades (three from Iyatayet) have thick tips that are beveled towards the edge on both faces and thinned below the point where they are to be inserted in the blade slit of a harpoon head. Two other blades are unusually thick, with a strong bevel, but with no thinning for accommodation to a blade slit. No evidence appears among the blades or harpoon head fragments to indicate the hunting of whales other than beluga.

Harpoon dart heads are numerous, and various in size and form. Variety is indicated by the illustrated specimens, *8, 20–32.* All of these could have been used in sealing, but it is clearly impossible to decide whether they were propelled as spears or as arrows, or whether or not some of the smaller specimens were used in harpooning fish. The variety of such methods of hunting along the Alaskan coast of Bering Sea as indicated by Nelson (1899, pp. 118–72) for the latter part of the past century is apparently outside the pattern of Thule Culture and northern Eskimo hunting in general, probably because this variety is necessary only where fish make up a food mainstay equal to, or greater than, that of sea mammals. The Kobuk River sites thus show greater kinship in these respects with Norton Sound sites than with coastal sites along the Arctic Sea. A striking similarity in forms appears between the Nukleet specimens and those from Kobuk sites, especially as follows:

>*8,* 20–22 like Ekseavik specimens (Giddings, 1952, XXVIII, 10–12)
>   23   like Old Kotzebue specimen (*Ibid.,* XII, 7)
>   27   like Ekseavik specimen (*Ibid.,* XXVIII, 4)
>   28   like Ekseavik and Old Kotzebue specimens (*Ibid.,* XXVIII, 5; XII, 5)
>   31, 32 like Intermediate Kotzebue specimen (*Ibid.,* XXVIII, 3).

The dart heads with barbs only on one side, *8, 24–26,* are also similar to Ekseavik specimens (Giddings, 1952, XXVIII, 1–3), but recall more specifically Cook Inlet barbed points of all periods (de Laguna, 1934, *39*). In spatulate stem, and in opposite barbing, *8, 27* also is like a Yukon Island III specimen (de Laguna, 1934, *40, 1*).

8, 30–32 are small heads identical with historical specimens illustrated by Nelson (1899, *57,* 18, 20).

Socket pieces for sealing harpoons include only six specimens, but these fall into three distinct types. One type, a cylinder of antler gouged out at the distal end for receipt of a wooden plug into which to fit the foreshaft or dart head, and at the proximal end for fitting over the wooden shaft, is represented by *7, 3*, a specimen which is provided with a lashing groove about the foreshaft socket. This object closely resembles a socket piece from Intermediate Kotzebue (Giddings, 1952, XXXVIII, 25) and another from Ahteut (Giddings, 1952, XVI, 2). Another type consists of a tube of antler similar in function to the preceding. *7, 2* has a series of grooves about the rounded distal end, either for decoration or for lashing, and is almost identical with a specimen from Ekseavik (Giddings, 1952, XXVIII, 22). *7, 7* is a shorter tube, lacking embellishment. The third type of socket piece is a composite form without known counterpart in other areas. *7, 1* is a long ivory half of such a socket piece. This is ridged on the outside, so that two halves fitted together would have a squarish cross-section. The inner surface is grooved lengthwise, pointed at the proximal end, and gouged out tongue-shaped at the distal end for receipt of a foreshaft, evidently of the sort shown in *8, 10*. *7, 9* is a fragment of the proximal end of a similar ivory piece, on which shows a lashing groove similar to one on the complete specimen. Socket pieces from all periods of Cook Inlet show a similar fitting together of two parts, but none of those illustrated (de Laguna, 1934, *41*) takes the special form of the Nukleet specimens. De Laguna has shown that this general type has a southern distribution:

The socket piece in two parts ... seems to be restricted to the Tena and to the Pacific Eskimo and Aleut. It is known from Kachemak Bay I to III, Kodiak, the Aleutian Islands, and Port Möller on the Alaskan Peninsula. Its occurrence on the Yukon seems to mark the northernmost extent of its distribution, and we might expect to find it among the Eskimo of the Yukon-Bristol Bay area, through whom it probably traveled to reach the Tena.

—de Laguna, 1947, p. 201.

Dart socket pieces (the smaller of which may have been used on fish arrows) take two forms. The cylindrical form gouged out at both ends is essentially the same as the larger harpoon socket pieces described above. *7, 8* is one of these, of antler, on which two lashing grooves are provided. *7, 10* is a split fragment of a similar socket piece of ivory, showing the shape of the distal socket. The other form of socket piece is illustrated in *7, 4, 5*. These are joined to a shaft by their wedge-shaped stem. The socket end of each has a shallow, drilled pit. Specimens very similar to these have occurred at Ambler Island and at Intermediate Kotzebue (Giddings, 1952, I, 22; XXXVIII, 24).

Several shaft fragments on which the distal end is intact show that they have been capped by socket pieces of the tubular form. *8, 1* is such a fragment—thickened just below the socket junction and provided with a lashing groove. *8, 4* is similarly thick where it joins the socket piece, while *8, 2* is undifferentiated. The joining of a tubular socket piece to a shaft in this fashion is a Thule trait to be seen as far away as Greenland in early sites

42

(Holtved, 1944, *7, 9*). The small specimen, *8, 3*, is probably meant for a harpoon arrow.

Another method of joining socket pieces to shafts is to be seen in the "stepped scarf face" such as Holtved has reported as a method of hafting hand drills in eastern Thule sites (1944, *24,* 13, 22). A large number of fragments of wooden shafts from Nukleet in which the distal end showed this unusual feature remained a puzzle until the socket piece, *10,* 7, was fitted into the grooves of shafts such as those pictured in *10,* 2–6. It is impossible to determine at present whether these were the parts of sealing darts or of heavy harpoon arrows.

A wooden object, *7,* 6, for which no comparative material has appeared, is possibly the foreshaft for some sort of sea-hunting lance. The lower end is whittled with a beaver tooth into a conical shape such as might fit loosely into a shaft socket. A notch just above this feature could be the equivalent of a line hole for securing the foreshaft to the shaft. The opposite end is wedge-shaped, as though for the attachment of a bifurcate blade of harder material.

Harpoon ice picks of various forms are shown in *7,* 11–14. *7,* 11 and 12 are so nearly identical in appearance with specimens from the Kobuk and Point Hope Western Thule period as to suggest their contemporaneity (Giddings, 1952, XVI, 12; XII, 8; Larsen and Rainey, 1948, *42,* 95).

Finger rests for harpoon shafts include two ivory specimens, *8,* 12, 13, and possibly the antler object, *8,* 14 (which, however, resembles somewhat a throwing board peg illustrated from Miyowagh [Collins, 1937, *33,* 24]). *8,* 13 has a bulbous head in which are four drilled pits for the inclusion of decorative pigment or other material, and its base is narrowly grooved for shaft attachment.

A harpoon rest to be attached to a kayak is shown in *8,* 19. It has been whittled from spruce wood with a beaver tooth.

Other evidences of sealing (see evidence of netting, pp. 51–53) include drag handles and attachments, wound plugs, float toggles, mending discs, mouthpieces, and possibly the double pointed object described on p. 75 (*30,* 8). A simple wooden toggle, grooved about the thickened mid-section, from under the floor of House 1, is presumed to be the handle of a seal drag-line. A form of cord attacher that appears to be peculiar to the north Bering Sea region is illustrated in *33,* 1–3, and Fig. 17. All three of these are from the later deposits at both Nukleet and Iyatayet and are illustrated in like form from historic villages on the south side of Seward Peninsula (Nelson, 1899, *66,* 1, 17) as separators for the heavy loop of rawhide that was used as a drag handle. *33,* 1 is a decorated specimen of ivory. A .5-cm.-wide hole through the narrow end divides and emerges as two separate tubes of equal width in the opposite end. Decoration takes the form of parallel grooves about the narrow end and four sets of "double circle-dot"

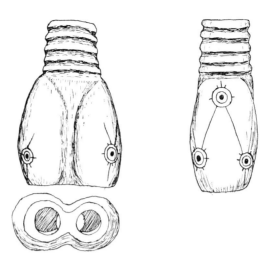

Fig. 17. Cord attacher of ivory – Iyatayet site. (Actual size.)

designs about the body of the specimen. The other two specimens, both from Nukleet, are undecorated, but closely similar in execution to the Iyatayet specimen. Two wedges of spruce wood, *8, 17, 18,* appear to be wound plugs or "air plugs"[1] such as have a wide distribution in time and space in northern sites. *8, 5–7* are float mouthpieces of wood. *8, 7* is thicker than the others and is provided with a lashing groove. Specimens like these are illustrated from several St. Lawrence Island sites of different periods (Collins, 1937, *32,* 13–15, Miyowagh; *73,* 16, Ievoghiyoq; *73,* 15, Seklowayaget). *8, 7* closely resembles Collins's (1937) *73,* 15, and may be the mouthpiece for a water bag, as the latter is described. *8, 8* is a mending disc, lightly grooved about the circumference, and similar to specimens from Miyowagh and Ievoghiyoq (*Ibid., 32,* 16–18; *73,* 19). *8, 15, 16* are float toggles, also comparable to specimens from St. Lawrence Island early periods (*Ibid., 32,* 20; *73,* 20).

Snow goggles, such as are commonly associated with Eskimo ice hunting,[2] are represented by a whole specimen (*34,* 3) and two fragments (*34,* 4, 5), all of spruce wood. The whole pair of goggles from the earlier deposits at Nukleet has been fashioned with a beaver-tooth knife and has long, narrow slits. This form of parallel-edged, narrow slit, giving wide-angle vision laterally, is known from Ekseavik (Giddings, 1952, XXXIII, 16) and from the Tigara Burials (Larsen and Rainey, 1948, *92,* 1). An equally narrow, but

---

[1] "To insure [seals'] floating while being towed, it is a common practice to make slits in the skin at various points and, with a long pointed instrument of deerhorn, to loosen the blubber from the muscle for a space of a foot or more in diameter. Then, by use of a hollow tube, made from the wing-bone of a bird or from other material, air is blown in and the place inflated; wooden plugs are then inserted in the slits and driven in tightly to prevent the air from escaping. By the aid of several such inflated spots the seal is floated and the danger of losing it is avoided." (Nelson, 1899, p. 131.)

[2] But also worn by the inland Ingalik on occasions (Osgood, 1940, pp. 183–5).

44

differently formed, slit is to be seen on historic goggles from the Bering Sea area (Nelson, 1899, *64,* 1, 4, 6). It is to be noted that the goggles illustrated from Miyowagh had oval or rhomboid slits (Collins, 1937, *58,* 1, 2; *60,* 6), while a pair of goggles from Ipiutak had round holes in place of slits (Larsen and Rainey, 1948, *26,* 14). On this meagre evidence we might look for an evolutionary refinement towards a form of goggle that cuts out the maximum glare while affording the maximum angle of vision. However, the other two Nukleet specimens appear to have had oval slits, and little angular range, although they may have been contemporary with the complete specimen.

Summary

The artifacts concerned with sea hunting are in all cases those that could have been employed only in the taking of seals in open water or along open leads in the winter ice. This is to say no direct evidence exists for whaling or for *maupok* and *utok* hunting on the sea ice. Whaling harpoon heads, heavy harpoon parts, large spear heads, boat sled runners, and other objects commonly associated at peninsular points in the Bering Strait area with the organized pursuit of whales are wholly absent. The present villagers in the area say that baleen whales were formerly hunted occasionally at Cape Denbigh and at Besboro Island, but their accounts show no real understanding of the dangers, procedures, and cults connected with the hunting of whales in other areas. The few pieces of baleen and whale bone found in the site could easily have been acquired by trade or taken from stranded whales. It thus appears that neither early nor late peoples of Nukleet were true whalers.

The absence of sealing stool parts, rod indicators, and the like does not prove that Nukleet people never waited at breathing holes for seal, nor does the absence of scratchers prove that the highly skilled methods of creeping close to basking seals were formerly unknown,[1] but they serve in a negative way in pointing up the importance of sealing by kayak that is still practiced by some few of the men in the area today. This consists of patrolling open waters in a kayak and harpooning with the aid of a throwing board; at other seasons a kayak is employed to move from one large ice floe to another in search of seals at open leads. The harpoon ice pick is a part of the floe-sealing complex today, and its distribution at Nukleet does not indicate a different connotation in earlier times. All of the other recognized adjuncts of sealing—harpoon darts, harpoon rests, float parts, etc.—are those that in recent times have been included in the kayak hunting complex.

The hunting of beluga must be included under the general heading of seal-hunting. No specific traits are recognized as pertaining only to the

---

[1] These and other methods of ice hunting are described for the Norton Sound region in the last century by Nelson (1899, pp. 128–9).

pursuit of these small white whales. These mammals were presumably taken by the same several harpooning devices as were seals. The seasonal concentration of beluga in the area and the recent practice in the Norton Sound–Kotzebue Sound region of communal herding of these mammals into shoal waters by means of kayaks suggest that the beluga bones at Nukleet were deposited after spring and fall communal hunts in open water.

The sea-hunting complex at Nukleet cannot, then, be broken down in terms of pursuit of large mammals (beluga, bearded seal, walrus) as against small seals, but only in rough terms of the season. By implication, the hunting of small seals was a more individual enterprise at all times than was the hunting of beluga. The large, wooden mesh gauges described under "fishing" were probably used in the fashioning of seal or beluga nets and representative of another basic hunting method, but of this we have no further proof. (See notes on seal and beluga netting, pp. 52–53.)

As will be pointed out in a later section, the distribution of animal bones at Nukleet shows shifts of emphasis on the kinds of animals hunted. This may have as much bearing on game cycles or migration routes as on the preferences of the hunters. Changes through time are not those of the efficiency of the sea-hunting complex, but of the styles of its material components. The earliest harpoon heads are nearly all decorated with engraved designs. Only a few specimens of the middle period are treated with extra-functional design, and by the late period there remains no sign of a tradition of decorating harpoon heads. Strictly utilitarian principles also seem to guide the fashioning of other later objects concerned with sea hunting. The elaborate, composite socket piece is forgotten after the earliest period, dart heads become more standardized, and objects are generally coarser in execution in more recent times. An exception to this tendency is seen in the separating-tubed cord attacher for a seal drag (33, 1–3) that appears to have a late origin and to be customarily decorated.

As to spatial relationships, the earliest period appears most strongly in accord with Early Punuk trends on St. Lawrence Island. This is supported by the identity of the styles and engraved designs of harpoon heads on the lowest levels at Nukleet. Possible Birnirk crossties also appear at this time in the treatment of spurs on heads outside the Early Punuk tradition, and some similarity to South Alaskan developments is seen in the composite socket pieces, which do not have a known northerly distribution.

The middle period, on the other hand, shows little cultural affiliation with St. Lawrence Island, but falls into the tradition of Ekseavik and related North Alaskan sites, including a strong increment best known from Cook Inlet in southern Alaska. The final period shows a general divorcement from the north, an intensification of local patterns, and a continuing general resemblance to Cook Inlet.

As to cross-dating on the basis of almost exact duplication of both form and style in specific artifacts, the early period combines Early Punuk, Ahteut, and Jabbertown separate traits on presumably the same time level; the middle period equates with Ekseavik on the same terms; and the late period fails to equate with any other known area.

Features of Nukleet sea hunting that seem to have a peculiarly local cast are: harpoon heads with plain, resharpened, distal ends; toy (?) harpoon heads of bird bone; harpoon socket pieces in two long halves; the lance foreshaft (?) (7, 6); a stepped scarf face for attaching dart socket pieces to shafts; and cord attachers for seal drags (33, 1–3).

Fishing (Table 3)

The taking of fish in quantity strongly stamps the culture of the present Eskimos of the Norton Sound area. The periodic runs of salmon and herring are drawn upon heavily along the coast and up the Shaktoolik River. By means of netting, the fish are dried on racks and preserved for off-season use. Other fish, less necessary for survival, are taken throughout the year by methods other than netting. Fish spears are still known, though rarely used. Rock cod and other deep-water fish are occasionally taken by hook and line, and tomcod are gigged through the spring ice.

Archeological evidence of fish netting and trapping is usually represented by fewer objects, and less variation, than is evidence of spearing and hooking. The Nukleet collections thus offer an abundance of artifacts concerned with the taking of one fish at a time by an individual, while only net sinkers and a few floats and other tools show the use of nets at any period. Our description of fishing in the early periods at Cape Denbigh is, therefore, one-sided in that it must lay stress on individuality and supplementary activity rather than on economic factors of great quantities of food.

Fish arrows such as those described by Nelson (1899, pp. 160–161) are represented in all levels by barbs smaller than those of a leister but similar in form to those clustered about the end of a spear. Fish arrows appear to be absent, or unimportant, in areas other than bay or river sites of west-central Alaska, although small barbed points from Cook Inlet (de Laguna, 1934, 42), St. Lawrence Island (Collins, 1937, 33, 16–22), and the Aleutians may have been used for shooting fish. The most direct relationship between the Nukleet site and others, in this particular, is with Kobuk River sites. Thus, 9, 11–12 are barbs very similar in form to specimens from Intermediate Kotzebue (Giddings, 1952, XXXVI, 11, 24), while 9, 13 shows identity with a barb from Ekseavik and Old Kotzebue (Giddings, 1952, XXVIII, 7; XIV, 11–12), and perhaps with Ahteut (Giddings, 1952, XVIII, 7). The variety shown in barbing and hafting the Nukleet specimens (9, 10–15, 17–19) seems more an individual matter than one concerned with evolution and the passage of time.

Table 3. FISHING

TYPE	PLATE	Levels 1-2	3-5	6-8	9-11	12-14	Miscellaneous	H-1	IY
Fish arrow barb	9, 10-15, 17-19	8	7	5	3	2	5	2	1
Fish arrow shaft	9, 2-5	.	.	1	1	1	.	1	.
Leister prong	9, 7-8, 16	2	2	.	4	.	1	2	.
Salmon harpoon head	9, 9	.	1	.	.	.	.	.	.
Center prong	9, 6, 24-28	1	2	3	2	1	2	.	.
Fish hook barb, antler	9, 20	3	1	.	1	.	1	1	.
Fish hook barb, ivory	33, 7	.	1	.	1	.	1	.	.
Fish spear side prong	9, 22	.	.	.	.	1	.	.	.
Toy ? side prong	9, 1	.	.	.	.	1	.	.	.
Fish spear barb, antler	9, 21	.	1	.	1	.	1	1	.
Fish spear barb, ivory	9, 23	.	.	.	.	1	.	.	.
Fish hook shank	11, 10-11	.	1	.	1	.	.	.	.
Fish line guide ?	11, 9	.	.	.	.	.	.	1	.
Gorge	11, 7-8	1	1	3	.	.	.	1	.
Line sinker	11, 12-14, 16-17	.	4	1	.	.	1	1	4
Shee hook shank	11, 15	.	.	.	.	.	.	.	1
Mesh gauge, small	11, 4-6	.	1	.	.	.	1	1	.
Mesh gauge, large	11, 1-3	.	4	4	.	4	2	.	.
Net shuttle	13, 6-7	1	1	1	.	.	.	.	.
Fish line reel	12, 6	.	.	.	1	1	1	.	.
Net float	13, 1, 2, 4	.	3	2	.	.	.	.	.
Net stretcher		.	.	.	.	.	1	.	.
Net sinker, bone	13, 3, 5, 8	3	12	4	.	.	5	5	2
Net sinker, stone, one notch	12, 7-10	7	11	2	2	2	2	4	3
Net sinker, large		4	.	.	.	1	.	.	2
Ice strainer	12, 1-5, 11	11	28	12	6	1	6	9	4
Fishing ice pick]		1	9	1	1	.	1	2	1

48

Several fish arrow shafts are identified by grooves for receipt of barbs at their distal ends. *9*, 2–3 are examples of these with only two grooves, while *9*, 4–5 each have three evenly spaced grooves.

Some of the larger barbed points were probably used as leister prongs, rather than as those of arrows. *9*, 7–8, 16 indicate the range of types. *9*, 8 closely resembles specimens from Ekseavik and Ahteut (Giddings, 1952, XXVIII, 8; XVIII, 9), while the thick prong, *9*, 16, is like a specimen from Ambler Island (Giddings, 1952, I, 1). Prongs of this sort are also to be found on St. Lawrence Island (Collins, 1937, *33*, 11, 13–15) and at Cook Inlet (de Laguna, 1934, *42*).

The long, barbed point with a spatulate tang, *9*, 9, closely resembles in form the salmon harpoon heads from the Kobuk, especially one from Ahteut (Giddings, 1952, XVIII, 8), although this Nukleet specimen was apparently fixed to its shaft, rather than detachable as were the Kobuk pieces.

A class of opposite-barbed points, *9*, 6, 24–28, may have been center prongs for either bird spears or trident fish spears, although none was found hafted.

The trident fish spear (salmon spear) is more reliably indicated by the base of a side prong of wood for such an implement, *9*, 22; by an ivory barb such as fits in the end of a side prong, *9*, 23; and by the slender wooden object, *9*, 1, end-notched in the fashion of certain side prongs, which appears to be part of a toy salmon spear. The barb, *9*, 23, is known in this special form only from 13th and 15th century sites in the Kobuk and Point Hope areas (Giddings, 1952, XVIII, 3–5; Larsen and Rainey, 1948, p. 173). The small antler barb, *9*, 21, is possibly a barb of another sort for a salmon spear, although this is purely speculative.

Fish hooks are extremely scarce at Nukleet. Only three specimens can be identified as shanks. These are illustrated in *11*, 10–11, and 15. The first two are straight shanks to the base of which were probably lashed barbs of antler or ivory. The other appears to be a crude specimen of the fish-shaped shanks common at Ekseavik and present at Intermediate Kotzebue (Giddings, 1952, XXIX, 17; XXXVI, 17). Barbs for fish hooks are illustrated in *9*, 20 and *33*, 7.

The simple gorge, which has often been described as a gull hook[1] but which is here classed also with fishing implements because of its recent use as a lingcod hook on the Kobuk River (Giddings, 1952, pp. 36, 40–41), is present in the later deposits at Nukleet. *11*, 7 and 8 are ivory specimens.

---

[1] "Gulls are taken about the northern shore of Norton sound and the coast of Bering strait by means of bone or deerhorn barbs, pointed at both ends and having a sinew or rawhide cord tied in a groove around the middle, the other end of the cord being fastened to any suitable object that will serve as an anchor; or a long line is anchored at both ends and floated on the surface of the water with barbs attached to it at intervals. Each barb is slipped lengthwise down the throat of a small fish which serves as bait. As the gulls in their flight see the dead fish floating on the water they seize and swallow them; when they attempt to fly away the barbs turn in their throats and hold them fast." (Nelson, 1899, p. 133).

Other evidences of line fishing include line sinkers, a fish line reel, and a probable fish line guide tip. The latter, *11, 9*, is a forked object of antler, one tine of which has been broken away. This was probably inserted into the end of a wooden line guide used in ice fishing. Tips comparable to this have recently comprised closed loops rather than forks in the Norton Sound area (Nelson, 1899, *68, 9*, 12). Worthy of note is the superficial resemblance of this to curious forked objects from the Tigara rack burials at Point Hope (Larsen and Rainey, 1948, *93*, 19–20). The line sinkers from Nukleet are closely similar to those of Early Punuk and Punuk periods on St. Lawrence Island (Collins, 1937, *36*, 11, 14; *75*, 12–13) and to those from Intermediate Kotzebue (Giddings, 1952, XXXVI, 1–2). These are of bone, ivory, and walrus teeth (*11*, 16) and are alike in having a single line hole at each end. *11, 13* is additionally provided with a pair of small holes at the center, presumably for attaching small hooks by means of light line. The range of size in these sinkers is shown in the illustrated specimens (*11*, 12–14, 16–17). Fish-line reels are wooden strips deeply notched at each end. Two of these, like *12, 6*, were found in the oldest levels.

Ice strainer rim fragments are among the most commonly encountered artifacts at Nukleet. If strainers are associated mainly with fishing, as we think they are, this probably has more to do with the setting of traps than with line fishing. "Fish fences" of the sort reported for the Kobuk River (Giddings, 1952, p. 34) and reported by Nelson (1899, pp. 183–184) for the Bering Sea area require the cutting of many holes through river ice in order to set spruce saplings through to the stream bottom. The 77 of these strainer rims recovered are far out of proportion to hooks and other appurtenances of line fishing; hence, we are obliged to include trapping under ice as one of the principal means of obtaining fish—most likely whitefish in the spring and fall.

The Nukleet rims are made of strips of antler cut so that the outside of a segment of antler forms the outer surface of the strainer. The hafted strainer probably took the form shown by Nelson (1899, *67, 9*). The netting, probably of baleen or rawhide, was attached to the rims at closely spaced intervals, as indicated on the illustrated specimens (*12*, 1–5, 11). These rims appear at all levels, but they are particularly concentrated in the middle levels, and scarce near the bottom of the old section. Slotted specimens (*12*, 3–4) are relatively rare and appear to be characteristic of early and middle periods. Specimens with drilled holes occur in all levels. A fragment of a strainer rim with drilled holes occurred at Old Kotzebue (Giddings, 1952, XIV, 17), but further evidence of use of strainers does not occur in the major Kobuk sites.

Associated with strainer rims are fishing ice picks (Giddings, 1952, pp. 36–41; Nelson, 1899, p. 174). 16 of the antler picks are represented, with a concentration in the upper middle levels. These picks of sharpened, split antler characterize Kobuk River sites and are usually distinguishable from harpoon ice picks because of their greater relative width and their lack of finish.

The use of nets is much better documented than is that of traps. Sinkers of two types, floats, shuttles, and mesh gauges give us an idea of the kinds of nets set and the method of their setting. Most of the Eskimo archeological sites excavated before 1940 were peninsular or strictly coastal sites where fish remained a very minor source of food. It is perhaps for this reason that until the last few years the possibility of an early knowledge of netting was hardly considered. As late as 1947, de Laguna reviewed the widespread use of notched stones all the way from Lake Baikal, in Neolithic sites, to the American Northeast, in archaic times, and advised caution in interpreting them as net sinkers (de Laguna, 1947, p. 214). During the past few years, however, notched stones like those still in use as net sinkers by Bering Sea Eskimos have turned up as characteristic and numerous elements in river-mouth sites all the way from the Kobuk to Bristol Bay (Giddings, 1949; 1952; Larsen, 1950). They are particularly numerous in early paleo-Eskimo sites. As it would be difficult to explain these objects as line sinkers without showing why line fishing should have been practiced on so enormous a scale in early times, it seems to us more reasonable to relate them to nets (on which their counterparts are still used) and admit netting to a respectable antiquity in the Alaskan area.

The particular forms that stone net sinkers took in Nukleet times are illustrated in *12,* 7–10. These do not differ essentially from those of the preceding paleo-Eskimo deposits in the area, but they may be distinguished locally in most cases by the thicker and harder pebbles chosen to be notched on two edges. Only a few specimens are ringed entirely about by pecking, as is *12,* 10. 7 large, double-notched stones similar in form to the illustrated specimens were perhaps end-sinkers for anchoring nets offshore. Notched stone sinkers are relatively scarce at Nukleet, as compared with the Norton levels at Iyatayet, where they bulk large in the total count of stone artifacts. Aside from the probability of their continuance out of Norton horizons within the Cape Denbigh area, these sinkers are known in identical form from Ambler Island (Giddings, 1952, I, 2–3) and from the Yukon Island III period at Cook Inlet (de Laguna, 1934, *16,* 1–11). Nelson illustrated a net with sinkers of this kind attached (Nelson, 1899, Fig. 54, p. 189).

Stone sinkers were found at Nukleet in all levels, but antler and bone sinkers such as those in *13,* 3, 5, and 8, first appear in the middle levels. *13,* 3 is a section of antler perforated at each end, as are similar specimens from Ekseavik (Giddings, 1952, XXXI, 13); *13,* 5, of whale bone, resembles a sinker from Ambler Island (*Ibid.*, II, 13). The manner of attaching sinkers of this sort is illustrated by Nelson (1899, Fig. 52, p. 188; Fig. 53, p. 189). Sinkers like this are widely distributed in Eskimo sites from Punuk times forward.

Net floats are seldom encountered in archeological sites, probably because of their very perishable nature—particularly when made of cottonwood bark. Five floats are from the middle and later deposits at Nukleet. All of these are plano-convex in outline, with the opposite line holes near the plane edge. The range of these floats is shown in *13, 1–2, 4. 13,* 1 and 2 are boat-shaped—that is, wide at the surface that would parallel the top of the net and keeled on the opposite surface—and *13,* 1 has been hollowed out slightly with a beaver tooth. *13,* 2 and 4 closely resemble a specimen from Ekseavik (Giddings, 1952, XXXV, 13), but differ from a diamond-shaped specimen from the later Ambler Island site. Nelson (1899, Fig. 53, p. 189) illustrates the method of attaching this kind of float.

Net shuttles and mesh gauges are older in this area than they were formerly thought to be. According to de Laguna (1947, p. 213), "It is generally conceded that the netting shuttle is relatively late in Alaska and that it was introduced from Siberia in protohistoric times along with the net gauge and the tobacco pipe." At Nukleet, mesh gauges occur in quantity in the lowest levels of the A Cut and in the middle levels of the B Cut. The small antler specimens (*11,* 4–6) are scarce, and none was found in as low a level as were the majority of the large wooden specimens (*11,* 1–3). If the earlier mesh gauges were made of wood, as this suggests, we may have an explanation of their absence in other archeological sites where preservation is not as good as at Nukleet. *11,* 1 is a spruce specimen that has the carving of a human face on the distal extension of the handle. *11,* 2 is a similar gauge with engraved line decoration on the handle and a mending slit in the blade. *11,* 3 is the handle of another gauge of this type. *11,* 4, of antler, is a double-purpose tool, the proximal end having been grooved for receipt of a beaver tooth and scored about for lashing. *11,* 5, of antler, is made over from a sled shoe (one of the few evidences of sledding in the site) and comes from the House 1 excavation.

The large wooden gauges are executed in so different a style from those of antler (the usual modern Eskimo type) that they seem likely to have been made for a purpose unrelated to the taking of herring, salmon, and other fish. Nelson describes the customary netting of seals and whales by natives of Norton Sound (Nelson, 1899, pp. 126, 131) and describes the seal net as having a "mesh large enough to admit easily the head of a seal . . ." (*Ibid.,* p. 126). The 17-cm.-mesh net created with the aid of the gauge, *11,* 1, would be much too open for the largest salmon, but would be large enough to admit the head of a large seal, or perhaps a small beluga. The evidence from Nukleet thus points towards the use of gauges in making seal and whale nets as well as in making fish nets at a time when Thule culture existed over a good part of the Eskimo area.[1]

Three net shuttle fragments all occur in the later deposits at Nukleet, but they may still be the earliest reported archeologically from the Eskimos. The wood and antler specimens illustrated in *13*, 6 and 7 indicate the type.

Summary

The artifacts from Nukleet that concern fishing show that the hooking, spearing, and netting of fish are integral to subsistence at all periods. Netting is particularly well documented in the relatively large numbers of floats, sinkers, and net-making tools. It is far more significant than other fishing methods in terms of quantity of food. On the other hand, netting is more likely to be practiced only during large, predictable runs of fish such as salmon and herring, while spearing and hooking may be employed at all seasons. We recognize no data at Nukleet concerning the preservation of fish, and can only suppose that the same drying and freezing methods of today's Eskimos made it possible for the Nukleet people to store up quantities of fish against slack seasons. Although the frequency of net sinkers increases noticeably towards late times, our sample is too small to indicate whether or not this represents a basic change affecting the food economy.

The large number of ice strainer fragments, showing an increase towards the latest period, is to be correlated with fishing ice picks and their increase, as evidence of a middle and late period emphasis on fishing through holes in the ice. We are unable to say whether these objects were more related to the jigging of tomcod and similar hooking, or to the use of a leister. Possibly this emphasis is to be correlated with food shortage and the need of more off-season food in later times.

Comparative data on fishing are less satisfactory than on sealing or land hunting, and for this reason outside influences on Nukleet fishing are not clearly defined. However, it appears that fish arrows were much more commonly employed here than in any other known Eskimo site, and that leisters were of secondary importance. The complex of fishing at Nukleet is most comparable with that of the Kobuk River sites, although hooking seems to have been less important here than at the latter sites.

The earlier fish arrow barbs remind one more of similar barbs from the early cultures of St. Lawrence, in terms of delicacy and elaboration, than of those of the Kobuk sites. Otherwise, the nearest duplication of design

---

[1] Nelson (1899) also describes large-meshed nets for taking mammals: "For trapping beavers in their houses square nets, 4 or 5 feet across, with meshes large enough for the beaver's head to pass through, are fastened over the entrance to the animal's house below the surface of the water, so that in going out or in the animal will become entangled and drown. These nets are sometimes used in the same way for otters" (p. 123). Nelson further says flocks of ptarmigan were caught in long salmon nets (p. 133), and that salmon nets were employed at the Yukon delta for taking molting geese and their young (p. 135).

The Ingalik made their beaver nets of babiche line (Osgood, 1940, pp. 215–216).

Table 4. TOOLS AND

PLATE	16, 1–3	16, 4–6	16, 10			15, 1–2, 8–9	15, 7	15, 3–6, 10, 11 14, 15	16, 8, 12, 13	16, 7, 9, 11, 14	16, 15			27, 13–15	14, 15–16
TYPE	Knife blade, slate, single edge	Knife blade, slate, double edge	Slate blade, like Cook Inlet	Knife blade, unfin., double edge	Knife blade, unfin., single edge	Knife handle, side blade	Knife handle, wood composite	Knife handle, antler, composite	Ulu blade, with tang	Ulu blade, tangless	Ulu blank	Ulu blade fragment	Slate blade fragment	Ulu handle	Beaver tooth knife handle, side haft
Levels 1–2	5	2	·	1	·	1	·	1	1	·	1	2	19	·	·
3–5	9	6	1	1	2	·	·	5	1	2	2	5	48	4	·
6–8	4	6	·	3	·	1	1	2	4	1	1	7	22	2	2
9–11	4	·	·	3	·	·	1	·	1	1	·	3	15	·	·
12–14	1	3	·	·	·	1	·	·	·	·	1	1	12	1	·
Miscellaneous	1	1	·	4	·	·	·	·	·	1	5	3	17	1	·
H–1	1	5	·	5	·	1	·	1	·	·	1	7	28	1	·
IY	·	7	·	2	·	·	·	1	7	2	4	22	51	·	·

is between Nukleet and the Kobuk and Point Hope sites. Thus, a fish spear barb of a special form (9, 23) has been reported only from the lower levels at Nukleet and from Ahteut, Ekseavik, Old Kotzebue, and Point Hope burials.

Special features of Nukleet fishing are fish arrow shafts, a toy (?) side prong for fish spear, and a form of net float (13, 1–2). In another sense, the abundance of both ice strainers and fish arrow barbs is unique.

Tools and Manufactures (Table 4)

The one practice that most sharply sets Nukleet apart from archeological sites elsewhere on Arctic coasts is that of whittling, planing, and gouging mainly by means of a hafted beaver tooth. Many objects made of wood, and some of antler, show clearly the shallow, gouged marks that result from the use of this implement, the parts of which were also found in quantity. Other than this, the tools and manufactures are identical in the main with those of other Eskimo slate cultures, even though distributions may differ between this site and others.

Men's knives of slate include both end-bladed and side-bladed specimens, but side-bladed knives are rare, and composite knives appear to have been used here much less than in other contemporary sites. The scarcity of the

Beaver tooth knife handle, end haft 1	Beaver tooth knife handle, end haft 2	Beaver tooth	Whetstone, large natural pebble	Whetstone, irregular slate or shale	Whetstone, long, rect. 4-sided	Whetstone, long, rect. slate or shale	Whetstone, irregular sandstone	Whetstone, flat beach stone	Whetstone, thick beach pebble	Whetstone, long thin pebble	Whetstone ?, beveled edge	Polishing stone ?	Grindstone fragment	Beach pebble, hammered one face only	Tooth sharpener	Hammerstone	Pick fragment, stone	Splitting adz head	Adz blade, beveled	Adz blade, no bevel	Adz blade, double-ended	Adz blade, thin slate
14, 1-3, 10, 14	*14, 4-6, 11-13*	*14, 7-9*		*17, 4-5*	*17, 7, 11, 13*	*17, 6, 10, 14*	*17, 1, 8*	*17, 3*		*17, 9, 12*	*17, 2, 15*	*17, 17*	*17, 18*		*15, 12, 13*	*20, 7-8*	*20, 5*	*20, 1-4, 6, 9*	*19, 2, 6*	*19, 4, 7-8*	
·	·	·	4	13	1	4	3	4	1	4	·	·	13	1	·	4	1	4	2	2	1	2
1	2	4	2	34	4	7	10	15	3	12	2	1	36	·	3	7	2	10	3	6	2	4
2	3	13	·	10	3	6	2	9	1	5	·	·	14	·	·	5	1	4	·	1	·	3
·	2	6	·	8	·	2	1	11	·	2	·	1	5	·	·	·	·	2	1	·	·	2
·	·	6	·	4	·	2	3	4	·	1	·	·	11	·	·	·	1	1	·	·	·	·
3	3	1	·	3	·	2	·	·	2	·	·	·	3	1	1	·	·	·	·	3	·	·
·	·	·	·	14	1	4	1	4	·	2	2	·	5	·	·	1	·	1	3	2	·	2
·	·	·	·	13	6	8	10	6	1	1	2	1	6	·	·	2	1	4	5	8	·	7

last two types is probably accountable to emphasis on beaver tooth knives for most work that did not concern skinning animals and cutting meat.

Single-edged, end-hafted knife blades of slate are shown in *16*, 1–3. These are flattened opposite the sharpened edge. This would have made it possible to support and direct the blade by means of extending the forefinger past the haft, a custom recently manifested in skinning animals. Knives of this sort are found in Old Bering Sea and Okvik sites (Collins, 1937, *39*, 15; Rainey, 1941, Fig. 31, *1*) and later sites on St. Lawrence Island and are characteristic of Thule culture. Close identity appears between *16*, 1 and a specimen from Ahteut (Giddings, 1952, XVII, 15) and between *16*, 2 and a specimen from Old Kotzebue (*Ibid.*, XIV, 1). A small jade blade, *33*, 12, should perhaps be included here.

Double-edged, end-hafted knife blades of slate have a similar distribution to the preceding type, and were probably used mainly for slitting and such cutting as requires the knife to be held at right angles to the forearm. *16*, 4–6 are representative specimens of this type. *16*, 4 has evidently been secured to the haft by means of a pin through the drilled hole in the stem. *16*, 5 has a lateral projection on the stem to facilitate hafting. *16*, 6 is a plain blade, identical with a specimen from Ahteut (Giddings, 1952, XVII, 4). Un-finished, or very crude, slate blades of the above types also appear in the collections.

Table 4. TOOLS AND

TYPE	Adz head stone	Adz—worked fragments, stone	Adz handle	Adz head, antler	Awl, wood	Awl, ivory	Awl, bone splinter	Awl, antler	Misc. barbs	Gauged drill, bone	Gauged drill, ivory	Gauged drill, antler	Wedge, antler	Wedge, whale bone	Two-hand scraper
PLATE	19, 1, 3, 5		18, 4, 5	18, 1–3	23, 5	23, 15	22, 6–8 23, 12, 14, 16, 17	23, 4, 6–11, 13		15, 18, 25	15, 16	15, 17, 26	18, 6–8	18, 9	22, 1–4
Levels 1–2	·	6	·	·	·	·	3	1	1	1	·	·	11	2	1
3–5	2	12	1	1	3	1	4	6	1	2	·	2	24	3	4
6–8	1	5	·	·	1	3	3	6	1	13	·	·	11	1	1
9–11	1	1	·	·	2	·	2	4	6	11	1	·	4	1	1
12–14	·	·	·	·	2	1	4	3	2	11	·	·	2	·	·
Miscellaneous	·	1	·	·	·	·	6	1	·	8	·	1	2	·	1
H–1	2	4	·	1	·	·	·	1	·	·	·	·	11	·	1
IY	4	19	1	1	·	·	·	2	·	1	·	·	6	5	3

A double-edged blade is represented by the fragment *16, 10*, but this is recognized as a distinct type of slate blade more often associated with Indians or other peoples about the circumpolar region than with Eskimos. The stem is tongue-shaped, and polished all over, and the base of each blade edge is notched inward and upward. This is evidently a base of a long, thin, parallel-sided blade such as Gjessing describes and illustrates from Maine, Alaska, and on to northern Norway (Gjessing, 1944, pp. 20–25). Some of the blades illustrated by de Laguna (1934, *31, 1–13*) from Yukon Island II and III periods at Cook Inlet fall into this general category, but aside from an undocumented collection in the University of Alaska Museum (presumably made recently in the southern Bering Sea area) these blades appear to be uncommon in Eskimo collections.

The handles from Nukleet, such as might have held blades of any of the end-hafted slate blades, are all composite. Most of these are made of antler, but three specimens are broad handle halves of wood. Two of these are halves of the same knife handle, *15, 7*, designed to hold a broad-stemmed blade. Composite handles of this type are known from Ekseavik and Intermediate Kotzebue (Giddings, 1952, XXXII, 6; XXXIX, 2) and appear to be a regional variant of the Eskimo one-piece handle which does not show up at Nukleet.

Composite knife handle halves of antler appear to have a relatively late

Bark peeler	Drill bearing, astragalus	Drill bit, flint	Drill bit, slate; jade	Drill, or toy, bow	Firedrill shaft frag.	Firedrill bearing, wood	Pick, bone, etc.	Maul, bone	Flaker point	Flaker handle	Flint side scraper	Flint end scraper	Flint retouched flake	Flint nondescript scraper	Chert flakes	Flakes, jasper and obsidian	Blade-like paleo-Eskimo types	Misc. polished stone fragments	Drilled stone frag.	Soapstone, worked fragment	Pumice	Coal	Tci-tho scraper
22 5, 9	24, 9-10	15, 19-21	33, 13-14	4, 3, 11-12			21, 3-5	21, 1	15, 27	15, 28	15, 22, 29	15, 23, 24							17, 21, 22				
1	2	3	1	·	·	·	1	·	·	·	·	·	2	·	3	·	·	1	·	·	·	·	·
1	5	1	·	8	3	·	3	·	2	·	2	3	1	1	5	1	1	2	2	1	3	·	4
2	1	1	·	12	2	1	2	1	1	1	·	1	2	·	4	1	·	·	·	·	1	·	·
1	·	1	·	3	3	·	1	·	·	·	·	1	·	·	5	·	·	·	·	·	·	·	·
1	·	·	·	5	·	·	·	·	·	·	·	2	·	·	6	1	·	·	·	·	·	·	·
1	1	1	·	1	2	3	·	·	1	·	·	·	1	·	4	2	·	·	·	·	·	·	·
·	·	1	1	1	3	·	1	·	·	·	1	·	3	2	7	1	2	·	·	1	·	·	1
1	·	·	·	3	·	·	2	1	·	·	·	·	·	·	·	·	·	·	·	·	·	1	·

distribution. Some of these are shown in *15, 3–6, 10, 11, 14, 15*. The two specimens with very small blade slits, *15, 14–15*, probably had metal blades, while all others could have been designed for slate blades of various sizes. Composite knife handles in this form are known from all areas and periods of Eskimo prehistory. Close duplications of form are seen between *15, 4* and a specimen from Ekseavik (Giddings, 1952, XXXII, 3) and between *15, 5–6* and specimens from Intermediate Kotzebue and Ambler Island (*Ibid.*, XXXIX, 12; IV, 5–7).

Knives with side blades are represented by four handles of antler, all but one of which came from the more recent levels. *15, 1–2* are whole specimens, and *15, 8–9* are tip fragments with narrow slits in the side. *15, 9* comes from the bottom of Cut B. Blades were probably all of metal, although none of these remains in place. Similar knife handles were found at Ekseavik, Intermediate Kotzebue, and Ambler Island (*Ibid.*, XXXII, 7, 12; XXXIX, 13–14; IV, 8).

214 slate blade fragments are those of either men's knives or women's semilunar knives. Ulu (semilunar knife) blades are relatively rare in a fully recognizable form, however. The range of shapes and sizes of these is shown in *16, 7–9, 11–13*. Stemmed ulu blades like *16, 8* and *12* are perhaps more numerous at Nukleet than are stemless specimens. This form is well documented to the south, where it appears in quantity at Cook Inlet in

the Yukon Island III period (de Laguna, 1934, *33*, 1, 6–7, 9), but it is rare elsewhere in the Eskimo area. It is also found in certain of the Tigara burials at Point Hope (Larsen and Rainey, 1948, *90*, 27, 29). The other illustrated specimens lack a well-defined stem and are not sharply distinguishable from slate ulu blades that are known from the time of the earliest Eskimo slate cultures. However, regional styles may be indicated in the close similarity of *16*, 9, a perforated specimen, to Old Kotzebue and the Tigara burials (Giddings, 1952, XIV, 3; Larsen and Rainey, 1948, *90*, 28); of the high-backed specimens, *16*, 11, 13 to a blade from Ahteut (Giddings, 1952, XIX, 4); and of the large blade, *16*, 14, to another from Ahteut (*Ibid.*, XIX, 2). These are indications that the stemmed blade is the later form at Nukleet and that it was received from the south. *16*, 15 is an unpolished slate blade in semilunar form that has been chipped about the edges. This and others like it are probably unfinished ulu blades.

Nine ulu handles and fragments are all of wood. Three of these, including *27*, 13 (the socket of which is partly split out) are designed for stemmed blades of the type described above (*16*, 12). All are roughly crescentic in outline, like those illustrated (*27*, 13–15), and little change through time is indicated. *27*, 14 bears a simple decorative design, identical on either face.

Beaver tooth chisels or drawknives were of at least two types. One kind of haft was essentially an extension of the tooth—a handle of wood or antler with the tooth set in a groove at one end (*14*, 1–6, 10–14). The cutting edge of the beaver incisor could be drawn towards the user in the manner of a gouge. The handles of this sort that have curves or projections (*14*, 4–5) are nearly identical with specimens used recently by the Ingalik as wood chisels to be pushed away from the user (Osgood, 1940, pp. 85–86). Another form has a tooth set into the side of a cylindrical handle so that the cutting edge is parallel to the length of the handle (*14*, 15–16). This resembles the Ingalik "drawknife" (*Ibid.*, pp. 87–88).

14, 1 is a double purpose tool of antler tine. It is hollowed out on one side of the broad end to form the bowl of a spoon or ladle, while on the opposite side of the small end it is grooved to receive a beaver tooth.

14, 2 is a handle of seal rib with the groove and lashing lip at the smaller end. *14*, 3 is a similar handle made of the small end of a walrus penis bone. The groove end is partly broken away.

14, 4–5, 12–13 are handles made of small branches of spruce, the greater part of which is unaltered. *14*, 13 has been used also as a drill bearing. *14*, 6 is a molded and smoothed handle made of spruce. *14*, 11 is a curiously notched wooden handle, the tooth groove lying opposite the notches at the blunt end. The notches may have been made as finger rests, or the handle could have been remade from some unidentified shaft.

14, 14 is an antler tine grooved as a beaver tooth knife handle. All of the end-notched handles are provided with a lashing lip.

58

14, 7–9 are beaver incisors and an altered fragment such as might have been hafted. Thirty of these were found at Nukleet.

Most of the whittled pieces of wood, and some of those of antler, from the lower levels of Cut B have been cut with beaver tooth knives. This is a practice that does not allow close comparison with other known Eskimo archeological sites, although a few of both beaver incisors and handles appear in the Kobuk sites, especially at Ekseavik (Giddings, 1952, XXXI, 7), Old Kotzebue (*Ibid.*, XV, 3), and Intermediate Kotzebue (*Ibid.*, XXXIX, 15). The wood products of Kobuk sites do not show a predominance of beaver tooth whittling, however. Apparently the practice had become unimportant in the latest periods at Nukleet, although some use of beaver tooth knives was made in historic times in the same general area, as shown by Nelson (1899, Fig. 25 and accompanying pages) for the Eskimo and Osgood (1940, pp. 83–88) for the Ingalik (Athapascan). The use of beaver teeth is widely documented, of course, for Indians of the northern and eastern forest belt.

Beaver tooth marks may be plainly seen on some of the illustrated material from Nukleet, especially the following pieces: *7*, 6; *8*, 7, 19; *13*, 1–2; *32*, 7; and *34*, 3–6, 8.

Little can be said of Nukleet whetstones, except with reference to earlier whetstones in the same area. The whetstones illustrated in Pl. *17*, are similar to those to be found in any Eskimo slate culture. A classification is possible on the basis of materials and probable special use, however. This is set forth as follows:

1. Large, natural pebble with one or more rubbed surfaces. Fine-grained, igneous or metamorphic rock for edging slate blades.
2. Smaller, flat beach stones like above (*17*, 3).
3. Irregular sandstone (*17*, 1, 8) for coarse slate grinding.
4. Sandstone slab with beveled edge (*17*, 2, 15). These may have been used as "saws" for cutting stone, but the edges lack the U-shape characteristic of Kobuk River saws (Giddings, 1952, p. 66). A few pieces of saw-marked stone show that the sawing technique was known locally (*17*, 19).
5. Irregular slate or shale (*17*, 4, 5) for edging slate blades.
6. Long, rectangular, 4-faced, slate or sandstone (*17*, 7, 11, 13).
7. Long, 4-faced, thin, slate or shale (*17*, 6, 10, 14).
8. Long, thin pebble of igneous or metamorphic rock (*17*, 9, 12). Many of these found in the site could not be identified as whetstones, but had obviously been specially selected instead of the more abundant pebbles of other shapes to be found on the beach below the mound. Some showed definite wear, as in the edging of knives.

Besides these commoner types of whetstones there were fragments of thick slabs that had been ground on one or both faces (*17,* 18). These appear to represent large grinding slabs such as those of the upper Kobuk River (Giddings, 1952, VIII, middle). No complete specimen was discovered, however.

A many-sided, small stone of metamorphic origin that has been polished smooth on several surfaces, *17,* 17, is thought to be a polishing stone for objects of ivory and antler, or possibly for pottery. Large animal teeth, pierced for suspension, may have been knife sharpeners worn at the belt (Geist and Rainey, 1936, p. 102), or simply ornaments (*15,* 12, 13).

Hammerstones are relatively rare. One of these is a flat, igneous beach pebble hammered on one face only, as though in driving stakes repeatedly. Other hammers are battered at one end, and could have been hafted (*20,* 7, 8).

The tip of a hafted pick is perhaps represented by *20,* 5. The tip is sharpened from both broad faces as well as laterally along the thin edges. A similar specimen comes from Iyatayet.

Large splitting-adz heads, usually of silicified slate, are very similar to those described by Larsen and Rainey (1948, *10,* 4–6) from Ipiutak. *20,* 1 is a thick, rather crude specimen with a pair of struck lashing grooves on either side. *20,* 2, 3, 4, 6, and 9 are thinner and more carefully shaped. These are polished in the planes that come together to form the cutting edge. *20,* 9 differs from the others in being polished on all surfaces. All of these except *20,* 1 are tip fragments, hence the complete head is difficult to reconstruct as to size and shape. Apparently, however, these are prevailingly single-bitted. Similar adz heads are known from Ekseavik (Giddings, 1952, XXXI, 1, 6) and Cook Inlet sites (de Laguna, 1934, *18,* 1–3). Strangely enough, in view of the Ipiutak reference, this type of splitting adz does not seem to have been used by the people of Norton culture at Cape Denbigh.

Adz blades, of the relatively short forms that are set into heads of antler and ivory, may be divided into those that have an axe-like blade and those that are sharpened by steeply beveling at the blade edge, thus adding a third plane to the two that would normally form a blade edge. *19,* 4, 7, 8 are adz blades lacking a bevel. This is a widespread and common form of Eskimo adz blade. The beveled adz blade (*19,* 2, 6) at Nukleet has about the same distribution in the site as does the non-beveled variety, and it seems to have a comparable spread in Eskimo culture. Our interest in the beveled blade is mainly that it appears to have been somewhat more important in this site, the earlier Kobuk sites, and Ipiutak than elsewhere, and that at Ipiutak it was found predominantly in the burials (Larsen and Rainey, 1948, p. 85). The beveled adz blade is clearly designed for refined planing, while it would be of little use for chopping such as could be done with the non-beveled blade in preparing rough boards. If the beveled adz blade is then the

60

tool of a craftsman in wood, its presence or absence in a site takes on added meaning.

Late period adz blades include three rather short specimens that are sharpened on both ends. While these could have been used in connection with a separate head, it seems more likely that they were mounted as one-piece heads, to be used in either direction. These are unbeveled blades.

All of the blades described above are of hard stone—silicified slate or metamorphic and igneous beach stones. Blades of non-metamorphosed slate, however, occur in the same form as the unbeveled, single-edged adz blades. These are clearly too soft for working wood and bony material, and it is thought that they were scrapers or drawknife blades. Twenty of these were found, but none was hafted.

Stone adz heads of too large a size to have been fitted into a socket are thought to have been hafted directly to a stout handle. *19,* 1 is a jade specimen from Iyatayet, probably procured by its users from the upper Kobuk River. *19,* 3 and 5 are heads of silicified slate. This type is flattened as a planing adz head, but lacks a bevel.

48 fragments of adz blades are unidentified as to type.

Adz heads of antler are represented by only three specimens. *18,* 1 is a long, thin head, planed on its under surface to receive a handle. This is a rather rare type of head known from Old Kotzebue (Giddings, 1952, XIII, 11) and earliest Greenland Thule sites (Holtved, 1944, *28,* 15). A simpler form of head is the short antler segment lightly scored for lashing. Two of these are shown in *18,* 2 and 3. *18,* 2 retains a non-beveled blade in its slot. Heads of this type were common to the early Kobuk River sites (Giddings, 1952, XXIII, 3—Ahteut; XIII, 7–8—Old Kotzebue; XXX, 4—Ekseavik) and eastern Thule (Holtved, 1944, *28,* 6).

Two adz handles of antler are very similar to Kobuk River specimens. *18,* 4 is similar in shape, and in drilled holes for lashing, to specimens from Ekseavik and Old Kotzebue (Giddings, 1952, XXX, 3; XIII, 6). *18,* 5, from Iyatayet, has lashing projections and lips like those of a handle from Ahteut and another from Ekseavik (*Ibid.,* XXIII, 1; XXX, 1).

Sharpened implements of various sorts are illustrated in Pl. *23.* It is convenient to classify as "awls" those specimens that have no clearly specialized use except as punching instruments. Some of the "awls" represented here may actually have been parts of devices—as snare pegs, pins, plugs, and even hair ornaments—but of such uses we have no direct evidence. The Ingalik have a variety of awl-like implements similar to these, but hafted for various uses (Osgood, 1940, pp. 63–67). The 59 implements classed here as awls may be divided by materials into those of wood (*23,* 5), ivory (*23,* 15), bone splinter (*22,* 6–8; *23,* 12, 14, 16–17), and antler (*23,* 4, 6–11, 13). Aside from pointing out that awls of both antler and bone splinter are encountered throughout the Nukleet levels, we might indicate some specific similarities with other sites. *23,* 16, for example, is like a specimen from the Old Bering Sea culture (Collins, 1937, *30,* 16); *23,* 16 and 17 both have counterparts in Yukon Island III collections from Cook Inlet (de Laguna, 1934, *44,* 28–35); and the ivory, double-ended piece, *23,* 15, is similar to an awl from Bering Sea culture (Collins, 1937, *30,* 17). The last-named specimen is somewhat constricted near center and could have been used as a gorge.

Awls may also be included in a miscellaneous class of pointed, small objects that we list as barbs in the absence of any direct indication of how they might have been used.

Pointed objects of another kind are classed as gauged drills. These are irregularly shaped objects of bone, antler, and ivory, of a size to be held conveniently in the hand, all of which have in common a shaped, cylindrical point of a uniform thickness throughout. *15,* 16–18, 25 and 26 are representative samples. These gauged drills are known from Early Punuk or Old Bering Sea times on St. Lawrence Island (Collins, 1937, *48,* 1–9), from Greenland Thule sites (Holtved, 1944, *29,* 7, 14–15), and from the Yukon Island III period at Cook Inlet (de Laguna, 1934, *36,* 2, 3, 5–7). The Greenland specimens are treated by Holtved as marline spikes, and Rainey equates the type with "... cleaners for harpoon heads and other hunting implements since at present men carry such tools to remove ice and snow when it clogs the hunting gear." (Geist and Rainey, 1936, p. 103.) Whether or not these tools had multiple uses in early times, it is clear that the type is a special one that could have spread from St. Lawrence Island both southward and eastward in America.

Wedges of antler were present at all levels at Nukleet. These range in size as shown in *18,* 6–8. Wedges of this kind are widespread in Eskimo culture, although antler is largely replaced by ivory on St. Lawrence Island. More unusual is the heavy whale bone wedge, *18,* 9. This was apparently hafted and used both in an axe-like fashion and as a wedge to be hammered on top in splitting wood.

Two-hand scrapers of caribou metatarsal and metacarpal are cut in a lateral plane to afford two sharp edges for drawing across an object to be treated. Three fragmentary specimens, *22,* 1–3, are scrapers on which the condylar ends were left intact as handles. This form of two-hand scraper is known from Ipiutak (Larsen and Rainey, 1948, *22,* 15), Ahteut, Old Kotzebue and Intermediate Kotzebue (Giddings, 1952, XXIII, 10; XIII, 4; XL, 8), and Greenland Thule sites (Holtved, 1944, *27,* 6). Another kind of scraper, known in identical form from the Ambler Island site (Giddings, 1952, III, 9), is shown in *22,* 4. This is the posterior half of a metatarsal, the inner edges of which were sharpened. All of twelve specimens from Nukleet are cut laterally, and all but one are of the type which includes condyles. This is in contrast to a form of two-hand scraper cut sagittally, and sharpened on only one edge, which seems to have been used exclusively at Eksea-vik, and which is known also from Ahteut (Giddings, 1952, XLIV, 22; XXIII, 9).

Bone implements with a spatulate tip, *22, 5, 9,* are similar to specimens from the Ambler Island site (*Ibid.,* III, 9) and are identified with similar implements used recently both along the Kobuk River and in the Norton Sound area (Nelson, 1899, *38,* 12–13) as bark peelers. These appear at all levels at Nukleet and carry some implication of removing bark from standing birch trees, although they could also have been used in peeling local willows to secure inner bark for net-making.

Drilling techniques are documented by relatively little material. None of the mouthpieces recently used widely by Eskimos occur in the site, and it is to be inferred from this that strap drilling was unimportant or absent. Drill bearings of caribou astragalus appear in the middle and later levels, however, indicating the use of a bow drill with one hand while the other hand holds the bearing. While it would have been possible to hold these pieces in the teeth, as de Laguna implies was done by Eskimos (de Laguna, 1947, p. 170), none of the Nukleet specimens shows signs that this was the practice. *24,* 9 and 10 are specimens of this form of bearing, which charac-terized Birnirk (Mason, 1930, p. 386) and Thule culture (Holtved, 1944, *24,* 24–25), but is rarely recorded from elsewhere in the Eskimo area.

Drill bows do not appear at Nukleet in readily identifiable form. How-ever, a number of nock ends of a small, relatively thin bow appear at all levels in nearly the same form, as shown in *4,* 3, 11, 12. These are nearly all made of the stout "compression" wood such as forms on the outcurved trunk of bent spruce trees, and it seems likely that they would act as an efficient spring to keep a drill bowstring taut. If these were toys, as another possibility, they do not show the same changes in form that accompany full-sized hunting bows. Further evidence that these are drill bow fragments comes from Kobuk River sites, where specimens like these (Giddings, 1952, I, 21) occurred at Ekseavik, Intermediate Kotzebue, and Ambler Island, as the only probable parts of drill bows.

Shafts for the inclusion of drill bits are not positively identified in the Nukleet material, although some of the small shafts with square sockets, such as *10,* 1, could have been designed for this purpose. As to drill bits, however, eight of these occur in flinty materials (*15,* 19–21), and one each in jade and silicified slate (*33,* 13–14). The jade and slate specimens, from near the top of the deposit, are polished on all surfaces, have square stems, and were sharpened by beveling the tip.

Fragments of fire drill shaft fragments, identified by the charred, convex ends, and a few plank fragments of cottonwood containing charred pits, show the presence of fire drilling. These do not occur in the lowest levels, but too few were found in all to justify conclusions from this distribution.

A few large, hafted implements of bone, antler, and ivory are classed as picks and mauls. *21, 1* is a section of whale vertebra hammered about the large surface showing in the photograph and the one opposite. This was probably hafted, as indicated by lashing marks about the spine. *21, 3* is an antler pick scored about one end for hafting, and wedge-shaped at the other. *21, 4* is a similar pick of whale rib, and *21, 5* is the tip of a walrus tusk grooved at the thick end for hafting. *21, 3* is remarkably like a specimen from Ipiutak (Larsen and Rainey, 1948, *22, 6*), and the other two picks are similar to Ekseavik specimens (Giddings, 1952, XXX, 6, 8).

The extreme scarcity of flint-working products at Nukleet sets it apart sharply from earlier cultural horizons at Cape Denbigh. The use of flint was not entirely lost to Nukleet people, however, as is shown by the recovery of a few drill bits, scrapers, projectile points and raw flakes, in addition to flaker points and handles. The total count of only 34 chert flakes and 6 flakes of jasper and obsidian shows that little flaking was actually done on the site—perhaps only that which was required in sharpening the few flinty artifacts fashioned elsewhere and used on the site. Three side scrapers (*15, 22, 29*) are keeled, and pointed at either end, recalling Norton culture specimens from Iyatayet. These could have been recovered from older sites in the area, but we should point out that a similar specimen was found at Old Kotzebue (Giddings, 1952, XIV, 6) where there was less likelihood of this sort of appropriation. End scrapers of chert are shown in *15, 23–24*. These are also reminiscent of both Ekseavik and Old Kotzebue (*Ibid.,* XXXIV, 17; XIV, 4). Five others of this type were found in all levels of Nukleet. These and three nondescript retouched flakes make up the total inventory of Nukleet flint products found during the 1948 season. *15, 27* is a flaker point of split animal rib with one beveled tip. This could have been lashed to a handle, and three smaller specimens were probably placed in the groove of such a handle as *15, 28*. This handle is made of wood and has a lashing lip at one end. It is similar in form to an ivory specimen from Ipiutak (Larsen and Rainey, 1948, *43, 16*).

Miscellaneous objects found at Nukleet were two small pieces of whittled soapstone, four rubbed pieces of pumice, and two drilled pieces of white limestone. *17, 22* is one of the latter which shows that two drill holes have been placed close together, perhaps for the purpose of splitting the stone. *17, 21* has a single drilled hole.

Objects of worked baleen include the perforated strips, *24, 1* and *3*, and a pair of spliced lines, *24, 2*. These specimens, unidentified as to use, nevertheless inform us that baleen was used when available in early and middle periods of the occupation of Nukleet. Unworked baleen fragments were collected from all Nukleet levels except the sod level, totalling 48 pieces. 17 more pieces came from late period deposits at Iyatayet. It is impossible to say from this evidence that baleen whales were hunted, since raw slabs

64

or finished products could have been obtained through trade, and some baleen probably could have been salvaged from dead whales that washed ashore locally. It is to be noted, however, that three-fifths of the baleen from Nukleet was localized in the middle levels.

Fragments of worked ivory, antler, bone, and wood that are not complete enough for identification are enumerated as follows:

	Ivory	Antler	Bone	Wood
Nukleet	85	279	111	1123
Iyatayet	5	14	9	16

Proportions within Nukleet site are difficult to analyze because of the much better preservation by frost and the close-packed nature of the midden in the older sections. There can be no doubt, however, that ivory was more abundant in earlier times (see analysis of bone counts, pp. 92–94 and Table 9).

Besides the commonly encountered materials listed above, we found four pieces of unworked mammoth ivory and four fragments of mammoth tooth, distributed through all but the lowest level of Cut B. Some miscellaneous objects may also be described in this section. *23, 1–3* are some of the 46 pointed wooden objects found at Nukleet, mainly in the earlier levels. These undoubtedly served a number of purposes, none of which is definitely indicated, such as snare pegs, meat forks, and skin-drying pegs.

25, 3 is one of many bits of fiber line observed during excavation at all levels. The grasses and roots that made up this line were usually too fragile for preservation, disintegrating rapidly as they thawed and dried. Our impression is, however, that fiber lines largely took the place of the rawhide lines so commonly encountered in other Eskimo sites.

The spruce shaft fragment, *25, 5*, is wrapped at the intact end with rawhide line.

The nondescript object, *25, 8*, is the whittled-off section of a small tree branch with a bundle of grass loosely knotted around it.

Another curious object, *25, 4*, is a simple pebble wrapped in thin birch bark and secured with sinew lashing. Its use as an amulet, a line sinker, or a button all seem possible.

A puzzling object is the polished igneous pebble with a groove down its center, *17, 16*. The outward resemblance to a shaft smoother is negated by its irregular groove and high polish.

Summary

Tools and manufactures at Nukleet include knives for cutting wood, skin, and flesh, and the abrasive stones required for preparing and re-edging the blades of these knives; adz components, and the stones for grinding adz blades; pointed implements of organic materials for punching skin, bark, and wood; spatulate implements for peeling bark from trees; beaver tooth knives for whittling and planing wood and antler; wedges for splitting wood into planks; scrapers of bone and stone for treating raw skin and for finishing objects of wood and antler; drill components for the perforation of thicker materials than those effectively treated with awls; a few hand hammers for breaking or pecking stones; and little else. Some of these assumptions of complexes and functions are, of course, speculative. Nevertheless, none of the objects included in this section is entirely strange to northern ethnography, and we would be short-sighted in overlooking the more obvious associations.

The artifacts in this category are, in short, the equivalent of the modern tool chest—those implements required in making and maintaining the primary articles concerned with shelter, food getting and preparation, and social adjustment. This inventory is not remarkable for its individual items; in terms of its emphases and absences, however, it is reflective of the special environment and cultural background of the Norton Bay area.

The splitting and gross dressing of logs of driftwood was accomplished in all periods by the use of wedges and adzes. Wedges are mainly of antler, as are those of the Kobuk River sites. Heavy adz heads, suitable for the splitting of logs and in some cases for the planing of rough boards, are more prominent here than in most Eskimo sites. These take the form of Ipiutak adz heads and are made of silicified slate as are those of the early Point Hope site. Strangely enough, this distinctive type is present in Nukleet and late Iyatayet deposits but seems to be lacking in the earlier Norton culture deposits at Cape Denbigh. Inheritance of this trait thus seems to be directly out of an Ipiutak base, rather than out of a generalized paleo-Eskimo tradition. Distribution at Nukleet suggests an increasing importance for this kind of adz towards the later periods. If the splitting adz connotes the halving of logs for house building, as seems possible in view of the many split poles and logs found in the Nukleet later levels, we may have here evidence of economy in the use of driftwood as the major reason for similarity in this isolated trait between late Cape Denbigh and early Point Hope.

The variety of adz blades and thin adz heads at Nukleet is similar to that of the Kobuk River sites and other coastal sites to the north. The principal use for adzes with these cutting qualities would have been the controlled trimming and planing of both wood and antler that goes with the production of implements and the finer details of construction.

Men's knife blades of slate, for setting into the ends of either one-piece or composite handles, seem to have been used mainly for slitting and piercing rather than for whittling. Side-bladed knife handles are rare, relative to such sites as those on St. Lawrence Island, and no blades are identified as those of side-bladed (whittling) knives. Whittling, both of wood and harder organic materials, was accomplished by means of the beaver tooth knife.

66

The beaver tooth knife was also known along the Kobuk River from the earlier periods forward in time, but little evidence exists as to what its special uses may have been. At Nukleet, on the other hand, we see that a great deal of the whittling and planing, as well as the gouging out of concave surfaces, was done with beaver teeth. Both at Nukleet and along the Kobuk River, this use of beaver tooth knives is similar to that described for the neighboring Indian areas. However, we have no evidence from anywhere else, including the interior of Alaska, that beaver teeth were used at any time as a principal whittling tool, as was the case from at least the 13th century at Nukleet. It thus appears that we shall have to include the beaver tooth knife as an integral part of Eskimo material culture in those areas where beavers are available, and as an old trait in the Norton Sound area.

Abrading tools are to be found at Nukleet such as would account for both the manufacture and maintenance of slate blades of all kinds. Grindstones are represented only by irregular slabs and fragments. No special care seems to have gone into the preparation of grindstones, such as was implicit in the special jade-grinding stones of the upper Kobuk River, but Nukleet grindstones are numerous enough in all periods to account for the basic fashioning of slate blades in place, from the abundant supply of raw slate to be found along the beaches near Shaktoolik. Whetstones range through the various grades of grain size that generally go with care and repair of slate blades throughout the Eskimo area.

In a general absence of flint work in all periods at Nukleet, we see a departure from the patterns of the Alaskan area north of Seward Peninsula, where flint products continued to be skillfully made in quantity until the period of European contact, and a kinship with the St. Lawrence Island sequences after Old Bering Sea times is seen in this dropping of flaking techniques in deference to techniques in slate.

The *tci-tho* scraper, a prominent trait in all Kobuk River sites, scarcely appears at Nukleet, and only in relatively crude form, as is the case in Cook Inlet sites.

The two-hand scraper of caribou leg bone and the spatulate bark peeler of bone may both point towards the inland regions, as do beaver teeth, but both are firmly fixed in western Eskimo culture. These elements, together with the astragalus drill bearing, are likely to be old North American traits inherited from the paleo-Eskimo. In most other respects, the Nukleet tools and manufactures show a close relationship to those of St. Lawrence Island cultures.

It is noteworthy that most of the traits in this category are fairly stable through time, contrasting in this respect with the changing styles in hunting methods and emphases.

Table 5. FOOD PREPARATION AND HOUSEHOLD

	Dipper, wood	Bowl frags., wood	Bucket bottom, wood	Bucket top ?	Bucket rim, small	Handle—for bucket or bag	Birch bark, sewn	Pot hook, antler	Spoon, antler	Shovel blade	Rake, antler	Drying rack frame	Scapula scraper, scaler ?	Grass matting
PLATE						26, 1–5	24, 6–8 / 25, 2, 6–7	26, 8, 9	34, 6–8	26, 6–7	21, 2		24, 4–5	25, 1
Levels 1–2	·	·	1	·	·	·	·	1	·	·	·	·	4	·
3–5	2	13	10	·	1	4	·	1	2	·	2	·	5	·
6–8	1	7	13	·	1	1	1	·	3	·	·	1	2	·
9–11	·	2	1	1	·	2	·	·	·	·	1	·	6	1
12–14	1	·	6	1	·	2	2	·	·	1	·	2	1	·
Miscellaneous	·	5	5	·	2	·	·	·	1	·	·	·	8	1
H–1	·	·	2	·	·	1	·	·	·	·	·	·	1	·
IY	·	·	2	·	·	3	1	·	·	1	·	·	·	·

Food Preparation and Household (Table 5)

The artifacts from Nukleet that relate mainly to a woman's role in preparing food and keeping the house in order are neither numerous nor varied. Exclusive of pottery, which is treated in a separate section (p. 103), the most distinctive of these are the fragments of utensils made of birch bark and the bits of grass matting.

Dippers, or scoops, and one-piece bowls of wood were uncovered in fragments in various of the frozen levels. None of these is distinctive enough to be used comparatively, however, nor are these objects rare enough in Eskimo culture to give them any particular significance. The same observations hold true for fragments of composite buckets or bowls made of a planed board looped back on itself and sewed, and closed with a circular or oval bottom. Forty whole and fragmentary bottom pieces of wood show this form of container to have been fairly common, and various as to size.

The range of bucket and bag handles, of wood and antler, found in various parts of the cuts are illustrated in *26, 1–5. 26, 2–3* and *5* are all from the bottom of Cut B, but they display no particularly distinctive character, unless in their uniform simplicity.

Two pot hooks of antler, *26, 8–9,* one cut from two adjacent tines of a caribou "paddle" (*26, 8*) and the other evidently steam-bent from a single long tine, are closely similar to specimens from the Thule culture of Greenland (Holtved, 1944, *30,* 17, 21).

A shovel blade of antler paddle, *26,* 6, resembles, in the shape and position of lashing slits for a handle, another of scapula from Iyatayet, *26,* 7. This form of shovel—probably a scoop used about the house—is old in the Bering Strait region (see Collins, 1937, *50,* 6—Miyowagh, and Larsen and Rainey, 1948, *21,* 5—Ipiutak).

Rakes of antler paddle may be more regional in their distribution. The crude specimen illustrated (*21,* 2) and two other broken rakes are similar to specimens from the Kobuk River (Giddings, 1952, X, 2) and the hafted specimen illustrated by Nelson (1899, *35,* 2).

Spoons, exclusive of wooden fragments classed as dippers, were made of strips of antler whittled thin for a bowl and narrowed laterally for a handle. *34,* 6–8 illustrate three of six such spoons. *34,* 6 closely resembles a spoon from Intermediate Kotzebue (Giddings, 1952, XLI, 38).

Scapula scrapers like *24,* 4–5 appear in all levels and in relative abun-

Fig. 18. Grass matting upon removal from Section 1, Cut A, Nukleet.

dance. These were probably multi-purpose tools, although Kobuk River people recognized the type as primarily a fish scaler. These objects characterize the Thule-related sites on the Kobuk (Giddings, 1952, XVIII, 2—Ahteut; XXXI, 10—Ekseavik) and are similar to specimens found in early Thule sites in Greenland (Holtved, 1944, *26, 7*).

Drying racks may be represented by three fragments of wooden frame perforated at intervals. If these pieces are correctly identified, we can say of them only that frames of the "ladder" type were used in early Nukleet periods. A ladder-like drying-rack frame was uncovered in House 12 at Intermediate Kotzebue (Giddings, 1952, p. 81) but this kind of frame does not seem to have had a wide distribution in early periods.

Grass matting appears to have been used throughout at least the middle and later periods at Nukleet (Fig. 18). Only three pieces were found in 1948, but Wendell Oswalt, in 1949, recovered several large sections of matting and many fragments in house excavations at the site. The 1948 specimens, one of which is illustrated (*25, 1*), all represent the same kind of loosely twined matting, with stitches slanting upward to the right. Nelson illustrates a mat (Nelson, 1899, *74,* 14–15) that seems closely related to the Nukleet specimens. Osgood describes similar matting for the Ingalik (Osgood, 1940, pp. 144–145), de Laguna found matting used as shrouds by prehistoric Tena and people of Prince William Sound (de Laguna, 1947, p. 217), and Oswalt describes kayak seats of matting, as well as archeological specimens from Hooper Bay (Oswalt, 1952, p. 65, Pl. *8*). The Nukleet matting is probably the earliest yet reported for the Eskimos, although closely twined textile, probably basketry, was used as early as the 13th century in the Kobuk River region (Giddings, 1952, pp. 95–103), a single piece of twined textile was found by Collins (1937, p. 245) at Miyowagh, and charred examples of both coiled and twined basketry turned up in the earliest of the paleo-Eskimo sites at Bristol Bay (Larsen, 1950, p. 184 and Fig. 57).

Birch bark is frequently encountered throughout the Nukleet midden, even though birch does not grow in the immediate vicinity. Most of the birch bark was unworked, or showed only the marks of cutting (*24,* 7, 8). However, a few sewed rims and larger fragments showed the use of the bark in folded baskets (*24,* 6). The large basket fragment, *25, 2*, has a rim-stitching with spruce root that closely protects the cut edge of the bark. Just below the rim, on the inside, can be seen a bit of additional strengthener of wood stem (the Ingalik now use cranberry wood—Osgood, 1940, pp. 133–134) that was loosely stitched to the basket side. This particular basket, part of which was too rotten for preservation, was frozen in place 3 feet deep in Cut A. It still contained a crust of cloudberry seeds in its bottom and sides, as though it had been full of berries when covered over. *25,* 6–7 are fragments of birch bark baskets from Iyatayet.

Fragments of a birch bark container of another type were uncovered in the Nukleet period midden at Iyatayet during 1950. The form of this object appears to have been that more usually seen in wooden or baleen composite buckets, the sides of which consist of a loop of flexible material sewed on itself and enclosing an oval, or round, bottom. About the birch bark sides of this vessel had been incised and painted both human figures and geometric designs (see pp. 109–12). Larsen and Rainey hypothecate a basket of this construction as a prototype of the common Eskimo composite bucket, and interpret sewed birch bark in the Ipiutak site as parts of this kind of vessel (Larsen and Rainey, 1948, p. 111). I have earlier remarked that while the composite vessel could conceivably be sided with birch bark removed from driftwood, folded birch bark vessels are likely to crack unless folded while the bark is fresh from the growing tree and collected in the spring of the year (Giddings, 1952, pp. 86–117). In obtaining their folded baskets, the Nukleet people must have been either directly familiar with the upriver country where birch trees grow to considerable size or must have traded freely with others who lived in the forested area.[1]

Summary

The traits concerned with food preparation and household furnishing and activity are scarce, but they all fit into the general pattern of the western Eskimo. Birch bark baskets and grass matting are not widely associated with Eskimo culture, although the Norton Bay people have made grass matting as well as baskets of woven grass. The finding of these products in the early archeological levels of Nukleet shows them to be old Eskimo traits; hence their use among Eskimos in recent times does not necessarily reflect either trade with or borrowing from Athapascans of the interior. Both the use of birch bark and the weaving of grass at Nukleet are held in common with similar early practices along the Kobuk River, where twined basketry impressions in Ahteut and Ekseavik pottery and fragments of sewn and folded birch bark were found. This means that as early as the 13th century A. D. these traits were firmly established among Eskimos who lived near to the forest border or within the forested area at the base of Seward Peninsula.

Other inland-slanted traits are the antler rake and the scapula scraper, presumably a fish scaler. These are both prominent in all periods along the Kobuk River.

Other Nukleet traits concerned with food and household are to be found in most coastal Eskimo sites of all periods. While parts of a composite bucket are fairly stable throughout the mound, however, the carved wooden utensils such as dippers and bowls appear to become more common in the later Nukleet periods.

---

[1] See the variety of Ingalik birch bark baskets (Osgood, 1940, pp. 133–142).

Table 6. CLOTHING, PERSONAL ADORNMENT,
ORNAMENTATION

TYPE	PLATE	Levels 1–2	3–5	6–8	9–11	12–14	Miscellaneous	H–1	IY
Sewing needle	29, 3, 4	·	·	1	·	2	·	·	·
Winged needle case	29, 2	·	·	·	1	·	·	·	·
Sinew reel	29, 5	·	·	1	·	·	·	·	·
Cutting board	29, 6	·	1	·	·	·	·	·	·
Comb	34, 1–2 / 32, 7	·	·	·	1	1	1	1	·
Grass insole	25, 9	·	·	1	·	·	·	·	·
Labret, ivory peg	30, 11–15, 22, 29	·	3	2	1	·	1	·	·
Labret, ivory plug	30, 9, 10, 16–19, 23, 25, 26	1	4	·	·	2	1	·	2
Labret, antler peg	30, 20, 21	·	·	1	·	1	·	·	·
Labret, ivory, oval	30, 28	·	·	·	·	1	·	·	·
Labret, medial, stone	30, 27	·	·	·	·	·	·	1	·
Labret, wooden plug	30, 24	·	1	·	·	·	·	·	·
Pendants	29, 31, 33	·	7	2	3	5	1	2	·
Ornaments, fasteners, etc.	29, 31, 33	1	9	4	10	5	·	·	4
Brow band	Fig. 21	1	3	3	7	6	·	·	·
Engraving tool	30, 1–7	·	3	1	2	1	·	·	·
Compass ?	30, 8	·	·	·	1	·	·	·	·
Graphite	17, 20	1	·	·	·	·	1	1	4
Paint—red ochre		2	2	3	·	1	·	·	·
Paint—yellow ochre		1	1	·	·	·	·	·	1
Paint—white ?		·	1	·	·	·	·	·	·
Quartz crystal		·	·	·	·	·	·	·	1

Clothing, Personal Adornment, and Ornamentation (Table 6)

Clothing and sewing equipment are but slightly represented at Nukleet. Three bone needles all come from the older section of Cut B. *29, 3–4* are two of these. *29, 4*, from the bottom of the deposit, is noteworthy for the extreme smallness of its eye, with its implication of fine-drawn sinew thread and meticulous sewing.

29, 2 is a short, basally flanged variant of the winged needle case. This ivory specimen, with its ticked-line decoration, is apparently in the identical style of a fragmentary specimen from Intermediate Kotzebue (Giddings, 1952, XLI, 27), and not unlike a recent needle case from St. Michael (Nelson, 1899, *44, 32*). The plain antler tube, *29, 9*, is possibly an earlier form of needle case. It comes from the bottom of Cut B and resembles supposed bone needle cases from Ipiutak (Larsen and Rainey, 1948, *23, 6*; *48, 4*).

Other objects probably concerned with sewing are the wooden pieces, *29, 5–6*. The first, with notched ends, is identified as a sinew reel, and the second, thinned and notched for suspension at one end, bears the knife marks of a cutting board such as women use for their trimming and thread-cutting.

A compact, flat bundle of grass, *25, 9*, found frozen in place 3½ feet deep in Cut A is apparently an inner sole for a skin boot. Grass is still widely used as boot lining by the Eskimos, as it is by most circumpolar people.

Labrets and brow bands were used throughout the Nukleet periods. The presence of labrets of the simple plug type at the very bottom of Cut B is surprising in terms of previously known distributions of the labret. The labret in an elongated, heavy form has been demonstrated from paleo-Eskimo sites 1000–2500 years old in the north, and from perhaps even older sites in the Aleutians, but the simpler "plug" or "hat-shaped" labret has been considered a fairly recent development among the Eskimos generally. The use of labrets, though of different form, centuries earlier than the Nukleet periods in the same area, would lead one to assume a continuity of the older into the newer form somewhere in the area where both have occurred. Cape Denbigh, near the heart of the area of labret distribution among the Alaskan Eskimos, may also be in an area where labrets were never given up, as they appear to have been for several centuries north of Seward Peninsula. There is no evidence that labrets were worn by the peoples of Ahteut or Old Kotzebue, and only one, very doubtful, specimen was found in the older houses at Ekseavik. On the other hand, labrets were numerous at Intermediate Kotzebue.

The range of Nukleet labrets is shown in *30, 9–29*. These are made of antler, ivory, tooth, wood, and stone. The single stone specimen, *30, 27*, is shaped like labrets of the Norton people. It could have been discovered by a Nukleet individual and redeposited in House 1, where it was found. One of the oldest specimens, *30,* 28, is a small, thin, ivory labret from the bottom of Cut B. This is oval in outline and resembles the Norton labrets found at Ipiutak (Larsen and Rainey, 1948, *48,* 13–15) and the stone specimen from Nukleet, at least in outline. It seems possible that this is a transitional form between the large oval labrets and the plug- or nail-shaped labrets more recently popular. The "nail-shaped" labrets, *30,* 11–15, 20–22, 29, may in some or all instances have supported discs or appended ornaments, although no other evidence of this form of composite labret was found. *30,* 24 is a wooden plug of the sort said to have been used to widen a labret hole or to close it temporarily when exposure to cold would have rendered cold-conducting, harder materials unbearable. Other illustrated specimens are of the simple plug form widely worn in recent times.

Brow bands were even more numerous than labrets from bottom to top of the Nukleet midden. All but two (ivory) specimens are made of antler. These vary little in shape and are in this respect like brow bands from the earliest St. Lawrence Island sites (Collins, 1937, *15,* 11—Miyowagh; *30,* 26—Hillside; *58,* 6–8, 12—Miyowagh), Ipiutak (Larsen and Rainey, 1948, *24,* 15–21), Tigara burials (Larsen and Rainey, 1948, *92,* 2), or Old Kotzebue (Giddings, 1952, XV, 9). However, nearly all Nukleet brow bands are decorated with engraved designs, and these can be loosely correlated with depths in the midden, as well as with designs described from other areas. Brow band designs are therefore valuable aids to arranging the design form of both Nukleet and Iyatayet in time perspective.

The range of size, methods of lashing, and design patterns of Nukleet brow bands are indicated in Fig. 21. The 20 specimens of the illustration are arranged in order of their probable age, as indicated by their position in the mound. Numbers *1* to *5,* and 7 are from Cut A, and are not to be considered as progressive in time except with relation to the other pieces. Numbers *6* and *8* through *20* are from Cut B, and are arranged in order, with *6* and *8* the uppermost, from the 3-foot level, and *20* from a depth of 7 feet. It will be noted that although the elements of design are simple and geometric throughout and the elements listed by Mathiassen (1927, II, pp. 120–125) as those of Thule Culture are all present, the arrangement of these elements as motifs varies considerably and recognizably with the progression of time. These designs are treated in more detail on pages 97–103.

Hair combs include three antler specimens, one fragmentary, and one of wood. The antler combs, *34,* 1–2, from the earliest and later levels, are distinguished in no appreciable way from Eskimo combs widespread in time and space. The wooden comb, *32,* 7, on the other hand, has a handle carved in the form of a round-headed, featureless, human being. Forearms are lightly indicated. A similar comb from Old Kotzebue has a human head carved above the center of the handle (Giddings, 1952, XV, 8).

Engraving tools of a variety of kinds are illustrated in *30, 1–7*. The unusual bone tool, *30, 8*, has been thinned towards a convex basal working edge, the tips of which show wear as though drawn back and forth over softer material. Such an implement might have served to engrave parallel lines, or to execute circles, or both, on a wood or antler base. Possibly, however, it was a short one of those implements described by Nelson for attaching cords to seals that are to be towed behind a kayak:

> In order to pass the cord between the slits in the skin without difficulty, small, slender bone or ivory probes are sometimes used, having a notch at the upper end and a groove along both sides. The cord is looped and placed over the notched end; the hunter holds the two ends in his hands and passes the doubled cord through from one slit in the skin to another.
>
> —Nelson, 1899, p. 130.

This specimen comes from the bottom of Cut B.

An ivory engraving tool, *30, 6*, is of the precise form known from the Ievoghiyoq site (Punuk) on St. Lawrence Island (Collins, 1937, *81*, 17–18) and is similar to Early Punuk specimens (*Ibid., 60*, 10–11). Although this specimen lacks a tip, it probably was designed to carry a small iron bit, as did St. Lawrence Island specimens (*Ibid.*, p. 180). The thinner but similarly shaped specimen, *30, 7*, may also be an engraving tool, although it was not designed to accommodate a separate bit. Both of these are from the older parts of Cut B.

The composite engraving tool of wood and ivory, *30, 2*, was found in middle levels of Cut A and is therefore likely to be of a later period than those considered above. The wooden part is notched at the tip—evidently for receipt of a metal bit. Perhaps the owner kept bits of different gauges lashed to similar wooden plugs, selecting the one that suited his purpose and quickly inserting it in the ivory holder. The ivory part of this tool is deeply engraved with bands, ticked lines, and man-like representations, as may be clearly seen in the illustration. The only other combination of this sort that we know is a functionally different, but structurally similar, "drill shaft" from Miyowagh (*Ibid., 60*, 9). This specimen (probably Early Punuk) has had a drill bit lashed to the tip of the decorated ivory part, while the wooden cap, resembling a cigar in a cigar-holder, was fitted into a drill bearing. Although the Nukleet specimen is undoubtedly later than that from Miyowagh, their close relationship indicates a continuity that has somehow failed to show up in other archeological sites.

Both *30, 1* and *3* are provided with a groove such as would have accommodated a rodent tooth. The first is otherwise a plain shaft of wood, while the second is widened towards the middle and engraved in the fashion of ivory specimens from Ipiutak (Larsen and Rainey, 1948, *8*, 15–24, esp. 17). Similar engraving tools characterize the Ekseavik site on the Kobuk River (Giddings, 1952, XLIII, 24; XLIV, 8, 21). *30, 4*, of antler, lacks a groove at either end, but appears to have been capped at one blunt end, and may have been a special form of engraving tool handle. Although the curious ivory object, *30, 5*, is unlike any other engraving tool of which we know, the long groove towards its tip may have accommodated a bit of some kind. There is no evidence of lashing about the outside, however.

Other indications of engraving and decoration include a single large quartz crystal from Iyatayet, such as would have been rare and attractive and might have been used for cutting hard materials; several smears of disintegrated red ochre in the early levels and 4 rubbed pieces from near the surface; seven pieces of rubbed graphite (*17,* 20); three pieces of yellow ochre; and a single piece of rubbed, white, chalky stone. Nelson (1899, p. 198) observed for Norton Sound that "coloring matter is obtained from various sources. The dark reddish shade which is given to tanned sealskin is obtained by soaking the inner bark of the alder in urine for a day and washing the skin with the infusion. White is made from a white clayey earth; yellow and red from ocherous earths; red is also obtained from oxide of iron; black is made from plumbago, charcoal, or gunpowder, the two latter being mixed with blood; green is obtained from oxide of copper."

A large collection of miscellaneous small items includes pendants, fasteners, and problematical objects, many of which were probably worn about the person. These will be described in some detail, with speculations as to their identity; cross-comparisons will be made where possible, since some of these may prove later to be valuable culture-markers.

Unlike most coastal Eskimo sites, Nukleet apparently contains few of the large seal and bear tooth pendants variously described as knife sharpeners and pendants. A seal tooth, *29,* 11, and a bearded seal or dog tooth, *31,* 31, are both untreated except for grooving for lashing about the tip of the root. They show no signs of wear, and were probably pendants. A seal tooth, *31,* 2, perforated for suspension, is engraved about the middle with two lines enclosing slanted straight lines and at the end to represent a head like that of a sea bird. Two small canine teeth, *31,* 16–17, and the tooth *33,* 9 are all from the lowest levels of Cut B. Each of these has a very small drilled hole at the tip of the root, recalling necklaces or decorative strings of matched teeth such as Indians have sometimes worn. The small seal tooth, *33,* 8, from House 1, may also be a necklace tooth. Probable necklace teeth are also illustrated from the Kobuk (Giddings, 1952, V, 13—Ambler Island; XLI, 23—Intermediate Kotzebue) and Point Hope (Larsen and Rainey, 1948, *92,* 5–6).

A thin, rhomboid pendant of jade, *29,* 12, lay four feet deep in Cut A. This object, the use of which is not clear, gives us two valuable bits of information. If it comes from the jade deposits on the upper Kobuk River, as seems likely, this piece is evidence of trade to the north; and it apparently antedates the period of intensive jade working on the Kobuk (17th and

76

18th centuries A. D.), indicating the development of a large-scale jade industry to meet in part the opportunities of trade. (See references to jade in Giddings, 1952).

Small ivory ball pendants, *31,* 19–21, resemble in form and size the chlorite and antler specimens described by Holtved from Greenland Thule sites (Holtved, 1944, *37,* 17, 33). These objects all come from the same section and bottom level of Cut B and may have been the property of a single person.

A long, thin pendant of ivory from the upper levels of Cut B, *31,* 22, is identical in shape with specimens from the Kobuk River (Giddings, 1952, XLIII, 23—Ekseavik; XLI, 24–25—Intermediate Kotzebue) and the Punuk site, St. Lawrence Island (Collins, 1937, *82,* 7).

The ivory pendant in the form of a caribou hoof (?), *31,* 3, is from recent levels and appears to be unique.

The ivory chain and pendant, *31,* 4, from the middle levels of Cut B, is a standard product of other areas in early times. Similar chains and pendants are illustrated from the Old Bering Sea and Punuk periods of St. Lawrence Island (Collins, 1937, *31,* 4; *82,* 32–34) and from Ipiutak (Larsen and Rainey, 1948, *70,* 2–3). The pendant for such a chain was found at Old Kotzebue (Giddings, 1952, XV, 13). Although chain links are by no means confined to these early period sites, the form of this chain and pendant are very similar to St. Lawrence Island specimens, and a close relation to Early Punuk culture is further indicated by a series of drilled pits filled with black pigment about the center of the pendant.

A bulbous pendant of cottonwood bark, *31,* 32, comes from the bottom of Cut B. This could be some kind of float, although we have no indication of how it might have been used.

The small ivory pendant, *33,* 10, is a late-period specimen, quadrangular in cross-section near its tip.

Two small ivory objects, *31,* 14–15, from the same area and low level in Cut B are ovoids, concave at the ends and slightly flattened laterally. *31,* 14 is decorated with an engraved cross on each flattened side, while *31,* 15 has four short engraved lines ticked outward from the rim of each concave end. The concave ends show traces of a whitish deposit, suggesting that they were either painted or filled with an inlaid material. They appear to be unique, and no use for them is suggested unless it might be that of a form of dice.

Three short tubes, *31,* 5, 8–9, are similar in size, but variant in materials and surface treatment. *31,* 5 is an engraved ivory tube from Cut A. It is decorated with longitudinal and diagonal paired lines enclosing series of squares, with lines about the ends from which triangles point inward, and by a central band of shallow pits. Although these separate elements might be found on Punuk pieces, the execution of this engraving is rather crude and lacks geometric precision. The other two tubes are from Iyatayet. *31, 8* is made of soapstone. It is decorated by five deep grooves fairly evenly spaced about the circumference, and by series of short grooves joining these lines lengthwise. *31, 9* is a highly polished tube of amber, lacking engraving. Cylinders of ivory and antler very similar to these were found at Ipiutak (Larsen and Rainey, 1948, *27,* 11–12), but their use there is not indicated. Tubes of this sort are too short to hold needles, and the stone and amber specimens have rather constricted openings near center. They appear to have been strung in some manner, perhaps as beads.

A shorter cylindrical piece of ivory, *31,* 13, is an ornamental fastener, wide on one side which is dotted with shallow pits filled with black pigment, and narrow and plain on the opposite side where a line or cord has been attached. It comes from the upper part of Cut A.

A singular practice is indicated in the tightly joined seal claws, *31,* 18, and in several separate claws, the roots of which are split in such a fashion as to suggest that they had been joined to others in this way. We have no indication as to whether or not these claws were bound for suspension as ornaments or tools, however.

The thin oval ring, *31,* 23, appears to be a mounting of some kind. It is rounded and polished on the surface illustrated, and flat and rough below, as though for setting into a prepared cavity in softer material. It comes from the older part of Cut B.

The square buttons or mountings of ivory, *31,* 24–25, are also from the older deposits of Cut B. These small objects may have been attached to skin bags, or clothing, although their exact use is not apparent.

Another type of unidentified small object is represented by three ivory pieces of different sizes, *31,* 26–28, all from the bottom of Cut B. These are apparently line guides of some kind, such as might be set into a shaft of wood.

Small, thin antler rectangles, *31,* 30 and *33,* 15, appear in early as well as late levels. These were also found in 15th century Kobuk River sites (Giddings, 1952, XV, 18–20). A use for these as swivel pins is suggested by swivel parts with similar plates in place from Ipiutak (Larsen and Rainey, 1948, *57,* 1), but swivels are oddly absent from the Kobuk periods concerned. The only swivel part from Nukleet is the ivory specimen, *31,* 33, from the upper levels of Cut B. It is also suggested that these rectangles may have been gaming pieces.

The small ivory toggle, *31,* 29, is similar to bladder float toggles illustrated by Nelson (1899, *56,* 22), but its delicacy suggests some more decorative use, such as in connection with sewing equipment.

The walrus-tooth carving of a bird, probably a ptarmigan, *31,* 34, comes from Cut A. Although it brings to mind the bird-and-fox gaming pieces widespread in eastern Thule culture and represented in the later periods of

Fig. 19. Walrus head button of ivory.

St. Lawrence Island culture (Collins, 1937, *83,* 7–11), this object lacks the perforation in the tail for stringing that characterizes the pieces used elsewhere in games.

31, 10 is a flat carving in ivory to represent a whale. The extremely small size of this object sets it apart from most Eskimo animal carvings. It comes from the older levels of Cut B.

Animal heads are represented on the tips of three implements of unidentified purpose from the later deposits. *31,* 1, is a walrus tooth carved at the root to represent a wolf (?), and battered at the base as though used as some kind of hammer or mortar. *31,* 7 portrays another possible wolf head at one end of a poorly preserved ivory pointed implement. *31,* 11, also of ivory, resembles the preceding object in having an animal head at one end (walrus with tusks broken off), a suspension hole near center, and a dully pointed opposite end. This is possibly a boot-sole crimper or a feather-setter.

A delicate handle fragment of antler, *34,* 9, from Iyatayet, is carved to resemble a bear's head at one end.

Two other animal carvings, from the older parts of Cut B, are strikingly reminiscent of early St. Lawrence Island art forms. One of these, the bear head line attacher, *33,* 6, is stylistically similar (ears, shape of head, jet plugged eye sockets) to carved animal figures from the Okvik sites on the Punuk Islands (Rainey, 1941, Fig. 25, *1–3*). This specimen has three rows of circular pits on the neck region that are joined by engraved lines and retain the bases of feathers—as though the object, when in use, had been decorated by a crest of feathers. A large hole through the underside enters the throat region and emerges at the neck. *33,* 4 is an unusually fine piece of animal sculpture. It is an ivory button representing a walrus (Fig. 19) and is shown in the photographic illustration from the underside, where a toggle has been formed by gouging two holes together so the object can be fastened firmly to a larger object. Buttons closely similar to this are described by Collins (1937, *13,* 4, 6, p. 50) as elements of Old Bering Sea culture.

Among other decorated or ornamental pieces as yet unidentified are the carved wooden fragment, *29,* 1, with paired lobes along the wider edge; the tongue-shaped, thin antler object, *29,* 10; the ivory rectangle, *31,* 6;

and the small ivory wedge fragment, *33,* 11, on which shows a bit of Okvik-like, light-line engraving of parallel and ticked lines. All of these are from near the bottom of Cut B. *33,* 5 is a curved antler piece somewhat in the shape of a wrist guard, but lacking lashing slots, from a later Nukleet level. It has three double concentric circle elements at the upper edge. *31,* 12 is a small ivory peg, or wedge.

Summary

The few items concerned with sewing and the preparation of skins for clothing offer little help in distinguishing Nukleet from other Eskimo sites. Sewing needles with very small eyes, indicating to a certain extent meticulous sewing techniques, are not remarkable even in the lowest Nukleet levels, for these are also present in the earlier Point Hope and St. Lawrence Island sites. The winged needle case, from the middle period of occupation at Nukleet, offers close identity with another from Intermediate Kotzebue and is thus significant as a time-marker. Perhaps, as was indicated for Kobuk sites, the traditions of skin-working and the tailoring of clothing are not strongly influenced by environmental factors such as would periodically affect hunting and fishing, but tend to remain stable for long periods.

The presence of lateral labrets of essentially recent type in all levels indicates the diffusion of the labret among western Eskimos. Simple plug labrets have usually appeared in archeological sites as late introductions from the south. The discovery of labrets at Ipiutak, however, demonstrated the antiquity of the trait. The absence of labrets from all St. Lawrence Island sites, from regions east of northern Alaska, and from Alaska mainland sites later than Ipiutak but earlier than immediately prehistoric times has seemed to indicate a rather late revival of labret-wearing from some faraway center to the south. Labrets are absent in the earliest Kobuk River sites (unless a problematic object from Ekseavik is a labret), but appear in quantity at Intermediate Kotzebue. A pair of labrets was found in the Jabbertown site at Point Hope (Larsen and Rainey, 1948, p. 114), however, showing that they were worn by at least some peoples in the area during the time of Ahteut, and now we see that Nukleet people probably considered it *fashionable* to wear labrets at the same time. Thus we have no need to postulate a late diffusion from the south, but may assume that labrets were worn sporadically and regionally between the time of their height of fashion in paleo-Eskimo culture and the second, recent revival in the west, and that Nukleet was one of the regions where the custom may never have gone out of style.

Brow bands also have a sporadic distribution through time and space. Their presence at Nukleet at all levels, and, presumably, with the same emphasis from period to period, suggests strongly that labrets and brow bands should be considered parts of the same complex of ideas about adornment. The stability of both labrets and brow bands (presumably items of male and female adornment, respectively) lends strength to a view of the Norton Bay area as one where trends along certain main currents of diffusion were but lightly impressed upon a basically conservative and old culture.

Decorative elements and motives in the engraving art are best illustrated on brow bands from successive levels. The arrangements of elements into motives and designs are like those of other archeological sites of the northern Eskimo areas and help to establish the cross-dating, as well as to point up the strong relationship between eastern and western Thule art.

Pendants and ornaments decrease in numbers, while decorated brow bands remain stable in all periods. The earliest deposits contain pendants and ornaments that strikingly resemble those of Early Punuk finds on St. Lawrence Island, and the relative importance of these objects in the two areas and time periods is further suggestive of some kind of cultural connection.

Travel and Transportation (Table 7)

Nukleet, like the earlier Kobuk River sites, yields a relatively large amount of evidence of snowshoeing, and less of other means of transportation.

Dog traction shows up only in the form of eight sledge shoe fragments and two shoe fragments that were remade into other artifacts. These are all from either the sod level or immediately beneath sod and evidently relate

Table 7. TRAVEL AND TRANSPORTATION

PLATE	27, 3–8	27, 9–12	27, 1, 2	28, 1, 3–6	28, 2	31, 33
TYPE	Snowshoe fragment	Snowshoe needle	Sledge shoe	Kayak part	Pierced block	Swivel part
Levels 1–2..........	.	.	4	.	.	.
3–5..........	2	1	.	.	.	1
6–8..........	4	2	.	7	.	.
9–11..........	1	1	.	.	1	.
12–14.........	5	.	.	.	.	.
Miscellaneous.........	1	.	.	.	.	.
H–1	.	.	4	.	.	.
IY	.	.	.	.	.	.

either to the last occupation of Nukleet or to non-resident campers on the site after the mound had already taken its present form. Even though some or all of these shoes represent the time of last occupation of the site, this does not necessarily imply dog traction. As the writer has concluded from evidence obtained in Kobuk River sites (Giddings, 1952, pp. 62–63), sledge shoes appear before any of the other appurtenances of recent Eskimo dog traction, such as swivel parts, harness toggles and fasteners, and whip handles and ferrules. None of these are to be seen in the Nukleet collections. The sledge shoes, therefore, may have been designed for a built-up sledge that appears to have been used in this area by seal hunters before the spread of large-scale dog traction.

27, 1–2 are representative samples of the sledge shoes of antler from Nukleet. These had drilled holes rather than lashing slots and presumably were designed to be pinned to a sledge runner by means of wooden or antler pegs, as were those of Intermediate Kotzebue. *11,* 5 is a sledge shoe that has been later fashioned into a mesh gauge.

The only other artifact that could possibly be related to dog traction as we know it from many archeological sites in Alaska and towards the east is a swivel part of ivory. This specimen, *31,* 33, lay between 1 and 2½ feet deep in Cut B, and although no sledge shoes were found below sod in this area, it is possible that it has to do with sledding.

Snowshoe parts, mostly of birch wood, are about equally distributed among the Nukleet levels. The finding of both frames and crosspieces in the lowest levels of Cut B was rather surprising in 1948, for at that time the oldest snowshoe parts known for western Eskimo sites were those found in the 15th century site of Ekseavik on the Kobuk River (Giddings, 1952, p. 62) and in Thule-related deposits nine feet deep in the Kukulik mound (Geist and Rainey, 1936, p. 162). However, snowshoe parts were found by Helge Larsen in 1950 in an excavated house of the Ipiutak culture at Deering, Alaska (Larsen, 1951, pp. 83–87). Perhaps the greatest significance of the Nukleet shoes is that they include, in the middle levels, at least one frame fragment of modern Athapascan type. This specimen, *27,* 5, is a birch fragment, the cross-section of which is a rounded triangle. As photographed, two lashing holes show inside a ridge which lies to the right. As in modern Alaskan Athapascan shoes, the lashing was attached to the inner ridge of this shoe, thereby protecting the lashing from wear about the rims. *27,* 3–4 are crosspieces from snowshoes. *27,* 7–8 are two frame fragments of the commoner type of shoe, only the crosspieces and heavy central webbing of which penetrated the rims. Fine webbing in this type either was strung only between crosspieces or was stretched over the outer rims of the frame. *27,* 6 is a fragment of such a frame broken off at one of the crosspiece's sockets.

Snowshoe needles comprise three of wood, *27,* 9–11, and a broken one of antler, *27,* 12. The wooden needles appear to be unique, and perhaps help to explain the absence of snowshoe needles in sites elsewhere in which preservation of wood is poor. Snowshoe needles of antler and ivory appear in a Point Hope burial of Western Thule association (Larsen and Rainey, 1948, *88,* 10), at Ekseavik (Giddings, 1952, XXXIII, 20–21), and in later sites generally.

Aside from the indirect evidence of boating provided by toys (pp. 89–90), the actual parts of kayaks of essentially the modern Norton Sound type were found in Cut A. The bow piece of cottonwood root, *28,* 1, is obviously designed for a kayak of the same general type as that which Nelson illustrates from St. Michael (Nelson, 1899, *79,* 3). The lower edge of the Nukleet specimen has a series of lashing slots where it was secured to the keel piece and a single slot and grooves where a single lashing held down the central rib on top. The forward projections are broken off, but if we may judge from the proportions, the upper, small projection was not much longer than the width of a hand, while the stout lower projection extended considerably farther. This would mean that the finished kayak of this style would differ somewhat in the shape of its bow from the craft illustrated by Nelson, but would still resemble the St. Michael example much more closely than any of the other western Alaska kayaks illustrated (Nelson, 1899, *79*). The two crosspieces of spruce, *28,* 3–4, are evidently designed to support the central ridge of a kayak. These indicate the width of the kayak at the point where these ribs were used to have been about 60 cm., or only 10 cm. narrower than the greatest width of the kayak illustrated by Nelson (1899, p. 220). Since these crosspieces may have come from anywhere along the central section of the kayak, this information tells us only that the kayak in question was comfortably wide and in keeping with recent kayaks of the Norton Sound–southern Bering Sea area rather than with the slenderer northern and eastern kayaks.

The two wooden objects, *28,* 5–6, are apparently spear or paddle guards for the sides of a kayak, such as those described by Nelson (1899, pp. 226–27).

Two wooden pieces, of which *28,* 2 is one, from different parts of the lower levels of Cut A are unidentified, but may be the parts of skin boats. Each has a wide slot extending through the center, as illustrated.

Summary

The rather surprising evidence that snowshoes were in common use from the earliest Nukleet times is to be coupled with the fact that the early shoes were far from crude in execution. These indications lead us to wonder to what extent we can attribute the world's greatest excellence in the making of snowshoes to Athapascans. In the absence of archeological proof that either the babiche-cutting technique or the stringing of snowshoes is old in Athapascan culture, we can only point to this positive evidence that an Eskimo coastal people made fine snowshoes as much as seven centuries ago.

The kayak parts from Nukleet are principally from the middle periods of occupation. The kayak of some five centuries ago was essentially the same model as that currently in use in the Norton Sound area. If the several kayak styles to be seen elsewhere between southern Alaska and Greenland have been equally stable, a great age is indicated for the kayak as an element of Eskimo culture.

Evidence for dog traction before the latest occupation of Nukleet does not appear in the collections. Nor do the sledge shoes necessarily mean that dogs were used to pull the sledges that undoubtedly are represented in the last period, as the author has attempted to show elsewhere (Giddings, 1952, pp. 62–63). The Nukleet evidence strengthens the usual assumptions that extensive dog traction took hold among the western Eskimo only two or three centuries ago.

It must be noted that none of the traits at Nukleet concerned with travel and transportation can be seen as derived from cultures of the St. Lawrence Island type. Both kayaks and snowshoes may have been old on the American side of Bering Strait when Early Punuk art and sea-hunting forms were introduced.

Table 8. COMMUNITY

PLATE	34, 10–12			34, 13	32, 1–14	32, 16–17	32, 15, 18	29, 7, 8
TYPE	Armor plate	Drum rim	Drum handle	Buzz	Doll	Boat model	Dish model	Lancet
Levels 1–2.........	2	.	1	.	.	1	1	1
3–5.........	3	.	.	.	1	6	2	.
6–8.........	.	1	2	1	1	.	2	.
9–11.......	.	1	.	.	6	3	.	.
12–14.......	.	1	.	.	5	2	1	.
Miscellaneous	.	1	.	.	2	5	3	.
H–1	.	.	.	.	4	1	2	.
IY	.	.	1	.	.	1	.	1

84

Community (Table 8)

The classes of objects that we judge to have more to do with the community as a whole than with any of the categories of food-getting, housing, and the like, are those concerning warfare, shamanism, ceremonials, and childhood play.

Signs of feuding, group rivalry, or warfare are seen only in the five pieces of armor plate found in the uppermost levels at Nukleet. These, *34, 10–12,* are thin plates of antler, each of which has three pairs of drilled perforations at the edges for lashing to other plates. Armor plate in this form appeared on St. Lawrence Island by the time of Ievoghiyoq (Collins, 1937, *76,* 20–23) and had reached the Kotzebue Sound area by the 16th century (Giddings, 1952, XL, 1–7), when it was important at the Intermediate Kotzebue site. Armor plate does not seem to have been much used north of Seward Peninsula, but it continued to be made until recent times in the coastal areas nearest to Bering Strait. Nelson (1899, *92*) illustrated ivory plate armor in nearly complete form from the Diomede Islands. A difference worth noting between the Punuk armor plate from St. Lawrence Island and that from the Alaskan sites of Nukleet and Intermediate Kotzebue is that the former is often slotted for lashing and made of bone (?), while the latter is always drilled and made only of antler. (See Collins, 1937, pp. 224–5; Geist and Rainey, 1936, pp. 111, 142, 159.)

Three fragments of wooden drum rim, one from the earliest levels, show no distinguishing features, nor do four plain drum handles—two of antler and two of wood. The antler handles are sections of thin antler cut square at each end and notched halfway through near one end.

The fragment of a "buzz" (bull-roarer), *34,* 13, is made of spruce wood and shows traces of red pigment. Although probably a toy, its use as a ceremonial object is not precluded.

Two objects are familiar to us from Kobuk River sites and are classed as lancets, such as shamans used, as suggested from a specimen from Point Atkinson and another from Point Barrow, described tentatively as such by Mathiassen (1930, p. 26). *29, 7* is a polished slate specimen from Iyatayet, the beveled and sharpened blade of which stands above a wide, irregular stem evidently meant for hafting. Identical specimens were found at Ekseavik and Old Kotzebue (Giddings, 1952, XV, 14; XLIII, 25–26). These are all like the specimen described by Mathiassen. A jade blade from the sod level at Nukleet, *29,* 8, of a small size and less distinctive shape, is like jade specimens from the upper Kobuk River, where it probably originated.

A surprisingly large number of carvings of the human figure were found at Nukleet, mainly in the earlier deposits. As is usually the case with Eskimo specimens of this sort, we are unable to say whether these were mainly dolls or ceremonial figures. Small human figures of several kinds have been used recently in connection with whaling ceremonies, both at Point Hope and on St. Lawrence Island, and it seems likely that symbolic objects of this sort might have played a part in serious social observances of many kinds in times past. On the other hand, Eskimo children almost everywhere are provided with dolls, some of which can be expected to be preserved in rubbish heaps. The significant fact at Nukleet is that these human carvings are perhaps more relatively numerous than in any Eskimo sites other than eastern Thule.

A total of 19 whole and fragmentary dolls (as we shall call them for the sake of brevity) are preserved from the Nukleet test cuts and House 1 excavation. They are carved from wood or bark. At least one of these is recognized as the part of an object in daily use—the spruce wood comb, *32, 7*. With one possible exception, *32, 9*, these are shown as naked, or clothed only in short trunks or breech clout. Physiognomy is not stressed, but details of the remainder of the body are often carefully indicated. Heads are always broad, approaching roundness, and it is particularly note-worthy that no single physical form prevails. Arms are usually indicated, though not always at full length. Representative Nukleet dolls are shown in Pl. *32*.

32, 1 is the fore view of a faceless, naked male doll of spruce. The thin, short forearms and the stubby foot are out of keeping with the good proportions of the rest of the figure. The greater part of the right leg has been broken away.

32, 2 is a doll of bark. Eyes and nose are crudely indicated on the broad head, and the arms are represented by stubby projections, as are those of seven others in the photograph. The legs are partly broken away.

32, 3 is a whimsical small doll of spruce, the prominent breasts of which pronounce it female. This was hardly intended as a serious representation of a human being, and may have been that of a mythical being.

32, 4 is a rather crude bark doll with a large head, one leg of which was unfinished when it was discarded. The other leg is missing, possibly broken off in the whittling.

32, 5 is the back of a carefully sculptured male doll of wood, showing accurate observation of the muscles of the back. The legs were apparently meant to be cut off at the knees, but the intact part of a left arm shows signs of having been proportionate to the body. The head and right arm were apparently broken off after completion.

32, 6 is a doll fragment of spruce, evidently representing an attenuated individual like *32, 1*.

32, 7, the comb mentioned above, shows the human figure with a feature-less head, sloping shoulders, and forearms blending with the top of the comb.

32, 8 is a fragmentary, crude, bark doll, the intact foot of which is stubby like that of *32, 1*.

Fig. 20. Dolls from Iyatayet Site. (*1*: Norton culture; *2* and *3*: Nukleet culture.)

87

32, 9 is another crude bark doll, possibly indicated as wearing a parkee with hood up. The lower part has been broken away.

32, 10 shows the back of a male doll that appears to have been realistically proportioned, but not as a person of "classic" Eskimo build. Men of the Kotzebue Sound and Norton Sound areas sometimes reach a height of six feet and are relatively long-legged. The cottonwood bark of which this figure was made has partly split away on both sides, obscuring features. The legs have been broken away, but the arms were originally as shown in the photograph.

32, 11 is another bark fragment, the eyes and mouth of which may have been painted on, as indicated by faint scratches where these features should be.

32, 12 is a crude male figure in bark, the indicated genitals of which show that it was meant as unclothed.

32, 13 is the fore view of a broken female doll of bark, indicated as wearing short trunks.

32, 14 is another fragmentary bark doll, no distinguishing features of which remain.

A small representation of the human figure (not shown), similar to *32, 2*, is a simple cut-out in thin birch bark. Two dolls from the Iyatayet 1949 excavations are shown in Fig. 20, *2* and *3*. The first of these is a female doll of cottonwood bark on which eyes, nose, and mouth are crudely indicated. Feet are shown as slight forward projections similar to those of *32, 1* and *8*. The second is an ivory male figure, portrayal of feet and hands of which has been avoided by over-thinning the arms and blending the lower legs together. Facial features are indicated. Both of these dolls are shown as wearing short trunks, and both are stocky of body build. The ivory specimen has a groove about the sides of the face, joining under the chin. This grooving shows that the doll was meant to be suspended, perhaps as an adjunct of some ceremony.

The two Nukleet period dolls from Iyatayet are contrasted in the same photograph with a doll from Norton culture deposits of the same site, Fig. 20, *1*. This is a dark brown ivory specimen. Neither arms nor facial features are indicated, although the upper part seems to have been finished and partly polished. The legs are left rough, and possibly unfinished. This doll differs from all the later ones in the long-oval, pointed-chin treatment of the head. This treatment of head shape in figurines is characteristic of Okvik (Rainey, 1941, *28*, 1, 3; *29*, 1, 4, 5), early Old Bering Sea (Collins, 1937, *12*, 5–7), Near Ipiutak (Larsen and Rainey, 1948, *81*, 17), and possibly Yukon Island II (de Laguna, 1934, *52*, 2) cultures. Round heads similar to those of Nukleet seem to be the rule, on the other hand, in Early Punuk and later St. Lawrence Island cultures (Collins, 1937, *59*,

16–17; *83,* 12–13). A marked similarity in the treatment of legs is noted between a doll from Kialegak, St. Lawrence Island (*Ibid., 83,* 12) and the male doll from Iyatatyet. This specimen is further discussed on page 146.

In view of the rather large number of dolls from the Nukleet period at Cape Denbigh, perhaps we are justified in reading some meaning into the treatment of the human physique. One might imagine that figurines as realistically carved as some of the specimens considered above would reflect to no small degree the standards of beauty of the peoples concerned. Thus, we might see in the general change towards round-headed dolls after paleo-Eskimo times on the Alaskan mainland, and after Old Bering Sea times on St. Lawrence Island, a recognition of broad-headedness as a desirable feature. Coinciding as does this trait with a general change in material culture in both regions, there is even more reason to see an increasing dominance of broad-headed peoples over earlier ones whose faces were long.

The present-day western Eskimos are, as Hrdlička pointed out, highly mesocephalic to moderately brachycephalic (Hrdlička, 1930, p. 249). This is in contrast to the eastern Eskimos generally, and to the people who established the Thule culture in the east in particular. If the physical type of a people tends to be closely portrayed in doll form, we might expect dolls of the Thule culture in the east to be predominantly long-headed. This is not the case, however. Holtved illustrates the variety of dolls found in Thule sites of Greenland (Holtved, 1944, *40*). Among 28 dolls portrayed, only four have markedly oval faces. The remainder have round heads similar to those of the Nukleet period. In portrayal of the head, then, there seems to have been more adherence to widespread tradition than to sculptural accuracy. In another respect, however, the Thule dolls conform throughout. This is in stressing a long trunk above very short legs. There is clearly a strong bond of continuity between the Nukleet dolls and those of Greenland Thule sites, although short legs and long trunk are stressed in the east and not in the west. Strikingly enough, there seems to be more kinship between these two groups of dolls, separated by thousands of miles, than between either of these and the Okvik or Norton dolls of the Bering Strait region.

Other toys, or models, include 11 small dishes of bark. *32,* 15 is in apparent imitation of large, carved bowls, or trays. *32,* 18 is quite different from any of the others, the deep central part being rimmed by a relatively wide, upturned rim. This is possibly the model of some form of basketry, wooden bowl, or pot of which we have no record.

Models of boats include 19 fragments of both open boats and kayaks carved from cottonwood bark. Two of the more complete specimens of kayak are illustrated (*32,* 16–17). Each of these shows a trace of a bow projection similar to that of present-day kayaks of the Norton Sound region.

Other fragments offer little additional information except to indicate that small boat models were made in all Nukleet periods.

Other toys are indicated in the harpoon head, *6, 26*, the arrow shaft, *3*, 1, and possibly in a few other small objects described elsewhere.

Summary

Evidence concerning the broader aspects of social organization is always scanty in archeological sites, other than burials, of the Eskimos. Nukleet offers only a few items that shed light upon ideas of group protection, ceremonialism, shamanism, and the rearing of children. Nothing can be said of death practices except that burials of some periods of occupation of Cape Denbigh were made on the surface of the ground at the top of the cliffs facing northwestward. All these burials are now either weathered away or destroyed by the trampling of reindeer, although some of them are said by Eskimos to have been collected by scientists in earlier years. Surface burial on high ridges parallels the practice on St. Lawrence Island (Collins, 1937, p. 246; Geist and Rainey, 1936, pp. 80–81), and presumably precedes the tepee-burials of recent times in the Norton Sound region.

Drum rims and drum handles are scarce at Nukleet, as compared with other large coastal sites of the Eskimos, and they offer no distributional or stylistic information of value.

Armor plate is also scarce, and it is limited to the uppermost deposits. The preparation of heavy plate armor in itself suggests a looking forward that does not presently characterize most Eskimo endeavors, and leads one to accept the reality of inter-tribal feuding in those areas such as St. Lawrence Island and other Bering Strait points where armor plate has been found in abundance. It seems unlikely that warfare figured strongly either at Norton Bay or Kotzebue Sound, however, since armor plate is sparsely represented. Perhaps the presence of a few plates of armor at both the Intermediate Kotzebue site and Nukleet represents more a fashion or pattern of self-protection than the actual need of preparation for or against armed attack.

If we are correct in interpreting the delicately executed, small slate "lancet" as a shaman's accessory, we have at Nukleet at least this one trait of shamanistic identity between Norton Bay and the whole of the coast northward to the Point Barrow region.

The remainder of the artifacts from Nukleet that relate to the whole community appear to do so through ceremonial magic, or the play of children, or both. Ethnographic sources show that models of boats and utensils and miniature human figures play a part in whaling and other game-getting ceremonies at St. Lawrence Island, Point Hope, and elsewhere. Similar figures are made in the same areas for children to use in their imitative

90

activities. In view of the relative scarcity or absence at Nukleet of such commonly employed ceremonial objects as the drum and masks, we should not expect to find a great many ceremonial miniatures. Therefore, it is proposed that the great majority of the relatively numerous dolls and models at Nukleet were dropped by children, and that these toys were characteristic of the site at all periods. Exceptions may be the two human figures with suspension grooves around the sides of the heads. The manner of grooving these figures is remarkably like that illustrated by Laughlin from the Aleutian site of Chaluka and described as a "household image" (Laughlin and Marsh, 1951, frontispiece and p. 82).

The high incidence of dolls in the lower levels may relate somewhat to the better preservation of organic materials in the permanently frozen parts of the mound, but it looks as if dolls were numerous only during the earlier periods of occupation. It seems very significant that both in numbers and in styles of execution these dolls more closely resemble those of early Thule sites of Greenland and northeastern Canada than those of other known western Eskimo sites.

Miscellaneous

Some of the materials excavated at Nukleet do not lend themselves to classification within the main categories of activities based upon presumed function of artifact type. These include animal bones and worked fragments that may not be identified except as to material. Also included are a few objects complete in themselves, but of such a nature that they may not be classified on the basis of our present knowledge. The latter are few in number and appear to represent no highly significant facet of culture.

Table 9. ANIMAL BONES

	Percent of bird bones	Percent of beluga bones	Percent of bearded seal bones	Percent of small seal bones	Percent of caribou bones	Percent of walrus bones	Total bones in sample
Levels 1–2........	18	5	18	50	6	3	5172
3–5........	15	3	18	53	9	2	5940
6–8........	11	3	17	53	12	4	2823
9–11.......	19	2	9	52	18	0	990
12–14......	14	2	15	52	17	0	1134
H–1	15	2	16	62	5	0	1736
Nukleet..........	15	3	16	53.5	11	1.5	17,795

Bone Counts and Their Significance (Table 9)

The unworked animal bones uncovered in the Nukleet mound seem to have meaning in terms both of food supply of the local residents at various times and of possible shifts in populations of the game animals themselves.

Our aim at Nukleet was to save all bones for identification. Practically, however, this was neither possible nor likely to be productive of significant data. Fish bones, for example, may number in thousands and still represent only a few individual fish. (Fish bones, and those of small rodents, are difficult to sort out from other debris where they are present in quantity, and an attempt to sort them out is time-consuming.) Consequently, we decided to limit statistics to the bones of larger mammals and birds. It is likely that many small bird bones escaped attention, but it is also likely that consistency was maintained throughout the site in the proportion of these small bones saved to those lost. Bones of the larger mammals were treated with the same degree of thoroughness as were artifacts. It is, therefore, likely that our statistics for the whole site are relatively proportionate, even though bird bones are more reliably indexed against total bones recovered than against the total of birds represented in the site.

Two ways are open to the archeologist who wants his collection of animal bones identified. The more scientific way is to box up all bones and ship them to a specialist in this sort of identification. The biologist who undertakes such an examination is usually hard-pressed for time and either delays his analysis for months or years, or submits only a cursory analysis to the archeologist. The other way of securing identifications is to employ local observers who are familiar with the bones of animals in their environmental region. The Eskimos are meat eaters primarily, and we have found through long experience that most Eskimo men and women do not hesitate to identify a bone proffered them as that of a local animal or of an unknown animal. Their identification is not confined to parts of the skull or the more scientific diagnostics of condyles and the like, but extends freely to all bones of the body. This non-scientific, but nonetheless accurate, identification of the separate bones and the ways they fit together is a result of the daily dissection of food animals and the picking clean of the bones in the course of eating a predominantly flesh diet.

We have a great deal of confidence in the identification of the bones made by our Eskimo helpers—particularly in that made by the women, who normally do most of the family meat-cutting. On bone-counting days, the Eskimo men and their wives usually spent several hours in progressing from the bone pile of one level to that of another, sorting out the bones of the broader divisions of animals into separate groups. The occasional disagreement that we noted among the consultants was usually settled quickly by one of the women after a graphic demonstration of what part of the

92

skeleton of a particular animal was concerned. Our demands did not extend to differences between closely related species, but to the sort of animals that were considered distinct in appearance, habits, and environmental preference. Thus, the bones of small seal are not distinguished from each other, but from those of the bearded seal and the walrus, the habits of which are largely distinct from those of small seal.

The bones thus collected and identified from the Nukleet test cuts of 1948 number 17,795. The sample is large enough to have meaning in terms of hunting and subsistence emphasis and to escape the culturally imposed distortion that can easily arise from the selection for identification of only special series of bones from each kind of animal. (Counts of crania, for example, can be entirely misleading if the heads of one species are customarily thrown into the sea while those of others are not subject to this ceremonial treatment.)

The vertical columns of Table 9 contain percentages of total bones for the levels indicated and the total of bones in the sample. The animals concerned in this tabulation are those of birds, beluga, bearded seal, small seal, caribou, and walrus. The lower two horizontal columns are separate percentages for House 1 as a whole, and for Nukleet as a whole, regardless of time periods.

It is to be noted that the percentages of bones of both birds and small seal remain fairly constant from the lowest levels of the test cuts to the top, while the percentages for the other animals change through time. The rather uniform decrease in percentages of caribou bones parallels uniform increases in percentages of the bones of all the large sea mammals.

One possible interpretation of these indications is strictly cultural. As Nukleet people slowly lost their interest in caribou, they developed their ability to secure the large sea mammals—beluga, bearded seal, and walrus. This view incorporates the idea that refinement of processes of hunting large sea mammals from boats enables hunters to secure enough food from the sea to minimize the need for ranging far overland in search of caribou. It brings up questions of the divorcement of a sea-hunting culture from possible early dependencies on the tundras and forest, and might be seen in the perspective developed by Birket-Smith and others for originating classic Eskimo culture from inland cultures.

Another view, however, is that with the depletion of caribou through over-hunting, or with the shifting of the feeding range of the inland caribou herds, Nukleet huntsmen were forced to turn to other sources of meat. Only so many small seal are available throughout the year, but with additional gear and hazard the beluga can be taken seasonally when they enter the shoals, and walrus and bearded seal can be secured by hunters ranging widely over the ice and the open sea.

Whatever the view taken, we cannot escape the implication in these bone counts that over a period of four or five hundred years Nukleet culture slowly reoriented itself in terms of basic food supply. If ceremonial observances, personal prestige, and even philosophical interpretations of life in the past were geared largely to the game animals, as they have been in recent times, we might hypothecate more than a temporary shift of hunting emphasis in the evidence of the bones and consider the implicit changes as even more far-reaching than will be indicated by the changing styles of material culture.

Raw Materials for Manufactures

The raw materials chosen for various manufactures are indicated for the most part in the finished artifacts described under other headings. However, the tabulations of unidentified worked fragments shown in Table 10 give some additional points of emphasis.

It is to be noted that some organic materials were secured from animals either rarely hunted or definitely unknown alive to the people of Nukleet. Baleen was found in limited amounts at all levels. The extreme scarcity of any other evidence of large whales in the site leads one to assume that baleen was secured largely by trade with whaling groups at the favorable peninsular points along lanes of whale migration, although dead whales washed ashore could have been exploited now and then. The presence of cut mammoth ivory and bits of mammoth teeth in the site reflect no hunting habits. The present natives of the Norton Bay area know the value of mammoth teeth as sinkers for nets and collect mammoth ivory for carving useful objects. These materials and other bones of extinct mammals wash out of frozen silt banks continually during the open season at several points in the Norton Bay area. No evidence was found at Nukleet that mammoth teeth were cut with sandstone saws and made into artifacts, as was the case at Intermediate Kotzebue (Giddings, 1952, p. 69), although it would not be surprising to find such an exploitation of the local elephant materials here.

In considering the columns of Table 10 concerning worked fragments of walrus ivory, sea mammal bone, antler, wood, and ground stone, it should be kept in mind that the figures represent actual counts of objects at levels in which opportunity for preservation varies, and at which the volume of earth concerned is by no means constant. The figures show, in spite of these difficulties, that work in walrus ivory tended to decrease upward in time, while work in the denser bones of beluga and walrus increased. This tendency is more noticeable in the artifacts, such as harpoon heads, where artistic care in the fashioning of the earlier pieces tends to correlate with work in ivory, while antler, and even coarser bone, sufficed in the later periods.

94

Table 10. MISCELLANEOUS

TYPE	PLATE	Levels 1–2	3–5	6–8	9–11	12–14	Miscellaneous	H–1	IY
Shaft for square tanged implement	10, 1	·	2	2	4	3	2	·	1
Baleen, worked frags.	24, 1–3	·	·	2	·	1	·	·	·
Baleen, unworked		·	5	28	7	7	1	·	17
Mammoth ivory		1	3	·	·	·	·	·	2
Mammoth tooth		·	1	1	2	·	·	·	·
Ivory (walrus), worked fragment		11	18	16	18	15	5	2	5
Bone, worked frags.		24	41	11	12	12	4	7	9
Antler, worked frags.		50	85	39	34	30	23	8	14
Wood, worked frags., mainly shafts		9	141	308	242	239	173	11	11
Pointed wooden implements	23, 1–3	·	5	11	7	17	6	·	·
Fiber line	25, 3	·	·	1	·	·	·	·	·
Pebble wrapped in birch bark	25, 4	·	·	·	1	·	·	·	·
Stick with lashing	25, 5	·	·	1	·	·	·	·	·
Stick tied with grass	25, 8	·	·	1	·	·	·	·	·
Grooved round stone	17, 16	·	·	·	1	·	·	·	·
Ground stone, frags.		20	61	25	19	33	4	6	·
Braided grass		·	·	1	·	·	·	·	·

The much higher proportion of antler to ivory in these worked fragments of all periods is, of course, largely a reflection of relative accessibility of these materials. In view of the vastly greater amounts of caribou bones than walrus bones in the site, it looks as though walrus ivory must have been sought at a greater distance from the site than would have been practical for purposes of securing food. Trade in ivory may have flourished between walrus-hunting localities and bay sites such as Nukleet, where walrus do not now appear in great numbers.

Some degree of correlation of raw materials is possible between Nukleet and other sites. However, it is difficult to separate the preference of craftsmen as to the material they use from their necessity to use local materials that occur in abundance. The emphasis on antler at Nukleet, for example, is similar to that at the Ipiutak site, but at Nukleet scarcity of ivory is suspected to be the determinative factor, while at Ipiutak "the preference for antler as a material for weapons and tools despite the apparently unlimited supply of walrus ivory" (Larsen and Rainey, 1948, p. 147) can hardly be explained on the same terms. Again, Nukleet distributions appear to be completely out of line with those of St. Lawrence Island sites until it is recalled that caribou apparently never inhabited the island and that the few pieces of antler found in sites there must have been imported from Siberia (Collins, 1937, p. 247).

Some significance may be drawn from a test of the bones found in 14 Ipiutak houses. Here "53 percent of all the bones, except dog bones, were from seal, 23 percent from walrus, 12 percent from bearded seal, and 10 percent from caribou. The remaining 2 percent consisted of bones of birds, fox, squirrel, polar bear, whale, wolf, and beluga, in this sequence, ranging from 60 bird bones to two beluga bones" (Larsen and Rainey, 1948, p. 68). A comparison of the distribution of all Nukleet bones with this sample from Ipiutak gives a percentage (slightly adjusted to allow for the smaller groups of each series) as follows:

	Small Seal	Bearded Seal	Walrus	Caribou	Beluga	Bird	Other
Ipiutak	53	12	23	10	–	1	1
Nukleet	53	16	2	11	3	14	1

The significant differences here seem to be in the greater emphasis on birds and beluga at Nukleet, and on walrus at Point Hope. Nukleet is environmentally favored by miles of cliffs on which sea birds nest in great numbers and by shoal waters in which beluga gather in large herds where they may be easily killed at low tide. Point Hope is in the direct path of walrus migrations. Except for these environmentally determined factors, the food economy appears to have been remarkably similar between the Point Hope site of 1500 or more years ago and the Nukleet site over a period of several hundred years ending near the present time.

Only two classes of fairly complete objects represented in quantity are still unidentified. One of these is the shaft with a deep socket in a widened end which is evidently meant to receive an additional part, the tang of which is square in cross-section (*10*, 1). The socket is usually formed by cutting in from one side. The other class is a more general one comprised of pointed wooden objects (*23*, 1–3) which may have had more than one use. Snare pegs, awls, and meat forks are considered possibilities.

Decorative Art

The decorative art of Nukleet, known mainly from engraved designs of antler and ivory objects, is geometric and conservative. It is conservative in the sense that its elements and motives nearly all appear in either the archeological horizons of the region later than Old Bering Sea and Ipiutak or in the work of recent people both north and south of Seward Peninsula. Although the human figure and animal forms are sometimes realistically carved in the round, the engraving does not include pictorial realism like that of the historic Eskimos. While no particular engraving from Nukleet appears to be entirely original, the use at the site of most of the basic motives known from the general region within the last millenium in a single pool of design attests to originality of a different kind, most comparable in this respect to Punuk art of St. Lawrence Island.

The basic elements and motives of eastern Thule culture, as delineated by Mathiassen (1927, II, pp. 121–23), are present. They may be seen in the brow bands illustrated in Fig. 21, as follows:

a) "The line with short cross lines" (ticked line)—no. *2*.
b) "The double line with alternating cross lines"—nos. *9, 19*.
c) "The double line of alternating, small, hatched fields and larger, blank fields"—nos. *1, 5*.
d) "The Y-ornament"—no. *2*.

Mathiassen has recognized a degeneration of art from Alaska to the east, listing five elements or motives in the Point Barrow and Point Hope regions of Alaska that are not concerned in eastern Thule culture (Mathiassen, 1930, p. 82). They are the "tree figure" (Fig. 21, *13*—ends of central panel), oblique spurs on one side of a line (not known from Nukleet, but present at Ekseavik), the compass-made circle with central dot (21, *13*), and the compass-made circle and dot with outward-ticked lines (21, *9* Pl. *33*, 1–3).

Turning now to de Laguna's (1947, p. 263) distribution table of Tena art forms, we find in common not only the elements mentioned above, but

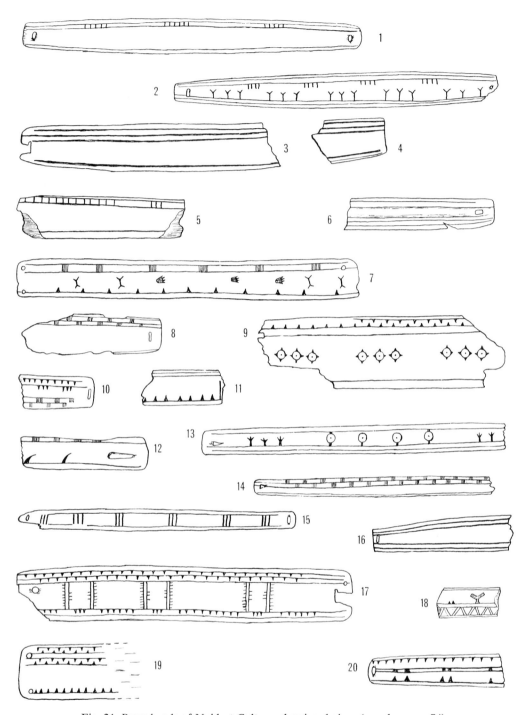

Fig. 21. Brow bands of Nukleet Culture, showing designs (see also page 74).

also "short, vertical spurs on one side of a line" (Fig. 21, *2, 10, 20*), the "curved line with spurs on one side," "grouped spurs" (Fig. 21, *2, 10, 17, 20),* and "round, bored dots" (Pls. *6,* 28; *33,* 6). The "owner's mark" on arrow heads is rare in Nukleet culture, but occasionally present.

Elements that occur in Tena art, as listed in the same table by de Laguna, but not at Nukleet, may carry some significance. They are: "angular dots in a line," "short transverse lines in groups," "oblique spurs on one side of a line," "line with alternating vertical spurs on both sides," "line with alternating oblique spurs on both sides," "lines with paired oblique spurs," "ladder pattern with oblique cross bars," and the "band of cross-hatching." It is to be noted that five of these eight elements comprise short lines that lie at a sharp angle to the guide line, and that Nukleet engraving is consistent from early to late in the absence of oblique lining of this sort. This adherence to the ninety-degree angle, Y-figures, and nucleated circles is curiously common to Nukleet and Punuk art (Collins, 1937, pp. 192–202), and aids in distinguishing the styles of both of these cultural phases from either very early northern styles or those of southern Alaska.

This is not to say, however, that Nukleet engraving is Punuk engraving. As has been stated already (pp. 39–40), the styles and decorations of some of the earliest Nukleet harpoon heads are indistinguishable from those of Early Punuk heads. Similar agreement does not appear between any Nukleet harpoon heads and those of middle, or "classic" Punuk. It is with this latter period on St. Lawrence Island that most of the general agreement occurs in Nukleet art. Nucleated circles appear at Nukleet only in the middle period. These elements seldom stand alone, however, but are further elaborated by appended triangles (Fig. 21, *9*), one or two connecting lines (21, *13*), an outer circle added from the same nucleus, and variations of the double circle with outward ticks or long lines (Pls. *6,* 21; *33,* 1–2, 5). These treatments of the nucleated circle are still to be found in the southern Bering Sea area of Alaska.

Some degree of separation of art elements is possible on the basis of time lapse at Nukleet. Thus we may isolate elements that seem to occur only, or mainly, within early, middle, and late periods, as follows:

Early

1. Spaced, solid rectangles between close, parallel lines (Fig. 21, *20*—middle panel).
2. Half-arc above line, resembling killer-whale dorsal fin (21, *12*).
3. Groups of three vertical lines between widely spaced parallel lines (21, *15*).
4. Panels forming zigzags between widely spaced parallel lines (21, *18*—bottom).
5. Panels forming Y-figure; panels cross-hatched (21, *18*—center).

6. Filled dots in rows, joined by lines (Pl. *33,* 6).
7. Vertical panels with lateral ticking, between widely spaced parallel lines (21, *17*—center).

Middle and Early
8. Triangles with bases on line (21, *7, 9–11, 17–20*). Sometimes alternating (21, *17*).
9. Opposite rows of evenly spaced triangles based on line with apices intermeshing (21, *9, 19;* Pl. *31,* 6). Illusion creates negative running scroll. Common to middle and early periods.
10. Hatched rectangles alternating between three parallel lines (21, *8, 10, 14*). Common to middle and early periods.
11. Line with grouped, short cross lines (Pls. *11,* 2; *29,* 1). Only found on wooden objects.

Middle
12. Nucleated circle with four appended triangles (21, *9*).
13. Nucleated circle with one or two (opposite) stems connecting to widely spaced parallel lines (21, *13*).
14. "Tree" figure—or human figure?—(21, *13,* Pl. *30,* 2).

Late
15. Y-figures stemming from line (21, *2*).
16. Double Y-figures—stem to stem (21, *7*).
17. "Bear-paw" figure (21, *7*).
18. Double line with regularly spaced cross lines (21, *1, 5*).
19. Double nucleated circle, usually with lines extending outward (Pls. *6,* 21; *33,* 1, 2, 5).

All Periods
20. Drilled dots—filled with pigment.
21. Simple ticked line.

Although this sorting out of elements on the basis of time at Nukleet is to be taken as no more than an index to preference—implying only vaguely that some late elements may have been unknown in earlier times—it is noted that Punuk elements increase in middle and late periods and that resemblances to Okvik, Ipiutak, and Aleutian art occur mainly in the early Nukleet period. Thus, the nucleated circle, altered though it is at Nukleet, appears here only in middle and late periods, along with increased use of a simple Y-figure. Element 1 above is duplicated on a pick from Okvik (Rainey, 1941, Fig. 22, *4*); element 4 is to be seen on a stone labret from a cave on Atka Island (Jochelson, 1925, Fig. 88); and elements 7 and 10 appear on a brow band from Ipiutak (Larsen and Rainey, 1948, *24,* 21) which closely resembles in overall execution a brow band from Nukleet

100

(Fig. 21, *17*). Another brow band from Ipiutak compares closely with bands from Nukleet (Larsen and Rainey, 1948, *24*, 19). It is decorated with hatched alternating rectangles (element 10) as are bands from the lower levels (Fig. 21, *14*) and middle levels (21, *8, 10*) at Nukleet.

The significance of close resemblance between early Nukleet brow bands and some of those from Ipiutak, in the absence of such pronounced agreement in other respects between the two sites, is far from clear, but if brow bands were classed together with labrets as objects of facial adornment, we might see a remnant of the old Ipiutak culture transplanted in the Norton Sound area.

A possible connection of art forms of Nukleet with those of the Aleutian Islands is seen also in the arrangement of nucleated circles and appended triangles on the face of a dart head from Umnak Island (Jochelson, 1925, *23*, 3), and in the use of element 10 on a fragment of throwing-lance head from a cave on Atka Island (*Ibid.*, Fig. 68).

The choice of design elements at Nukleet does not, surprisingly enough, correspond closely with that of any Kobuk River period—probably because relatively few engraved objects occur in the Kobuk River sites in which organic materials are preserved in quantity. Oblique ticked lines characterize Ahteut, Ekseavik, and the Kotzebue sites but fail to appear at Nukleet. The following Nukleet elements occur at the Kobuk sites mentioned: 7, 8, 15, 19, and 20.

Turning again to the St. Lawrence Island cultures, it is only when the sweeping, free-hand earlier elements and motives formalize into Punuk art that close similarity appears with Nukleet art. Illustrations in the Collins (1937) monograph and that of Geist and Rainey (1936) show so great a variety of combinations that each of the significant elements in Nukleet art could have been a development of Okvik and Old Bering Sea prototypes, with a formalization similar to, but not necessarily stemming from, that of the later Punuk period. For example, in the two figures in which Collins (1937, pp. 47, 82) shows the principal decorative motives of Old Bering Sea art, the Nukleet elements and motives that appear to be derivative are as follows:

Old Bering Sea Style 1. (p. 47)	Nukleet element No.	
5	21	
6	7	
12	1	
Old Bering Sea Style 2. (p. 82)		
2 b	8	
2 c	18	
2 d	8	alternating
6	19	
7	12	
16 a	12	

101

Table 11. POTTERY

TREAT-MENT	TEST CUT	Levels 1–2	3–5	6–8	9–11	12–14	Miscel-laneous	H–1	IY*	Totals
Plain	A	532	757	340	11	33	60	121	915	3,499
	B	150	325	96	72	40	47			
Rim	A	67	121	54	5	·	37	24	179	578
	B	29	36	14	3	7	2			
Line-decorated	A	26	14	2	·	·	·	21	3	84
	B	10	8	·	·	·	·			
Paddle-marked	A	1	1	2	1	·	·	5	119	145
	B	1	2	7	2	4	·			
Lamp	A	1	3	2	·	·	·	2	9	19
	B	·	2	·	·	·	·			
Average thickness mm.	A	8.8	8.9	9.5	9.7	·	·	·	·	·
	B	8.3	8.6	9.0	·	9.2	·			

Rims										
Rim 1		58	97	38	4	2	28	11	107	345
Rim 2		25	44	19	1	3	3	5	44	144
Rim 3		5	1	·	1	1	4	1	7	20
Rim 4		6	8	7	1	1	·	1	4	28
Rim 5		·	·	·	·	·	·	1	·	1
Rim 6		·	2	1	·	·	·	1	11	15
Rim 7		·	2	2	1	·	3	·	3	11
Rim 8		1	·	·	·	·	·	·	·	1
Rim 9		1	1	·	·	·	1	2	·	5
Rim 10		·	1	·	·	·	·	·	·	1
Rim 11		·	1	·	·	·	·	2	2	5
Rim 12		·	·	1	·	·	·	·	1	2

* 1949 sherds included

102

From the foregoing considerations, it looks as if Nukleet engraving art has retained many ancient elements out of a background shared with Punuk art and has combined them into a greater variety of motives than any other comparably late western Eskimo regional art in continental America. Punuk formalized art disappeared on St. Lawrence Island several centuries ago, but Nukleet art has persisted, with but minor modification, to the present time.

Pottery (Table 11)

The most striking difference between Nukleet and any other excavated Eskimo site lies in the actual and relative abundance of pottery in levels of the later period of occupation. Pottery is distributed throughout the early levels in about the same quantity and quality as might be expected of any Eskimo coastal site. However, a new style and technique of pottery-making appeared towards the latter part of the middle period—that is, after basic bow and arrow changes had been made and after harpoon heads had begun to take on a more local cast. This later Nukleet ware is classed apart from other Eskimo pottery on the basis of (1) abundance, (2) temper, and (3) form and decorative treatment.

The forms and decorative treatments of Tena pottery described by de Laguna (1947) are in the same tradition as the later Nukleet pottery, although in execution the Nukleet potters seem to have modelled with an eye to greater regularity and to have decorated with more geometrical precision. De Laguna speaks of a "renaissance" of southern Eskimo pottery (1947, p. 235) and very convincingly derives the new styles from Kamchatka and the Kuriles, while pointing out that the time and exact route of its introduction are in many ways obscure (*Ibid.*, pp. 226–247). The evidence from Nukleet largely bears out de Laguna's conclusions that we are dealing with a pottery complex that derives little out of the older base of north Alaskan pottery form and methods, and it indicates the time of arrival in rather definite relative terms. However, the ways in which this transmission may have taken place across the lower Bering Sea, or the North Pacific Ocean, are still obscure (Oswalt, 1953).

The numbers of sherds present within a level at Nukleet increase sharply with the appearance of the "foreign" ware. This increase shows up graphically in the first six columns of Table 11. It will be remembered that Cut A at Nukleet is nearly all younger than the lower parts of Cut B. Thus, levels 1–8 in Cut A correspond in time and content very closely to levels 1–5 in Cut B. The new form of pottery appears in the Nukleet mound at about level 8 in Cut A, and level 5 in Cut B. In all cases the first appearance is marked by a great increase in sherds. The plain sherds listed in column 1 show a total of 252 sherds for the lower levels and 2104 for the upper levels. Columns 5–6 offer an index to the incidence of the new pottery complex, since "line-decorated" refers only to the treatment of the "foreign" ware.

The earlier pottery—that which was made during the time of the laying down of the lower and middle parts of Cut B—is in no appreciable respect different from that of coastal sites north of Seward Peninsula through the time (*ca.* 1400 A. D.) of the Old Kotzebue site. Vessels took the form of wide-mouthed bowls, narrowing to a conical or rounded base. These were often decorated by overall paddle-marks consisting of spirals or concentric circles; else they were plain. The temper was sand and feathers, and the firing was relatively poor, so that the ware tends to crumble or exfoliate. Although some paddle-impressed sherds occur in upper levels at Nukleet (Table 11), they are probably displaced examples of the earlier ware.

The "foreign" ware thus seems to have swept into common use without an essential incorporation of earlier local methods. Where the early pottery was in most instances smooth-surfaced, the later[1] pottery was roughened outside because of a coarser temper of pebbles and a white material that appears to be shell. In place of feathers, the later ware contains grass predominantly. Firing is regular and rather thorough, evidently in a reducing atmosphere. Sherds are gray to buff and tend not to crumble or exfoliate. Vessel forms are those of bucket or situla, the bases always generously wide and flat or slightly concave (*35,* 10, 12). The commoner decorative designs are indicated in Plate *35.* *35,* 1 is a rim part of a straight-sided vessel, the outside of which was decorated with two indented circumferential rings just below the rim, and by another series of four raised rings several centimeters lower along the side. Joining the lowest of the lower series of rings was a series of V-elements, apex down, the part of one of which shows in the photograph. *35,* 4 is similarly decorated, with the exception that the V-elements (one of which shows) are placed under the upper series of rings. The inner surface of each of the above sherds shows that a series of rings has been impressed evenly around the inside of the vessels, as though by drawing the slightly spaced fingers of one hand about the inner circumference. Wide grooves of this kind also appear on the outside of the sherd *35,* 2. This sherd boasts in addition two bands of punctations such as might have been made with a fingernail or some blunt-ended object. A suspension hole is to be seen on this sherd, placed well below the rim, as was the practice in those relatively few cases where suspension holes are present.

35, 3, 5, 8, and 11 are sherds of the late ware that show the commonest form of decoration—a simple series of two to five regularly spaced indented

---

[1] This later ware, here described by the author before he left Alaska in 1949, falls mainly in Oswalt's (1955, p. 37) "Yukon Line-dot" category, and was presumably included by Oswalt in his survey.

circumferential rings. *35, 7* has, in addition to the rings, a ring of round punctations. The sherd *35, 6* is plain except for a groove just below the rim, a groove possibly for a rawhide collar by which the pot might have been suspended. *35, 9*, with its freehand lines in a single pair, resembles in the manner of its grooving and in the smoothness of its surface the Tena pottery illustrated by de Laguna (1947, esp. Plate *24*).

Other data in Table 11 help to point up the differences between the older Nukleet pottery and the "foreign" ware. The average thickness of vessels (taken from walls undisturbed by rim or base irregularities) decreases noticeably with the advent of the new ware. Although the change is of the order of only about one millimeter, this is sufficient to have meaning in terms of quality of the respective wares.

Rim forms are numbered in Table 11 from 1 to 12 and are identified in the outlines of Figure 22. These forms may be briefly described as follows:

1. Square. This is the form that a rim would normally take if intended to be turned bottom-up on a flat surface for drying. It is the commonest form in all periods.
2. Rounded. A rim of this kind indicates that the pot was dried in an upright position. This is a simple form of rim found in all periods.
3. Pinched-up. This is a slightly thickened rim that has presumably been provided with a central ridge by pinching up with thumb and forefinger. A pot with this rim must have been dried upright. Known in all periods.
4. Everted lip. The pot could have been dried upside-down. Lip eversion would have afforded a means of possible suspension. All periods; common, late.
5. Inverted lip, pinched-up. Apparently a late idea, unrelated to utility, unless in providing a means of lifting the pot by means of a fingerhold within the rim.
6. Inverted lip, squared. Possibly dried upside-down, inverted lip relating to finger hold. Late period only.
7. In-sloping rim. This is the form a rim would take if a plain pot with down-sloping sides were dried upside-down. Late period only.
8. Rounded, thickened rim. Late period; rare.
9. Inverted lip. Similar to Rim 6, but probably dried upright. Late period only.
10. Slightly everted lip. Variant of Rim 4. Late period only.
11. Out-sloping rim. A stylistic variant apparently unrelated to use. Late period only.
12. Beveled inner rim. A stylistic variant of Rim 1. Late period only.
13. Everted lip, squared. Opposite of Rim 6. Probably related to suspension. Late period.

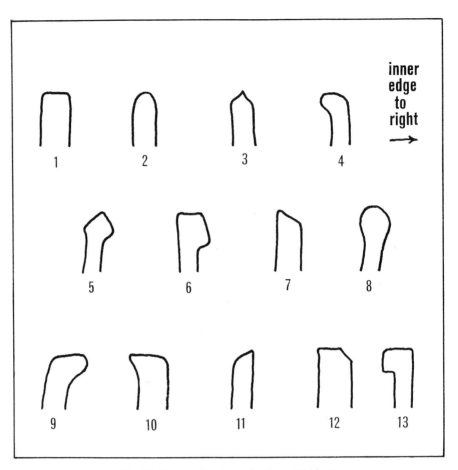

Fig. 22. Types of pottery rim from Nukleet.

These data indicate that although pots were dried both upright and upside-down in all periods, variations of rim treatment were much more common in the late ware than in the early.

Although cooking pots were radically altered at Nukleet with the adoption of the later pottery tradition, this may not have applied to lamps. The lamp fragments from Nukleet are all from later deposits, but these are essentially like those from Iyatayet that seem to belong to earlier times. The lamps are round to oval platter-like vessels with flat bases and shallow, upturned rims. None is decorated. A different form of lamp appears in the Norton Sound area after the time of Nukleet, as we found in 1941 excavations at Koyuk Village. This is a rounded bowl, decorated on the inner surface by a series of concentric circles. This form of lamp is identical with lamps illustrated from the Tena (de Laguna, 1947, *24*, 10), and recently in use between the mouths of the Yukon and Kuskokwim Rivers.

106

Comparative figures on the abundance of pottery in a site are hard to come by. No two diggers are likely to have the same habits of counting sherds, because obviously there is always a smaller and a still smaller fragment, especially in the crumbly Arctic wares, to be counted or discounted. In the counting habit of a single archeologist, however, there may be a consistency. On the chance that I have been fairly consistent in my counts during the past twenty years, I offer some simple ratios between potsherds and artifacts in sites where preservation of wood and bone was good, as follows:

Kobuk:

Ambler Island	ca. 1750 A. D.	.12
Black River	− 1600 A. D.	.12
Intermediate Kotzebue	− 1550 A. D.	.17
Old Kotzebue	− 1400 A. D.	.24
Ekseavik	− 1400 A. D.	.21
Ahteut	− 1250 A. D.	.58

St. Lawrence Island:

Okvik culture house	− 200 B. C.	(?)	.15

Nukleet, Test Cut:

Levels 12–14	(estimated dates, at	.15
− 9–11	approximately equal	.14
− 6–8	intervals, between	.61
− 3–5	1100 and 1700 A. D.)	1.36
− 0–2		2.80

These figures simply bear out field observations on frequency of potsherds. The figure for the oldest aspect of culture on St. Lawrence Island is given because, in the author's opinion, pottery was more abundant in it than in most other sites and levels of that Asiatic island. On the North American side of Bering Strait, it is noted that while in the Kobuk sites pottery decreased in importance through time, it increased at Cape Denbigh. The decrease in pottery along the Kobuk probably relates in some way to the high degree of hot stone boiling in baskets and wooden tubs that prevailed in that area until well into the historic period. The highest figure in each of the series is somewhat out of line with the other figures because of poorer preservation at Ahteut and in the uppermost levels at Nukleet; yet, in the later occupation of Nukleet, pottery seems to have been more prominent than in any other known Arctic site.[1]

Deposits of Nukleet Culture at Iyatayet

All of the excavations at Iyatayet North site penetrated the top layer of Nukleet culture at the site. As explained in a following section (p. 119),

[1] See page 108 for the Nukleet pottery in the Iyatayet site.

we avoided the deeper deposits of this later period as much as possible because of the generally poor preservation of organic material in the site and the duplication of most artifacts. The well-preserved, late-period House 1 floor is described in detail on pp. 124–25 and the presumably single-period House 6 excavation is treated as a unit below. The range of pottery of Nukleet period at Iyatayet North site is indicated in Appendix I, and South site pottery is described on p. 112.

House 6, South Slope

The south slope of the stream at Iyatayet gave abundant outward signs of being a midden like that of the north slope. A test cut in 1948 had shown us, however, that materials of neither Norton nor earlier cultures could be anticipated here. The objects recovered from the test cut were all those of Nukleet culture, and the underlying, sterile, rocky base gave no promise of a further yield. Besides, the south slope was somewhat sheltered, the frost more tenacious, and the ground slower to thaw under day-to-day excavations.

The cut had impinged upon a structure of some kind. The lower walls—presumably of a tunnel—indicated that a house was buried somewhere up the slope. Objects found in the tunnel were of early Nukleet forms; hence it seemed that a house might be excavated on the south slope that would act as a control to the recent houses on the north slope in which there was always a mixture of late with early materials. Excavations in 1950 bore out these suppositions and brought forth valuable new evidence of an earlier Nukleet culture.

Gerald M. Henderson undertook the excavation of House 6 on the south slope. He handled both the excavation and analysis separately from that of other Iyatayet features, and produced an illuminating report, "A Neo-Eskimo House Excavation at the Iyatayet Site on Cape Denbigh" (Henderson, 1952). We shall draw certain specific or summary facts from this report where they are needed to amplify or clarify aspects of Nukleet culture.

The house itself displayed interesting details of construction. Its floor had been outlined by four upright posts forming a trapezoidal floor plan somewhat wider at the front than at the back (Fig. 23). The house had been excavated at the rear into virgin earth and leveled off by moving earth and midden towards the front. The retaining wall thus formed presumably held up benches on either side, as shown in the floor plan. The precise extent of these benches could never be determined, however, because their level had apparently been formed on a fill of midden which, upon rotting together with fallen wall and roof timbers, was not clearly traceable. The rear part of the wall outlining the house floor was constructed by placing one hollowed log within the groove of another, as seen

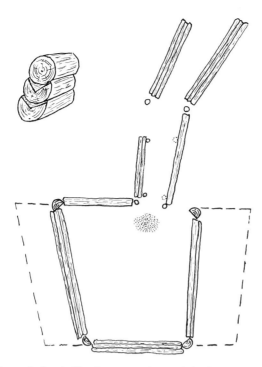

Fig. 23. House 6, South Site, Iyatayet; plan and detail of wall construction.

in the upper left detail of Fig. 23. This type of construction was also noted in the Nukleet test cut (p. 17). The walls of House 6, as they could be partly identified in the welter of fallen logs, had stood at an angle against a frame of horizontal logs at the top of the four posts of the floor corners. A hearth area lay near the tunnel entrance, rather than at the center of the house floor. A shallow step led downward from the house into the tunnel.

It was possible to isolate a large number of artifacts and potsherds from the House 6 excavation on the assumption that they belonged to the house itself. This was because the preservation of fallen roof and wall logs was good enough to have furnished a buffer against the percolation of later materials to the house floor. A variety of objects are thought to represent a woman's work within the house. These include the pieces of pottery vessels, fragments of wood-bottomed bowls, buckets or tubs with baleen or birch bark sides, broken pottery lamps, fragments of a ladder-shaped drying rack, and such miscellaneous objects as suspension hooks and an antler rake.

An unexpected trait of wide-ranging significance turned up in this excavation. This is a fragmentary composite bucket, the upper part of which was incised and painted birch bark. In Henderson's words,

There are four birchbark fragments which represent the sides of composite vessels similar in form to those made of baleen. Two large fragments from the floor of the

109

Fig. 24. Fragments of a decorated birch bark basket.

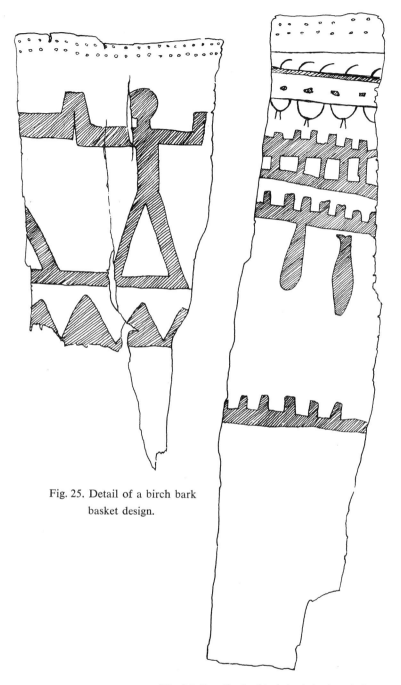

Fig. 25. Detail of a birch bark
basket design.

Fig. 26. Detail of a birch bark basket design.

111

house in front of the tunnel entrance are illustrated in [Fig. 24]. These show the same type of double rows of cross stitching paralleling the cut edge as in the smaller stitched baleen fragments. The thread here used was spruce root and not baleen. There is a vertical band painted dark red along the seams of both sections. Some of the areas were left unpainted to produce a negative design. On the segment illustrated in [Fig. 25], the designs near the edge were scratched through the painted surface. It is interesting to note that one of the designs running parallel to the cut edge is a series of dashes which might be an imitation of the under-and-over stitching used on the underseam of the baleen containers. A negative design on one of the painted fragments is the outline of a horizontal human figure, with the head nearest the seam, the arms extended upward, and the legs spread apart. The stick-like legs are standing upon a vertical line, beyond which to the left is a row of triangles. The designs on the second fragment [Fig. 26] were not produced by negative painting. The surface near the seam was first painted, and the designs were then scratched on the bark to expose the lighter under surface. Scallops with spurs at the top, and straight and broken lines are incised into the surface. Below these designs straight and broken lines are rendered positively in paint.

A third decorated piece from Level 3, which does not represent the complete thickness of a side fragment or any stitched seam, is decorated with incised cross hatching. A fourth small fragment of birchbark from Level 4 may be part of a container side. One cut edge is paralleled by a row of holes, as if for stitching.

...The late Dr. Frank G. Speck (1941, p. 240) has suggested that the direction of the grain on the long side of a folded basket might serve as a sorting criterion for eastern and western distributions. The Western Cree and Athabaskan baskets were cut with the grain *parallel* to the long side, as in the Nukleet example. To the east the Ojibwa and Salteaux, as well as the eastern Algonquin, including the Montagnais and Wabanaki divisions, cut and sew their containers so that the grain of the bark along the longer side runs *perpendicular* to the rim.

—Henderson, 1952, pp. 29–31.

Pottery was very prominent in the whole excavation, amounting to more than 1,300 sherds, or an average of two sherds to an artifact. The pottery that belongs to the house itself—that is, the sherds (about 190) that could be identified with the floor region of house and tunnel—seems to be like the pottery found in the lowest levels of Cut B at Nukleet. Many of the vessels bear curvilinear paddle marks on the outer surface, while some are plain. The lamps represented are shallow, spherical bowls, while the cooking pots are round-bottomed (usually with a flattened area at the base) and decidedly globular.

The count of animal bones kept by Henderson from his excavations in and about House 6 shows an interesting departure from the figures for Nukleet. Table 12 shows the distribution of more than a thousand animal bones. Although it can be very misleading to compare the proportions of mainly a single house accumulation with a whole site, such as the Nukleet cuts represent, we nevertheless see that caribou were far more important in all periods at the Iyatayet House 6 excavation than at Nukleet. The levels indicated in the table range from the uppermost, immediately beneath sod (Level 1), to Levels 4, 5, and Tunnel, which are the levels most surely associated with House 6 occupation. Iyatayet is thus indicated at the time of occupation of House 6 to have been a good caribou hunting ground and not primarily a sealing station.

Table 12. ANIMAL BONES, SOUTH SITE, IYATAYET

Animal			Levels				Total	% of
	I	II	III	IV	V	Tunnel		Total
Caribou	233	113	20	19	17	28	430	40.9
Small seal	177	45	24	21	18	22	307	29.4
Bearded seal	97	70	24	9	3	10	213	20.2
Beluga	34	3	1	4		7	49	4.6
Walrus	2	14		1	1	5	23	2.2
Bird	18			2			20	1.9
Other	3	1	1*	2	1	1**	9	0.8
Total	564	246	70	58	40	73	1051	100.0

* Beaver skull   ** Bear tooth

The other artifacts from the oldest part of the House 6 excavations are compatible with those of the earliest levels at Nukleet. There appears to be no occupation of the south slope, however, to correspond to the latest occupation at Nukleet. Most of the pottery from this excavation (presumably not of House 6 itself) is similar to that of a period somewhat earlier than the final period at Nukleet.

The only non-Nukleet period objects recovered from the south slope excavations were an angle burin like those of the Denbigh Flint complex and a few chips of cherty material. This nearly complete isolation of culture is interesting from two points of view. It shows that the soil of the south slope has probably been deposited (through sliding down the slope?) since Norton people lived at Iyatayet—else some Norton flakes or sherds would have been deposited across the ravine. Again, it shows that the people who occupied House 6, and presumably other Nukleet period houses on the south side, were not very determined collectors of the curious flints that almost surely were continuously exposed by digging on the north slopes. The purity of the Nukleet culture deposits exposed in the south site, only a few feet from the terrace of the north site, adds to our confidence in sorting out the non-Nukleet materials that appear in the later levels of the north site.

The Nukleet Culture

Nukleet was occupied more or less continuously from about the twelfth to the eighteenth century. The people who lived there may have been descendants of a single limited group of families until the site was finally abandoned, for although one major wave of cultural innovation is to be seen in the archeological materials, the basic pattern of subsistence remained the same.

The food economy of Nukleet people seems to have been rather equally based upon sea mammals, fish, and caribou. The bones of seal and beluga far outweigh those of caribou at the site itself, and fish bones may not be equated with those of mammals in direct ratio. Nevertheless, the distribution of devices for taking these several kinds of food animals indicated that all three were sought during the whole time that the site was occupied. Sea birds and their eggs from neighboring rookeries undoubtedly furnished a source of summer food, but these would not likely be sources of midden material, for Nukleet people could be expected to leave their permanent houses and live in tents during the season of bird nesting. Wild greens and other vegetable foods would also have been eaten mainly during the season of camping in tents along the beaches. Quantities of cloudberry seeds were sometimes found in the midden, but the berries could have been originally stored for winter use as they are today. Bird bones in the midden include a high percentage of those of ptarmigan as well as those of waterfowl. The presence of the latter indicates at least some residence at the site during the warmer parts of the year when sea birds inhabit the region.

The Eskimos who now make up the population of the Shaktoolik–Norton Bay area live on the sea coast at the mouths of rivers. This is partly because the local economy has to be adjusted to the acculturative requirements of missions, schools, and trading posts. These institutions do not function well unless people can be concentrated in rather large villages for the greater part of the year. Transportation by sea has encouraged seashore locations. The old people recall, however, that villages of permanence are fairly recent. The Shaktoolik group has shifted its winter village site several times within the past century, locating for a while on an old beach line at the mouth of the Shaktoolik River, then a few miles up the river within the timbered area, then back at the river mouth, again up the river, and finally at the site chosen for the present school building, church, and store.

The greater stability indicated for Nukleet until the time of its abandonment may be partly accounted to the absence of dog traction on a large scale until some 250 years ago. A similar shift from permanence in the house and village to a semi-nomadic existence has been noted along the upper Kobuk River within roughly the same time span. The dog team makes possible rapid movements between separately located hunting and fishing grounds during eight months of the year and permits more of a choice of winter dwelling sites than would have been possible when travel was limited to walking and boating.

The reasons for first settling at Nukleet rather than along neighboring beaches at the edges of flat coastal plains probably had to do with catching

114

fish and sea mammals close by at all seasons. Caribou could be taken within a few miles of the village at the times of seasonal migration. On the other hand, Nukleet offers few inducements for house building. It is unlikely that Eskimos would have depended much upon the neighboring stand of spruce trees, even if trees had surrounded the village in prehistoric times (Giddings, 1952, p. 106), and the ring sequences of far the greater number of logs preserved from the site show them to be of wood that did not grow locally. Driftwood is never plentiful at the site because of the limited beach space upon which it can lodge, and all driftwood for building and fuel in former times would have had to be carried up the steep slopes from the beach to the site. Again, house excavations would have been possible only in damp and dense soil, or in the middens of earlier inhabitants. The advantages of Nukleet as a lookout point from which to scan the surrounding sea and land would have been a consideration at all times, although recent peoples in the area have not chosen high points upon which to camp or build, preferring to be near the water edge where food, fuel, and drinking water are easily obtained.

Changes through Time

Tree-ring dating has thus far failed to date for us the Nukleet sequences as far as the building materials and wooden artifacts of the site are directly concerned. Indirectly, however, the Kobuk River dendrochronology can be drawn upon to designate the broader periods of time for the occupation of Nukleet. Factors of time "slope," or "lag," must be taken into close consideration in any attempt to cross-date one site with another by means of aligning similar styles of art and workmanship. A form of harpoon head can be closely similar in form and decoration between Nukleet and a Punuk site on St. Lawrence Island, for example, without indicating the direction in which passage of the incorporated ideas has taken place. The distances between the Kobuk River and Norton Bay are so slight, however, that actual contact can be presupposed on the same time level. And when we add to this consideration the similar inland manifestations of sites of the two areas, and the fact that the Malemiut dialect is spoken across the whole base of Seward Peninsula, we are inclined to interpret similar changes in many aspects of culture between the two areas as roughly contemporaneous.

Identity or close similarity between Nukleet levels and the Kobuk sites has been pointed out time after time in the preceding sections. The best sequential examples of correlating styles are to be seen in arrowheads of antler, harpoon heads, and pottery, and all of these are more determinative in the early and middle levels than in the latest at Nukleet. The correlations of Nukleet levels with Kobuk sites are indicated as follows:

1550 A. D. to abandonment. Nukleet levels 1–4: Intermediate Kotzebue.

1400 A. D. Nukleet Cut A, level 5 to bottom; Cut B, level 5 to top of dense midden: Ekseavik and Old Kotzebue.

1250 A. D. Nukleet Cut B, all dense midden in sections 3 and 4: Ahteut.

Prior to 1250 A. D.? Lowest parts of dense midden in sections 3 and 5: no exact Kobuk equivalent.

It seems likely that the earliest Nukleet midden deposits of the middle sections of Cut B were laid down somewhat earlier than the time of Ahteut, if only because here are found numerous elements unknown from any of the Kobuk sites but similar to elements from Early Punuk levels in St. Lawrence Island sites. To be recounted are the several harpoon heads decorated precisely in the styles of Early Punuk, and the small, elaborate ornamental pieces most closely referable to the same source.

The most obvious changes through time are those that have to do with land and sea hunting, and with pottery. Changes in these complexes have also been noted in connection with Kobuk River sequences (Giddings, 1952, p. 112). Both the Kobuk sites and Nukleet have shown greater stability through time in other respects. The harpoon and its appurtenances seem to have changed more in form and decoration than with respect to function. The changes from delicately formed early harpoon heads to the thick and undecorated late ones probably have nothing to do with taking sea mammals more effectively. All of the changes appear to be those of fashion rather than of greater efficiency or materials available. We may suppose that men, on their sea hunting expeditions, came into contact with neighboring hunting parties and copied the styles that currently prevailed across the whole Seward Peninsula area—styles reaching back to the areas where whaling and other sea hunting were most highly developed.

The shift in archery practices can be explained on a more utilitarian basis. A new form of arrowhead hafting and the simultaneous acceptance of the sinew-backed bow some time before 1400 A. D. were related to the techniques of obtaining caribou and other land animals. The improvements in archery that caused no inconvenience or sharp break with tradition would have been accepted if only because they promised an increase in food supply and competitive success among archers.

Harder to explain is the shift from pottery vessels with conical or round bases, after 1400 A. D., to the flat-bottomed, bucket-shaped vessels of all later periods. The coincidence of a new pottery form with a tremendous increase in the use of pottery is to be considered in a somewhat different light from either of the preceding complexes in that it falls within the presumed sphere of women's activity. We see no comparable changes in the materials of household maintenance, dress, or those aspects of fishing that presumably were carried on mainly by women. The new pottery is known in a more highly developed form at Nukleet than farther to the north,

116

where pottery seems nowhere to have reached the elaboration of form or the quantitative importance that it had at Nukleet in the later periods. This Nukleet innovation probably offered no more efficient a means of containing and boiling liquids, but it may have marked a shift in preferred methods of cooking (as in the shift from stone boiling in baskets to fire-exposed boiling in pots), or the discovery of an abundant source of pottery clay.

Changes in styles of decoration and in ornamentation seem also to have followed widespread fashion to a large extent, as is to be seen in the reflection of Early Punuk-like pendants and other small objects in lowest Nukleet levels, in the Ekseavik-like drop pendants in middle levels, and in the increased number of labrets in the upper levels. Decorative art elements also seem to have been appropriated at Nukleet out of a continuum of diffusion at various periods, including the "circle-dot," although the newer elements were so thoroughly incorporated with the old that Nukleet art seems to have remained very stable throughout the period of occupation of the site.

Stability of Nukleet Culture

The changes that took place at Nukleet with the passage of several centuries are sharp enough to allow speculation upon influences from and into other parts of the Eskimo area, but they are not the kinds of changes that would upset a basic economy or imply successions of people. The last families to occupy Nukleet could easily have been descendants of the first persons to choose the site for their home. The shift of emphasis from caribou hunting to greater concentration on the large sea mammals, as indicated in bone counts, was very gradual, and no other factors show a change in the basic economy through time. The food economy remained essentially the same throughout the time of occupation.

Similarly, we see that those aspects of everyday life concerned with manufactures and the tools of manufacture, the preparation of food and clothing, the care of the house, and community life entertained few radical changes from early to late. The grinding and polishing of slate, the working of wood with adzes and beaver tooth knives, and the preference for antler over other hard organic materials all remained essentially the same. Fishing techniques changed hardly at all, as indicated by the distribution of netting parts and ice scoops throughout the site, and by the conservatism of other fishing implements. The uniform distribution of brow bands and toys, especially dolls, shows a stability in the adhesives of a community from early to late.

Familiarity with the products of the inland forested region also appears to have remained about the same at all times. This can be judged by the consistent use of birch bark, beaver teeth, antler, and barking tools. Seasonal residence inland is strongly implied, but is not likely to be proven by excavation away from the coast, unless some of the hypothetical inland camps may have been also winter house sites.

These signs that Nukleet culture was already firmly established within the Norton Sound region at the time of first residence at Nukleet itself indicate a considerable antiquity for the combination of traits. Unfortunately, there is no direct evidence as to whether or not it grew out of the Norton culture sites of the same region. As we shall see, the Norton culture levels underlying the levels of Nukleet culture at Iyatayet contain a very different combination of artifacts and were deposited much earlier. A quantitative comparison of any one aspect (such as fishing or hunting) of the separate cultures is impossible, however, because of the scarcity of organic material in the earlier levels.

The abandonment of Nukleet and Iyatayet, probably in the 18th century A. D., creates no problem of migration or replacement, despite the traditions that surround these sites. The economy and habits of the present population of the Norton Bay area are essentially those of the earlier inhabitants of Nukleet, even though large-scale dog traction has lent greater mobility, and many acculturative elements have been added. The artifacts and assemblages of Nukleet are in almost all cases recognized by the natives of Shaktoolik as variants or exact duplicates of those still in use, or only recently given up to make way for European goods and patterns of behavior. Nukleet culture is literally an extension backward in time of the culture of modern Norton Bay people. We are less certain that the Norton culture and much earlier manifestations at Cape Denbigh stand in the same line of developments. Nor are we at all sure that the dialects spoken by the predecessors of Nukleet people in the Norton Bay area were Malemiut or Unalik—or, for that matter, Eskimo.

118

III. SITES OF THE NORTON CULTURE

Iyatayet

The site called Iyatayet, on the northwest side of Cape Denbigh, gave no outward sign of concealing any cultural remains older than those of Nukleet when we first investigated it in June of 1948. A heavy mat of deeply rooted bunch grass clearly outlined the area of last occupation. This grass lay like a blanket over the slopes of both sides of Iyatayet Creek (Figs. 27–31), bounded by alder thickets on all sides. Excavations later proved that the bunch grass did in fact outline the later (Nukleet age) parts of the site, both on the south side of the creek and on the slope and terrace of the north side. This area had been enriched by the midden accumulations of centuries. However, the earlier occupations of the site had extended well past the boundaries indicated by alders and bunch grass. The mineral content of these older extensions no longer noticeably affected the vegetative cover, for the plants growing over them were identical with those of the surrounding slopes.

The first task was that of sampling the whole site as effectively as possible while waiting for the slow day-to-day thaw which, at Nukleet, had allowed only a few inches of progress a day. As it turned out, few parts of Iyatayet site were deeply frozen, though several days of slow thaw were required from the surface to the permanently thawed ground underneath. We avoided the thicker deposits left by people of Nukleet culture as much as possible in order to isolate and define the early cultures. This accounts for the discontinuities shown in the map of Iyatayet (Fig. 31). It should be stressed that preservation of Nukleet materials was far better at the type site, and that had our goal been further delineation of Nukleet culture, we should have chosen to expand excavations at Nukleet itself. Iyatayet was poorly stratified and poorly preserved; hence the overburden of Nukleet cultural material always placed a strain upon the time and effort of our small labor crew. The excavations of later seasons progressed from the original test pits outward in those directions where, first, there was the greatest probability of finding the oldest deposits and, second, the older deposits could be reached with a minimum of digging in Nukleet remains.

Excavations, 1948

A total of 15 test sections, 6 by 10 feet in area, were laid out in 7 places at intervals over the grass-covered part of the site (Fig. 31). Another area

119

Fig. 27. Iyatayet site from the air.

Fig. 28. Iyatayet camp and site. The lighter, grass-covered slopes mark the main site on the terrace, to the left, and the south site, across the creek.

120

Fig. 29. Vegetation on
Iyatayet site. Bunch grass
and alders.

Fig. 30. Iyatayet, from the south. Norton and Denbigh Flint deposits extend through
the alder thicket, to the right, and beyond.

121

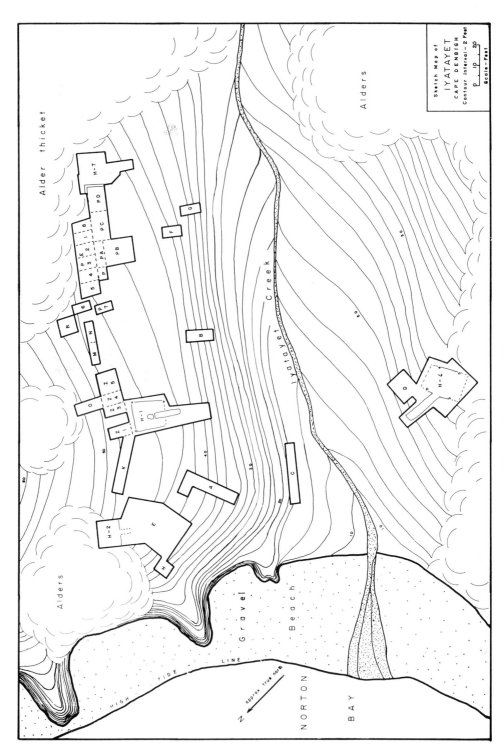

Fig. 31. Sketch map of Iyatayet site.

122

was staked out to cover what appeared to be the pit of a dwelling house. Cut A, 20 feet long, extended over the steep brow of the terrace. Once the thick sod was removed and the air had begun to thaw the mud underneath, we had great trouble with stratigraphy. The fine-grained soil was saturated with moisture and slid off down the slope as soon as it thawed. Bits of artifacts, partly exposed in the evening, had thawed out and floated or slid down the slope by morning. As in most of the steeper parts of the slope, materials here appeared to have been thoroughly mixed at earlier times and stratigraphy meant little. In general, however, the lower part of this cut contained a coarser soil which tended to hold its place while thawing and drying out. Near the center of Cut A, at about the 38-foot contour level, a narrow patch of coarse sand containing only objects of the Denbigh Flint complex extended from wall to wall.

Cut B began as a 10-foot-long section and was extended 4 feet farther down the hill as the season progressed, partly to insure drainage. Rather clear-cut stratigraphy was discerned in its lower part in the form of an old sod line beneath which were found only deposits of Norton and Flint complex culture. This was one of the few well-defined division markers between Norton culture times and the arrival of the Nukleet builders.

Cut C, 30 feet long, lay along a contour level at the foot of the steep slope. Here we found no stratigraphy whatever, but a conglomeration of objects from all three culture periods—the result, we surmised, of hillside wash, or creep, before the last abandonment of the site. The absence of an undisturbed Norton culture deposit here indicates that Iyatayet Creek, or the sea itself, had washed across the relatively flat ground at the creek mouth after the site had been abandoned by people of Norton culture.

Cut D, which tested the south slope across Iyatayet Creek, was originally 6 by 10 feet in surface dimensions and was later expanded (in 1950), as described on pp. 108–9. In this cut were found the traces of a tunnel floor and walls, frozen—as had been the site at Nukleet—and in a much better state of preservation than any of the late material on the north slope across Iyatayet Creek.

Cut E began as a narrow strip at the south margin of this large excavation. Here we found a clear-cut separation between Nukleet and earlier materials. Materials of the Denbigh Flint complex were often concentrated at the top of the sterile, disintegrated bedrock, though not in sharp separation from Norton culture deposits. This was one of the two most promising areas uncovered during the first season.

Cuts F and G helped to define the distribution of materials but offered little encouragement to excavating further in their vicinity. The Flint complex had been disturbed, though the earlier flints seemed concentrated near bottom, in contrast to the Norton flints at higher levels. The upper levels of Cut F contained quantities of rotten wood, suggesting nearness to a Nukleet period structure which we chose to avoid.

All of these tests, with the exception of Cuts C and A, showed that Nukleet people had built extensively at or very near the brow of the hill, where the depth of deposits reached as much as seven feet. The House 1 excavation was laid out originally to encompass the walls and tunnel of what we discerned from clearly defined surface indications to be a Nukleet-period dwelling structure (Fig. 32). The excavation was carried far enough in 1948 to expose the floor (Figs. 33 and 34) and most of the tunnel, and the pit in which the house was located was further excavated in 1949. House 1 belongs, perhaps, to the last period of occupation of the site. It was a large, rectangular house, 15 by 17 feet in floor plan, its tunnel opening into the house one-third of the way between the front and rear walls, directly in front of a large fireplace. The floor had been covered with split logs and planks (now only compressed streaks of rotten fiber) laid directly on the earth base of its excavated pit. The abundance of ash and charcoal uncovered directly in front of the tunnel opening lay upon only a thin coating of earth upon the wooden floor. The floor itself had not been burned. This seems to indicate either that the fireplace had not been persistently used or that it had been further protected from the floor by materials removed before the house was abandoned. The flooring had run lengthwise of the house—that is, in line with the direction of the tunnel. Base logs and their fragments were exposed between corner posts as indicated in Fig. 32. The outside walls had been of split uprights, retained apparently by the base logs. The roof is indicated to have been mainly supported by corner posts and two additional posts, one on either side of the tunnel, in line with the front wall of the house. In contrast to the base logs and flooring at the back of the house, wall and other timbers were poorly preserved. Unlike House 6, an earlier house on the south slope (pp. 108–13), the walls of the tunnel appeared to have consisted of poles laid outside of two series of posts defining the tunnel floor. The entrance to House 1 had been through the floor within the house itself, recalling a similar form of entrance in a probably contemporary house at the Intermediate Kotzebue site (Giddings, 1952, pp. 20–21, Fig. 14).

Two observations concern the dating of the house: 1) this was one of only two house pits (the other not excavated) which were clearly discernible from the surface, indicating a terminal period of building at the site and 2) present on the floor were artifacts similar to those of Intermediate Kotzebue or later times in the Kobuk-Kotzebue region—that is, later than 1500 A.D. A polished jade adz head, *19*, 1, is very similar to those used along the upper Kobuk River in the 17th and 18th centuries. The site thus seems to have been finally abandoned some 300 years ago.

Immediately under the fragments of wooden flooring of House 1 was

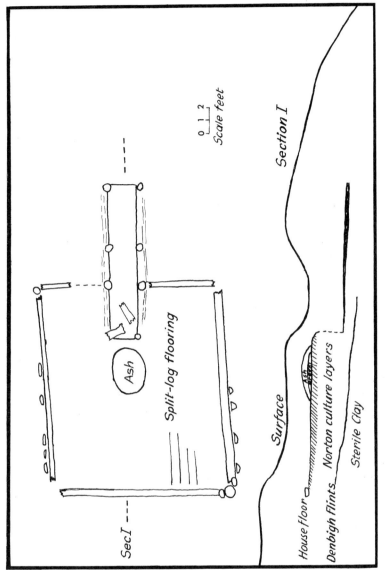

Fig. 32. Plan of House 1, Iyatayet.

125

found the first undisturbed deposit of what became known as Norton culture. The floor thus marked a clear separation of at least two periods of culture at Cape Denbigh. Here also, still deeper under House 1, were first isolated the sterile layer and the underlying thin deposits of the Denbigh Flint complex (Giddings, 1949, pp. 85–86).

Excavations, 1949

Where the previous year's excavations had been exploratory, those of 1949 were aimed at interpreting the successions of culture. Cut K was laid out on a fairly level section of the site, where it was hoped that drainage would offer no serious problem and where stratigraphy might be expected. Only Sections 2, 4, 5, and 6 were dug. The soil remained dry enough to excavate in levels and vertical walls. It became clear, however, that stratigraphic separation of phases within the Norton culture deposits was not possible and that, with the disappearance of organic binder at some earlier period, the Norton culture soils had repeatedly run together and mixed, as mud will do on a slope. Soil discoloration, together with streaks of mussel shell chitin and streaks of gravel, made it possible to separate, with some certainty, the Nukleet from the Norton culture soils (Fig. 35), but at no point above the dense, disintegrated bedrock was the separation clear-cut in the absence of cultural evidence.

A section twelve feet long was added to the upper limit of Cut A in a search for further evidence of Flint Complex level in place, but this section had been disturbed throughout, indicating the nearness, perhaps directly uphill, of a late period house.

Cut E was expanded northward in a series of parallel cuts in which were found extensive, undisturbed deposits of Norton and earlier materials, as well as clear-cut intrusions of Nukleet-period midden (Fig. 36). The latter were well-preserved in spots and, though not comparable to the deposits at Nukleet, afforded most of the antler and ivory objects. Except for Nukleet-period midden and traces of house construction, Cut E provided almost no preservation of bones or organic artifacts. Scattered throughout the fine-grained soil, however, were the stone objects and pottery of Norton culture together with objects and flakes displaced from old Flint complex deposits. One narrow deposit of Flint complex flakes and artifacts was isolated from later cultural deposition. This was found at the northwest corner of Cut E extending into Cut H, a trench made essentially for tracing out this deposit of earliest materials. Here, as in Cut A, materials of the Flint complex seemed to have been redeposited, for they did not lie plastered to the clay or podsol, as in other parts of the site, but directly on yellowish, gritty, disintegrated bedrock. The deposit in both cases, however, was covered with sterile soil separating it from soil containing Norton culture deposits.

126

Fig. 33. Pottery lamp in wall of House 1 excavation, Iyatayet.

Fig. 34. Floor of House 1, Iyatayet.

127

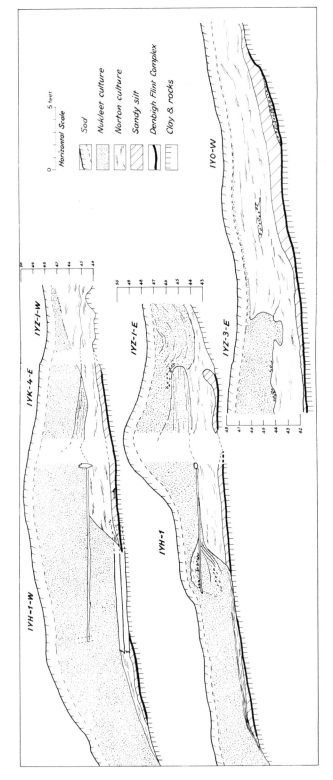

Fig. 35. Profiles in and above House 1 excavation, Iyatayet.

128

All of the materials listed as in place in the Denbigh Flint complex level and bearing the location *A, E,* or *H* are related to these perhaps secondary deposits. The remains of parts of two Nukleet period houses, dim though their signs were, appeared in Cut E.

House 2, at the north end, presented a fairly regular floor level, at the edges of which the rotten impressions of upright timbers were discerned, enabling us to define, particularly at the outer edges and on the west side, the edge of floor deposit. The tunnel was better defined in its layer of compressed woody inclusion at the floor level. A fireplace, indicated by a deposit of ash and burned stones, lay just beyond the point where the tunnel floor ended, about two feet below the floor level of the house.

At a level a few inches lower than the House 2 tunnel floor, and east of it, were five post molds which seemed to define a floor level of the usual width of a house tunnel. This floor widened between the western set of posts, but here traces of floor disappeared into the undifferentiated soil of the remainder of the cut. This is designated House 3, and from the concentration of Nukleet culture materials at the tunnel floor, we judge it to be a trace of early Nukleet period building.

A better defined feature was a roughly circular inclusion of gravel near the southeastern part of Cut E (*see* Fig. 31 for location). This was beach gravel, which clearly had been brought up the slope at some expense of effort; hence it may be considered the floor of some kind of structure. A heavy deposit of ash near the south edge of the top of this gravel suggests that it was part of the flooring of a house or tent. The gravel had been laid down on soil containing Norton culture materials and it contained a concentration of objects related to Norton culture, together with a few displaced pieces from the Flint complex. No further features were discernible in the mud which covered and surrounded the gravel inclusion.

Cut O was laid out to test the extent, up the hillside, of the Denbigh Flint complex level. The profile, Fig. 35, shows the old level to have been nearly continuously present, thinning out and disappearing only at the uphill margin. Referring to the map of Iyatayet (Fig. 31), the profile IYO-W was drawn from the west face of Cut O, while its continuation downhill is taken from the east face of Cut Z-3 before Cut Z-4 was excavated. Profile IYZ-1 east is continued through House 1 (IYH-1), and IYZ-1 west continues in a line through the west wall of House 1. The gravelly inclusion within the old level, indicated in the profile IYO-W, was roughly oval in plan and about 3 feet long by 2 feet wide, the greatest length in the direction of the slope. Within from 1 to 5 feet of this gravel inclusion were concentrated chips of flinty material as well as artifacts, including several burins. It appears likely that this was once a fireplace— perhaps gravel was laid down on the sod of a tent interior to reduce the possibility of spreading fire to peat or sod. A small lens of gravel would

Fig. 36. Detail, Cut E, Iyatayet.

have lengthened itself downslope through gravity as it settled to a position in the present Flint complex level after all of its organic matter had disintegrated. The very presence of beach gravel high on the terrace is evidence of its being carried up the slope for some human purpose.

It is also to be noted in the profile that the Flint complex layer turns rather sharply upward before thinning to imperceptibility. Although we saw no other signs of excavation within the level itself, this could be the mark of some kind of levelling off of the ground at a campsite.

Cuts M and N, also near what seemed to be the upper limit of probable occupation, proved to have no Flint complex layer in place, although a concentration of the old flints appeared at the top of the bedrock material or scattered through the lowest levels of the cut. The Nukleet period deposit here was very thin and nearly all of the soil exposed in the relatively shallow cut (comparable in depth to those shown for the PE series) was of Norton culture with no recognizable organic inclusions.

Finally, in Cut P, were found encouraging signs of good preservation in the Norton culture deposit as well as in stratified lower levels in which the sterile, sandy loam and the Flint complex were undisturbed. This cut was extended into PA, where the back wall of a Norton culture structure was localized, then to PB in an effort to define a Norton culture house, and, finally, at the end of the season, to PC, where undisturbed stratigraphy proved very rewarding and where was found *in situ* in the old level the single fluted point recovered from the site. The signs of construction found in the lower edge of Cut PA, which led to the excavation of Cut PB, were

130

almost certainly those of a Norton culture dwelling. A row of upright posts, or split planks, had extended diagonally from the east end of PA Cut westward into PB Cut. The excavation which had been made in order to place these posts in the ground as the back wall of a house had broken the stratigraphy of the sterile, sandy layer and the Flint complex layer between 6 and 8 inches behind the wall outline. Preservation was so poor elsewhere, however, that we could discern only traces of a possible wood flooring immediately inside the wall and traces of posts, mainly in the form of stains in the ground, along two possible walls. A deposit of ashy soil containing bits of charcoal suggested a fireplace near the front of the house, but in the absence of a well-defined floor level and because the Norton culture deposits had been cut through by Nukleet culture builders, Cut PB was not completed in the downhill direction.

Excavations, 1950

The aim of excavation in 1950, even more than in previous years, was to locate and uncover as much as possible of the Flint complex level with a minimum of costly work in other deposits. The information gained in previous years clearly indicated that the best opportunities of this kind were to be found well back along the terrace, out of range of the dense and troublesome Nukleet culture deposits.

Cut Z, laid out as a series of parallel cuts between the House 1 excavation and Cut O, was completed in three of its proposed sections. (Section 2 was left as a control block.) As indicated in the Sections Z-1 west and Z-1 east, Fig. 35, the Flint complex level was lacking in Z-1 Cut except for patches of the level in place covered by sterile sandy loam at the lower edge.

In the bottom of Section 3 was exposed the Flint complex level in place, except for about 15 square feet in the lower west corner. Elsewhere, the sterile sandy layer ranged from 1 to 8 inches in thickness. The concentration of Flint complex material was thin, however, in this section.

A gravel inclusion within the Flint level in Section Z-4 appears to have been flooring for some form of surface dwelling, for the gravel must have been transported to the site by human efforts. A revealing section through this gravel and its overlying deposits at the east wall of Z-4 are shown in the photograph, Fig. 37, and the sketch, Fig. 38. The stratigraphy of this area is further discussed in connection with solifluction lobes and the dating of the site (pp. 191–201, and 244–46).

Cut PE began as a test of the uphill limit of the Denbigh Flint complex and proceeded from PE-1 in the order numbered. Walls one foot thick were left between the Sections 1–5 and 8. The walls were removed at the end of the season. In the PE series, the direction taken had to do with following

Fig. 37. East wall of Cut Z-4.

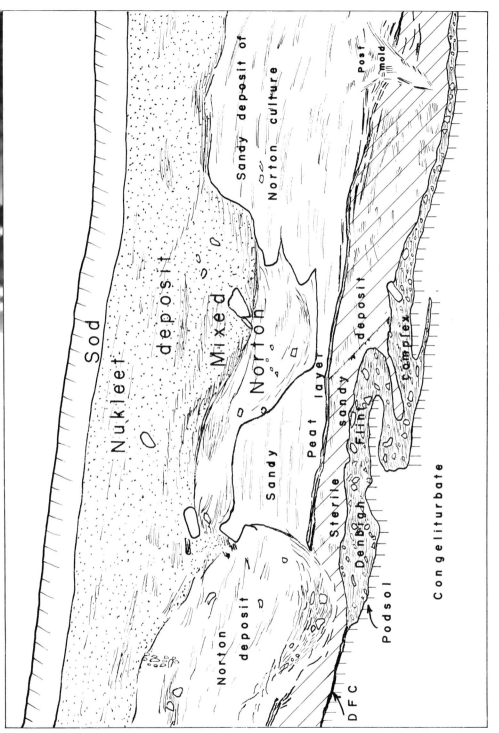

Fig. 38. East wall of Cut Z-4, diagrammatic.

133

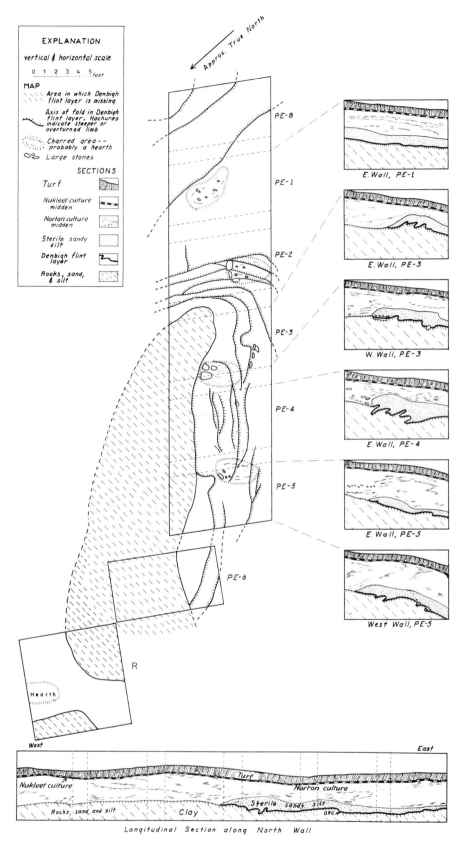

Approx. True North

PE-8

PE-1

PE-2

PE-3

PE-4

PE-5

PE-6

R

Hearth

E. Wall, PE-1

E. Wall, PE-3

W. Wall, PE-3

E. Wall, PE-4

E. Wall, PE-5

West Wall, PE-5

West

East

Turf

Nukleet culture

Norton culture

Rocks, sand, and silt

Clay

Sterile sandy silt

Longitudinal Section along North Wall

Fig. 39. Plan and sections, Cut PE, Iyatayet.

out folds in the Flint complex layer, as indicated in Fig. 39. The folds, both here and in the Z Cut, proved valuable criteria for dating and isolating materials of the Flint complex (see pp. 200–201). A continuation of PC Cut, as Cut PD, is worthy of note because at its east end we found traces of the base of a burned wooden structure which made it possible to anticipate the presence and location of a large and relatively well-preserved Norton culture house.

House 7, the house of Norton culture, Fig. 40, owes its partial preservation to burning, probably at the time of abandonment. Wall timbers, which had been standing apparently upright at the west wall, had fallen diagonally across the house floor, making it possible to collect large, almost whole, sections of pure charcoal. The fact that charring in these logs was complete, leaving no trace of unburned wood within, may point to a smoldering, persistent fire after an insulating wall and roof had fallen over the burning logs. Elswhere about the walls and house floor, signs of burning were either completely absent or very slight. A floor level existed, however; towards the rear of the house it lay at a level on top of eroded bedrock showing that an excavation had been made.

There were clear signs elsewhere, however, that Norton culture deposits had already covered the ground at the site of House 7 before the house pit was excavated. This was seen particularly at the northwest corner, where the bases of the wall logs, now charcoal, were set below levels of Norton culture that stopped short of the margin of the house itself. Upper levels of the Norton deposit, however, continued over the wall and without a break across the expanse of the house itself. Toward the front of the house, several places were noted where the charred timbers and the blackened floor beneath them lay above earth containing Norton culture deposits. The entrance passage floor also was packed in part on top of earlier Norton deposits. The house appears to have been excavated into Norton culture midden, or leavings, of an unknown thickness and to have been covered over, after it had collapsed in ruins, by a thick deposit of the Norton culture, followed by a thinner deposit of Nukleet culture. The floor of this house had apparently been earth, although uncharred wood cannot be expected to leave clear signs. The house floor was traced in all directions to a point where none of the charred or compacted surface could be discerned. The resulting floor outline, as shown in Fig. 40, has an essentially rectangular appearance, excepting the unusual extension forward near the entry way. A fireplace was clearly indicated by a fired area near the center of the floor, as shown in the plan—an area almost devoid of black charcoal, but reddened well into the ground as though by persistent fires, and marked by several large, fire-reddened stones. At the front of the house, the floor dipped almost vertically about 10 inches, in an arc. Flat stones lay like stepping stones forward of the drop, and the floor level con-

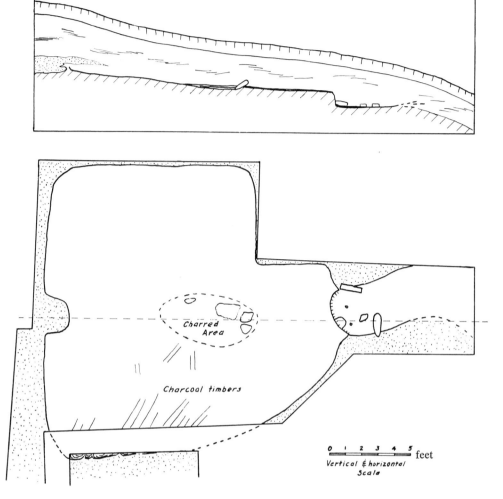

Fig. 40. Plan and profile of Norton Culture House 7, Iyatayet.

tinued clearly marked for about 5 feet before it diffused from a compacted
and darkened layer into an almost imperceptible blend with the color and
content of surrounding earth. The dotted line in the plan indicates the
probable widening of this entrance floor, as though beyond the doorway
of a rather short entrance passage. A curious absence of floor level midway
across the back of the house is also noted in the figure, possibly having
to do with some undetermined building feature.

To summarize the rather meager evidence, this Norton culture house
was built early, but not in the earliest period of Norton occupation of the
site. It was roughly 17 feet both wide and long, with a short entrance
passage and a forward extension of the house as a kind of anteroom be-

136

fore the fireplace. The house was heated, at least in part, by indoor fires, and its walls were of upright driftwood poles. There was little difference in level between the floor of the entrance passage and that of the house proper, yet the single step seems to have been held in position by a retaining wall of perishable material. (For further notes on dating, see pp. 244–46).

Also excavated during this season was House 6, the Nukleet culture house located on the south slope, as reported on pages 108–13.

Excavations, 1952

A fourth trip to Iyatayet was made in the summer of 1952, at the conclusion of a reconnaissance trip to the Arctic coast of Alaska. Alex Ricciardelli and I excavated Cut Z-5, an extension of the cut in which solifluction lobes had previously appeared, and Cut R, higher on the slope than any previous excavation. Our aim was to secure samples suitable for radiocarbon dating and to test further the nature of the solifluction lobes.

The Isolating of Norton Culture

The manner of formulating Norton culture is different from that used to define the other two archeological cultures at Cape Denbigh. The method is that of subtraction—a largely subjective process of removing the Nukleet and Flint complex artifacts and treating the remainder as Norton. The Norton people, following long after the campers at Iyatayet who had left behind flints of the Denbigh complex, settled upon ground which already contained in spots the washed-up materials from an earlier level, and they themselves no doubt displaced parts of the oldest cultural layer whenever they dug holes or house foundations. Some Denbigh flints are found throughout the Norton deposit. Following Norton times came a hiatus in occupation which is shown, in part, by a sod line between Norton and Nukleet deposits. One can guess that for centuries heavy grass grew upon the surface of the ground, as it has done on the abandoned site during recent centuries. Finally, the Nukleet people—the last occupants of the site— dug extensively into the terrace at Iyatayet, thoroughly mixing parts of both the Norton and the earliest cultural deposits with their own. Although in the main Norton culture is separable from that of Nukleet, it is never certain that some Nukleet stones have not drifted into the Norton culture mud after organic binder has rotted from the soil. In practice, there is little question about the separation of Norton culture artifacts from others in the Iyatayet site. The thousands of Nukleet period artifacts excavated at Nukleet itself offer a wide range of forms in stone and pottery. Almost none of these forms with their accompanying evidence of technique are to be found in the least disturbed parts of the Norton culture deposits. Even so, Norton culture at Iyatayet is largely defined by subtraction.

The objects of Nukleet culture in the same deposits with those of Norton and Denbigh Flint complex are removed with confidence. Separating the Flint complex artifacts creates considerably more doubt. While all of the unpolished artifacts of basalt and similar coarse, flinty stone can be set apart as Norton simply because they almost never occur in the Flint complex in place, it is more difficult to be certain of such forms as flake-knives, some side blades, and scrapers. Norton culture seems to have inherited, in these areas, techniques of Denbigh Flint complex with little change.

No stratigraphy could be discerned at first within the Norton culture deposits. Nevertheless, it was assumed that by excavating these deposits in levels of uniform thickness the content of the levels would express culture change through time. With the exception of two limited sections, however, this procedure offered little or no help. The exceptions were the K cut, where not much prehistoric digging or mixture of cultures had taken place, and part of cuts P and PE, where burning had preserved enough organic matter towards the end of Norton occupation to allow certain organic artifacts, bones, and stone implements to be associated as belonging roughly to the same time level and, presumably, to the time of last occupation of the site.

The Norton layer, where it is most nearly intact, ranges from 18 to 36 inches in thickness and consists of "a rich, red-brown or light yellow-brown mixture of humic material and silty soil, but in some places it consists of soft, friable, black, peaty material" (D. Hopkins, in Hopkins and Giddings, 1953, p. 19). Except for the limited areas mentioned above, neither organic artifacts nor bones are found in the deposit. Shells may be traced for a few inches or a few feet in wavy lines in some places, indicating, perhaps, a seasonal deposit of mussel shells as the only organic leavings of a once extensive midden. The shells themselves are not preserved, but only their chitinous covers, which appear as papery traces within the dark streaks of dirt. Discolorations in the soil sometimes may be seen to take the outline of a bone.

Artifacts of the Norton culture lie at all angles in the ground. This is in contrast with those of the Denbigh Flint complex, nearly all of which lie flat upon a single soil surface. The artifacts of Nukleet culture, with their better preservation, tend to follow strata of compressed organic matter. During a very dry season, as that of 1951, these deposits hold their shape during excavation. When the ground is thawed and saturated, however, the soil oozes away in continuous mud flows, creating practically insurmountable problems of excavation. Without doubt much rearrangement of stone

138

artifacts and pottery has taken place in the ground since wood rotted away and the deposits reached their present state of plasticity.

Further aid in defining Norton culture at Iyatayet comes from the sites of Madjujuinuk, Gungnuk, and Difchahak. Limited though the information is from these sites, it is highly significant that in none of them was found a microblade, a burin, a burin spall, an example of elaborate diagonal flaking, or any of the highly distinctive artifact forms of the Denbigh Flint complex. In these sites we found little obsidian and chert but much silicified slate and basalt, bearing out roughly the proportions of these materials as we gauged them in the Norton levels of Iyatayet. Also, the evidence from these three Norton culture sites included no overlap of artifact forms with those of Nukleet culture.

Collections of Norton Culture Levels

Objects of Organic Material

The way of life of the Norton culture people at Iyatayet must have been very much like that of the later Nukleet Eskimos, for the materials used in artifacts in the earlier period are like those of the later, and the houses of Norton builders were as permanent as those of their successors. These facts are clear, but they are based upon only scant information in the rather vast deposit of Norton culture earth examined. Evidence of housing comes largely from House 7, and this from burned timbers and related markings. Most of the artifacts of organic material were in a limited section of the IYPA cut in which fire has formed a more or less protective envelope over the bones and artifacts presumably deposited at one time. The artifacts shown in Plates *36, 37,* and *38* are not themselves charred, but they were unearthed among pulverized charcoal and ash in the soil. Rather than to suppose that this was the debris of a burned house or a section of midden later set on fire, we interpret this area as one in which the embers of a daily house fire were deposited near a house at the end of a day. Kobuk River Eskimos have explained to the writer that it was formerly customary in their area to remove the smoking remains of a fire when cooking had been completed in order that the smokehole might be tightly closed and the lamps lighted for illuminating and supplementary heating. The presence of both lamps and fireplaces in Norton culture suggests some similar arrangement.

Throughout the greater part of the Norton culture deposit the wooden and bony inclusions were no more than discolorations of the soil, with a few fibrous fragments of a cheese-like consistency that went to pieces upon exposure. Impressions of bone could be seen in the earth in some places, showing that these objects had been largely replaced with soil without distortion or undue pressure. Elsewhere the earth had been subject to more

139

disturbances, and the only continuities that could be seen were uneven layers of the dark chitinous covers of mussel shells and, less often, thin seams heavily blackened by charcoal.

The objects that can be identified as broken or whole artifacts of organic material are nearly all illustrated. We were fortunate in obtaining so wide a range of forms and implied functions in these few pieces.

End prong for bird spear. The fragment of a barbed point of ivory, *36, 1*, is somewhat like the rather fragile end prongs of western Eskimo bird spears (Nelson, 1899, pp. 151–52) and seems to fit into no other category. The barbs are distinctively created by notching two opposite narrow vanes that border the otherwise cylindrical central shaft. Notches alternate across the shaft. Another ivory point, *36, 3*, is more nearly complete and closely similar to Eskimo center prongs of either bird spear or fish spear. The lower part of the shaft shows rather heavy longitudinal scratching and lateral scoring near the base. The barbs, most of them rotted away, along two opposite vanes of the upper part have been formed by simply sawing thin notches at close intervals at right angles to the length of the shaft. Center prongs of this distinctive form are known from Okvik (Rainey, 1941, Fig. 13, *14*) and later phases of St. Lawrence Island culture (Geist and Rainey, 1936, *54, 5*).

Leister spear or fish arrow prong. Four objects are barbs (and fragments) such as have been identified most commonly in the Arctic as leister or fish spear prongs. There appears to be no way to distinguish spear from arrow barbs of this kind, since they have been used in various lengths on both types of weapons by the recent Norton Sound Eskimos (Nelson, 1899, pp. 160–61, 194–95). The tip of an antler specimen, *36, 2*, shows that its barbs have been set off by strong longitudinal grooving. An ivory fragment, *36, 4*, is from the base of a curved prong, the barbs of which were on the outward bend. It bears heavy longitudinal scratching. *36, 5* is the base of a small ivory prong, the barbs of which were shallow. *36, 7* is a complete prong of antler, the five barbs of which have been formed by lightly grooving two sides of the narrow vane of a strip of antler that is triangular in cross-section and then whittling out generous notches. The shaft below the notches is wedge-shaped for inserting into the side grooves of a shaft, but no lashing knob is provided.

Barb for fish spear prong. The trident fish spear is represented in the Norton culture by the distinctive barb of a side prong (*37, 21*). This specimen of antler is thicker along its curved edge and is wedge-shaped at the base for insertion into a side prong. Its lashing slot has been grooved from both sides, probably with one of the burin-like instruments of stone. The identification of this specimen would be more speculative if it were not for the discovery in the Near Ipiutak burials of a barb of precisely this kind inserted in the slot of a side prong (Larsen and Rainey, 1948, *78, 28*).

140

This form of barb is thus far a special trait of Norton–Near Ipiutak culture, but it is possible that some of the smaller Okvik barbs illustrated by Rainey (1941, Fig. 17, *3–8*) were similar to these in function.

Gorge. A gorge of ivory, *36, 15,* was apparently whittled away at the upper end after its original purpose had been served. As a gorge, it could have been used as either a gull hook or a fish hook in keeping with recent Eskimo practice (Giddings, 1952, pp. 40–41).

Arrow (?) shaft fragment. The flattened piece of spruce wood shaft, *36, 6,* appears to have been compressed while in the ground. It is of about the right size to have been the piece of an arrow shaft. It is liberally coated on the rounded surfaces with a maroon paint—probably discolored red ochre. Many of the arrow shafts excavated by the author in the Okvik culture house at Gambell, St. Lawrence Island, were red-painted as a base for limited designs in black (Rainey, 1941, p. 472).

Arrowhead for end point. A single antler specimen of an arrowhead notched for an end blade, *36, 11,* is nearly complete. Grooves at the base on either side, in line with the blade slit, show that this specimen was precisely like the Near Ipiutak arrowheads of Type 2 (Larsen and Rainey, 1948, *78, 12–14*). It is to be noted that the arrowhead illustrated by Larsen and Rainey (*Ibid., 78,* 12) that is most like the Iyatayet specimen retains in its blade slit an arrow point like many of those present in the Norton Bay site—that is, a thin chert point, oblanceolate in outline, presumably with basal thinning on both faces and a pronounced basal concavity. A blade that would seat itself firmly in the Iyatayet specimen would necessarily have such a basal concavity, as in some of the specimens of Plate *47.*

Arrowhead for side blades. The tip of an antler arrowhead grooved for the receipt of two side blades is shown in *36,* 10. The groove showing in the illustration cuts into a similar groove on the opposite side which extends nearly to the tip of the cylindrical shaft. Both grooves are curved so as to seat comfortably side blades like, for instance, figures 4 and 5 of Pl. *46.* The grooves, of about the same thickness throughout, were very likely made with a burin-like groover such as those in Pl. *41-b.* This arrowhead appears to fall into the Ipiutak "Type 1" (Larsen and Rainey, 1948, *32, 1–8*) which appears also in the Near Ipiutak deposits at Point Hope (*Ibid., 84,* 1).

Blunt arrowhead. A blunt arrowhead of antler, *36,* 16, has three prominent lobes and a round socket that has been formed by gouging rather than by drilling. The three-lobed tip of this specimen recalls most closely certain specimens from Near Ipiutak burials (Larsen and Rainey, 1948, *78,* 24–25), but blunt arrow tips with sockets and compound points have a wide distribution not only in western Alaska but in northeastern Asia (de Laguna, 1947, pp. 209–10). A socketed form much like this replaced

141

earlier forms in northwestern Alaska in the 15th century A. D. (Giddings, 1952, p. 51).

Harpoon head. The five harpoon heads represented by three nearly complete specimens and two fragments are all made of antler. They are outstanding in their consistent "primitiveness" as compared with the harpoon heads of most other sites of the Arctic, and they can be more nearly duplicated in rare forms of Near Ipiutak than in either Ipiutak or other early sites. One specimen, *36,* 17, has no line hole. A wide and shallow shaft socket is opposed by a wide band of indentation for lashing. Presumably the harpoon line was attached directly to this area, unless the deep groove shown in the photograph above the socket is an unfinished line hole instead of the side-blade groove that it appears to be. The spur is a rounded shelf extending only slightly beyond the proximal end of the socket. Two specimens from the anomalous House 24 at Ipiutak (Larsen and Rainey, 1948, *83,* 4–5) are similar to this in lacking a line hole. If the slot in the upper part of this head is designed for a blade, it must be for a triangular blade such as those in *46,* 10–16, which would fit into the groove and extrude a backward-pointed barb. *36,* 19 appears to have been like the specimen just described in having a short, semicircular spur, but it differs in having a shorter socket and a line slit, a part of which is to be seen at the broken upper edge. *36,* 20 is also slotted, by grooving from opposite sides, for line attachment, and it has an open socket, but its spur is broken away. This specimen appears to have been closely similar to a head from Near Ipiutak burials (*Ibid.,* 1948, *78,* 6). *36,* 18 is another bladeless harpoon head with open socket and a broad lashing indentation. It differs from the others in having a line hole which has been drilled and a rather long, lateral spur. The line hole has been formed by drilling from both sides. Except for lacking provision for side blades, this head is much like a Near Ipiutak head from the middens (*Ibid.,* 1948, *84,* 10). *36,* 21 is the fragment of a harpoon head that reveals only that it was another open-socketed specimen. In all five of these antler harpoon heads and fragments, the socket appears to have been formed by drilling. Presumably the drilling was done first in a thick piece of antler, and the remainder of the head was shaped with reference to the position of the drilled socket, probably by first cutting through the blank so as to bisect the drilled hole. Aside from a superficial resemblance of all of these bladeless heads to specimens from Cook Inlet (de Laguna, 1934, *38*), there seems no need to make close comparisons with collections other than those from Near Ipiutak sites at Point Hope, with which they are obviously in close accord. Larsen and Rainey (1948, pp. 69–70) have already called attention to the fascinating resemblance of some of the "primitive" Ipiutak and Near Ipiutak heads to ancient harpoon heads of Norway.

Harpoon foreshaft. A single harpoon foreshaft of antler, *36,* 22, falls

142

Fig. 41. Dart head from below Norton levels in House 1.

within one of the two principal types found at Ipiutak (Larsen and Rainey, 1948, pp. 74–76). It has a stem, the cross-section of which is a long rectangle. The shaft remains more or less rectangular for about two-thirds of its length, where it becomes cylindrical for insertion into a harpoon socket. The line hole has been formed by gouging from both sides. Closely similar forms are illustrated for both Ipiutak houses and burials (*Ibid., 6, 2–3; 38*).

Harpoon dart head. A dart head of antler, found in a pocket slightly below Norton levels where these lay under the floor of House 1, is represented in Figure 41. This rather flat object has all of its surfaces carefully rounded, but undecorated, and is provided with opposite notches for lashing as well as with three sets of opposite barbs. The resemblance of this object, presumably a seal-hunting dart, to dart heads of Azilian culture of western Europe is remarkable (see especially Niederlender, Lacam, et de Sonneville-Bordes, 1956, Fig. 9, p. 439).

Harpoon ice pick. The well-preserved ice pick of ivory, *38, 12,* is more or less a thick oval in cross-section throughout, thinning to a wedge at the upper end. It is scored all around its upper half. Although simpler than most harpoon ice picks, it is similar to those of the earliest cultures of the region, specifically Old Bering Sea (Collins, 1937, *29*, 13–15; *32*, 1–6), Okvik (Rainey, 1941, Fig. 11, *11*, *13*), and Ipiutak (Larsen and Rainey, 1948, *39*, 9–12).

Dart socket piece (?). The fragment of a shaft socket of sea mammal bone, split through the middle (*36*, 9), is probably the part of some form of harpoon dart assembly. Although this is a plain specimen, in contrast to the ornately decorated socket pieces of Ipiutak, it is similar to some of the latter in having a cylindrical socket of a size like those meant for the seating of foreshafts with wedge-shaped or rectangular stems into a wooden plug carved to fit the socket (Larsen and Rainey, 1948, pp. 73–74). Socket pieces of this size and bulbous at the tip are known from early (Collins, 1937, *33*, 26) and recent sites of the western Eskimo. It is seldom possible to associate them beyond doubt with a particular form of head or even with a single form of hunting (Giddings, 1952, p. 57). Socket pieces of a size and shape comparable to this have been used recently in the Norton Bay region for both sealing and fishing, and they have appeared with feathered arrow shafts (Nelson, 1899, Fig. 44, *1–2*) as well as with shafts propelled by hand.

Flaking hammer. Two objects appear to be flaking hammer heads of different kinds. *36*, 13, of ivory, is blunted about the upper end as though in repeatedly hammering a hard substance. Two vanes, or ridges, are roughly opposite one another. The small notch on the right edge in the illustration seems to be part of a hole drilled through a once higher vane. The opposite ridge is less pronounced and looks as though it was meant to furnish a firm mounting of the piece in a handle.

The other specimen, *36*, 23, is a more familiar form of flaking hammer head, closely similar to those of Near Ipiutak and Ipiutak (Larsen and Rainey, 1948, *11*, *81*, *83*, and *86*). The lower right side has been broken away from this otherwise symmetrical antler piece, which has a narrow lashing groove and a longitudinal groove on its upper, rounded, surface, but no markings on its flat under surface. This object and the probable flaker described below give confidence that the working of flints by Norton culture people was essentially like that described for the modern Utorqarmiut by Larsen and Rainey (*Ibid.*, pp. 92–93).

Flaker point (?). A split seal rib, both ends of which are blunted as though by pressure flaking (*38*, 11) is probably a flaker point like Near Ipiutak specimens (*Ibid.*, *86*, 2–3), presumably meant to be lashed into flaker handles (*Ibid.*, *1*).

A short ivory object, *37*, 16, longitudinally lined on the surface shown and blunted at both ends, is probably a flaker point of the kind that is inserted in a separate grooved handle. A point almost identical in shape and size with this one was found in a Near Ipiutak burial at Point Hope (*Ibid., 82,* 13).

Composite knife. 36, 14 is the half of a composite knife of ivory which has warped from its original shape. A rather narrow groove in the thin upper end is of a size that is more likely to have held a metal blade than a point of stone. A composite knife half of similar proportions occurred in the Near Ipiutak burials *(Ibid., 81,* 15).

Awls, bodkins, etc. A number of objects appear to have been pointed for use as awls or bodkins. *37,* 1 is a thin, cylindrical shaft, broken at both ends. *37,* 5–8 are all antler specimens, two of which (6 and 8) have been definitely sharpened towards one end. The double-ended ivory instrument, *37,* 10, is still sharp, and it is possible that the slightly wider upper end was meant to be hafted, as Larsen and Rainey suggest for similar double-pointed pins from a Near Ipiutak house at Point Hope (1948, *83,* 16). This specimen has been scratched longitudinally as though for decoration, and near its center the scratches form series of chevrons on one side. Double-pointed bone pins similar to some of these in outward appearance were found in Cook Inlet sites (de Laguna, 1934, *43,* 27–30).

Needle blank. A piece of bird bone, *37,* 17, has heavy longitudinal guide lines on one side only, as though for the production of slivers for needle-making. This is similar in size and treatment to a specimen from Yukon Island III culture (de Laguna, 1934, *44,* 26), and Larsen and Rainey (1948, p. 90) mention from Ipiutak "163 unfinished needles and bird leg bones from which needles have been cut. Several needles were cut from each bone in the form of slender rectangular strips which were probably later sharpened on a whetstone. . ." of special form like some of those in Plate *45.*

Gauged drill. An object of bone, *37,* 9, is a familiar form which we have called a "gauged drill" because the shaft near the sharpened end is drawn to a gauged thickness for one or a few centimeters, as though to allow the object to fit a drilled hole. These are known from Old Bering Sea sites (Collins, 1937, *48,* 1–9), from Cook Inlet and eastern Thule sites (de Laguna, 1934, p. 185), from Kotzebue and Ekseavik in the Kobuk region (Giddings, 1952, pp. 69, 72), and from Nukleet (*15,* 16–18, 25, 26). They have been interpreted variously as drills and line-hole cleaners. Possibly some of them are stoppers for bladders or skin containers.

Engraving tools. Three objects appear to be engraving tools of different kinds. A "pen-holder" specimen of ivory, *37,* 12, has four longitudinal lines engraved at equal intervals about its circumference, a terminal groove that is curved to fit a rodent tooth, and a lashing lip opposite the groove. This kind of implement is known from Ipiutak (Larsen and Rainey, 1948, pp. 82–84) and Okvik cultures (Rainey, 1941, Fig. 35, *10*) and persists as late as Ekseavik times (Giddings, 1952, pp. 72–73) and the time of middle Nukleet (*30*, 1, 3–4). A long ivory object, *37*, 13, may be a much cruder specimen of the same kind of engraving tool. It was originally somewhat rectangular in cross-section and decorated by two parallel, engraved longitudinal lines on what is now the convex surface. A beveled surface at the upper end may have been for tooth attachment. An engraving tool of a different kind, *37*, 11, is a delicate, cylindrical specimen of ivory, carved into the intricate form shown. The upper end is hollow for a short distance, and a part of it seems to have rotted away. Inside the hollow, however, is a dark stain which, according to Mr. Eric Parkinson, Preparator of the University Museum at Philadelphia, gives a strong iron test. It seems likely, therefore, that an iron bit was set in the tip of this instrument, as in Early Punuk specimens (Collins, 1937, p. 180). This object came from a deposit beyond the east wall of House 1 and from near the bottom of the paleo-Eskimo deposits. At this point, however, the paleo-Eskimo deposits were much disturbed, and relative age is not strongly indicated.

Beaver tooth. The presence of the fragment of a beaver incisor, *37*, 4, in the deposits is interesting for the questions it raises of inland-related practices. Unfortunately, there is too little shaped wood to show whether or not beaver tooth whittling was common in these deposits. The whittled marks on the bark object, *38*, 8, could have been those of a beaver tooth knife, but this is only a possibility.

Bone tube. A bone tube, *37*, 3, appears to be too short for a needle case. Possibly it was an object of ornamentation.

Doll (*see also* p. 88). The human figure carved in ivory, *37*, 14 (and Fig. 20, *1*), is unlike any of the Nukleet figurines in lacking both features and arms. The face region is a flat oval, pointed at the chin. The legs are only partly separated from the matrix, but the feet are indicated in a slight outcurving at the base of the carving. The oval face is to be compared with that of a carved human figure from a Near Ipiutak burial (Larsen and Rainey, 1948, *81*, 17), with the outline of which it is nearly identical. Carvings of the human figure from both Okvik (Rainey, 1941, Figs. 28–30) and Old Bering Sea cultures (Collins, 1937, *12*, 5–7) differ from this in having doubly pointed oval faces. A double-faced ivory face from Yukon Island II (de Laguna, 1934, *52*, 2) has a pointed head and rounded chin. Most other recent or archeological Eskimo carvings of the human figure show the face as rounded or egg-shaped (see pp. 88–89).

Fish scalers (?). Three pieces of caribou scapula show signs of having been prepared in the same way as were those at Nukleet and the Kobuk River sites (pp. 69–70), and, on the strength of the recent use of these implements on the Kobuk as fish scalers, we may tentatively class them as such. *38*, 7, 10, show that the vane of the scapula has been cut off. *38*, 9 is a head fragment of a scapula.

Miscellaneous. Among the unclassified objects are two that may have been meat forks or marline spikes, among other possibilities. *37, 15* is a bluntly pointed object of bone, and *38, 6* is a split rib, blunted at both ends. *36, 8* and *37, 2* are ivory objects that were possibly blanks in some process of manufacture. *36, 12* is the tip of an antler object, broken at the lower edge. *37, 18* and *22*, of antler and bone respectively, appear to be the broken-off tips of larger objects. *37, 19* is a flat, more or less rectangular piece of antler, possibly a gaming piece. *37, 20*, of antler, is conical in form and is possibly a cut-off tip of some implement. *38, 2* is a fragment of mammoth ivory, remarkable only for the bit of crude engraving including a "tree" design faintly showing along the upper right edge. *38, 4* is a fragment of a worked object of split seal rib. Worked wooden objects include a birch fragment, *38, 1*, the fragment of a spruce board, *38, 3*, and the fragment of a spruce shaft, *38, 5*, that bears a shallow groove on the surface shown. A large object of cottonwood bark, *38, 8*, takes the form of a hammer head with a deep hafting indentation on the surface shown. The opposite surface is slightly convex, and a lashing lip is provided at the narrower end. This is possibly a toy adz. Another possibility is that it was the part of a protective case for a blade or other breakable object. Guards of bark are sometimes made by Eskimos today.

Objects of Stone

The people of Norton culture knew about the polishing of thin slate blades like those which characterize all of the later Eskimo cultures, but they preferred to work in flinty materials, and their slate work is crude by comparison, as well as relatively scarce. They must have maintained trade routes, for some of the typical points and knife blades are made of chert, chalcedony, and even obsidian—materials that do not seem to occur near Cape Denbigh. Most of their flaking was done in the local basalt, which is not capable of as fine a preparation or finish as cherts and other rare stones and which, therefore, gives to most Norton culture workmanship a crude cast in spite of the occasional excellence of a piece in a better medium.

Even though the Norton people were flakers primarily, they left behind many tools for grinding and smoothing—whetstones, groovers, and the like—most of which apparently had to do with grinding points and shafts of organic material rather than stone. Whetstones appear, however, in several degrees of coarseness, as they do in the sites of most of the recent Eskimos. The sandstone, shale, and occasional other stones from which these objects were made appear to be of local origin. Some use was made of local quartz, an inferior material.

Labrets. Paired labrets such as those worn by Eskimo men in historic times have figured, as well, in most of the earlier accounts as a means of distinguishing Asiatic dwellers of the Bering Strait from the "ferocious" Americans. Men of the Malemiut group and their immediate neighbors continued to wear labrets until about the beginning of this century. The labrets worn by Alaskans north of the Aleutians in historic times have been mainly cylindrical, hat-shaped labrets inserted in holes bored in the lower lip at one or both sides of the mouth and larger discs and variants pinned to the lip by means of separate pieces inserted through the cheek or lip. Labrets do not figure in the St. Lawrence Island sequences of any period, and until recently it appeared that archeological evidence for labrets in the Bering Strait region was all fairly recent. With the discovery of Ipiutak, however, and the Bristol Bay sites far to the south (Larsen, 1950), labrets showed themselves to have been no recent importation from the Pacific coast Indians, but to have been long used as ornaments in the region of the western Eskimo.

The labrets of Norton culture at Iyatayet are of stone and jet, and they are all of the long, thin, medial type such as were most likely worn in a slit in the lower lip parallel to the mouth. The largest and most elaborate specimen, *39, 4*, is carved and handsomely polished from a single piece of jet. It weighs little and is smooth on all surfaces. This object was carved to fit a large jaw—one might guess that of a man. It is 80 mm. long, 12 mm. wide at the center, and the width of the inner flange ranges between 8 and 10 mm. The exposed flange is drawn to a bar about 4 mm. thick. This bar is presumably the only part that would show through the lip slot. Another, nearly complete, specimen, *39, 1*, is somewhat shorter and thinner. It is polished from a piece of slate and has a uniform thickness of about 3 mm. The outer edge is notched at three points. The fragment of another labret, *39, 2*, of polished shale, shows that it had been originally quite long and fitted to a wide mandible. Like the jet specimen, it is thicker along the inner surface—4–5 mm.—while the exposed flange is only about 3 mm. thick. A slight projection is formed at the end of the outer flange opposite a projection designed to fit within the mouth. The fourth labret is also fragmentary (*39, 3*). Made of polished shale, this one is shaped like the previous specimen of shale. This one is 7–8 mm. thick along the inner surface and 4 mm. thick at the outer flange. The wider portion shown in the illustration probably was formed near the end of the outer flange, as in the preceding specimen, although a break obscures this feature of the labret.

Medial labrets most like these from Iyatayet occur in the Bristol Bay sites. A labret from Chagvan Bay site and one from the Nanvak Bay site have the curved base like the jet specimen from Iyatayet, and one of them is closely like Norton specimens in that "the front part is a wide, thin plate, which must have extended like a shelf below the mouth" (Larsen, 1950, pp. 181, 183; Fig. 56 A, *18*). Large labrets were worn by Ipiutak people (Larsen and Rainey, 1948, *48,* 11–15), possibly by women as well as men (*Ibid.,* p. 114), but these are thicker and styled differently from those of Norton Bay and Bristol Bay, and, astonishingly, most appear to have been worn in lateral pairs.

Awkward though it would seem to mutilate a lower lip so greatly as to accommodate the largest of these Norton labrets, the thickening of the mouth portion of three of the specimens suggests that they were worn in a slot that reached across the whole of the lower lip. It would have been possible, of course, to insert the prongs of a labret such as these into two holes near the corners of the mouth, but of such a practice we have no ethnological evidence. It is worthy of note that these specimens seem to date from a period of between 1500 and more than 2500 years ago and are thus, together with Aleutian specimens (Laughlin and Marsh, 1951, p. 82) and one from Choris site (Giddings, 1961, Fig. 9, third from left), the earliest labrets of which we have knowledge in America as well as in the Bering Strait region.

Objects of baked shale. Baking shale for use as paint or collecting naturally burned shale for this purpose were practices which de Laguna reported as of considerable antiquity in the Cook Inlet sites of southern Alaska. Pieces of baked shale were cut into rectangular bars and other shapes, presumably to be further rubbed or scraped into powder for paint (de Laguna, 1934, p. 117). The shale itself seems to have come from the north shore of Kachemak Bay, but whether as raw shale that had been baked on purpose or as deposits that had been accidentally fired by burning lignite beds could not be decided from the 44 pieces obtained from various time levels.

A rather large number of samples of red shale like that of Kachemak Bay was found in the Norton deposits. No sample of this deposit is known from the later or earlier deposits in the same vicinity, nor, for that matter, elsewhere in the Bering Strait region, nor is a local deposit of red shale known to the people of Shaktoolik; hence, a possibility exists that from some common source of this red material trade had been established in more than one direction from very early times.

The baked shale of Norton culture was treated as a luxury product. It seems to have had no consistent practical use, but to have been cut and ground into a variety of shapes, much like the material used by a sculptor. The most variant of the 25 pieces recovered are illustrated. A large fragment, *40,* 1, 25 mm. thick, is probably the part of a much larger slab. Two edges and one face have been ground smooth, and a series of engraved lines produce a checkerboard effect on one face. Another specimen, *40,* 9, is also checkered, although it is much smaller and rubbed on all but a single broken edge. A third sample, *40,* 6, 8 mm. thick, shows dim check marks like the others, as though a larger checkered piece had been broken, rubbed on all edges, and marked with a single groove at a later time. A pyramidal piece, *40, 2,* with one edge partly flaked away, is essentially complete. The under surface is a polished plane, in contrast to the angled surfaces above. The top has been planed off and then ground into a shallow concavity, which has been drilled through by a 4.5 mm. drill. This specimen is unique, calling to mind in a general way the weight of a top or spindle of more recent times. A disc of baked shale, *40, 5,* is about 4 mm. thick at the center, tapering to sharp edges all around. A hole 7 mm. thick is drilled through the center. This specimen resembles in form the discs of one kind of recent labret, but there is no further evidence that lateral labrets were worn by people of Norton culture. A three-pronged piece, *40, 3,* is 7 mm. thick and ground on all surfaces. A roughly four-sided piece, *40, 4,* is provided with longitudinal grooves on each surface. This could have been used as a polisher for pins or other objects of organic material, although this usage is by no means implicit in the grooving. A flattened piece, *40, 7,* is ground on all surfaces and provided with two rather heavy grooves across one face. A fragment, *40, 8,* is the piece of a larger object. The lower edge in the illustration has been broken. The other surfaces are polished and rounded. The form of this piece is consistent with the fragment of a large medial labret, but the material is clearly impractical for such an object. A large "brick" of baked shale, *40, 10,* has been flaked all over, giving it the superficial appearance of a block of nephrite which has been shaped by hammer blows. It has then been ground on only the surface shown. This could have been a handstone for some special light abrading process for which there is no other clue. The 15 other specimens, mostly fragmentary, show a variety of scratches, some of which might have been made in sharpening awls or in cutting the blocks of baked shale, while most edges and faces are rounded or smoothed by some grinding.

The burning, or baking, of clay to produce red paint, a practice that seems related to procedures at Norton Bay and Cook Inlet, is recorded for Puget Sound tribes and neighboring peoples of that part of the Northwest Coast (de Laguna, 1947, p. 226). Other pigments were available, however. Smears of red ochre were occasionally found in Norton levels, indicating that this more vivid pigment was collected and used by Norton people. The baked shale has been ground so often that its use as a pigment seems probable, but we cannot discount the fact that it was also used as a raw material for the sculpture of a variety of forms. Perhaps the scratching or cutting of this material gave pleasure in itself, much as it pleases modern Eskimos to whittle at an occasional piece of soapstone that they find on the beach.

Ground slate blades. If an archeological site were to be sought in which to show flint workers just becoming initiated into the processes of slate grinding, no better deposits could be chosen than those of the Norton people at Iyatayet. Only 32 specimens of slate blades are identified as those of Norton levels, and these are all so coarsely treated as to distinguish them from all of the numerous slate blades of the succeeding Nukleet period. None of the Norton slates is complete enough to be classified as the blade of a particular form of knife. If the semilunar knife, the *ulu* that characterizes all of the "Eskimo" sites of the New World, is present, it is not obviously so. A single specimen, *41-a, 7*, has a long, sharpened edge which might be that of a straight-edged blade hafted in the fashion of an *ulu*. Many of the fragments have a flaked edge, or more than one, indicating that grinding and polishing slate were secondary processes and were indulged in only for the preparation of a cutting edge. *41-a, 5–6* may be fragments of similar large blades with an *ulu*-like edge of secondary polishing, as may also ten other fragments. It is to be noted that the above three specimens are all markedly scratched on both faces with V-shaped grooves. While it is possible that on some specimens, as *41-a, 5*, this was intended as a form of decoration, it seems more likely that most grinding was done by very coarse stones that left their marks on the slate.[1] Ten specimens are more lightly scratched, the scratches forming long V's. These also are secondarily polished, probably by means of a fine-grained whetstone only along the cutting edge. Examples are *41-a, 1*, a double-edged blade fragment, and *41-a, 3*, a broader blade, one edge of which is sharpened. Eight other specimens are lightly scratched, but they differ from all others in having only chipped edges, although the faces are ground. The flaking of one specimen, *41-a, 2*, is from one face only, while another specimen, *41-a, 4*, is flaked along one straight edge and one rounded end. Although it seems likely that Norton culture slates are always distinctive enough to be picked out of the later deposits at Iyatayet, we have confined the count of ground slates to those specimens that came from definite Norton culture levels. In all of the ground slates from the "pure" site at Nukleet, however, there were few, if any, fragments that might be confused with the distinctively scratched specimens from Norton culture levels at Iyatayet.

Groovers of polished stone. Unlike their clumsy scratching and polishing of slate, Norton people's workmanship in polishing certain tools that they made of harder materials was excellent. Their small groovers of gauged thickness, made of hard silicified slate or some stone of similar grain, are now known all the way across the American Arctic, where they occur frequently in very early coastal forms of culture that precede the

---

[1] After this was written, the author excavated an earlier site at Choris Peninsula (Giddings, 1957b) on the opposite side of Seward Peninsula from Cape Denbigh and found there slates like these (but even cruder) which had clearly been scraped into rough shape with flint side scrapers before the edges were polished. Some of the scrapers in Pl. 55 may have been used at Iyatayet for the same purpose.

"Thule" whalers. Their function was not recognized when they first came to light, however, mainly because they did not look much like the metal tools by which they seem to have been replaced.

The oldest archeological collection in which the groovers appear is probably that described by Solberg in 1907 from the Disko Bay region of West Greenland and identified as "drill points" (Solberg, 1907, Pls. 5–6). Collins later recognized specimens from the Old Bering Sea levels on St. Lawrence Island as similar in form to some of those illustrated by Solberg. The St. Lawrence Island specimens were flat pieces of ground stone consistently polished at one straight, smooth, working edge and at approximately right angles to this edge across the top (Collins, 1937, p. 149). Considering them to be specialized tools, the shape of which was intentional, both Collins and those who described Dorset culture in the eastern Arctic suggested that these objects might have been boot sole creasers (Collins, 1937, p. 149; de Laguna, 1947, p. 193).

In 1939 I discovered a large house ruin on the "hillside" at Gambell (Rainey, 1941, pp. 468–72) near Collins's two earliest Old Bering Sea houses (Collins, 1937, pp. 38–40), and in the course of excavating this house and a series of test trenches on the neighboring slopes, I found a number of these unusual implements. Preservation within this Okvik culture (earliest Old Bering Sea) house was very good, and a number of sections of ivory were found that had been either longitudinally cut through or prepared for splitting apart by grooving at two or more lines around the circumference. Each of the grooves had been made by an instrument of gauged thickness, the last full cutting impression of which was to be seen in pieces of ivory that had not yet been split. I recognized this technique at once as identical with techniques found in much later aspects of the St. Lawrence Island archeology. The difference was that on the Okvik house floor lay stone implements, some of which fitted so precisely into the grooves of the ivory that they seemed to be without question the implements with which the grooving had been done. It seemed at the time that instruments of this sort must have been replaced within Old Bering Sea times, or shortly thereafter, by tools which we had not yet come to recognize or by metal tips perhaps inserted in one of the special kinds of knife handle found in the site. These speculations were not published, however, and it was on other grounds that the small ground stone objects were later questioned as to their possible function as "boot sole creasers." In a small classic of archeological reasoning, Frederica de Laguna explained why she thought these objects, wherever found, were created for a special job more important than the creasing of rawhide boots:

The shape of the Canadian Dorset stone implement suggests, I believe, the use to which all the implements of this class were put. These Canadian blades are thin stone plates, ground flat on both surfaces. One edge, the back, was usually left chipped and probably fitted into a slotted handle, probably like those used for knives. The chipped or ground notch on the opposite, front, edge evidently held a lashing which secured it to the handle. The edge above the notch is ground straight and flat, so that its plane is at right angles to the two faces of the blade. Frequently the edge across the top was ground in the same way; sometimes it was ground to form an obtuse angle with one of the faces. The angle between the front edge and the top, as I have remarked, was frequently broken off, implying an energetic use. Incidentally, this argues against the tool having been used to crimp boot soles, since one does not have to press very hard to crease skin, and none of the bone creasers figured by Mathiassen are broken at the tip. I believe that the stone implements were used for cutting grooves in bone, not only in order to break the bone in two, but to make the holes so characteristic of the Dorset culture which are produced by cutting two grooves, one on each side of the specimen and crossing at right angles... In cutting, one of the two angles of the upper outer corner of the blade would have been used, and this would account for the common breakage of the stone implement at this place. If my hypothesis is correct, this implement would correspond to the chipped stone burins (sometimes called "gravers") of the Upper Paleolithic.

—de Laguna, 1947, pp. 193–94.

It should be noted that de Laguna was proposing in the last sentence only that the ground groovers with which we are concerned were meant to do a job similar to that which had been proposed also for a different implement—the stone burin of the Upper Paleolithic of the Old World. No intimation was made that these ground implements were to be equated with or were descended from flaked burins, nor that among American specimens true burins were to be found. We shall return to the problem of true American burins in a later section.

The 44 whole and fragmentary groovers from Norton culture deposits at Iyatayet include six of dark, granitic rock, ten of dark gray to black silicified slate, and all the rest of a light gray or buff to white silicified slate. Each of the whole specimens has a corner at which two ground planes across the thickness of the piece meet at approximately a right angle to form a small cutting edge. Thus, each piece has two edges that have been ground perpendicular to the two faces. Treatment of the other margins varies from flaking to fine polishing. Some of the specimens may be unfinished. *41-b,* 11, for example, is the fragment of a stem that is ground only on the face opposite that illustrated. The owner may have intended to polish both surfaces. *41-b,* 5 is a specimen on which both faces are polished, as well as the two meeting, edge planes, but it is simply flaked about the unused edge. *41-b,* 9 is a large specimen of black silicified slate, the working end of which has been broken off to leave a hook at the upper left-hand corner. The groover seems not to have been used after the break occurred, even though one sees no reason why it should not have been even more effective as a groover in this shape. Each of two specimens, *41-b,* 2 and 3, has its non-cutting edge smoothed by grinding and polishing, but without reference to forming another cutting corner. Three specimens, *41-b,* 4, 7, 10, are polished except for the edge opposite the working corner, which is beveled by the original flaking marks rather than by grinding. *41-b,* 12 is the stem of a large groover polished on both faces. The edge is beveled from both sides by chipping rather than by polishing. *41-b,* 1 is hollow-ground on either side. The lower edge is broken, and the cutting point is at the upper right corner, opposite a flaked edge. *41-b,* 6 is also hollow-ground, and the working corner is on the upper right. *41-b,* 8 has its working end partly broken off. The greater part of this specimen is a stem that is only partly ground, but a bit of the gauged section remains near the break.

Each groover is of almost uniform thickness near its working corner. These thicknesses range from 2 to 4 mm., averaging about 2.5 mm.

The distribution of these ground stone groovers in the west is without doubt very early. On St. Lawrence Island, they are associated only with the earliest phases of Old Bering Sea culture, including Okvik. Only five specimens from Collins's Hillside site seem to fall within this category (Collins, 1937, *39,* 19–22; *42,* 18). They were more numerous in the older Okvik house excavated by the author on the Gambell hillside. Rainey found only one specimen in the Okvik material of the Punuk Islands, however (Rainey, 1941, Fig. 32, *6*). In the Norton Bay region they were very common in the Norton culture levels at Iyatayet and present in the Gungnuk site (Norton culture) on Cape Darby. The only other example of them, excepting possibly that one pictured in the Bristol Bay collection (Larsen, 1950, Fig. 56A, *6*), is from Point Hope, where a single specimen is listed for one of the small "midden" excavations that is classed with Near Ipiutak culture rather than with Ipiutak proper (Larsen and Rainey, 1948, *85,* 22). The absence of these groovers elsewhere in western archeological sites is thought to result from the substitution of metal groovers for those of stone, for the practice of grooving antler, ivory, and the like did not diminish after the disappearance of these stone implements. One form of tool still used by some Eskimos, as Collins has pointed out (1953, p. 38), is the so-called "antler chisel," a form of composite knife, the metal tip of which is shaped somewhat like the polished stone groovers and used in splitting sections of antler or ivory. These metal burins, called "gravers," were described earlier by Hoffman (1897, Pl. *19*; pp. 785–6).

No groover of polished stone appears in Ipiutak culture proper, yet Ipiutak people practiced grooving of antler and ivory with gauged implements of some kind, perhaps as much as did any other archeological group in the Bering Strait area. Examples of gauged grooving are to be seen on almost any plate of antler and ivory objects in the Larsen and Rainey (1948) monograph, yet the pointed flint implements that were found in profusion in the site would seem poorly designed to produce anything but light or irregular engraved lines in hard organic materials. It looks as

154

though the Ipiutak people had not only an occasional piece of iron (Larsen and Rainey, 1948, p. 83) but enough to provide them with groovers adequate for reducing large amounts of antler and ivory to workable sections and slivers.

Until more dating can be obtained for Dorset culture sites of the eastern Arctic, we cannot say much about the final disappearance of the stone groover, but as far as the Bering Strait region is concerned, these groovers seem to have been replaced by metal between 2000 and 1500 years ago. A possibility of survival is seen in the bone cutter of chalcedony described for the Ingalik by Osgood (1940, pp. 94–95). This hafted instrument, drawn repeatedly towards the user, grooves bone with its tip which has been pointed by grinding.

Grindstones and whetstones. The artifacts of Norton culture that distinguish themselves least from those of Nukleet culture are the abrasive instruments used in fashioning or sharpening ground stone cutting implements. The most common type of whetstone, however, appears not to have occurred in the Nukleet site or levels. 56 specimens of these small whetstones are represented by some of those figured in Plate *43*. They are very small, flat whetstones ground on both faces, or on all four longitudinal faces if the specimens are fairly thick. All of them are made of a greenish-gray, fine-grained shale or a schist containing small mica flakes. Some have one or more concave surfaces, indicating short whetting motions, and others have been worn to a very small size before discarding. Most of these whetstones—35 in all—are thin and small, as in *43*, 1, 4, 7, and 8. Thirteen are broader and flat, as in the broken specimen, *43*, 3. Eight specimens, including *43*, 2, are both broader and thicker than the average and tend to be worn until broken through the middle. Most of the small whetstones have been broken. Four of those illustrated are mended from fragments found apart in the deposits. *43*, 4 consists of two fragments that lay only a few inches apart, but at different levels, in soft and muddy soil. *43*, 3 and 8 are similarly patched from fragments found within a few feet of each other in the ground. *43*, 2 is a mended piece, the fragments of which had been separated by only about ten feet, but this was the whole thickness of the Norton deposit at that point. It is from instances like this that we learn how futile it is to relegate heavy artifacts to specific levels within deposits that turn to oozing mud when thawed and wet.

Whetstones as delicate and breakable as these could have been used only for a final polishing or edging of implements already ground into shape. They are not highly abrasive. Perhaps they are stones designed primarily for edging the small groovers and adz blades of silicified slate and similar hard stone. At any rate, whetstones of this kind are not found in any of the later sites of the region in which argillaceous slates are numerous and important. This kind of whetstone occurs at Ipiutak (Larsen and Rainey,

155

1948, *10,* 9), but it appears to be far less common there than at Norton culture sites.

Another kind of whetstone that we guess to have been used frequently by Norton people is a long, thin, cylindrical beach pebble of dense igneous stone (*43,* 5 and 6). These were fairly common throughout the Norton culture levels. Use is not clearly defined by differential wear, and only a few were saved out of many encountered. The proportions of these to other natural beach stones in the site, which is high on a terrace, indicate that they were intentionally brought to the site. Similar pebbles, usually larger, occurred now and then in the Nukleet levels of the same site, but in nothing like the same proportions. It would be impossible to compare the distribution of pebbles like this with those of a beach site in which they might occur naturally in the gravel.

Only two fragments of what may have been large grindstones occur in the deposits. *42,* 12 is the edge of a larger slab, both faces of which have been ground. The slab is not flat, however, nor suitable for grinding a large, flat surface such as that of a slate knife blade, but has shallow pits on both faces such as would discourage the grinding of all but small objects. Both this and the following specimen are of medium-grained sandstone. *42,* 10 is a small, flat, irregular section of another grinding stone. Two notches may have been cut intentionally into one edge. It is ground also on the face opposite that shown and on the edge opposite that which is notched. Only one of the whetstone and grindstone fragments is coarse enough to have produced scratches like those on all blade fragments of argillaceous slate. This is *42,* 8, a whetstone of coarse scoria, four surfaces of which have been ground.

Thirty-one specimens of whetstone are flat, irregular pieces of sandstone, one or both faces of which are ground. The stain of red ochre on one specimen indicates that it was used, perhaps incidentally, in grinding paint. Five specimens, including *42,* 13, are relatively large whetstones of medium to coarse sandstone, two wide faces of which have been used, as have the two narrow edges. The illustrated specimen has been scratched on the face shown. Thirteen smaller whetstones are long and ground on four sides, as in *42,* 2. *42,* 6 and 7 are specimens of this type in which a shallow groove extends lengthwise of one face. Perhaps they functioned as shaft smoothers rather than as whetstones. Four sandstone specimens, including *42,* 5, are pentagonal in cross-section, all five faces having been ground. Two others are six-sided; one of these is illustrated in *42,* 11. Unusual grindstones are *42,* 4, an irregular, cylindrical piece that is worn by grinding at several places, and *42,* 9, which has three plane surfaces and one convex surface. The latter specimen could have been held in the hand and used somewhat as a planing stone. Nine whetting or polishing stones are

156

irregular pieces of shale ground on one or both faces. A specimen of this type is *42, 3*, which has been both ground and scratched on both faces. The scratching might have been made from pointing an awl-like instrument.

Whetstones with multiple rubbing surfaces, such as the five-sided specimen, *42, 1*, belong to Okvik culture (Rainey, 1941, Fig. 33, *7* and *8*) and occur in the Hillside site at Gambell (Collins, 1937, p. 154; *43, 1* and *2*), where they are closely similar to the stones of pentagonal cross-section in Norton culture.

Even though 69 grinding and whetting stones were found—other than the special thin ones of shale and schist and the beach pebbles—none of them, except, perhaps, the single specimen of scoria, helps to solve the question of why the argillaceous slate artifacts should all be distinctively scratched and scored in their preparation. On the other hand, the high polish of hard stone grooving instruments and adz blades may be explained by the polishers of schist and shale found throughout the deposits.

Adz blades. Excepting a few specimens of the local basalt, the adz blades of Norton culture are all made of silicified slate varying in color from greenish or dark gray to almost white. Some of them are highly polished on two faces as well as about the cutting edge, as though their maker took pride in their appearance as well as in their cutting efficiency. Type 1 is an adz blade the cutting edge of which is formed by a plane strongly beveled from the upper, overhanging, face. The bevel ranges between 60 and 80 degrees. *44, 7* is such a blade, squarish in outline, of green silicified slate, polished over most of both faces. *44, 9* is a similar specimen of gray silicified slate, polished only near the cutting edge. *44, 8* is similar, but smaller. *44, 6*, of dark silicified slate, has a strongly convex cutting edge and is polished only near this edge on the broader face. This particular specimen was figured in the initial report on Cape Denbigh as belonging in the "microlithic layer" (Giddings, 1949, p. 89; Fig. *2e*). There is little doubt that this was an error based on separating materials by six-inch levels at the moment at which the thin layer of Denbigh Flint material was first discovered. Such a specimen as this, quite typical of Norton culture, was not at any time encountered directly in the thin layer of Denbigh Flint complex material. *44, 3* is a handsome small specimen of light gray silicified slate, squarish in outline and highly polished on both faces. Two similar specimens are larger.

Type 2 adz blades are those with a low bevel of 45 degrees, more or less, from the upper face. An example is *44, 1*, of light-colored silicified slate, lightly polished only near the cutting edge. A unique specimen, polished lightly on both faces, is beveled against a polished surface only by flaking.

Type 3 adz blades have no bevel, but are sharpened by the meeting of two slightly convex polished surfaces. Examples are *44,* 10, of light silicified slate, polished on most of both faces, and *44,* 5, a similar but slightly larger specimen. Two other blades conform to this type.

Three specimens, each unique, may prove to have counterparts elsewhere in Norton culture. *44,* 4 is a narrow, thick object of light-colored silicified slate with a V-shaped section at the left edge. It is about 12 mm. thick throughout. The curvature shown in the figure is caused by a break. This object appears to be a wedge-shaped adz blade or chisel similar to those from Ipiutak (Larsen and Rainey, 1948, *10,* 14 and 15). *44,* 2 is an adz blade of basalt with a rounded edge that is polished only where necessary to form a sharp cutting edge. It is 22 mm. thick near the center, tapering to thin, flaked edges. *44,* 11, of basalt, is a crudely flaked specimen, irregular in shape and beveled to about 50 degrees. It resembles no other adz blade of Norton culture so much as it does the later crude thin jade blades of Kobuk River sites (Giddings, 1952, *7,* 4, 5, and 6). Included among the adz blades are two unfinished specimens and five fragments too small for typing.

Unlike many of the Nukleet adz blades, none of the Norton specimens has been cut by sawing. In this particular, a resemblance is noted to blades in the earlier periods of deposit at Kachemak Bay, and in their detail there is a similarity to two tongue-shaped specimens from Yukon Island sub-III 2 (de Laguna, 1934, p. 57; *19,* 9 and 10). Other adz blades of very similar form to those of Norton culture come from sites on Umnak Island in the Aleutians (Jochelson, 1925, *15,* 19, 25, 35, and 41), where adz blades are reported to be surprisingly scarce (*Ibid.,* p. 120).

Shaft smoothers. The abrasive blocks of stone with a prominent central groove that are known in the archeology of the western states and British Columbia as shaft smoothers are well represented in the Norton culture levels. Occurring also in the Ipiutak deposits at Point Hope (Larsen and Rainey, 1948, p. 86; *10,* 11) and more notably in those of Near Ipiutak (*Ibid., 81,* 12), these artifacts seem out of line with those of other sites of the Bering Strait region.

One pumice specimen, *45,* 12, has an irregularly rounded back. *45,* 1, of porous quartzite, is 25 mm. thick and also has a rounded back. In a total of 26 other specimens, 2 are of coarsely textured sandstone, 15 of medium grain, and 9 of a fine grain; *45,* 8, which has one end broken, is beveled on the back at the intact end, and is 14 mm. thick; and *45,* 9, a fine-grained specimen, 16 mm. thick, has a lateral groove around the front and one side—perhaps for suspension. *45,* 2 is keeled at the back, giving it a heart-shaped cross-section, and is 25 mm. thick. Others are more or less flat on the back. *45,* 13 is a handsomely ground specimen with a deep groove that is only 10 mm. thick. *45,* 10 has a groove more suitable for a thin dart shaft or the like than for receipt of an arrow shaft. It is 9 mm. thick. *45,*

4 is a fine-grained specimen, 18 mm. thick. *45, 5* is similar, but with a coarser grain and broken at one end. *45, 7* is a very thin specimen (4 mm.), one end of which is broken, but it is grooved as though for receipt of an arrow shaft.

Among the other specimens are one that is grooved on opposite faces and several that are scratched on one or more faces, as though in secondarily serving as a pointer.

In speculating on the reasons for rubbing a stone such as this along a shaft to make it smooth, we are obliged to guess why recent Eskimos have not used it. The reason seems to be that metal knives may be turned at right angles and used to round off any of the effects of whittling that might otherwise affect the efficiency of an arrow. Modern Eskimos employ either a crooked knife or a jackknife for shaft smoothing. In Norton culture days, however, if metal were not available, the fashioner of a shaft would be obliged, perhaps, to do his smoothing with a beaver tooth, a flint, or some abrasive. A flint, whether a scraper or a knife blade, would be likely to leave impressions of its flaking marks, while the tooth would be too narrow for rapid scraping. Hence, an abrader that could be rapidly run the length of a shaft, gauging thickness somewhat as it went, would have special merit and might continue to do so until a metal blade became available. Perhaps the spotty distribution of shaft smoothers in the eastern woodlands and roughly within the range of early use of copper knives is a matter of function more than tradition, and its presence in the western states may be a reflection of the lack of metal. However this may be, the striking resemblance between Norton smoothers and those of the Southwest attests to some early diffusion between the two regions.

Grooved sharpeners—"abraders." This class of grooved objects, mainly of sandstone, seems closely related in its distribution to the shaft smoothers, especially in their more perfected forms. We assume that they were used to smooth and point small shafts, such as awls and arrowheads, by either twirling and plowing them in a groove or working them back and forth as one might point a pencil. Many objects of antler, ivory, and wood, including some of the instruments illustrated in Pls. *36* and *37,* must have needed to be smoothed and pointed in such a way as this, especially if scraping edges of metal were not available.

These sharpeners may be described in two groups. In one group the instrument has a central prominent groove, while in the other it has multiple grooves. Four illustrated specimens and three others fall into the first group. *45, 6* is a domino-shaped block, 13 mm. thick, with thin grooves paralleling the deeper, central groove. *45, 11* is narrower, 14 mm. thick, and provided only with the central groove. *45, 18* is the fragment of a longer sharpener, 16 mm. thick, on which the single central groove is thin and irregular. *45, 15* is an uneven slab of sandstone, 17 mm. thick, the opposite face of which is ground smooth in contrast to the illustrated surface with its central groove.

Each of eleven specimens has more than one groove. *45,* 17 has a pair of grooves on one face. It is 8 mm. thick. *45,* 3 is a broken, boat-shaped specimen, 30 mm. thick, which has several grooves along both convex surfaces and a smooth concavity (right-hand margin of the illustration). The concavity is not that of a shaft smoother, however, for it bends in both directions. *45,* 16 is an irregular fragment, 23 mm. thick, with deep, uneven grooves on its narrower face and a single groove on the opposite face. *45,* 14 is a nearly square slab, 14 mm. thick, one face of which is crossed by two grooves at right angles to each other, and it is further marked by three short grooves that may have been added on a decorative impulse. These and the other specimens are of sandstone, with the exception of one of slate and one of pumice.

While the closest parallels to these abraders are to be found in sites in western Canada and the western and central states, it is to be noted that Jochelson illustrates a grooved round stone from Umnak Island that he surmises has been used "for grinding and polishing bone foreshafts and heads" (Jochelson, 1925, p. 64; *16,* 20) and, from a Kamchatkan site, a grooved "whetstone of porphyrite for sharpening bone needles" (Jochelson, 1928, *11,* 2).

It is to be noted that many of the grooves, both on the abraders and on shaft smoothers, are straight enough to have been cut with a stone "saw." Saws were rarely found in the Norton levels, however (p. 174).

Side blade. The term "side blade" is used here to describe both the small, arcuate flints like those of Ipiutak that are described as "inset blades," and larger flints that were almost certainly inset after one manner or another to be used on a single cutting edge. It is inevitable that some of the most delicately worked side blades of chert and other excellent material in Norton culture cannot be distinguished from side blades of the Denbigh Flint complex, some of which appear within the Norton levels, where they have been thrown up in excavation during Norton times. The side blades of Pl. *46* are chosen to give the range of side blades that belong without question to Norton culture. Some of the better-executed side blades made by Norton people may also occur in the collection abstracted from the later levels and regarded as displaced Denbigh Flint complex pieces. At least two conjectural forms of side blade are associated with arrow heads and harpoon heads of Norton types, as we have seen (p. 142).

Type 1 (48 specimens). The range of arcuate to leaf-shaped side blades is shown in *46,* 1–9. The rounder edge of each specimen nearly always shows finer retouch than its opposite, or inset, edge. Eight are of basalt, one of silicified slate, and the others are of cherty materials (gray and black chert, red jasper, and translucent chalcedony). Most of these side

160

blades are smaller than *46, 6*, and seven could have been fitted into arrow heads like *36*, 10.

Type 2 (36 specimens). These side blades are triangular in outline (*46*, 10–16). Seven are made of basalt, and one of silicified slate. The slot in the antler harpoon head shown in *36*, 17 would accommodate one of the points of a side blade such as this in such a way as to expose the convex cutting edge. Side blades like these are known from a single Ipiutak burial (Larsen and Rainey, 1948, *36*, 40), from Ipiutak houses (*Ibid.*, *2*, 31), and especially from Near Ipiutak burials (*Ibid.*, *80*, 28–29).

Type 3 (40 specimens). These are relatively crude flakes of no closely defined shape that have obviously been used as inset blades (*46*, 17–23). Of these, 18 are made of basalt and 4 of silicified slate—materials that do not lend themselves readily to extremely fine flaking. We have no indication of special methods of hafting these flints, nor even that they were all used for the same purpose. Perhaps they represent only a low standard of artistic perfection in preparing cutting edges for weapon points and knife blades.

Type 4 (6 specimens). These side blades are relatively large, ranging from ovoid to irregular to nearly circular in outline, as shown in *46*, 24–27. All specimens are made of chert and related material. It is surmised that they were set in either spear heads or the sides of knife handles (Larsen and Rainey, 1948, Fig. 21; p. 100).

Type 5 (4 specimens). These are long and slender side blades (*46*, 28–29), perhaps for lance head or special knife.

Type 6 (5 specimens). These are thin, broad blades, more or less diamond-shaped in outline (*46*, 30–31), the use of which is not known.

The range of execution of these blades is significant in comparing Norton culture with either Denbigh Flint complex or Ipiutak culture. A glance at Pl. *46* will show that the flaking is of no uniformly high order, while many of the specimens are little more than raw flakes retouched about the edges. This carelessness about the appearance of side blades is completely out of line with either of the other two cultures, reflecting either a different background of flint techniques or a deterioration of the flint work as ground slate began to take its place.

Small projectile points. A large number of small, bifaced flints with equally treated long edges occur within the Norton levels at Iyatayet. Some are without doubt displaced specimens from the Denbigh Flint complex. Most of them, however, occur in forms either completely different from those found in place in the Denbigh Flint complex or sufficiently distinct from the Flint complex in material and technique to justify our placing them within Norton culture. Those bifaced small points that we feel are probably displaced from the Denbigh Flint complex are treated separately, even though some of them may be specimens that actually continue from

Flint complex times into Norton culture. In the following pages are distinguished eight classes of small bifaces that seem most likely to have been used as arrow points, harpoon end blades, and the points of other projectiles, such as small spears or lances, that may have been used by Norton people. Unlike the projectile points of Ipiutak, these of Norton culture fail to separate into numbers of sharply defined types. Rather, they intergrade variously, in part as a factor of the use of inferior flaking materials such as basalt in making the same objects that were also executed more delicately in chert. The classification of these points is made on the basis of form rather than that of proposed function.

Type 1 (25 specimens). These are bifaced points varying in size and ranging from a strongly oblanceolate to a parallel-edged outline. They are nearly always basally thinned by the removal of one or more flakes from either face, and they may have either a concave or a straight base. Examples are shown in *47,* 1–8, 18, and 26. Specimens *47,* 2 and 5, together with eight unillustrated specimens, are made of basalt. The others are of gray (*47,* 1, 3–4, 18) and black (*47,* 6–8) chert and chalcedony (*47,* 26). Only two specimens, including *47,* 8, are lightly ground on each face. Others are unground. Several specimens are finely serrated about the cutting edges, as in *47,* 1, 6, 7, and 8. The basal thinning sometimes takes the form of a single, prominent channel on one face, as in *47,* 2 and 6, and several scars on the opposite face, as in *47,* 1 and 26. Nearly all of the specimens of this class could have been fitted into the end slots of harpoon heads. The broader specimens, such as *47,* 7, appear to be unusually wide for an arrowhead and might be more reasonably classed as harpoon blades. However, none of the harpoon heads actually found in the Norton levels were of the end-bladed variety.

Type 2 (46 specimens). The bifaced points of this class are triangular to parallel-edged in outline. Like specimens of Type 1, they are straight- or concave-based, but generally lack heavy basal thinning. Examples are *47,* 10–13, 15, 19, 23–24, 27–29, 32, and 34. Twenty-seven of this type are made of basalt, including *47,* 10, 12–13, 15, 29, and the others of cherty material. Only 3 specimens (not illustrated) show grinding on a face, and these only on one face each. Parallel flaking is to be noted on a few specimens, *e. g., 47,* 19, 24, but the flaking is in the main more haphazard than that of Type 1 specimens, and some are carelessly made.

Type 3 (25 specimens). Bifaced points of this type differ from those of the two preceding types in having one or both faces determinedly ground, perhaps to facilitate their insertion into a pincer-like slot of a harpoon head or arrow head. They have been produced by the same flaking processes as the other bifaces of flinty material, but then have been flattened by grinding on stones of fine to very fine grain. A few are highly polished after the manner of adz blades. Only three specimens (*47,* 25, 30, 36) are made of chert. The others are of basalt, including *47,* 9, 14, 20–21, 31, 35, or light-colored silicified slate, including *47,* 16, 17, 33. Four specimens, including *47,* 14 and 22, are ground on only one face. All others are ground on both faces, including *47,* 9, 16, 17, 20, 21, 25, 30, 31, 33, 35, and 36. Some of these are narrow, with serrated edges, as in *47,* 30, while others, as *47,* 25, are quite wide, and bases are more often straight across than concave.

Type 4 (15 specimens). One form of bifaced point corresponds closely with an Ipiutak type. This is a long, triangular point with a straight base that slants away from a line perpendicular to the long axis of the point. Where Larsen and Rainey (1948, p. 96) consider this as "most difficult to distinguish from Ipiutak Type 1," it is not so easily confused with other classes in the Norton culture. Only 5 specimens are made of basalt, and 1 of silicified slate. The 8 specimens illustrated are all of the better materials— 4 of black chert (*48,* 22–23, 25–26), 1 of jasper (*48,* 19), and 2 of chalcedony (*48,* 24, 27)—except for *48,* 21, of silicified slate, ground on both faces. The others show no grinding.

Type 5 (29 specimens). The rhomboid to 5-edged, thin bifaced points of this type are also to be closely identified with Point Hope sites—this time with Near Ipiutak instead of Ipiutak, however—where points of precisely the same form occurred prominently in Near Ipiutak burials (Larsen and Rainey, 1948, *81,* 14). The range of form is shown in *48,* 1–18, 20. Seven specimens are made of silicified slate, including *48,* 4, 9, 20, and nine of basalt, including *48,* 5, 8, 11, 15, 17. These are nearly all ground in part on one or both faces. Other specimens are of black (*48,* 2, 3, 7, 12, 14) and gray chert (*48,* 1, 6, 16) or chalcedony (*48,* 10, 13, 18). Some specimens further show by the serration (for example, *48,* 3, 5, 20) that they are meant for hafting as end points rather than as side blades or special tools.

Type 6 (36 specimens). Stemmed arrow points are prominent in Norton culture, although they are not greatly various in the form of either stem or blade. For purposes of classification it seems likely that the presence or absence of basal grinding will at some point have comparative value— hence, this type is based upon the fact that the stems are ground about the edges in such a way as to present a dull surface. In strong contrast to other bifaced points, the stemmed points are made almost exclusively of the local basalt or silicified slate. Only three specimens, *49,* 13 of black chert, *49,* 26 of jasper, and *49,* 28 of chalcedony, are of other than basalt (27 specimens) or silicified slate (6 specimens, including *49,* 5, 30). Some of these are much like the illustrated bifaces that Larsen and Rainey call "end blades" (1948, *14,* 13–18) and there is little doubt of related function, yet the range of size in the Norton culture strongly suggests that many of these were used as arrow points, whatever purposes the larger specimens may have had. The squared-off base of most of the specimens indicates that these points were meant to be hafted in the same manner, whatever the size of the specimen. The illustrated specimens of Type 6 are *49*, 5, 6, 10, 13, 16, 17, 20, 25, 26, 29–31. Four specimens have one or more faces partly ground.

Type 7 (42 specimens). Points of this type range through the forms of Type 6, but differ in the lack of basal grinding. In a total of 42 specimens, 32 are made of basalt (including *49*, 3, 7–9, 12, 14, 15, 18, 19, 21, 23, 24, 27, 32), one of silicified slate, one of quartz crystal (*49*, 11), and 8 of black (*49*, 1, 21, 22) or gray (*49*, 2, 4) chert.

Miscellaneous forms (22 specimens). In this category are included the odds and ends of bifaced points that stand somewhat apart from the other types. They could be the erratic products of local flint chippers or rare forms that may some day prove to have comparative value. Seventeen of these 22 points are illustrated in Pl. *50*. *50*, 1 is a stemmed point of chalcedony with serrate margins, the base of which is partly broken away. *50*, 2, 3, and 4 are leaf-shaped, stemless specimens, the first two of which are considerably thicker at the tip than at the base. *50*, 5 is similar, but longer and narrowed at its base. Two broken pieces, *50*, 6 and 7, both of black chert, have the square stem like other stemmed projectile points but appear to be more sharply defined at the shoulders. *50*, 8 is a small, stemmed, plano-convex point of chalcedony. *50*, 9 is a rare obsidian point, also plano-convex in shape. *50*, 10 is a small point of basalt, the stem of which has been defined by strong lateral notching. *50*, 11 and 12 are the fragments of long, narrow points of black chert, both showing a degree of diagonal flaking. The large chalcedony point, *50*, 13, is handsomely executed, and the stem is strongly ground. *50*, 14 is a thick point of black obsidian, a cross-section through the center of which is strongly triangular, while the opposite face is nearly plane. *50*, 15 is a crude specimen of basalt that may be the blank from which a point was in the process of being made. *50*, 16 is an unusually thick-stemmed point of chert. *50*, 17 is a stemmed point of silicified slate, somewhat like *50*, 10, but distinguished by an alternate retouch at the edges of the stem, which gives the stem the cross-section of a parallelogram. An unillustrated specimen, of basalt, is also similar to this.

Fragments of points and blades. The fragments of 487 specimens can be tentatively identified as those of points in the eight preceding classes. Nevertheless, none is definitely classifiable as to type, and they are placed together with the fragments of other cutting edges which may be those of side blades, end-hafted knives, and the like. In the order of their abundance, these are classified by material as follows:

Basalt	212
Chert and chalcedony	148
Black chert	98
Jasper	16
Silicified slate	11
Obsidian	2

Lance (?) points, blanks for blades (84 specimens). Large bifaced points, possibly hafted for use as knives, are illustrated in *51,* 4–8. The crude basalt specimens, *51,* 9–13, appear to be the blanks from which either lance points, such as those preceding, or small weapon points were in the process of being made. *51,* 1 is a specimen of silicified slate that has been retouched about its irregular edges. This may be a blank. If it is a finished implement, however, its method of hafting is not strongly indicated. The large basalt specimens, *51,* 2 and 3, are the blanks of large blades, perhaps lance points, in process of manufacture. While *51,* 3 is a fragment of a beach pebble coarsely flaked about all edges, *51,* 2 has been given a symmetry and cutting edge about its upper region, while its lower region has not been touched. If this does not illustrate merely a step in the process of manufacture, it may mean that some such points as this were hafted without further altering the stem region. The points *51,* 4–6 and 8 are remarkably suggestive of similarly shaped points that have been found repeatedly in sites of probable early age in the interior of Alaska and northern Canada.

Six other large points are similar to those illustrated, and 27 fragments of blades also appear to be like these. All of the latter are made of basalt except for 2 of silicified slate and 1 of chert. The basalt blanks for points or knives number 38, including only 2 of chert and 1 of silicified slate as materials other than basalt.

Knife blades (92 specimens). The bifaced flints illustrated in Pl. *52* represent a sizeable part of Norton culture artifacts. They have in common the careful working of one curved edge, presumably to be used as a cutting edge, and a coarser retouching of other edges to facilitate hafting of some kind. Specimens *52,* 1 and 3–8 are nearly like some of the forms that have been described as side blades. They have irregularities in thickness, how-ever, together with the blunting of an end, which suggests for each of these that they were hafted towards the end of a handle that covered from a half to three-quarters of the blade, including one end. The basalt blade, *52,* 2, is one of six specimens that resemble a short hunting knife blade. The opposite, shallow notches near the lower edge of this specimen are presumed to be intentional so as to provide a suitable lashing region.

The large, leaf-shaped blades, *52,* 9–12, somewhat irregular in outline, may also have been three-quarter hafted. On the other hand, each of these would have lent itself to hafting after the manner of an Eskimo woman's knife. *52*, 12 is ground on both faces, as are two other basalt specimens of the same shape. The basalt blade, *52*, 11, is similar to 14 other specimens of basalt and two of cherty materials.

The large basalt knife, *52*, 13, and three smaller specimens, *52*, 14–16, make up the most closely defined knife form. Each of these is carefully flaked about one edge, usually the more curved one, as in *52*, 13, 15, and 16, and irregularly flaked for hafting about the other edge. These were presumably hafted in such a way as to expose all, or nearly all, of the better prepared edge together with a point, after the fashion of skinning knives. 44 other specimens of this type are made of basalt, while only 3 are of chert and 3 of silicified slate. *52*, 17 is a basalt blade with a double-curved back edge like that of a modern hunting knife. Two similar specimens are of basalt. *52*, 18 is a narrow and long specimen of slate, flaked about the edges, but ground over the central parts of each face, as is another very similar specimen of basalt. *52*, 19 is a larger basalt blade, also polished on both faces.

Flakeknife. This is a class of specialized flints that probably served their makers a multiplicity of uses. They have been called "gravers" (Collins, 1937, p. 150; *41*, 11–12, 14; Larsen and Rainey, 1948, pp. 109–110) when sharply pointed, and "scrapers" of one kind or another where blunt-ended (Collins, 1937, *41*, 15–31). At the risk of adding a term where these others would serve, we shall describe as "flakeknives" the several kinds of flints that appear in Pl. *54*. With one exception, *54*, 12, they are produced by a single technique which is strongly reminiscent of Old World blade-and-core techniques. Each of these objects appears to have been struck from the end or edge of a prepared core. They differ from Old World blades, however, in that they are almost invariably the only flakes removed by this process. We have no evidence that a core was prepared from which these primary-ridge blades were struck ahead of a series of true blades. Rather, the core seems to have been prepared for the striking of only the single blade or flake from which implements such as these were to be refined by pressure flaking.

Unlike the flints that we have classed as knife blades and projectile points, these flakeknives show no strong signs of having been hafted. They could be held between the fingers, or with a finger curved over a blunted back, as piercers, shavers, groovers, smoothers, and whittling knives—as the kind of instrument, in other words, that would be handy to have in the tool chest or sewing kit, where a bulkier and more specialized hafted instrument might not be needed.

Flakeknives are almost invariably made of chert and similar materials. Only one is made of basalt and one of silicified slate. They fall into 5 types based on form:

166

Type 1 (29 specimens). This is a steep-ridged, narrow, and usually long instrument characterized by careful pressure flaking from each edge of the plane surface upwards towards the longitudinal ridge or ridges left in core preparation. Objects of this class are often nearly parallel-edged. Examples are shown in *54*, 6, 10–11, 15–20. In each of these illustrated specimens, the plane, or concave, face, which does not show, is untreated except for the flaking away from its edges. The small jasper specimen, *54*, 6, is quite thick at its upper edge, from which it draws downward evenly to a point. All of these specimens are relatively thick. *54*, 20, for example, is about as thick as it is wide throughout.

Type 2 (8 specimens). These flakeknives, when resting on their plane or slightly concave under-face, take the form of a comma. Examples are *54*, 5, 7, 8, and 9. The heavy end is often quite thick and would form a reasonable finger support for drilling, piercing, or marking purposes, as well as for cutting or smoothing.

Type 3 (3 specimens). Flakeknives of this type are broader and less steeply ridged than the other types, presumably as a result of their blade-like preparation before removal from the core. *54*, 2 and 14 each show the scars of a pair of flakes running lengthwise along the convex face shown. These have resulted from blows struck at opposite ends of these instruments while they were still part of the original core. In place of a single long scar, which might result from a true blade technique, these simulated blades result from pairs of blows struck towards one another. Each of the illustrated specimens is more strongly retouched along the long edges than at the ends, although the latter show signs of use.

Type 4 (11 specimens). These are double-curved flakeknives, the curvature of which is partly determined by pressure flaking about the edges. Examples are *54*, 1, 21, and 22.

Type 5 (17 specimens). Irregular specimens less carefully made than those of the preceding groups are included here. *54*, 3, 4, and 13 are examples in which little alteration of the original flake has been made by pressure retouching. The long flake, *54*, 12, is included with flakeknives as a suggested raw flake from which, through persistent retouch, a Type 1 flakeknife might be made. This specimen shows some flaking about the ridge that is seen in the illustration. The opposite face is plane and untreated.

Untyped fragments (11 specimens). These are flakeknives broken in such a way as to leave no further classifying feature.

Side scrapers (283 specimens). The objects here classified as side scrapers are in nearly all cases crude flakes that have been treated along one edge—and sometimes more than one—presumably for the scraping of wood and other hard organic materials. It looks as if any reasonably large or suitably shaped flake that could be picked up and held in the hand for

167

scraping wood or hard organic materials was used without consistency as to methods of retouching, or even purposeful pressure flaking at all. In Pl. 55, the specimens 1–13, 15, 17, and 19 are classified as side scrapers. Careful pressure retouch is to be seen on the left margin of 55, 2; on the lower right margin of 55, 4; and on the left margin of 55, 19. Other specimens, such as 55, 1, 6, and 15, have been crudely retouched to provide a steep cutting or scraping edge. Still others appear to have been used, sometimes repeatedly, without determined retouch. 55, 5 is a thick, black obsidian, plano-convex specimen, the left edge of which shows signs of use as a scraper. The prominent large flakes that extend upward from the left edge to the height of the convex surface, however, seem unnecessarily elaborate for a simple scraper. On the convex face of 55, 13 are to be seen the ripples that result from a blow near the lower center. The opposite face is plane. This specimen is retouched along its lower margin and a bit of the upper left margin.

About four-fifths of the side scrapers are made of basalt. Those of cherty material are usually small.

Choppers and blanks (34 specimens). In this category are placed 34 large objects of basalt or of modified beach pebbles of metamorphic rock. Three of these are illustrated in 55, 14, 18, and 20. Each of these might have been used for some crude chopping process, since flakes have been detached mainly about one convex edge. They could also be the blanks for the manufacture of ground, or partly ground, blades. 55, 16, a thin, metamorphic beach pebble, shows signs of battering about the unbroken, outcurved edges. This might be some kind of chopper or heavy scraping instrument.

Discoidal scraper (35 specimens). This class of very distinctive bifaced flints is to be directly associated with Ipiutak culture, where it plays an even more prominent part. All but 2 (basalt) specimens are made of good quality chert, black chert, and similar materials. Most specimens are nearly spherical, as in 56, 2–6, 9–12. Exceptions are shown in 56, 1, 7, 8. Most are also pressure flaked with equal care on each face, although large flake scars show on one or both faces of some specimens, as 56, 1, 6, and 10. As Larsen and Rainey also indicate for Point Hope (1948, pp. 103, 104), these discoidals usually have sharp edges, only some of which show evidence of having been used as scrapers. Artifacts as carefully made of scarce material as these strongly point to a special use, probably a method of hafting that is not to be duplicated precisely in known Eskimo practices. The presence of these discoidal flints in large numbers both in the Ipiutak sites and the Norton sites should be a valuable criterion in cultural cross-dating. Discoidals like these also appear in the Platinum site at Bristol Bay (Larsen, 1950, p. 184), though the proportions are not specified. At the moment, it seems less significant that an occasional discoidal biface turns up here and there in other archeological sites (for example, in Yukon Island III deposit [de Laguna, 1934, *30,* 32, and p. 70]).

End Scraper. The end scrapers, of basalt, with a few of quartzite, complement the discoidal scrapers, with which they most likely overlap functionally. Unlike the discoidals, however, the end scrapers are worked in such a way that only one curved edge appears to have been designed as a scraper edge. Most specimens have been crudely flaked beyond this working edge to provide them with a hafting surface. This category differs from the discoidal scrapers in being made of basalt and quartz, and in having less retouching on one face than on the other. It is to be noted that Norton culture appears to lack the plano-convex form of end scraper that is more usually encountered in the Arctic and in the world at large—the form in which the scraping edge is steeply flaked from an untrimmed under surface. (*See* p. 64; Pl. *70-b.*)

Type 1 (27 specimens). This consists of specimens ovoid in outline, the large end of which has been retouched on both faces for use as a scraper, as in *57,* 9, 14–18.

Type 2 (9 specimens). These differ from Type 1 scrapers in having a truncated ovoid outline, as in *57,* 10–12. The upper edge is the working end of each of these illustrated specimens.

Type 3 (3 specimens). This includes either large and coarse end scrapers or the blanks from which adz blades were to be made—*57,* 6–7. If they are scrapers, the working edge is less defined than that of other classes of scrapers.

Type 4 (6 specimens). This includes scrapers that are discoidal in outline, though a single, special working edge is defined by pressure flaking—*57,* 8, 13.

Type 5 (18 specimens). This includes irregular flakes, often the outer edges of pebbles, worked along one broad edge, presumably for insertion into a scraper handle—*57,* 4–5.

Type 6 (6 specimens). This is set apart from other classes of end scrapers only because its material is a white quartzite, the source of which is not known. The three specimens here illustrated, *57,* 1–3, and three other specimens were found in various localities within Norton levels.

All but the Type 6 specimens are made of basalt.

Lamps and other stone vessels. Lamps of both stone and pottery occur in Norton culture levels at Iyatayet. Stone lamps and fragments number 36, but the pottery lamps are confined to two specimens, both nearly whole. Although we cannot say that pottery lamps are later than those of stone, it is certain that they are less important within the site. The two specimens are not similar to the circular, saucer-shaped pottery lamps of the Nukleet period, nor are the two specimens closely like each other. Each of them appears to be an imitation in clay of a form that would normally be made of stone. One of the pottery lamps, *59*, 4, has a convex base and is smooth on all surfaces. Except for two chipped places, the rim stands uniformly 45 mm. above the base. The right-hand margin, as illustrated, is somewhat scooplike, rather than sharply upturned, as is the left-hand face. This specimen is typologically similar to the stone lamp, *58*, 1. The other pottery specimen (not illustrated) is a heavy, very thick and clumsy specimen, closely identical with the stone lamps *59*, 5 and 6, as though a crude imitation in clay of stone lamps of this form.

The stone lamps are greatly varied in size and shape. A large, triangular form, however, is so closely duplicated in three specimens (*58*, 3, 5, and 6) two of which are fragmentary, that we may treat this comparatively as a widespread type. The complete specimen, *58*, 6, is a pecked lamp of granitic material, the base of which is rounded. A thin, dark encrustation extends across the bowl. The thickness of the vessel, from its base perpendicular to a plane of its rim, is 45 mm. *58*, 5, closely similar in material and treatment to the preceding specimen, differs mainly in its thickness. From base to rim plane it is 70 mm. thick. The base of this specimen is also rounded, but its bowl is pecked flat, rather than concave as in the other two specimens of this type. The rim is sharply defined by flattening. This specimen is mended from three fragments, two of which were found close together in Cut M, the other in Cut E, some 70 feet away. *58*, 3 is another triangular lamp fragment, made of sandstone, and similar to *58*, 6 except that it is thinner and shallower (30 mm. from base to rim plane).

The fragmentary lamp, *59*, 1, may also have had a triangular outline. This schistose specimen stands 24 mm. thick from base to rim plane. Its base is convex, and its bowl concave.

Other large lamps and fragments tend to have a rectangular bowl, although their form is variable. Examples are *59*, 5, of vesicular basalt, *59*, 6, of sandstone, and *59*, 2, also of sandstone. The largest specimen, *59*, 5, stands 100 mm. from base to rim plane, and its base is flattened, as though for placing on a plane surface. *59*, 6 is crudely flaked about the edges, and the bowl has been pecked and "chopped" into shape. It is 70 mm. thick from base to rim plane. In contrast to these coarse specimens is *59*, 2, the base and bowl of which have been pecked and smoothed by some grinding process to form a flattened base and a bowl that deepens towards the concavity shown along the upper edge. This notch, or concavity, is presumably meant to accommodate a wick.

Another distinctive form of lamp is illustrated in *58*, 1, 2, and 4. *58*, 1 and 4 are of granitic material, and *58*, 2 is of sandy schist. Each is nearly round in outline with a wick ledge indicated by a shoal area near the rim. This area is shown in the upper margin of each illustrated specimen. *58*, 1 is 25 mm. thick from base to rim plane, *58*, 2 is 12 mm. thick, and

58, 4 is 30 mm. thick. The heavy specimen, *58, 4*, is further distinguished by a series of markings across most of its concave base. These are in the form of spaced, perpendicular lines forming a rough checkerboard pattern.

Several small stone objects are either lamps or some kind of mortar. They are characterized by a nearly hemispherical pecked basin. In the absence of signs of paint on any of these objects and the presence, in most of them, of a dark stain such as is usually found in stone lamps, it is suggested that these were small, perhaps individual, illuminating lamps. *59, 3* is a beach pebble of dense granitic material, 60 mm. high from rim to base, with a naturally flat base. The notch along one margin appears not to have been deliberately made, though it could easily have served as a wick ledge. Specimens of similar material, only the basins of which have been altered by pecking from original beach pebbles, are shown in *60, 6, 8, 10–13.* Each of these specimens shows signs of polishing which might further attest to some unexplained grinding process.

Other specimens, altered only slightly from beach pebbles, are *60, 7,* an elongated specimen, the base of which has a longitudinal ridge, *60, 9,* a naturally hollowed pebble but slightly pecked, and *60,* 14, 15, and 16.

A limestone fragment, *60, 1,* shows part of a deeply stained concavity. This may have been part of a large stone lamp.

60, 2 is an interesting and unusual specimen of a flat dish with a precisely angled, thin rim. Both the base and the bottom of the bowl are flat. The whole vessel has apparently been both pecked and ground smoothly. It was evidently part of a large vessel. The rim rises at about a 45-degree angle and thins toward its margin. A large fragment of the center of another piece such as this is treated in the same way and shows at one margin that an angled rim has been broken away. Although stone dishes of this kind are somewhat out of line with stone lamps at this site and elsewhere in the Arctic, we hesitate to assign them a function as cooking utensils or plates. It would be hard to explain why Norton people should have gone to great elaborations of grinding and pecking in order to prepare food in some way which we do not know for circumpolar people.

Still other small vessels that may have been illuminating lamps or served other purposes are shown in *60,* 3, 4, and 5. Each of these specimens has a shallow, elongated bowl indicated in the pictured fragment. *60, 3,* of metamorphic stone, suggests a long, rectangular vessel. The base is rounded and the basin is 11 mm. deep. *60, 4* is a specimen of similar material—a thin-walled vessel fragment with a deep basin, broken except for a narrow rim at the bottom left of the illustration. Its base is rounded. *60, 5* is a shale specimen, 1 cm. thick, with a shallow, polished basin only 4 mm. deep. Dark brown to black stain is found within the bowls of specimens *60,* 1, 3–12, and 14. Of the unillustrated specimens, two fragments are those of rims like the flat-based vessel, *60, 2.* Four specimens are fragments like *60,* 12 and 13. One vessel fragment is like *60,* 3. Two specimens are elongated bowls like *60,* 7, and two fragments are those of basins like *60,* 8.

The stone lamps of Norton culture are unlike anything to be found in the Nukleet period or more recent archeology of the region. A stone lamp closely like the Norton triangular lamps is illustrated by Nelson (1899, Pl. *28,* 6), but this was acquired as a gift from someone at St. Michael and most likely is an archeological specimen. The lamps of the Aleuts, according to Jochelson (1925, pp. 73–74), were of two types, distinguished by size, name, and use. The larger were meant for warming a person who squatted above or placed it under the folds of his clothing for comfort or a kind of sweat bath. It was not normally employed for heating houses, for which an abundance of driftwood was usually available. The smaller lamps were used for illumination within the house or temporary tent in which a hunter lived. Archeological specimens from the Aleutians seem to have been even more varied than those recently in use, and it is among the Aleutian lamps that we find close parallels for each of the types in Norton culture.

The triangular lamp of the Aleutians (Jochelson, 1925, *18,* 1), the oval lamps of Cook Inlet (especially those from Yukon Island III [de Laguna, 1934, *25*]), and the oval, or triangular, specimen from Platinum Village site (Larsen, 1950, Fig. 57, 7) are all closely related in form and outline. They differ mainly in the degree of angularity. The dating of specimens outside the Norton Bay area is uncertain as yet, however. Laughlin and Marsh (1951, p. 82) imply that the earliest stone lamps from the lowest levels of their Aleutian excavations are rounded, deeper, and less elaborately worked than later specimens, and Bank (1953, p. 43) speaks of the "round bottomed, crude lamps from earlier cultural strata" in his excavations at Unalaska Bay. Although as yet undated, the Platinum Village site has many close parallels with Norton culture, with which it probably cross-dates at some period. The "sad-iron shaped" lamps excavated by Jochelson in Kamchatka show an obvious stylistic relationship to the early stone lamps of Alaska, yet it is impossible to decide whether or not any of the illustrated specimens (Jochelson, 1928, *14,* and *15,* esp. *14,* 10 from Kuril Lake) can be compared on the same time levels with Norton deposits.

Small stone lamps are reported from Cook Inlet and elsewhere in southern Alaska and the Aleutian Islands, where they take forms often seemingly dictated by the prevailing shape of beach pebbles. Perhaps the closest similarities with lamps of Norton culture are between Jochelson's (1925, *18,* 16) and the Norton specimen, *58,* 4, in which a prominent wick lip is provided. Deeply hemispherical Norton specimens resemble certain small Aleutian specimens called lamps (Jochelson, 1925, *18,* 8). In addition to stone lamps, Laughlin and Marsh (1951, p. 82) speak of "two types of larger stone vessels. . . a cooking stove and a cooking bowl. . . ." It is possible that when the Aleutian collections are published in full we shall see close similarities between the lamps and other stone vessels of Norton culture and other horizons in the Aleutians.[1]

Hand drill. The drills thought to have been held between the fingers and rotated in drilling organic materials of various degrees of hardness are those left broad and rough except about the retouched drilling tip. Eight examples of twelve specimens of hand drill are shown in Pl. *53.* A specimen of black chert, *53,* 13, is thin and delicate, as though meant for piercing soft materials such as rawhide, or drilling soft wood. A coarse chip of black chert, *53,* 16, has had a drill point (tip broken) flaked from its thin end. *53,* 18 is a thick basalt flake, the naturally thin end of which has been retouched. A flake of black chert, *53,* 20, has been altered by careful all-over flaking into a thin hand drill, the tip of which is broken. *53,* 21 is a drill of basalt, only lightly retouched about the right margin of the stem. *53,* 23 is a blade-like flake, the plane lower surface of which has been retouched only at the narrowed drill point. *53,* 24 is a raw flake of basalt, only the tip of which has been altered by retouching, and *53,* 25 is a bifaced hand drill of basalt. One specimen not illustrated is of black chert; the others are of basalt.

Hand drills of flinty material are widespread in the Eskimo region, extending even to those cultures where polished slate predominates. They were scarcer at Ipiutak, however, than might have been expected in a non-slate culture (Larsen and Rainey, 1948, p. 105).

Drill bit. The stone drills of Norton culture that have been flaked, and sometimes partly polished, in such a way as to suit them for binding to the end of a wooden shaft, but not for holding between the fingers, are classed as the bits of some form of composite drill. In Pl. *53* are shown 13 unpolished specimens of a total of 19, and 6 of 11 polished specimens. *53,* 2 is a bifaced basalt specimen, the tip of which is wedge-shaped. *53,* 3, 8, 10, and 11 are basalt bits of various flat forms. *53,* 6 is the thick, triangular-sectioned tip of a broken basalt bit. *53,* 9 and 19, also of basalt, are flat tips apparently broken from longer specimens. *53,* 5 is the stem section of a similar broken specimen of silicified slate. *53,* 22 is presumably a hafted drill, the stem region of which is narrowed. This flat basalt specimen has its tip beveled on one face, as shown. *53,* 12 is a thick specimen of chert, the stem region of which is quadrangular in cross-section, while the bit has a triangular section. *53,* 14 and 15 are thin specimens of black chert, flaked about all edges and apparently shaped to fit in the socket or slot of a drill shaft.

Specimens *53,* 1, 4, 17, 26, and 27 are all polished about the drilling

---

[1] R. F. Heizer's excellent report (1956) on the Uyak site, which I received after the Norton section was written, contains descriptions of stone vessels similar to those of Norton culture and is pertinent in other respects to the problems of the later cultures at Cape Denbigh.

tip and are distinguished from the unpolished specimens in having the tip more nearly circular in cross-section. The long, complete specimen, *53, 26*, shows flaking scars at its flattened stem and is beveled from both faces to form a wedge-shaped tip. *53, 7*, also of basalt, is flat and polished only along the edges.

It is to be noted that both the flaked and the polished forms of drill bits are found at the old Platinum site at Bristol Bay (Larsen, 1950, Fig. 56B, *14* and *15*). Aleutian drills seem to have been flaked varieties, both for hafting (Jochelson, 1925, p. 67, Fig. 37 C and D) and for hand use (*Ibid.*, Fig. 37 A and B), although the latter is not specified. The nearest approach to a duplication of the whole range of Norton drills is to be found in the Hillside site of St. Lawrence Island's Old Bering Sea culture, however, where Collins reports polished specimens (Collins, 1937, *41, 3* and *4*) with wedge-shaped tips, broad-stemmed flaked specimens, probably hand drills (*Ibid., 41, 5, 6, 9*, and *10*), and others closely like the Norton drills. An almost precise duplication of form is seen between the black chert specimen, *53, 14*, and a fourteenth century A. D. specimen from the Kobuk River (Giddings, 1952, *34, 14*). The most specialized type, *53, 26, 27*, and perhaps two unillustrated fragments, do not appear to be closely duplicated in neighboring sites.

Stone saw. Grooving and splitting by means of "saws" or thin slabs of gritty stone was not a common practice among Norton culture people, who did not work jade, and whose treatment of similar hard and brittle stones was usually that of flaking into rough form and then only partly grinding or polishing. Nevertheless, three specimens of sandstone saw and a saw-grooved fragment of some unidentified sandstone implement were recovered. *61, 1* is a saw fragment about 5 mm. thick except where it has been hollow ground through use along both faces of its lower edge. It is broken at the left end and at the notch in its working edge. *61, 2* is another saw fragment, the lower edge of which is worked.

Stone saws may have been used to cut the grooves in the shaft smoothers and other grooved stones of Norton culture (Pl. *45*), though the specimens described here are too small for most of that grooving.

Stone sinker. The range of size of Norton culture double-notched stones is shown in *61, 3–7*. These stones were used almost without question as net sinkers, as similar ones have been used in the region recently (Nelson, 1899, p. 189; Fig. 54). Altogether, 224 such sinkers were obtained from Norton levels. They are made of igneous or hard metamorphic beach pebbles and are to be distinguished from the scarce stone sinkers of Nukleet culture (*12, 7–10*) by their invariable thinness and the placing of notches at the ends in preference to the narrowest section of the pebble. By their numbers, these sinkers indicate a preference in Norton times for stone over

174

the bone and ivory sinkers of most recent Eskimos, although perishable sinkers may also have been used.

Miscellaneous. A thin, hollowed-out object of coarse shale is closely similar in shape and size to the mussel shells that frequently wash up on the beach at Iyatayet. In 1939, in a thick deposit of Punuk period mussel shells at the site of Kitneapalok, St. Lawrence Island, I recall finding a precise duplicate of a mussel shell executed in walrus ivory and decorated on its outer surface with a typical Punuk engraved design.

Pottery

The pottery of Norton culture is easily distinguished from all later pottery of the Eskimo area thus far on record. While a local transition from earlier to the later forms might be expected, the Ipiutak time gap in pottery-making, presumably affecting all of northwestern Alaska, thus far serves as an effective barrier between the two ceramic continuities. The earlier pottery was first recognized at Point Hope, where it occurred in middens, burials, and a house of Near Ipiutak culture (Larsen and Rainey, 1948, pp. 166–68). Partly because of this pattern, the Near Ipiutak features at Point Hope were at first considered to be later than those of Ipiutak culture. The few sherds which came to light in the Near Ipiutak features on the earliest beaches at Point Hope were of the linear-stamped variety.

The broader meaning of the early Point Hope ware was not seen until 1948 when Helge Larsen found check-stamped sherds of a thin, well-fired ware like that of Near Ipiutak at both Chagvan Bay (Larsen, 1950, p. 181) and Nanvak Bay (*Ibid.,* p. 183) in southwestern Alaska, and I found both check-stamped and linear-stamped sherds associated with the Norton culture levels at Cape Denbigh (Giddings, 1949). Evidence of the priority of this ceramic tradition to Ipiutak culture was delayed, however, until a range of radiocarbon dates was available for the Norton deposits. The recognition of a spread of the thin, check-stamped or linear-stamped pottery along the entire coast of western Alaska encouraged a comparison with, on the one side, Japanese pottery almost identical in appearance, and, on the other side, check-stamped and linear-stamped pottery from the eastern United States.

It was on the strength of such widespread possibilities of cross comparison as these that I persuaded James B. Griffin to undertake an analysis of the Cape Denbigh pottery. After a preliminary study and description of the sherds, some 1,000 recovered during the first three seasons of excavation, I shipped the Norton pottery to him at the Museum of Anthropology in Ann Arbor. After his preliminary report (Griffin, 1953), Wendell Oswalt, while studying at the University of Michigan, incorporated some of this Cape Denbigh pottery in his system of classification (Oswalt, 1955). The names applied in the Griffin and Wilmeth paper (Appendix 1) are mainly those originated by Oswalt and Griffin. In his preliminary statement in 1953, Griffin announced his "intention to refer to the oldest pottery materials as the Norton ceramic complex and to recognize within it a number of pottery types in the same manner as has been done in the Southwest and the Eastern United States." The name "Norton" complex may thus be used for the designation of all of the pre-Ipiutak pottery now on record in Alaska, even though some exceeds the time range usually applied to the Norton culture itself.

With the exception of two pottery lamps, evidently made in imitation of stone lamps (p. 170; Pl. *59,* 4), we have no trouble in distinguishing between the pottery of Norton and that of Nukleet, even where these occurred in thoroughly mixed deposits. Since both the earlier and the later forms of pottery are treated in Appendix 1, however, I shall only say here that the pottery of Norton culture is that designated "Norton check-stamped," "Norton linear-stamped," and "Norton plain," together with a few sherds indicated as rare forms. While coarse stamping of pottery is known from earliest St. Lawrence Island sites (Collins, 1937, pp. 168–9; Fig. 17; Pl. *52;* Rainey, 1941, Fig. 34) and from very recent sites on mainland Alaska, the fine check-stamped, linear-stamped, and dentate treatments described in Appendix 1 are the marks of recognition of pre-Ipiutak pottery on the western Alaskan mainland.

Madjujuinuk

A pure site of Norton culture was traced out by a kind of detective work in which we later took pride. On a morning in August, 1950, VanStone, Henderson, Nakarak, and I set out in a boat to test all of the spots that we could find in the vicinity of Iyatayet in which it seemed possible for people to have placed their more permanent dwellings. We found this a fairly easy task, for on the western shore of Cape Denbigh there is but one other small creek like that at Iyatayet, and almost everywhere the coastline consists of bird cliffs or insurmountable walls above which no human beings of good sense would think of camping. Moving southward to the Cape itself, after failing to find a site at the second stream mouth, we saw only a few grassy pockets in which it was conceivable that people might have lived. In one of these we found chips of flinty material, but no encouragement to dig deeply in the frozen ground. On the return trip, we retraced the shoreline of the wide bay just south of Iyatayet and noted a small, dry ravine that cut deeply down from a fairly level terrace about a hundred feet above sea level. At the foot of this ravine was a little bay formed at the base of an abutment of naked rock in the ledges of which sea birds nested. Although we saw no likely place for more than a tent site on a rim of beach gravel, the things that Nakarak told us led to further examination of the place. He said that it had a name, Madjujuinuk, which meant "no winter sunshine," that driftwood frequently lodged on its rocky beach, and that tomcod could be caught here in great quantities between January and April.

VanStone took a shovel and made his way through the sprawling alders that concealed the rock of the steep slope, to the terrace edge. Almost at once he shouted that he had found something. We spent the remainder of the day testing among the tenacious roots of alders and willows on the terrace and found that a rather large site existed in the form of a blackened cultural layer between one and three feet deep, and that it had in it objects like those of Norton culture.

The site would no doubt reward a more extensive excavation, but because it showed even less frost preservation than the Norton levels, we did not take the time from our work at Iyatayet to make a new camp at Madjujuinuk. The objects shown in Pl. *64* come from the limited excavations at the site.

Side blades are represented by the complete basalt specimen, *64, 3,* the obsidian specimen, *64,* 4, the fragmentary basalt pieces, *64,* 5 and 6, the irregular basalt biface, *64,* 7, that seems to be a "triangular" side blade like those of Iyatayet, the tiny, broken-tipped side blade, *64,* 15, of chalcedony, and the larger basalt pieces, *64,* 16 and 17.

The complete arrowhead, *64,* 2, of chalcedony, is a carefully flaked, thin specimen with a slanted base, recalling Ipiutak Type 2A (Larsen and Rainey, 1948, *2, 12*) and certain Iyatayet arrowpoints, *48,* 19, 21, 25, and 26. Specimens *64,* 3, 8, and 9, of basalt, may also be arrowpoints. The face opposite that shown of *64,* 9 is the plane surface of a flake scar except where it has been lightly retouched at the edges.

The fragments, *64,* 1 and 13, and the whole specimens, *64,* 10, 16, and 17, all of basalt, represent knife blades.

The black chert flake, *64,* 12, is lightly retouched at the left edge of the face shown, perhaps for use as a knife edge of some kind. *64,* 11 is a basalt hand drill, the opposite face of which is a plane flake surface trimmed only at the edges. *64,* 18 is a thick fragment of silicified slate, possibly the blank for an adz. The flaked apex of a longitudinal ridge is upturned in the photograph.

The roughly triangular object of silicified slate, *64,* 19, is thickest at the lower end and plane on the opposite face except for slight flaking about the edges. Although it could perhaps have been used as some kind of scraper in its present form, it is likely to have been the flaked blank from which a small adz blade was to be beveled at the wide end and ground on the faces as in *44,* 3, 8, and 10.

The olive-shaped, grooved pebble of fine-grained sandstone, *64,* 21, is reminiscent of the grooved stones from Kachemak Bay, where de Laguna regards the specimens "grooved about the longer diameter," as this one is, as belonging to the periods Yukon II and III (de Laguna, 1934, p. 55; *17,* 3). The Madjujuinuk specimen has a very narrow groove, presumably for the attachment of a thin string. The resemblance of this object to oval bola weights of bone and ivory, such as have been used more recently in the region, is noteworthy (Nelson, 1899, *51,* 3, 14, and 16; Giddings, 1952, *12,* 16). Stone bola weights would appear strange to the Eskimos of today, however; to these natives the object would more likely be called a fish line sinker.

Fishing is more surely indicated by the net sinker, *64,* 22, which is a double-notched basalt beach pebble like those of Norton culture at Iyatayet.

The fine-grained sandstone whetstone, *64,* 23, has been used only on the face shown. The small, thin whetstone fragment, *64,* 14, is typical of Norton culture.

The large object of vesicular basalt, *64,* 24, is semi-cylindrical, the unseen surface being ground flat and pecked at the very edges. Battering at the upper end (the lower end is broken away) gives this object the look of a hammer or maul that was meant to be hafted on a flat-headed, adz-like handle.

The check-stamped potsherd, *64,* 20, and also another one, are identical in texture and form with pottery from Norton levels at Iyatayet, but a third has some kind of textile impression on its outer surface—probably that of a cord-wrapped paddle.

In addition to these illustrated specimens from the site, there are three thin whetstones of shale like *64,* 14, two arrow point fragments of silicified slate, and seven flinty blade or scraper fragments of undetermined type. A sample of charred bones and charcoal proved to be too small for radiocarbon dating.

A count of discarded flakes of flinty material is as follows:

64 light colored silicified slate
43 basalt
18 chert
 1 obsidian

In style of workmanship and use of materials, as well as in nearly all of the artifacts themselves, this site corresponds closely with the Norton levels at Iyatayet.

Gungnuk

One of the greatest hindrances to locating very old archeological sites in western Alaska is the presence of recent ones in nearly every direction. On our reconnaissance of the western shores of Norton Bay and the coast of Golovnin Bay in 1950, we found the interesting house pits and mounds of fairly recent inhabitants at many points along the shore. Perhaps it would have paid us to camp at the large sites and explore carefully for signs of a very early culture. Our aim was to discover "pure" old sites, however—that is, sites of culture earlier than those of the neo-Eskimos of the region, in which we should be free of mixed collections such as those of the later deposits at Iyatayet. The only such discovery was made at the site called Gungnuk, and this was a site of Norton culture, rather than a microblade site for which we were specifically searching.

The west side of Norton Bay, unlike the east one, is deep enough to be entered by fairly large vessels. Captain Cook, in 1778, was pleased to find that he could secure fresh water and other materials here when forced to turn back from the inner waters of the Bay (Cook and King, 1784, pp. 476–77).

We began our survey from Moses Point, where we landed on the modern emergency landing field of the Civil Aeronautics Authority. We secured the use of a boat and motor, and the services of its owner, Mischa Charles, a man of mixed Russian and Eskimo descent. Charles took us several miles up the Tubuktulik River, but we failed to locate archeological sites or to learn of flint finds from the several families of Eskimos who were fishing at their regular summer camps. Returning to the coast, we moved eastward to the mouth of Kwik River, where a very extensive archeological site exists on both sides of the river. House pits of considerable age lie along several old beach lines on the right-limit bank of the river near sea level, and a more recent series of pits and the remains of quite modern houses are to be found on the left-limit banks. Probably the Kwik River village is that described by Cook in 1778, when he says that "on the west side of Bald Head the shore forms a bay, in the bottom of which is a low beach, where we saw a number of huts or habitations of the natives" (*Op. cit.,* p. 477).

Small tests in the older house pits quickly showed us that pottery of the Nukleet period was present. Although it is possible that older material exists in the same region, we decided not to take the time needed for excavation in a mixed site.

No further sites, other than those of very recent Eskimos, were seen along the coast until we had reached a point about eight miles southwest of Elim. Here again were a few signs of recent and somewhat earlier building, disclosed by dense and green grass about depressions. This creek

179

mouth is presumably the point at which Cook's party first landed in the Norton Bay region:

Having continued to ply back all night, by daybreak the next morning [September 10th] we got into six fathoms' water. At nine o'clock, being about a league from the west shore, I took two boats and landed attended by Mr. King, to seek wood and water. We landed where the coast projects out into a bluff head, composed of perpendicular strata of a rock of a dark blue color, mixed with quartz and glimmer. There joins to the beach a narrow border of land, now covered with long grass, where we met with some angelica. Beyond this the ground rises abruptly. At the top of this elevation we found a heath, abounding with a variety of berries; and further on the country was level, and thinly covered with small spruce trees, and birch and willows no bigger than broom stuff. We observed tracks of deer and foxes on the beach, on which also lay a great quantity of drift-wood; and there was no want of fresh water.

—Cook and King, 1784, p. 478.

When Cook returned to the watering place on Cape Darby two days later, he encountered a family of natives who presumably fished near by (*Ibid., pp. 480–81*).

A site known to our guide by tradition was located about seven miles from the tip of Cape Darby. House pits were obscured by a combination of soil creep and thick moss, but we determined that they also belonged to the Nukleet, rather than to an earlier, culture. This site lies about fifty feet above sea level, on a gentle slope at the top of a bluff.

The large site of Atnuk, reported, but incorrectly treated, by Hrdlička (1930, p. 200), which is the most venerated of archeological sites known to local Eskimos, lies in a sizeable stream valley about two miles from the tip of Cape Darby. Here we saw respectably thick midden deposits eroding along the creek bank. The exposed artifacts and stone fragments showed at a glance that the greater part of the site was quite recent. Bits of iron and glass were found well below the surface of these deposits. We tested neighboring terraces and isolated spots in hopes of finding some earlier cultural stratum, but, although the thaw was deep, we were unsuccessful in this search.

On rounding Cape Darby, we found several miles of almost sheer and forbidding cliffs, among which it would have been impossible for campers to have found a decent foothold. The cliffs gradually tapered off, however, until, at the first large stream, McKinley Creek, wide and flat terraces came into view. A little bay is formed at the mouth of this creek by a rocky reef, and in it we found a good sandy beach on which to land. The place about this creek mouth is called Gungnuk. We set up camp on the beach and soon discovered, on an old terrace at the right bank of the creek, the leavings of flint-using people. Confining our search at first to the 20-foot terrace—a wide, flat expanse of boulder-covered ground—we found

180

quantities of chips of silicified slate and like materials, along with a few of chert. Tests with a shovel were disappointing, for the whole terrace appeared to be so rocky that people could not have built there. Farther to the right, however, and 100 or more yards from the creek mouth, we found a gravelly beach upon the ridges of which several shallow depressions were to be seen. To our surprise, tests quickly indicated that none of these was a neo-Eskimo house. We settled upon one of several depressions that appeared to be roughly rectangular. This one had a clearly indicated tunnel, opening from a wide side of the depression toward the sea. We excavated this feature, determining as best we could the floor level and dimensions. The floor level was surprisingly shallow—less than a foot at center—even though the walls of the rim were quite clear around the depression. This condition of the surface features, not distinguished by a difference in the surface vegetation from the surrounding thin mossy cover, may be explained by the heavy gravel and boulder content of the soil, which would naturally resist erosion. The house, to judge by the surface signs, as well as by the distribution of flakes, must have been 12 or 13 feet in length and 9 feet in width. The floor (Fig. 42) was easily traced about its central portion, in an area some 7 feet square leading to and through the tunnel region, where there was a concentration of stone chips and charcoal flecks. Nothing organic was preserved other than the bits of charcoal. An area near the center of the house was indicated to have been the fireplace by a strong discoloration of the soil beneath it. The tunnel floor was traced for about 7 feet beyond the house proper, in a width of about 2 feet. The tunnel and house floor were nearly on the same level, but in place of a drop from house into tunnel, the tunnel floor sloped a few inches higher than the house floor. The tunnel of this and at least two other depressions likely to be those of houses pointed towards the beach.

Objects from the Gungnuk house are in nearly all cases closely like those of Norton culture at Iyatayet. The more complete or distinctive specimens are shown in Plates 62 and 63. Plano-convex flakeknives are shown in Pl. 62. 62, 1 is a steeply keeled specimen of red jasper, the upper end of which flattens and becomes wedge-shaped because of the single large flake scar that shows in the illustration. 62, 3, of gray chert, is a rounder specimen, broken at the upper end. 62, 4 is a flat flakeknife of dark basalt, broken at the lower end. 62, 5 is an end fragment of a thin flakeknife of red jasper. 62, 6 is the tip of a black chert flake, possibly a flakeknife or side scraper fragment, the right and lower left margins of which have been retouched.

A side blade of silicified slate, 62, 7, is retouched from the evenly curved edge on both faces. 62, 8 and 15 are the broken bases of arrow points (or blades) of black chert, both basally thinned, but differing in form. 62, 8 has the

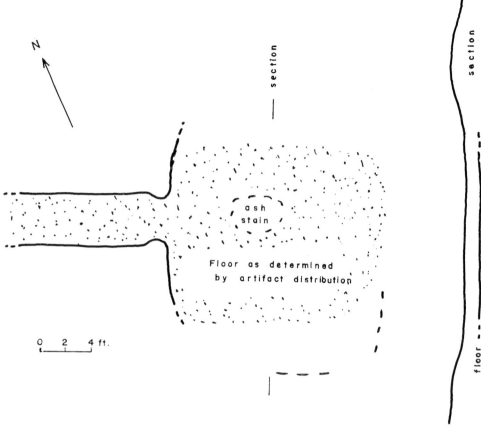

Fig. 42. Excavated house plan and profile, Gungnuk.

slanting base of a Norton Type 4 arrow point, while *62, 15* probably resembled the Iyatayet specimen, *50, 4*. The sturdy red jasper biface, *62, 9*, appears to be a knife blade like the Iyatayet specimen, *52, 16*. The black chert fragment, *62, 18*, is retouched along the right edge and appears to be part of a side scraper modified from a larger flake. *62, 11* is a flake retouched on the right edges, perhaps also for use as a scraper.

A single burin-like groover of silicified slate, polished on both faces and transversely to form the working face at the upper left and on top, is shown in *62, 12*.

Whetstones of shale duplicate those of Norton culture at Iyatayet. *62, 2* and *13* are both worked on both faces and are thinner, through use, at the broken, lower end. *62, 14*, also worked on both faces, is of uniform thickness (2–3 mm.) throughout.

The fragment of a shaft smoother, *62, 16*, has a shallow longitudinal groove on the face showing, while the opposite face is rounded from edge to

182

edge. *62,* 17 is a broken adz blade of silicified slate which has been first flaked into shape and then polished, like those of Iyatayet. The face showing is convex and beveled at about a 30-degree angle, while the lower face is a polished plane. *62,* 19 is a large, thin slate object, perhaps a knife of some kind, the opposite face of which has been ground flat at center, but not at any of the edges. Net sinkers, *62,* 21, 22, are like those at Iyatayet.

Hammers are shown as the metamorphic beach pebble, *62,* 10, which shows some results of hammering on both ends, and the heavier specimen, *63,* 3, which is battered only about the wide end.

The stone lamp, *63,* 1, is pecked from a large beach pebble of fine-grained sandy schist, the outer surface of which is unaltered. A smaller lamp, like those of Iyatayet, may be represented by *62,* 20, although this metamorphic beach pebble had a natural hollow only lightly pecked, if at all.

The large, oval object of metamorphic rock, *63,* 2, is a segment struck from a beach-worn boulder. The face shown is the flat cleavage surface. This object looks as if it had been battered intentionally about all of the edges, and may have been used as a hand shovel. It is to be compared with the shovel-like objects from Ahteut (Giddings, 1952, p. 74; *22,* 1).

The Gungnuk material includes, in addition to those illustrated, 5 shale whetstone fragments, another burin-like groover fragment, 11 flinty scraper and blade fragments, and the fragment of a small lamp. Nothing from the site appears to be out of line with Norton culture at Iyatayet, and the form and treatment of artifacts is strongly like that of both Madjujuinuk and the Iyatayet Norton levels.

Difchahak

Difchahak is the name given by Shaktoolik Eskimos to a large, ancient village site located about one mile along the beach south of Shaktoolik. Along a broad and low old beach ridge behind the current beach upon which is located the Shaktoolik reindeer corral, we counted 99 closely spaced house pits. Somewhat circular in outline, because of their depth and long erosion, and showing traces of a tunnel for each pit, they seemed never to impinge upon one another. They might, therefore, have been occupied simultaneously, although so large a village would have been unlikely in recent times. The pits are very deep. One can stand in the centers of some of them and be completely hidden from surface view. It appears that the excavations for these houses were originally as deep as 6 feet. Unfortunately, all 99 pits had been scratched into by curiosity seekers before our arrival. We learned that most of this mischief had taken place while a group of territorial soldiers was encamped near the site during the second World War. Little damage seems to have been done, however, because most of the floors, together with the tunnel floors, are too deeply covered with earth to have fallen easy prey to souvenir hunters. The shallowness of the center of each pit accounts for the holes dug at that point. From our examination of a number of these holes, it appears that a fireplace was customarily located at the center of the house floor.

We excavated only the part of one house floor at Difchahak. This was not because the site was considered unimportant, however. We felt that Difchahak could be preserved as a site which could be excavated with little preparation because it lay next to the village of Shaktoolik. We had counted upon it as a site to be dug while we were storm-bound at the village. As events unfolded, however, the moment never came when we got to the time-consuming excavation of the very deep pits of this site.

In the limited excavation of 1948 in House 1 at Difchahak, we learned that the floor was rectangular and that a large fireplace, thick with ash, lay at the center. Recovered were two plain potsherds, two pieces of rubbed hematite, two stone sinkers of the Norton culture variety, a polished slate knife blade, a flaked arrow point of silicified slate, a slate labret like the thin specimens illustrated for Norton culture, three retouched chert flakes, and three unretouched flakes. Surface collections about the rims or disturbed centers of these pits yielded the following: a stone lamp fragment, eleven stone sinkers, a grindstone fragment, two linear-stamped potsherds, one polished slate blade fragment, three side scrapers of chert, an arrow point of chert, and a chert chip. All of these objects, with the exception of the polished slates, seemed closely related to Norton culture forms. Difchahak, on this limited evidence, seems to be intermediate in culture between the final Norton culture occupation at Iyatayet and the earliest of the known Nukleet cultures. One might guess that the descendants of Norton culture people of Iyatayet lived at Difchahak, although this is speculation which can be best resolved by the excavation of a number of the Difchahak houses.

The Norton Culture

The Norton culture is that of coast dwellers with an inland turn of interest who built substantial winter houses which they occupied year after year. Although little stylistic relationship is to be noted between objects of Norton culture and those of Nukleet culture, the way of life of the earlier people may have been closely similar to that of the later. A broad distinction may be made, however, between the earlier and the later cultures. Where Nukleet technology tends to be finished and prideful, if not elaborate, the Norton workmanship is more strictly utilitarian and rough-hewn. The Norton slate work is haphazard and scratchy. Most objects of stone are somewhat irregular, as though functional attributes far outweighed those of form and style, and the few organic objects of Norton culture lack the polish and decoration of early cultures such as those of Point Hope and St. Lawrence Island. Not even the harpoon heads, the objects most often elaborated in the coastal Arctic cultures, are more than functionally attractive. They seem to be made with a minimum of effort, even when they are meant to be provided with flint side blades. In general, the flaking of projectile points, knife blades, and the like, is of no particular distinction. Even though chert and other excellent materials were no doubt to be obtained through trade or other means of collection, the Norton people seem to have made do more often with basalt and silicified slate.

Iyatayet, during Norton culture times, appears to have been a village site like the winter settlements of recent Norton Sound Eskimos. Houses were substantially built, and middens grew up around them after many seasons of occupation. Judging from House 7, the houses were commodious —heated both by fireplaces and lamps—and, although lacking the deep tunnels of later periods, designed for winter habitation.

The seasons of residence at the site may be further determined by the distribution of bones. The bone count of Norton culture deposits relates only to the last period of occupation during Norton times, for nearly all of the bones come from the charred areas in Cuts IYP and neighboring sections. It will be observed from Table 13 that some differences occur between the percentages of Norton bones and those of Nukleet. Very few caribou are represented in the Norton sample, while small seal, walrus, and beluga bones show up prominently. Modern Eskimos usually take both beluga and walrus in quantity when these animals appear in early summer— that is, between the end of May and early July. A predominance of small seal may indicate intensive spring hunting at the ice edge to make up for a shortage of caribou. The absence of bird bones in the Norton deposits and their presence in the Nukleet middens suggests seasonal departure from the site during the time of bird collecting and egg hunting—that is, July and August. On the other hand, the abundant traces of mussel shells throughout Norton culture deposits indicate late summer occupancy. We observed that children of the Eskimo families who aided in the excavations scoured the beaches after each storm and its resultant high tide. They came home with clusters of shells that had broken loose from rocks and washed up on the sand. The clusters were dropped into boiling water and, although many of the shells were empty, the ensuing meal was eaten with great relish. Since the more violent storms come in August and September, our Eskimo helpers surmised that the Norton people had collected their mussel shells mainly during those months.

Table 13. ANIMAL BONES, NORTON AND OTHER SITES

	Count	Norton %	Nukleet %	Iyatayet South %
Caribou	15	2.0	11.0	41.0
Small seal	437	68.0	53.5	29.5
Bearded seal	114	18.0	16.0	20.0
Beluga	36	6.0	3.0	4.5
Walrus	34	6.0	1.5	2.0
Bird			15.0	2.0
Other	1			1.0

The prominence of notched stones, presumably sinkers for salmon nets, further attests to residence during the summer months. In another view, however, the best salmon netting areas today are near the mouths of rivers, and it might reasonably be supposed that most netting took place away from Iyatayet during the height of the salmon season. The uniform and abundant distribution of notched stones in almost identical proportions throughout the Norton deposits indicates a very strong reliance on fishing as a means of subsistence. Since only a single form of this sinker appears, it probably does not represent both seal netting and fish netting. Had seal nets been used, their weighting might have demanded sinkers of a larger size. Intensive netting in recent times has been directed to salmon, although other fish, at off seasons, are by no means excluded. If fish were taken in the quantities indicated by the distribution of sinkers, it is reasonable to suppose that they furnished far more than the food needed during the summer and that they were preserved by drying for use throughout the year. Much of the salmon taken in modern Eskimo river and harbor fisheries goes towards feeding the dogs, and may not be the principal element in the diet of human beings. As dog bones are nearly absent in both Norton and Nukleet deposits, and signs of dog traction are absent—or almost entirely so—from all Norton Bay sites earlier than the 18th century, it follows that

186

Norton people subsisted to a very high degree on fish. At least some individual fishing was practiced, as we see from the probable fish spear prong. Hook and line fishing does not seem to be represented in the limited organic collection. The importance of sealing is to be seen not only in the bone count but in the remarkably high proportion of harpoon heads to other perishable artifacts. While many of the concave or straight-based projectile points of flinty stone may have been sealing harpoon points, they offer no further statistical evidence.

Evidence for the hunting of caribou and other land mammals appears in the abundance of small projectile points which are presumably arrow points, the many side blades, also perhaps mainly for arrows, and the heavy stone points presumed to be spear or lance heads rather than knife blades. It is possible, of course, that caribou then, as in more recent times, were hunted at various seasons far away in the hills and that most of the eating of caribou meat took place away from the seal hunting and fishing villages.

The abundance of small stone lamps and the absence of very large ones seems to mean that oil was used primarily for illumination and for only supplementary heat, although cooking would, of course, be possible over these lamps. The smaller specimens seem designed solely for producing a single shaft of flame at the wick notch, rather than the continuous line or arc of adjustable flame obtained from the lunate lamps of the Arctic coast and the rectangular forms of St. Lawrence Island. The method of house heating here proposed for Nukleet—and known from the accounts of old people both in the Norton Bay area and along the Kobuk River—is that of heating the ground by building a large fire each day and later removing the embers and relying throughout the night on radiant heat from the ground, supplemented only by the light of lamps.

Another aspect of winter house living is seen in the prevalence of pottery in Norton culture levels. The round- or conical-based pots, together with a few bucket-shaped ones, would have been suited to the preparation of food in the coals of a household fire. The presence of perforations below the rims of some potsherds shows, however, that these vessels were suspended and, thus, might have been used over an oil lamp as well as in connection with an open fire. The quantity of pottery casts doubt upon stone boiling as a method of preparing food.

Means of conveyance are not directly present in Norton levels. It seems probable, however, that the extensive sealing that seems to have been practiced would have been similar to that of recent times. Breathing-hole hunting is impractical today because of the broken nature of the ice in the vicinity of Cape Denbigh. The most practical recent method of taking seal has been to start out pulling a kayak on a hand sled, then, upon reaching open water, to place the sled inside the kayak, launch the craft, and then proceed across islands of ice, harpooning the seal either in open water or as they bask in the sun.

Norton people's forms of tools differed from those of Nukleet, and it follows that their craftsmanship also differed in many respects. While raw materials in the form of flinty flakes and the like cannot be distinguished sharply enough to allow the use of statistics, it is clear that the stones chosen for flaking included far more of those available from the local beach and bedrock than of those which had to be obtained from some distance. Thus, basalt is the most prominent stone flaked by Norton people, although other poor materials—silicified slate and quartz, were also used. Some non-local flaking materials were obtained either from distant sources or by excavating into the site of the Denbigh Flint complex. The presence of the identical materials used in the Denbigh Flint complex—gray and black chert, translucent chalcedony, and obsidian, in particular—suggests that Norton people did, in fact, mine the sites of their predecessors. It is also possible that some of the objects made in the style of the Denbigh Flint complex but found within Norton levels were actually re-used by Norton people, and it seems even more probable that some generalized objects, such as flakeknives and scrapers, were habitually sought out of the earlier deposits and used as they were or only slightly altered.

The whetstones of Norton culture seem to have been for only the fine-grained whetting of silicified slate implements such as adz blades or groovers rather than for slate implements. Some few coarser stones were probably for edging slate blades. The slate itself was not prepared and treated as it was in sites probably contemporary in other parts of the Eskimo region. The edges produced seem to have been those for crude *ulus* or skinning knives. Slabs of slate were first prepared for edging, apparently by scraping with a stone side scraper (see footnote, p. 151); then they were ground only at the proposed cutting edge. None of the forms produced in slate by Norton people can be regarded as closely similar in either form or technique to the fine slates widely distributed about circumpolar and more southerly regions.

Although wood was almost certainly used extensively, the implements commonly associated with its use are not prominent. Neither well-defined wedges nor heavy adz heads or blades suitable for splitting were found in the Norton deposits, nor were hammerstones clearly identified. On the other hand, adzes are represented by the abundant insert blades made of highly silicified slate, polished to an excellent planing edge. The cutting of antler and other such organic materials is suggested by these adz blades, rather than the large-scale working of wood.

It is doubtful that the true burin was used by the Norton culture people. However, their burin-like groover of silicified slate or basalt was often flaked about its edges and seems to be a form of groover which replaced the

188

true burin once the burin blow was lost and the "Neolithic" practice of grinding and polishing took its place.

The many drill bits, some of carefully polished basalt, show the importance of drilling holes in organic materials for the joining and lashing of flexible frames and mounts. Rapid and effective drilling techniques are indicated, although probable hand rests for drill bearings strongly imply the use of a bow drill.

The whittling and shaping of wood and softer materials was likely done with flakeknives of flint and with beaver teeth, and the finishing was done with abraders such as the grooved shaft smoothers and grooved sharpening stones. Slabs of stone were used as saws for the shaping of the softer stones into materials for manufacture. The abundant bifaced scrapers, as well as a few unifaced scrapers, give evidence of work in preparing hides for the various purposes of Arctic dwellers.

Very little in the Norton culture deposits relates to the personality or the communal and religious life of the individual. The absence of engraved designs is inconclusive because of the limited finds of soft materials. Yet it is evident that the decoration of objects was not as widely practiced as it was in contemporary cultures of St. Lawrence Island. Red paint—presumably disintegrated pieces of red ochre—was encountered frequently in Norton culture levels, as it was in the Denbigh Flint complex layer. This calls to mind the use of red ochre in decorating wooden objects of the Old Bering Sea culture and the use of this pigment in painting bowls, implements, and even the human body by more recent Eskimos of Norton Sound. The objects carved of red (probably baked) shale seem to have had a main function of amusing those who whittled in this substance, although one or two of the fragments may have been more practically useful.

Labrets of stone and jet were probably worn medially in long slits across the lower lip. We have as yet no evidence as to whether these objects were worn by men or women, but the careful finish of each of the recovered specimens shows that meticulous attention could be given to decorating the person.

No drum parts were found (they would show continuity in religious and musical practices), nor have burials been found in association with Norton culture (the cranium from Cut IYZ–5 was not accompanied by other bones).

The presence of a drill bearing made of mammoth ivory in the Norton deposits shows that the fossil banks on the north side of Cape Denbigh were known and exploited as they are today.

The Norton culture is manifestly distinct from any of the forms of culture thus far identified, with one exception. This is the heterogeneous collection of burials, houses, and middens on the old beaches at Point Hope called, collectively, "Near Ipiutak." The elements of culture that set apart

Near Ipiutak most sharply from Ipiutak culture—stone lamps, ground slate, pottery, etc.—are prominent elements of Norton culture. Even more specific crossties exist in flint work. While Near Ipiutak may be an extension of the Norton pattern toward a northerly limit, the old Choris culture of Kotzebue Sound appears to be an immediate predecessor of both—the two cultures together representing more than a thousand years of elapsed time.

IV. THE DENBIGH FLINT COMPLEX

Definition of the Cultural Layer

The layer containing the Denbigh Flint complex at Iyatayet is exceptionally clear-cut and isolated from other culture-bearing strata. The flints described as *in situ* in this and earlier publications came only from the old layer where it was clearly covered by sterile, sandy silt and exclude those flints of probable Denbigh Flint complex origin that occurred in doubtful association.[1] This oldest culture layer was broken here and there by the excavations of peoples of later cultures and, over wide areas, by what appears to be the result of natural erosion down into the sterile, eroded bedrock. Where in place, however, it could be exposed from above in such a way as to eliminate the possibility of a mixture of later artifacts and could be closely examined.

Excavations were made with increasing care as they became deeper. Eskimo workers helped remove sod and excavate the Norton culture levels. As soon as one of us came near the bottom of the Norton deposits, we began to test with trowels for the layer of sterile sand which covers the Denbigh Flint complex. We quickly learned to recognize this layer by its evenly gritty consistency which contrasted with the feel of chips, rocks, and smooth organic matter in the Norton layers. Upon reaching this stage, the floor of the pit or section was carefully bared to the top of the sterile, sandy layer. Then I usually worked alone to expose the Flint complex layer in order to observe how each small, rare object related to others in this limited and significant deposit. The covering sandy layer varied in depth from a few millimeters to 45 centimeters or so. Generally, when I had exposed a reasonable working area to within about a centimeter of the Denbigh Flint level, I cut a small block and lifted it, laying it aside for examination. These blocks of sandy silt, if small enough, came free of most of the chips and artifacts, leaving them exposed in their original position on the top of the dense clay layer. I could then pick up each of the artifacts and those flint flakes large enough for a meaningful count, proceeding in this fashion throughout the segment under examination. Except where solifluction had turned the old culture layer over on itself, this procedure was both simple and quickly revealing.

---

[1] The only exception resulted from an error made in the first hour of discovery of the Denbigh Flint complex. Excavating beneath the floor of House 1 in 1948 and removing materials from the newly found culture level later called Norton, I bagged the very first flints—those found in, perhaps, a square meter of the old level in place—with other artifacts from the six-inch level to which they belonged. This accounts for the inclusion, in my 1949 paper, of an adz blade of silicified slate (Fig. 2–*e*) and the fragment of a small mortar (Fig. 3–*i*), both almost certainly from the later Norton culture, with artifacts from the "microlithic layer." Certain it is that after that first day no ground stone adz blades or pecked stone vessels were found in the Denbigh Flint complex layer.

Fig. 43. Cut PE in progress. David M. Hopkins and James W. VanStone examine soil profiles.

192

Fig. 44. East wall of Cut PE-4.

Fig. 45. East wall of Cut PE-3.

The layer itself, when exposed by lifting away the sandy silt, contained almost no organic material. The entire site yielded, at this stratum, only a few bits of charred bone and minute bits of charcoal. While the flecks of charcoal could be seen throughout the old layer, they were so small as to defy collection unless we scraped the surface of the exposed layer. This we did during the first years of excavation, attemping to get material enough for radiocarbon dating—but without success. In 1952, however, by scraping in two areas more richly coated with hearth remains, we obtained the earth and charcoal-containing samples sufficient for a small series of radiocarbon dates (pp. 244–46). An exposed surface of the old layer contained, generally, a carpet of minute flakes of the chert, obsidian, and other materials used by the Denbigh Flint workers. We left behind dozens of these minuscule flakes for each larger, though still small, flake collected. Objects as inconspicuous as burin spalls might have been lost had it not been for their relative size with respect to the other chips and the close scrutiny to which all of the exposed surface was subjected.

The old layer, in profile at the edge of a cut, was usually no more than a dark line above the thin, grayish top of podsol and below the brownish, sandy silt cover. Exceptions occurred in areas of solifluction where the old level had folded over on itself one or more times, but in such cases components of the layer had not been disturbed. Artifacts and chips were still held against an upper surface and separated by the usual sandy silt until the

194

Fig. 46. West and north walls of Cut PE-2, solifluction lobes partly removed.

fold righted itself and the layer again became the top one with respect to podsol (Figs. 39, 43–46.). The other exception to the rule governing the appearance of the Denbigh Flint complex was found behind, underneath, and to the east of the floor of House 1. In this area, solifluction lobes had incorporated part of an irregular, small, gravel-strewn surface, folding over the gravel in a manner very similar to the folding over of the same layer where it was thin in other parts of the site. This is shown in Figs. 37–38. The gravel of this "floor," which had clearly been carried to the site from a neighboring beach, may have provided the floor of some kind of surface dwelling.

Possible Dwelling Sites

The absence of signs of excavation by men of Denbigh Flint complex times in any form identifiable suggests that all of the flints and chips of the complex were deposited on a layer of sod rather than directly on the surface of the clay, or podsol, where it now lies. If people had walked on the precise surface where the flints now are, footprints would surely have created irregularities in the surface, not to mention other signs of the activities that normally take place around aboriginal camps. The absence of any indications of digging, or even of scuffing depressions around a campfire, attests to the presence of a dense moss or sod layer, perhaps not unlike that of the present day, upon which this early Denbigh population camped and deposited its refuse. The clay-like podsol top upon which the flints now lie would scarcely have been a suitable floor or camp ground in any weather. This exposed surface now becomes both sticky and slippery with the slightest rainfall. Anyone attempting to camp on such ground would be continuously sliding down the slope. Also, it would be difficult to explain why all of the objects—artifacts and flakes alike—found in place in the flat or folded sections, except the one where gravel occurs, were plastered to the podsol top. If they had been dropped at random and stepped upon, they could be expected to lie at angles in the thin ground surface below their permanent position. That they were not speaks again for a dense organic layer which had to be completely dissolved before the flint layer could assume its present condition.

Hearths are identified, however, in at least seven locations on the Denbigh Flint layer. Five of these are indicated in Fig. 39, in Sections PE-1, PE-2, PE-3, PE-5, and Section R. Each was recognized by a reddish discoloration, somewhat oval in form, accompanied by a few fire-colored beach pebbles and a greater-than-usual concentration of charcoal flecks. Artifacts and flakes in Section O were concentrated near a hearth area. A better-preserved, obvious hearth, from which we collected ample charcoal-bearing earth for radiocarbon dating, was that in Section R. Another deposit from which we took charcoal-bearing earth was an irregular, better-preserved hearth in Section Z–5, at the edge of the gravel "floor" of Sections Z4–Z5. All of these probable hearth areas could have been those of enclosed surface structures, though, of course, they could have resulted from fires built in the open.

David M. Hopkins, of the Alaska Terrain and Permafrost Section of the United States Geological Survey, visited Iyatayet in 1950 and joined me in a detailed study of the geological background and the archeological interpretation of the site (Hopkins and Giddings, 1953). While at that time we considerably overestimated the dating of the oldest level, partly because pertinent radiocarbon dating was not yet available, the descriptions and relative order in that publication may be consulted with confidence. Hopkins and I have revised our estimates of the dating of the Flint complex layers as often as we have had reason to do so from studies made after the joint report was issued (Giddings, 1955; 1960b). The reader who is primarily interested in a geologist's interpretation of the site is urged to refer to the cited report. I shall attempt, in the present context, to describe the site primarily from an archeologist's point of view, while at the same time drawing upon Hopkins's observations and interpretations.

Now let us review the physical makeup of Iyatayet and construct an ideal stratigraphy for an area in which the Denbigh Flint complex is in place. As we see from the map of Iyatayet valley, Fig. 31, a small creek,

196

usually of clear and drinkable water, rushes out of a narrow ravine into a widening mouth between slopes of a hillside. Both slopes are densely carpeted with a tough sod which, nearest the creek, is made of tussocks of bunch grass interspersed with herbs and sedges and, higher up, turns softer through the prevalence of sphagnum moss and underlying peaty soil. The Flint complex layer exists only on the bench northeast of the creek and extends no farther down the slope than about the 40-foot present contour. Since the old layer is invariably buried, however, its original position as a ground surface was as low as, but no lower than, the present 35-foot contour. Although Norton culture deposits are found over nearly all of the slope shown on the map northeast of the creek, both at low and high elevations, and the Nukleet deposits are found on both sides of the creek outside the areas of alder thicket, it is presumed that the mouth of Iyatayet Creek did not have its present contours at the time when people deposited the Denbigh flints. The relatively flat area of the present bench where it is found may thus have extended on nearly the same level across the valley, only to be destroyed as the creek widened its mouth subsequent to that first occupation.

Marble or limestone bedrock crops out at cliffs indicated above the beach near the mouth of the creek. Overlying this bedrock, elsewhere on the bench, is a poorly sorted body of weathered bedrock and a soil introduced by mud flow or solifluction in a past cold period. This mixture may be called "congeliturbate" (Hopkins and Giddings, 1953, p. 7; Bryan, 1946, p. 640). It is topped (wherever the Denbigh Flint complex is undisturbed in place) by a one-inch layer of sticky, ashy-gray silt. These layers, taken together, resemble the two standard horizons of an ancient podsol (Hopkins and Giddings, 1953, p. 9). I should prefer to describe the sticky top of this layer in popular terminology as "clay." It is as slippery as clay and it may be rolled between the fingers into clay-like balls. However, a sample of this material was described for me by the United States Department of Agriculture in 1949 as "whitish silt loam." On top of the podsol lie flints of the Denbigh Flint complex and these are covered by the coarse, sandy silt which is covered, in turn, in at least one segment of the site, by a pronounced sod line of peaty nature.

Three radiocarbon dates are available for this peaty material. Referring for the moment to Fig. 37, the east wall of cut Z-4, samples P-104, P-108, and P-105 (Rainey and Ralph, 1959, pp. 372–73) were taken from an area from one to three feet farther into this wall and represent the lower end of the peaty layer where it seems either to have become broken into separate segments or to represent a successive deposit. Sample P-104 represents the uppermost sample of peat from this area where the band seems to split into several zones of depth. P-108 represents a layer below the previous sample but above sample P-105. The legend for P-105 is "Soil above Denbigh Flint complex pebbles, but below peaty layer where peaty layer was covered with sterile, sandy layer." When I labelled the original sample with these words, they seemed clear enough. However, they are without question confusing to one who has not seen the site or examined the photograph under present consideration. At any rate, this sample, P-105, was collected from a darkened area of peaty soil which I considered at the time to form a lower margin of a single layer of peat which grew above the sandy layer covering the Denbigh Flint complex.[1] Thus, these radiocarbon samples, taken together, should give us inclusive dates for the sod or peat that is preserved in this locality above the Denbigh Flint complex. The date for P-104 averaged 3000 ± 170 B. P., or 1043 B. C.; that of P-108, 3080 ± 210 B. P., or 1123 B. C.; and that of P-105 averaged 4040 ± 280 B. P., or 2083 B. C. (Rainey and Ralph, 1959, pp. 372–73). On the strength of these dates, then, the well-established old sod which grew after Denbigh people had abandoned the site, and before people of Norton culture arrived, was formed between 2000 and 1000 B. C. (*See also* pp. 244–46.)

Let us observe at this point that the flints of the Denbigh Flint complex must already have been lying in their present position—that is, flat on the top of podsol—for solifluction lobes had already formed and the layer was equally distributed on the upper and under sides of the fold. Thus all organic matter, with the exception of the charcoal flecks and minute charred fragments of bones above noted, would have been already in its present condition at the time when the sod cover formed. If there had been undecayed organic matter of any substance in the layer while the peat was forming, the flints of at least those portions of the overturned folds would not have adhered to their overlying podsol roof, but would have fallen into the silt below. This point seems very important in an interpretation of the age of the Denbigh Flint complex and must be carefully weighed before conclusions of a late date for the Denbigh Flint complex are reached.

Above the peat lies more sandy silt. From the area illustrated in Figs. 37 and 38, it would appear that this silt had accumulated to a considerable depth, killing and deeply covering the old sod before the site was again occupied by people of the Norton culture. Stone objects of Norton forms are found deep in the deposit, and one or two were recovered from the very top of peat. However, it appears likely that most of these objects had sunk through this relatively muddy deposit and do not represent an original walked-on surface. Most of the Norton deposit shows many signs of having been thoroughly mixed by the melting and thawing of a water-soaked matrix. Very seldom can an original Norton surface be traced for any distance through the deposit. Unlike the sterile, sandy layer below the peat, this

---

[1] The labelling of sample P-105 by Ralph and Ackerman (1961, p. 12) as "charcoal mixed with earth . . ." was done in error, as I have ascertained from Miss Ralph. The sample contained no charcoal as far as we know, and it was not associated with a cultural deposit.

sandy layer contains a large amount of organic matter in various states of disintegration. Sometimes it takes the form of bits of recognizable wood turning to a brown paste under the trowel, the leaf-like, chitinous parts of mussel shells, or various other organic elements, unrecognizable usually, that have a buttery feel under the shovel or trowel.

In a segment of the site which is solidy frozen at the beginning of the season, these levels above the peat thaw rapidly but tend to flow down the slope as they are melted. Thus, one may leave a cleanly scraped slope in the evening, with its artifacts and fragments still anchored in the ice, and return the following morning to find that they have slid downhill and de-posited themselves in a wall of soft mud. It is only in dry weather that photographs of the kind here used may be taken of the middle, or Norton culture, layers at Iyatayet. In contrast, the lower deposits, covered as they are by this sterile, sandy layer, are undisturbed, unless washed directly into, by the processes of freezing and thawing. Finally, a layer of recent or neo-Eskimo deposits is relatively thin, extending no more than a few inches be-low thick sod where it does not represent excavation or midden deposit or redeposit of recent material through erosion.

Iyatayet is not now a deeply frozen site. While the neo-Eskimo site of Nukleet on the opposite side of the Peninsula, located on a northeasterly slope, is perennially frozen, the ice in the cultural deposits at Iyatayet is limit-ed to the upper three or four feet—retained there for a good part, if not all, of the summer only by the thick mat of insulating grass and moss. Preservation of organic materials in the Norton and neo-Eskimo layer is uneven in distribution. Nearly all of the organic artifacts from Norton cul-ture levels come from burned areas or those preserved by ashes or burn in the near vicinity. Parts of House 1 were well preserved by frost; hence the large collection of organic pieces made here. Elsewhere, neo-Eskimo mate-rials as well as those of Norton culture were considerably rotted. In con-trast, on the opposite side of Iyatayet Creek, House 6 was well preserved in frost, presumably because of its sheltered position. Ice in the ground was earlier an important factor in the formation of the site, however. The exami-nation of solifluction lobes in other parts of Alaska has shown that the process of solifluction is best served by the presence of an elastic but firm retaining layer on the surface beneath which seasonal thaws allow a pro-gressive degree of creep or flow. If there is perennially frozen ground, this thawed portion tends to move downhill by gravity retained under its elastic coat and thus to break continuity in the uphill direction while its contained layers fold upon themselves at the bulging forward face. This is illustrated in Hopkins and Giddings, 1953 (Fig. 7, p. 18).

Fossil Solifluction Lobes

Two fossil solifluction lobes—that is, the results of an ancient solifluction process unrelated to the present surface—were exposed during the 1950 season. By the time of Hopkins's visit in August of that year, we had exposed in a series of pits (Figs. 39, 43–46) a wide area representing the lower edge of a large such lobe about 40 feet across its downhill face. In the map and cross-section of the exposed part of this feature (Fig. 39) is shown an area in which the old culture layer is intact in the region of a series of folds and beyond, eastward, but is broken in a segment to the north (shaded portion). The original cuts were PE-1 through 5 and PE-8, in one continuity, and PE-6. Here, under thick sod, the Nukleet layer was very thin. No building or excavation by the later people had been done here. Consequently, with the exception of a few Nukleet artifacts lying mainly on the surface exposed after removal of the turf, we excavated directly into Norton culture deposits. As indicated in the plan and profiles of Fig. 39, the Denbigh Flint complex was in place, undisturbed, wherever the sterile, sandy silt was found also undisturbed. Between the undisturbed areas, Denbigh flints were scarce and mixed into Norton deposits. The breaks in the Denbigh Flint layer could hardly be explained by the processes of hillside erosion; hence we recognized during that season the probability that the part shown by the shaded area in the plan represented a parting of the old flint layer as the result of slippage and folding down the slope.

A test of this supposition was made during our brief 1952 visit when we extended the cut PE-6 uphill (Cut R) and found again the continuity of Denbigh Flint complex with its sterile, covering layer, thus establishing the amount of slippage the old layer had made in order to produce folds of the complexity found at this site. Later in the same season, with new understanding of the solifluction lobes high on the slope, we were able to interpret the folding of gravel deposits (Fig. 37) in the "Z" series of pits. This deposit has already (p. 131) been briefly described in connection with the Norton culture.

The profile photographed in the east wall of Cut Z–4 (Fig. 37) and sketched and labelled in Fig. 38 now offers a convenient means of summing up the stratigraphy at Iyatayet. The depth of deposit in which cultural materials occur—from the top of sod to the Denbigh Flint layer—is here about seven feet. Overlying the congeliturbate and a thin layer of podsol is the one place thus far isolated where the Denbigh Flint layer thickens to incorporate gravel in quantity—perhaps the segment of a floor or large hearth. Over this lie up to 18 inches of sterile, sandy silt which is sealed off from the cultural layers above by a dense, though thin, layer of peat. Downhill, near where a post was driven through to peat in early Norton times, the peat seems to separate into thinner layers. This peat and peaty soil were radiocarbon-dated, as indicated on p. 198. Above the peat was a some-what laminated, sandy soil, sparse in artifacts (all of Norton culture) and lacking the soft, muddy consistency of other Norton deposits. Two disturbed areas are indicated, evidently the results of digging or erosion in Norton times, and these are filled at the bottom with objects of Norton culture only, and capped, as indicated in the sketch, with, first, a thin mixed zone of dark, muddy soil and then a deposit of nearly pure Nukleet culture. This second instance of folding indicates that at least two solifluction lobes of considerable size formed at Iyatayet after the Denbigh Flint complex had settled into its present condition and presumably after most or all of its organic content, together with its covering of sod, had rotted out and completely leaked away.

The order of deposits on Iyatayet bench now seems to have the following meaning: During the time of glaciation in other parts of North America, Iyatayet Creek was subjected to the mixing of hillside sedimentation with eroding marble bedrock which formed a frozen congeliturbate. With the coming of a warmer period, presumably post-glacial, a typical podsol formed to cover the congeliturbate. The ground may have been deeply thawed for a good part of this period. The Denbigh flints were deposited periodi-cally by campers on a sod covering the clay, but no cultural remains were deposited after a period of colder climate that followed podsol formation. During the cold period a second strong sod formed and retained a post-Denbigh Flint culture accumulation of sandy silt, and, under this, solifluc-tion lobes formed, encompassing Denbigh flints as the only cultural material. The peaty layer shown in Fig. 37 and labelled in the sketch (Fig. 38) results from this insulating layer. On the other hand, the peat itself appears to have formed in a period less severe than that of the solifluction lobe—a period when the climate was much like that of today. In subsequent centuries, under cooler conditions, another sandy silt was deposited and when the climate had ameliorated, people of Norton culture began to occupy the site and continued to do so with regularity as the climate remained warmer than that of the present. Finally, after another period of abandonment, came the Nukleet occupation during which the climate was essentially like that today. The dating of these deposits is appraised on pages 244–46.

Techniques

The flint work of the Denbigh Flint complex is a composite technology that might be said to draw upon nearly the whole span of European stone flak-ing. The removal of both Mousterian-like oval flakes and parallel-edged, blade-like flakes from cores, by essentially the Levalloisian technique of striking repeatedly from one end of a pebble; the highly skilled production of microblades by methods of the Mesolithic; the application of burin blows in a range of styles first perfected in Aurignacian times; and the Neolithic bifacing of flints by means of diagonal parallel strokes all combine to give the complex a Eurasian air. The meticulous fineness of Denbigh products, culminating in the burin spall artifact, is, however, a speciality not attained, as far as we know, outside of Arctic North America.

The Microblade Technique

The microblades and cores of the Denbigh Flint complex bring up many more questions than we anticipated in 1948 upon first finding these fragile objects. An archeologist from Europe would have thought of them as a trace of the later blade technique that had lasted for thousands of years in the Old World before metals finally replaced flint. The microblade was not yet fully acknowledged as an artifact in America, however. While the Mexican obsidian blade still provoked argument as to whether it was a direct and belated gift from across the sea or an independent invention, the microblade in Middle America, and in Hopewell culture sites farther north, was largely ignored, or treated as wastage in some more important process. The same was true of the microblade that was consistently present in Dorset culture sites of the eastern Arctic. In their inland Alaskan manifestations, however, the microblade and core had come into sharp focus when N. C. Nelson (1935, 1937) and Froelich Rainey (1939, 1940) had proposed them together as a kind of intercontinental "index fossil." Nelson had pointed out the identity of the wedge-shaped cores of the Campus site in Alaska with some that he had picked up in the Gobi Desert of Mongolia, and in doing so had established a goal and prediction for archeologists in the American Arctic.

The finding of not only raw microblades but their carefully reworked derivatives in the same thin deposit at Cape Denbigh was unexpected for two reasons. First, microblades were thought to be old enough in Alaska and northwestern Canada to be classed with "early man" finds rather than with continuities known from the Eskimo sites. An exception or so (Giddings, 1952, pp. 73, 76; Pl. 46; de Laguna, 1947, p. 124) did not alter the fact that they had no significant place in western Eskimo prehistory. Second, the retouching of microblades had been reported only very rarely either to the east or to the west, and what there was of this seemed confined to rather simple end retouching or side notching (Johnson, 1946, p. 184; Leechman, 1943, pp. 370–71; N. C. Nelson, 1937, p. 272; Rainey, 1939, p. 388; Wintemberg, 1939, p. 90). Thus, upon turning up a flint stratum that contained microblades in abundance and delicately bifaced flints made of microblades,

202

we saw at once that this stood for a form of culture previously unknown in the region.

The microblade and core, we can now be sure, are not the products of frequent reinvention throughout the world. They are, instead, vastly refined miniatures of the blade-tool industry that prominently appeared over much of the Old World in Upper Paleolithic times. The microblade is not simply an undersized blade made in a blade-using economy. It is rather the product of technical refinement so special in the Old World as to have replaced, and perhaps displaced, the blade as a basic product of flint technology. The microblade, wherever found, is eminently designed for hafting. It functions awkwardly alone, except, perhaps, for such things as thread-cutting or surgery. However, if it were fitted into a groove to form a cutting edge, or into a notch or cavity to allow only a working tip to protrude, it would provide an effective part of an often intricate tool or weapon.

The microblade is relatively long and uniformly thin (Pl. 72, 2). Its edges tend to be parallel for the greater part of its length. As the microblade separates from its core, the under surface turns in a downward curve over the matrix. A cross-section through the blade shows that this ventral face is nearly straight, while the dorsal face is angled, its form depending upon whether two or more longitudinal flake scars are present from the removal of earlier microblades (Fig. 47; Pl. 65).

Microblade Cores

The shape taken by a microblade will depend, of course, upon the preparation of its core. The only two whole cores from Cape Denbigh happen to be roughly cubical, and productive of microblades only at one of the faces thus formed. The striking platform in one specimen (Pl. 72, 1) approximates an angle of 75 degrees, and in the other (Pl. 65, 2—the striking platform is opposite the end shown), 85 degrees, to the direction of microblade removal. Unlike conical "polyhedral" cores, these are "semi-polyhedral," resembling in this respect alone the widespread Arctic thinly wedge-shaped core, examples of which are illustrated from Mongolia (Maringer, 1950, Figs. 14, 15, et seq.), the Kobuk River (Giddings, 1952, Pl. 46, 14–16), and the Campus site near Fairbanks, Alaska (N. C. Nelson, 1937, Fig. 16), to single out a few. The striking platforms of all these appear to be also nearly at right angles to the microblade scars, in contrast to some of the cores described from North Greenland (Knuth, 1954, Fig. 104F) and Disko Bay (Larsen and Meldgaard, 1958, p. 65) which have the striking platform at a considerable angle to the direction of microblade scars. Microcores of the Lena Basin seem to lack the narrow, wedge-shaped forms, but include, at Kullata, for example, both polyhedral forms (Michael, 1958, Fig. 81, 1, 2, 7) and thick semi-polyhedral ones (*Ibid.,* Fig. 81, *12, 13*) like those of the Denbigh Flint complex.

While only two cores are identified from whole specimens, seven fragments appear to be those of microblade cores intentionally broken up after they no longer could produce microblades of useful size. In view of the non-local origin of nearly all of the flinty rock of this earliest Cape Denbigh material, it is not surprising that large pieces of chert, obsidian, and the like were never discarded. Two specimens of broken core are of obsidian, one is of red jasper, and three are of chert. Each of these fragments shows a bit of striking platform, parallel scarring, or basal ridge such as would be compatible with the form of the two whole specimens. No other type of microblade core is indicated. (See *Core Scraper,* p. 227.)

The scarcity of microblade cores at the site presumably has to do with the imported nature of nearly all of the flinty material used by the Flint complex stone workers. Obsidian, the cherts, and the chalcedony must have been brought in either by trading or by travelling to a source of these materials, probably in the Brooks Range, where all of the cherts, at least, are known to occur in stream gravels (Thompson, 1948, p. 64). Relatively few large flakes and no raw cores of any of these materials are found in the oldest level; hence it appears that anything that might be used was hoarded and eventually used up in artifacts and small waste flakes. Exhausted microcores might also have been further fractured in the production of minute implements. A few of the raw flakes saved from the site show parallel scars like those of microcores. The last microblades struck from the larger of the two obsidian cores range from 22 to 27 mm. in length; those of the other core, from 20 to 23 mm. Of 82 microblades complete, or nearly so, 14 specimens at the upper end of the range fall between 40 and 45 mm., while at the lower end are seven specimens between 18 and 23 mm., and one is only 14 mm. in length. The others are distributed in this respect more or less evenly between the extremes. This indicates that cores at Iyatayet were shaped at first to produce large microblades and then had successive microblades struck from them until they had become too small to handle—specifically, when microblades had reached a length of only about 20 mm. The two whole cores recovered appear, therefore, to have been no longer useful when discarded.

Microblade Artifacts

A total of 379 microblades, exclusive of bifaced derivatives, are included in the following analysis. More than two-thirds (266) of this total were found *in situ* in the Denbigh Flint complex layer. 113 were microblades and fragments found elsewhere in the Iyatayet site and presumed to have been displaced from the oldest level (see pp. 138, 191–95). No disparity appears in the proportions of materials used in microblades, nor in their overall treatments in comparing the *in situ* group with the displaced group, even though the flinty materials known to have been used by the Norton people were in all respects disproportionate to those of their predecessors at Iyatayet.

The following tables of microblade measures (in millimeters) and distribution show in detail how obsidian compares with the chert-like flints in its choice as microblade material.

Table 14-a. MICROBLADE MEASURES

	Obsidian	Chert, etc.	Mean length, Obsidian	Mean length, Chert, etc.	Mean width, Obsidian	Mean width, Chert, etc.	Mean thickness, Obsidian	Mean thickness, Chert, etc.
DFC microblade, complete, retouched	20	9	34	29	8.7	7.3	2.0	2.2
Displaced microblade, complete, retouched ..	11	5	33	30	9.6	6.4	2.3	2.2
DFC microblade, complete, not used	16	12	24	36	9.0	7.6	1.8	1.7
Displaced microblade, complete, not used	8	5	27	25	8.1	5.4	2.0	1.9
DFC microblade, retouched fragment	39	16	23	21	9.1	9.0	1.7	1.8
Displaced microblade, retouched fragment ..	22	26	20	20	8.4	8.4	2.1	1.6
DFC microblade, fragment, not used	51	104	18	19	7.8	7.3	1.4	1.4
Displaced microblade, fragment, not used ..	15	21	18	20	7.7	7.6	1.3	1.3

Table 14-b. MICROBLADE DISTRIBUTION

Materials	Percentage of Microblades *in situ*	Percentage of Displaced Microblades
Obsidian	47	48
Chert	45	47.5
Chalcedony	4	0.5
Jasper	3	2
Black chert	1	–
Silicified slate	–	2

These figures indicate that there is no essential difference between the microblades found *in situ* in the Flint complex level and those displaced in the Iyatayet site. The retouched microblades tend to be slightly wider and thicker than those showing no sign of retouch, as though the larger blades might have been struck especially for the use to which the retouch indicates they were put. The retouched fragments, it is to be noted, fall within a rather limited range of 20 to 23 mm. in length. It seems likely that this has something to do with choosing straight sections of microblades where neither the thick, bulbous end nor the thin, curved tip would interfere with insertion into a slot as a side blade.

The figures on width and thickness may be compared with those compiled by Irving (1953, p. 62) for Alaskan and Asiatic microblades. The width/thickness index of Cape Denbigh microblades is 22.5, as compared with 27 for Imaigenik site—closely related in typology to the Denbigh Flint complex[1]— in the Brooks Range, 31 for the University of Alaska Campus site, 31 for a group from Hokkaido, and 28 for a large group from Jehol Province. This indicates a considerably broader and thinner flake at Cape Denbigh than at any of the other localities. We might further observe that the obsidian specimens at Cape Denbigh give a width/thickness index of 21, as compared with 24 for the cherty specimens, indicating, perhaps, a better control of obsidian than of other materials.

Microblades frequently show signs of use as cutting edges, or as more complicated implements. As noted in the preceding tabulation, some one-third of the microblades in place and more than half of those displaced are "retouched." A magnifying glass is required for a careful study of microblade use, for much of the retouch is simply that which is necessary to fit a fragment of a microblade into a slot of some kind. Details of retouch on some microblades and fragments are shown in Fig. 47 and in Pl. 65, 3, 5–9, and 12. The extent to which microblades are retouched probably relates to original function. Artifacts made of microblades are distinguished on the basis of shape and retouch as follows.

Unifaced Side Blade

A large number of broken microblades are fairly straight and would readily fit into slots, as in knives and weapon heads of the European Mesolithic and Siberian Neolithic. In many cases the break at one or both ends of the suspected side blade appears dulled or slightly ground. The break may thus have been calculated, rather than accidental. One or both edges, and sometimes the ends, of these specimens are lightly retouched, possibly by inadvertent pressure against an object at certain points, or by intentional preparation to fit without binding into prepared slots. Some such fragments are shown in Fig. 47, 1, 2, 5–10. A considerable number of these specimens are of about the same length (5–7), further suggesting preparation for use as series of side blades. The proposed side blades that have a more or less rectangular outline would lend themselves to insetting one above the other, after the fashion of certain Siberian Neolithic spearheads, especially those of the Isakovo period of the Lake Baikal region (Michael, 1958, pp. 42–43). On the other hand, many of the retouched microblades taper in outline while still straight enough for insertion into a nearly straight slot (Fig. 47, 1, 20). These might have been hafted like Maglemose microblades in spear heads and knives (Mathiassen, 1948, p. 67; Figs. 179–81). In the implements

---

[1] Recent observations at Cape Krusenstern and other sites of the coast indicate the probability, however, that the Denbigh-like manifestations of the Anaktuvuk Pass region fall late in the Denbigh Flint complex, and that the wedge-shaped cores and thicker microblades follow cores and microblades like those of Iyatayet.

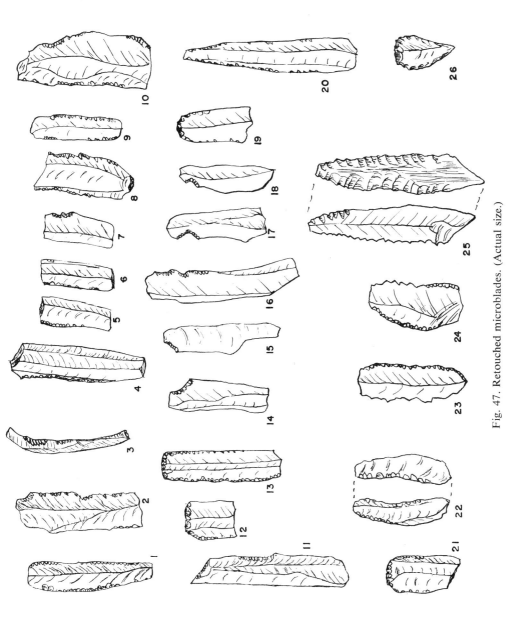

Fig. 47. Retouched microblades. (Actual size.)

figured by Mathiassen, the bulbar and wider end of a microblade is placed in the proximal position, forming a barb where it protrudes from the shaft, series of them providing multiple barbs. It is to be noted that Larsen (1951, p. 74) found microblades along with side-slotted projectile points 100 miles north of Cape Denbigh in the lower levels of Cave 2 at Trail Creek (see p. 255).

End-notched Microblade

A large number of the used microblades are notched at one edge of one end, usually the bulbar end, as shown in Fig. 47, *14, 15, 17,* and *18.* Pieces with this form of notch usually are not retouched extensively elsewhere. An exception is Fig. 47, *2,* which shows signs of use at two points, including an end. It might be supposed that implements such as this would be used in repeatedly cutting a soft material rather than in a more demanding process. These may be thread-cutters used in sewing or lashing. This form of artifact occurs in the Pointed Mountain site (MacNeish, 1954, p. 243, Fig. 66, *14*) and may be also represented from Sogho-nor, in Mongolia (Maringer, 1950, p. 141, Fig. 38), although Maringer describes the notching as double, for "fastening." Notched microblades are found in the Siberian Neolithic (e. g., Michael, 1958, Fig. 83, *14*—Kullata) and, occasionally, in Dorset sites (Collins, 1956*a,* p. 70; Pl. *4, 6*).

End Scraper on a Microblade

Some microblades have been used about a blunted tip, usually at a point of fracture rather than at the bulbar base of a microblade. Some examples are shown in Fig. 47, *12, 13, 19, 21,* and *26.* Many of these are short enough to have been hafted in shallow sockets as end scrapers, and one, *26,* is retouched about all edges on the face shown, clearly with a view to hafting. Similar instruments occur westward in the Siberian (Michael, 1958, Fig. 83, *1–14*—Kullata) and Mongolian sites (Maringer, 1950, Pl. *27,* 7) and eastward in sites of Dorset culture (Collins, 1956*a,* p. 69, Pl. *4, 6*).

Microblade Knife

Many of the retouched microblades appear to have been used about one or more surfaces in a whittling or scraping process. Examples are shown in Fig. 47, *3, 11, 16, 22–24. 25* is included in the figure as a possible knife, but was more likely to be a bifaced side blade in the process of manufacture from a microblade.

Burin on a Microblade

The five specimens shown in Fig. 48 are burins formed on fragments of microblades. With the exception of *5,* they are all from the Flint complex level *in situ.* It should be stressed that these are not "micro-burins" in the European sense of a by-product in the making of trapezoidal microliths (see Clark, 1932, Appendix 1, pp. 97–103). Rather, these are very small, true burins executed in the restrictive medium of a microblade. Fig. 48, *1* has had a single burin blow struck on a broken microblade which does not seem to have received special preparation. *2* is similar, the scars of two spalls showing. *3* is a microblade fragment split longitudinally, perhaps by the burin blow indicated by an arrow at the bottom of the figure. Two more burin blows have been struck at the opposite end, creating an effective double-ended burin. *4* is apparently a double-purpose implement, the lower end having been shaped as a drill, while a burin blow has been struck at the opposite end at a point indicated by the arrow. *5* has three effective burin faces, two at one end, and one at the opposite end, as shown by the arrows.

These burins on a microblade appear to be identical with burins occasionally found in Siberian Neolithic sites reported by A. P. Okladnikov, including the early Budun Bay site of Lake Baikal (Michael, 1958, Fig. 11) and the Middle Lena sites at Kullata and Ymyyakhtakh *(Ibid.,* Fig. 88, *1–5;* pp. 322–24). It appears that William Irving is also describing burins

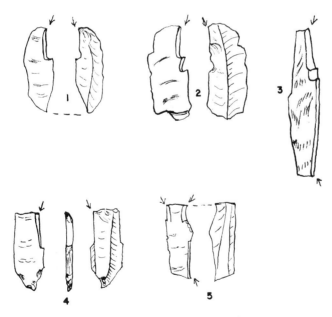

Fig. 48. Burins on microblades. (Actual size.)

(from Imaigenik) when he says, "Five [of 23 microblades] have been trimmed on one edge by the removal of a single longitudinal flake, in the manner of striking off a burin spall," (Irving, 1953, p. 62). These figures indicate a greater proportion of these burins than are known elsewhere east of the Lena drainage system. They occur also at Pointed Mountain site (MacNeish, 1954, p. 244) and at Southampton Island (Collins, 1956a, p. 70, Pl. 6, 6).

The bifaced side blades of the Denbigh Flint complex are believed to be, in the great majority of cases, reduced from microblades; hence these delicate implements, usually diagonally flaked, are to be considered along with the microblade technique, although they are treated in detail elsewhere in this report (pp. 229–32).

The microblade technique thus accounts for more than half of the artifacts of the Denbigh Flint complex. Microblades disappeared from coastal Alaska with the Denbigh Flint complex, some time before 2000 B. C. Almost none appear in the later sites of Kotzebue Sound and Norton Sound, though they seem to have persisted to some extent in the interior of northern Alaska. The parallel-edged instruments called "side scrapers" (Larsen and Rainey, 1948, pp. 105–8) or "flakeknives" (Giddings, 1951, p. 195) have been mistakenly classed by some (Laughlin and Marsh, 1956, p. 9) with microblades and blades, with which most have not even a strong superficial relationship. Although microblades and cores are present on an early time level in the Aleutians, they are not always clearly distinguished in the literature from other forms (Laughlin and Marsh, 1954). The microblade technique was highly developed in Greenland by, perhaps, 2000 B. C. (Knuth, 1952, 1954) and continued as a vital element in the Dorset culture (Collins, 1956a; Larsen and Meldgaard, 1958; Mathiassen, 1958; Rowley, 1940) until about 1350 A. D. in some regions of the east (Taylor, 1959, p. 38). Microblades were important at fairly early times also across the sub-Arctic and Arctic parts of Canada and interior Alaska, as indicated by collections from Dismal Lake and elsewhere in central Canada (Harp, 1958), from the Pointed Mountain site in the upper Mackenzie drainage basin (MacNeish, 1954), in the New Mountain phase of Firth River archeology (MacNeish, 1959, pp. 48–49), in Anaktuvuk Pass (Irving, 1953), and at the Campus site (Nelson, 1937; Rainey, 1939) in Alaska. The dating of many of these phases is still uncertain, however.

The Burin Technique

The burin technique, as it was practiced at Cape Denbigh, is the precise removal of gauged slivers from flakes serving as thin cores. It is, in a sense, the microblade technique in reverse. Where the microblade begins with pressure upon a broad striking platform, the burin spall (*lamelle de coup de burin*) is struck from a thin end toward the mass of its core. It does not splay out, as does the microblade, into a sharp-edged ribbon of flint curving downward toward the tip. It splits straight, instead, often with blunt edges that terminate in an abruptly upturned "hinge" fracture. A correctly delivered burin blow detaches, in most cases, a sturdy, needle-like spall of either three or four faces. The first spall to be removed from the edge of a trimmed core shows a single scar of removal, at the proximal end of which is found the bulb of percussion. The corresponding negative bulb remains on the core. Each spall removed after the initial one shows the negative bulb of the previous blow and, on the opposite face, the positive bulb of latest percussion.

Burins

The core from which the distinctive spall has been removed is called a *burin* (in Europe, sometimes *graver*). "Burin" implies a group of instruments made by a common technique; it does not always imply equivalence of function. Some of the Cape Denbigh burins may have been used in the manner of the modern steel implement of the same name—that is, as a tool for fine engraving. Most appear to have had a more practical use, however, serving as deep groovers with which to split or divide commonly used organic materials such as wood, ivory, and antler. Still others seem to have been drills, awls, scrapers, punches, and chisels.

The forms of Cape Denbigh burins, so far as the burin blows themselves are concerned, correspond to a high degree with the forms known from the Old World. The terminology for the burins of western Europe, worked out since the early years of this century, can be applied with some success to the American burins as well, because it is based on the arrangements of the scars of burin blows rather than on the matrix upon which the scars appear (Burkitt, 1920, 1925, 1948; Bourlon, 1911; Noone, 1934). The European terminology is ponderous at its best, however, and it has seemed advisable in this report to redefine it in terms that may be readily applied to the American specimens.

The hallmark of the burin is the negative bulb left by a burin blow. As Burkitt (1925, p. 68) has aptly remarked, "supposed graver [burin] facets should be carefully observed, as only those are genuine gravers that bear the mark of a blow along the length of the blade, proved by the presence of little negative cones of percussion at the working edge of the graver facet. There may be several of these facets, but one at least is necessary if the tool is to be regarded as a real graver." Many kinds of thin stone implements may have been used at one time or another, after the fashion of burins, but the technologically "true" burin is distinguished by its negative bulb.

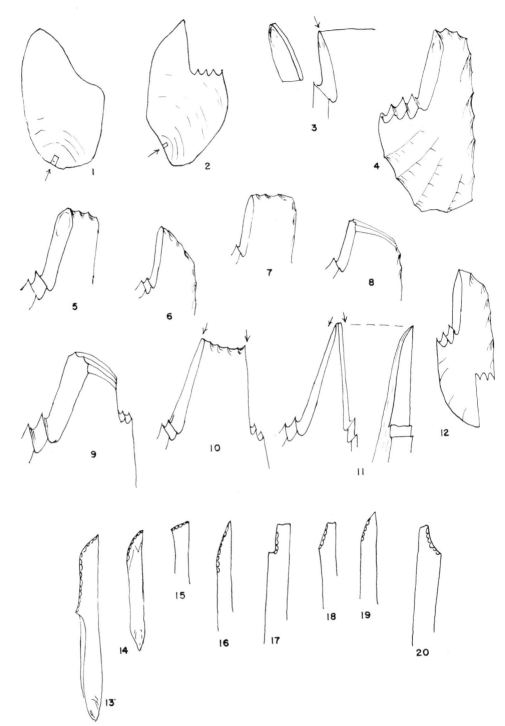

Fig. 49. Burin typology (diagrammatic), Cape Denbigh.

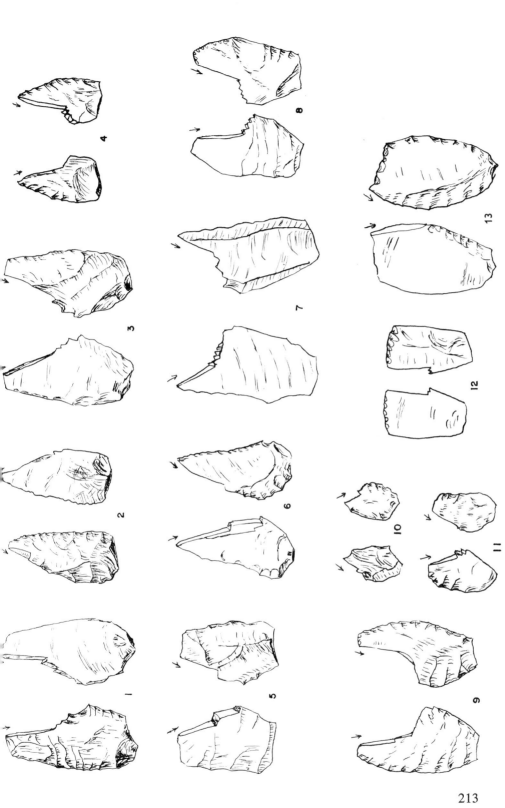

Fig. 50. Burins, Denbigh Flint complex. (Actual size.)

213

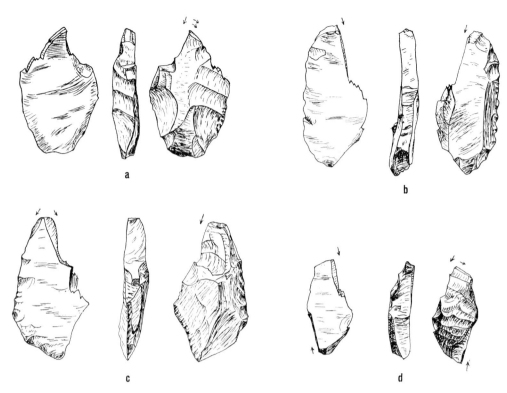

Fig. 51. Burins, Denbigh Flint complex. (Actual size.)

Most burins of the Paleolithic and Mesolithic periods of European pre-history were made on parallel-edged blades, which were in turn produced by the widespread blade-and-core technique. Cape Denbigh burins (Pls. *66-a, b;* Figs. 49–50), on the other hand, were usually fashioned from flakes of oval or lobate outline. We assumed at first that these flakes were struck at random, or that burins were made on any flake of suitable size that came to hand. A study of 146 burins (excluding burins on microblades, p. 209) found in place in the Flint complex level at Iyatayet, together with a smaller number of displaced specimens, shows, however, that the great majority were made on flakes struck in a uniform fashion from some kind of pre-pared core. Most of the burins that are not altered by pressure retouching at the proximal end retain here both a bulb of percussion on the plane face and a trace of the original striking platform. The flakes seem to have been predestined for burin making. The blow that detached one of them from its core did not direct itself parallel to the ridges left by the removal of earlier flakes (exceptions are shown in Pls. *66-a,* 8; *66-b,* 3; Figs. 48; 50, 7). Instead, the ridges on the original cores lay at a considerable angle past 90 degrees from that of the striking platform. The ridge-topped flakes from which burins were to have been made appear in most cases to have

214

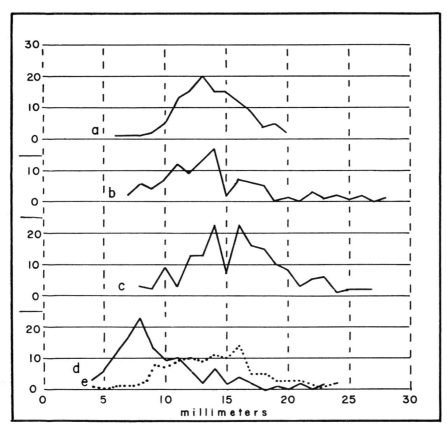

Fig. 52. Measures of burin scars, burin spalls, and burin stems.

a) Burin width at stem.
b) Burin stem length.
c) Length of burin spalls.

d) Length of last burin spall.
e) Estimated length of first burin spall.

been separated from the core in an asymmetrical leaf shape, or, preferably, a "mitten shape" (Fig. 49, *1,* and *2*). The latter form appears to have been ideal, since the first burin blow could be struck towards the "thumb" of the mitten with a good chance of its ending in a desired hinge fracture (Fig. 49, *3* and *4).* The thin, parallel edges of a blade or microblade were clearly avoided by most Denbigh burin makers.

The great majority of burins *in situ* (110 specimens) were complete and still functional as burins when discarded or lost; 35 were broken, usually near the distal end as though subjected to working pressure; and one specimen is doubtful as to whether it was broken or aberrant.

The average length of a complete burin was 2.64 cm. Since the burin spalls detached from a burin tend to become smaller as the core is used up, the burins at the time of their first blow would have averaged a few mil-

215

limeters longer. The average width at the stem near the base of the first burin scar was 1.31 cm., with a range as shown in Fig. 52, *a*. The width at the base of the final burin scar, however, was only .96 cm. The greatest thickness of a burin ranged from .2 to .8 cm., with a mean of .41 cm. The estimated length of the stem of a burin averaged 1.40 cm. on the 102 specimens for which this measure can be obtained. The curve in Fig. 52, *b* shows these burin stems to have conformed closely to a pattern with the exception of a few specimens of markedly greater length than the average. These stems were mainly those of burins made on the long, slender, and thicker instruments that we call "flakeknives." These burins, since they are long enough to be held firmly between the fingers, may have been used unhafted. The uniform dimensions of the more usual burin stems suggest that most burins were fitted into slots like those of recent Eskimos' end scraper handles.

Treatment of the stem involves, usually, pressure retouch about the edges of the convex face and the removal of a few to many thin, broad flakes from the plane surface opposite. Sometimes this was done (Fig. 50, *9*) to erase a prominent bulb of percussion resulting from the blow which had removed the original flake from its core.

The usual classification of burins is based upon the treatment with burin blows of the distal end of the implement. (In this classification, 66 of the burins *in situ* classify as angle oblique [Burkitt, 1920]; 17 as angle transverse; 14 as burins *busqués;* 8 as screwdriver; 15 as double burins, some verging on the screwdriver type; 7 as double-ended; and the others unclassifiable because of breaks or faulty last burin blows.)

Some burins (Fig. 50, *13*) have only one scar of a successfully delivered burin blow. The greatest number of the saw-tooth scars of burin blows on a single specimen is nine. The average, however, on 194 burin faces examined in this group is 2.5 scars to the burin face. Something can be said of the dimensions of the removed burin spalls. The average length of the last scar is .96 cm. An estimated figure for the length of first spall removed, based on visual reconstruction of the burin flake, is 1.41 cm. The range of these estimates and measures is given in Fig. 52, *d, e*. These fall well within the range of measures of separately recovered burin spalls (p. 220).

Trimming scars were present on the plane face of 67 specimens, and absent on 53, exclusive of the edge treatment of the distal end from which burin spalls were removed. Trimming at this end was only on the convex face of each of 61 specimens that were not beaked or double-faceted, while 51 were evenly trimmed on both faces. Those burins that show only a single trim would, if used on organic material as groove cutters, tend to cut an asymmetrical groove as against the even, double-curved groove of the double-trimmed burin.

In the following key to the burins of Cape Denbigh, distinction is made between burin blows removing unmistakable burin spalls and the presses

216

detaching curved spallettes from the crown of a beaked burin or related piece. Burins made by the latter process are designated "shaved."

The columns to the right show the numbers of burins of various types found in place in the Flint Complex layer.

A. Flake burins (non-microblade)

    I. Single facet   DFC
        a) Angle   *in situ*

	DFC *in situ*
Transverse (Fig. 49, *7*): single-face trim	11
double-face trim	9
Oblique (Fig. 49, *6*): single trim (Fig. 49, *4*)	40
double trim (Fig. 49, *5*)	30
shaved (Fig. 49, *8*)	8
b) Beaked	
With notch (Fig. 49, *9*)	1
Without notch	1
II. Double facet	
a) Separated	
Concave between (Fig. 49, *10*)	6
Convex between	4
Straight between	5
b) Convergent (Fig. 49, *11;* Fig. 51, *c*)	4
III. Double end (Fig. 49, *12*)	
Single-single	5
Single-double	2
Double-double	0
Beaked-single (Fig. 51, *d*)	0
Beaked-double	1
Unclassified	21
B. Microblade burins (Fig. 48)	– 5
TOTAL	148 5

A burin that is "single faceted" is one in which the working end has been formed by the scar of a single burin blow delivered against a trimmed end of the implement (Fig. 49, *3–9;* Fig. 50, *1–13;* Pls. *66-a,* 1, 5–7, 9; *66-b,* 2, 5–8; *72,* 11). The trimming can be on one (Figs. 49, *4;* 50, *1, 2, 6–8, 13*) or both (Figs. 49, *5;* 50, *4, 9, 12*) faces of the end of the burin ("single" or "double" trim), or the end of the burin can be "shaved," by pressing off one or more spallettes (with the microblade technique) parallel to the end of the burin, either on an untrimmed or previously trimmed end, to take the place of even trimming (Fig. 49, *8, 9;* Fig. 51, *b*). A variant is Pl. *66-b,* 1. This treatment is similar to the spalling that creates a "beaked" burin (Fig. 49, *9;* Fig. 51, *a;* Pls. *66-a,* 9; *66-b,* 2; *72,* 10). The "shaved" angle burin is here distinguished from the beaked burin by the adherence of its spallettes to the convex face of the burin where they substitute for the more usual trim, and by the thinness of the burin tip.

The materials for burins were carefully chosen by the Denbigh flint-workers. No burin is made of the obsidian commonly used for other artifacts at the site. Varieties of gray chert were used in making 72% of the burins, translucent chalcedony in 10%, black chert in 8%, red jasper in 6%, and highly silicified slate or poor quality chert in the remaining 4%. (*See* p. 221 and Table 15 for burin spall and side blade materials.)

Twelve burins either show signs of secondary use as instruments other than burins or of having been made into burins from artifacts rather than from the usual raw flake. An angle oblique burin of chert has had the negative bulb of the last burin blow obscured by scarring as though the tip of this nearly used-up burin was finally employed as a drill. Five other specimens show similar secondary use as drills.

One convergent burin appears to have been made over from a broken projectile point. The original had been rather large and diagonally flaked on both faces. One burin, originally an "angle oblique," had been retouched about its burin face and the scars of earlier burin blows in such a way as to make it useful as a concave scraper—perhaps for smoothing shafts. Two specimens seem to have been long, slender flakeknives, on one end of which a burin blow was struck as an afterthought. A single thin specimen has had a burin blow struck on the edge of a broken side blade. One of the rare burins on a microblade (Fig. 48, *4;* Pl. *65*, 3) has the end opposite the burin scar retouched as a drill or graver point. While it would be possible to use the stems and edges of some burins in a scraping process, only a few stemmed burins were made over from side and end scrapers, a possibility once suggested for another group of Alaskan burins (Solecki, 1951, p. 57).

The greatest uniformity in the Denbigh burins is seen in those angle oblique specimens that were more or less mitten-shaped from inception and were generally used up before discarding. They appear to have been hafted and to have functioned by being drawn toward the user in a grooving process. When a burin of this kind is placed on its plane face with the point of burin blow upward before the observer, it is usually found to be right-handed—that is, the burin scar and the "thumb" lie to the left. 87 percent of all the burins subject to this observation are right-handed. The distal section of angle burins tends to be somewhat evenly gauged in thickness. This would have been advantageous in cutting a parallel-sided groove rather than a groove which continually widens at the top. If most of the burins were used in dividing sections of antler and ivory into triangular strips for further reduction to projectile heads, shafts, awls, and the like—a process known from other Arctic archeological sites and for recent Eskimo groups—we can easily understand the function of most Denbigh burins. Where the

218

angle oblique or angle transverse burins would have cut an effective groove because of the razor-sharp edges of a newly created negative bulb on the burin scar, the advantage of beaking a burin tip by removing spallettes at right angles to the burin face is less obvious. I am inclined to see the beaked treatment as less a functional necessity in the Denbigh site than as a tradition of workmanship. Still assuming the region of the negative bulb to be the working end of a burin which is primarily a groover, the fluting about this tip that characterizes a beaked burin destroys part of the edging of the negative bulb if it is applied after the principal burin blow. This seems to have been the usual procedure in the beak technique. Several single-faceted burins have had only one or two spallettes removed after the fashion of a beaked burin (Fig. 49, 8). The spallettes take the place of a single-trimmed edge in all of these; hence I have classed them as "shaved" specimens of angle burins rather than as simple forms of beaked burins.

Each of the double-faceted burins (Fig. 49, 10, 11; Pls. 66-a, 2, 8; 66-b, 3, 4, 9) is held in some doubt as to its function as a hafted groover drawn in the manner visualized for most of the Denbigh burins. These specimens usually have a stem equally as suitable for hafting as is that of the commonest form of angle burin, but the distal end is provided with burin faces at either edge. The edge between the burin faces is usually double-trimmed and somewhat concave in outline. Such an instrument in which the concavity of the distal edge is rather wide could have served as a tool for some specialized chiseling process. The burins most nearly like European "screwdriver" forms are actually double-faceted burins, the burin faces of which nearly come together at the tip, creating either a sharp point or a chisel-like, beaked tip eminently suited to punching holes or drilling. These burins do not show that they have been roughly used as drills, however, and if they were turned by the hand at all, this must have been in drilling soft material. One suspects that these screwdriver burins were also hafted, but used in a special grooving process quite unlike that of the angle oblique and related forms.

A limited number of burins have been made of unifaced flakes much thicker than the average and were apparently shaped into flakeknives before being given a burin blow. Although each of these is classified in the terminology based on the burin scars, it is clear that they are unique as a small group within the larger category of burins.

The double-ended burins (Fig. 49, 12; Pl. 66-b, 10) create a question of their own. It is easy to see that a suitable flake might be given a burin function at either end, thereby insuring against breakage. The double-ended burins are usually small, however, and offer no adequate means either of gripping between fingers or hafting firmly. It is to be noted that the double-ended specimens are "right-handed" at both ends, suggesting that they were meant to be used in the same manner as single-ended burins.

The burin spalls from Cape Denbigh (Pls. *66-a,* 3, 4; *67)* were recognized from the very first as unique objects. They bore no resemblance to flakes from other flint sites in which I had dug, and it was soon deduced that they came from the small objects that were later identified as burins. The burin spall is not easily confused with any other artifact or by-product of the flaking technique. It differs markedly, even when struck imperfectly, from its nearest relative, the microblade. A burin spall is not likely to be produced by accident. The Denbigh burin maker without doubt practiced long in judging the angle of his press or blow before he mastered the technique.

It is helpful to divide the burin spalls into three classes: 1) the first spalls to be removed from the outside of a burin, 2) the four-sided spalls correctly struck after the first, and 3) the imperfect products of the burin blow. The first burin blow along the edge of a flake intended to be a burin removes a thin sliver, triangular in cross-section. Two faces of this sliver are from the prepared edge of the burin flake, while the third face, with its bulb of percussion at the point of burin blow, is the scar of separation from the burin proper. These first spalls, if they develop no curve, are likely to break satisfactorily at the end in a hinge fracture. Burin spalls of this class show clearly whether the original burin flake was trimmed from one or both edges, or whether it had been trimmed at all for the blow.

Blows subsequent to the first remove straight slivers, four-sided in cross-section, bearing at the distal end the mark of a hinge fracture, and at the proximal end the negative bulb of a previous burin blow and the positive bulb of the most recent blow (Fig. 49, *3*). A burin spall of this ideal form is a strong column throughout and the kind that was frequently chosen for hafting as a tool (Pl. *67*).

The third class of burin spalls includes those that result from a blow given at the wrong angle, causing a curve to develop, those driven through flaws in the stone, and those designed to straighten out a burin face. All such spalls tend to shatter towards the distal end, offering no area for proper retouch.

The average length of the 168 unbroken burin spalls in place in the Flint complex level is 1.51 cm. The range of these specimen falls between .8 cm and 2.7 cm., as shown in Fig. 52, *c*. The mean width of burin spalls is .30 cm., a figure representing perhaps the average thickness of the working ends of burins. The thickness of the burin spall, on the other hand, averages less (.17 cm.), partly, perhaps, because it was desired by the maker that the spall be so shaped for use, but mainly because excellent as well as faulty or misdirected burin spalls are necessarily included in the average.

The material chosen for burin spalls coincides closely, as we might expect, with that chosen for burins at Iyatayet (p. 218). This is evidence that both burin spalls and burins were manufactured at the site and that no large increment of either was brought in separately. Of 219 measured burin spalls found *in situ,* 72% were of chert, 10% of chalcedony, 7% of black chert, 7% of red jasper, and the remaining 4% of other materials (including one spall of obsidian among those of silicified slate and quartzite). (See also Table 15, p. 232.)

From the beginning of our excavation of the old level, burin spalls were treated as though they were artifacts. It is unlikely that any well-defined specimens were missed where they occured in place; yet it was not until 1953 that the true nature of the burin spall as an artifact was recognized. The series of observations that led to identification of burin spalls as engraving tools has been recorded by the author elsewhere (Giddings, 1956). In brief, the first microscopic examination of these spalls had been limited to the end which showed the bulbs of burin blows. These scars, of course, relate to burins themselves and appear at first to be the ends that have received the most functional treatment. When I learned, however, that the opposite end—that which breaks off in a hinge fracture—often was altered after its break by some form of pressure flaking, I understood that many burin spalls—perhaps most—were objects desired, perhaps more than the parent burin, for some specific use. The burin might thus serve mainly as a core for the production of the burin spall artifact. The result of use at the end opposite the bulbs of burin blows is evident on 122 of the 219 burin spalls found in place. Most of those showing no such use are faulty specimens driven from the burin in such a way as to thin the opposite end, which fails to break in a suitably thick hinge fracture.

By no means all of the burin spall artifacts are retouched only at the point of hinge fracture. Those specimens in which this fracture is clearly formed, however, are often retouched along the line of the hinge fracture to give them the appearance of a miniature end scraper (Pl. *68*) or, perhaps, to cite a more modern instance, the appearance of the tips of steel engraving tools. Many specimens are only slightly retouched at the point of hinge fracture and show signs of use farther along an edge, usually the left-hand edge as the spall is placed negative bulb up and the working end away from the observer (Pl. *67*). Other variations in these worked edges are shown in Fig. 49. Two of the forms illustrated (Fig. 49, *17* and *20*) have notches at the end resembling those of some worked microblades (p. 208). Burin spall artifacts of this type may, therefore, have been thread cutters or, at any rate, similar in function to the worked microblades. The remainder, however, are thought to have been engraving tips designed for hafting.

The burin spalls with a triangular cross-section, showing that they were the first struck from the edge of a prepared flake, make up 24 percent of those *in situ.* A discrepancy is to be noted between this figure and the mean of hinge fracture scars on burins, which indicates only 2.5 spalls to the burin. No doubt more spalls were struck than managed to leave clear-cut hinge fracture scars.

The figures for burin spalls with respect to right- and left-handedness correspond closely to those for burins, though the criteria are quite different. Each spall is placed with its cutting edge forward and its negative bulb (if it is a four-sided spall) upward. Among 122 spalls for which this observation could be made, 75% showed a left slant, 13% a right slant, and 12% no appreciable slant but signs of retouch straight across the region of the hinge fracture. If the burin spalls that show retouch were normally hafted in a penholder type of handle, as we have reason to believe they were (Giddings, 1956), the specimens showing left slant could have been drawn towards the user in an engraving motion like that employed by modern right-handed engravers who use small metal tools. Even though the functions of burins and burin spalls as artifacts are seen to differ considerably, the figures for both sets of artifacts, which presumably represent handedness, show a remarkable consistency. If we leave out the burin spalls which show no strong left- or right-hand slant, we find that proportions are 86% right-handed and 14% left-handed in the remaining specimens. The right-handed burins were found to make up 87% of the collection against 13% left-handed.

Shortly after I learned of the artifactual nature of burin spalls, I wrote to Dr. Helge Larsen in Denmark asking him to examine burin spalls from early Greenland sites, just then turning up, and learned that reworked specimens were present in a site of Sarqaq culture in Disko Bay. They have since been described from several sites of Sarqaq to Denbigh age and affiliation (Larsen and Meldgaard, 1958, p. 51, Fig. 19; Harp, 1958, p. 229; Giddings, 1956a, p. 262) and they occur in each of the Denbigh Flint sites from which I have a sizeable sample from Cape Prince of Wales and Kotzebue Sound. The burin spall artifact thus appears to be distributed in North America wherever burins of the "Denbigh types" occur. As far as I know, they are strictly a product of the American Arctic.

Other Flaking

If the oldest Denbigh people had picked up pebbles on their own beach from which to produce their artifacts, we might be able to reconstruct the grosser flaking techniques. They were so conservative of their flints, however, that they left hardly any cores or flakes of large size. Furthermore, the sites of Denbigh Flint complex recently discovered around the northern shores of Seward Peninsula and Kotzebue Sound show even less evidence of coarse flaking than does Iyatayet site. The production of an occasional parallel-edged, unifaced blade resembling blades of the Old World probably involved no complicated blade-core technique, however. The larger flakes (most of them either retouched as scrapers or knives, or used without preparation) show that parallel-edged flakes were sometimes removed before an oblong or irregular flake which was struck from immediately below the point of impact of the first flake. Since the flaking tended to be from one end of a cobble or pebble, the flakes usually are elongate. Presumably a skilled microblade maker could judge a ridge on a partially flaked core in such a way as to remove, if he chose, a parallel-edged flake closely resembling a true blade. Both the later people (those of Choris culture in particular) and the earlier people (those of Palisades II) appear to have produced true blades from true blade cores, though none of the cores has yet come to light.

Unifaced Forms

Flakeknives

The unifaced flints to be described here as flakeknives include several forms which have been designated by others as side scrapers (Collins, 1937, pp. 150–51; Larsen and Rainey, 1948, pp. 105–8). "Flakeknife," while also an inadequate term, is preferred for two reasons: 1) the term "side scraper" has been frequently used both in Alaska and elsewhere to identify certain rather large, essentially straight-edged flints that may be either held in the hand or provided with a handle, sometimes of baleen lashing—such implements have recently been used in various scraping processes; 2) while the Denbigh specimens could nearly all have been used as scrapers for such purposes as smoothing shafts, they could also have been used primarily for their cutting edges in shaping and whittling processes of various kinds. Most of the specimens are derived from rather thick flakes with a lengthwise curvature, sometimes pronounced, of the ventral face ("dorsal," in these descriptions, is the more strongly convex face—the one upon which retouch regularly occurs), but a sizeable number are fashioned from parallel-edged flakes approaching the form of blades or microblades in the European sense of these terms.

While no large cores exist to show that the true blade technique was practiced at Cape Denbigh, a few of the flakeknives have come off their cores ridged on the dorsal surface and parallel-edged, as they might be if they had been struck from prepared cores. Examples are seen in Fig. 53, *2* and *3* and Pl. *69, 6.* One of these, a strongly curved specimen, has been struck so as to remove a carefully prepared ridge from a core of some kind, possibly a core from which other long, parallel-edged blades were to be removed. Fig. 53, *4* appears to have been a similar initial blade removed from a core, while seven other specimens seem to have been formed by essentially the blade-making technique. An extreme example of blade production is probably

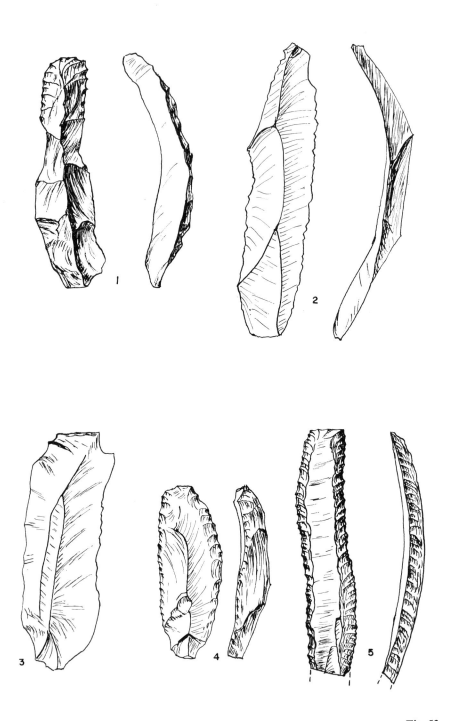

Fig. 53.

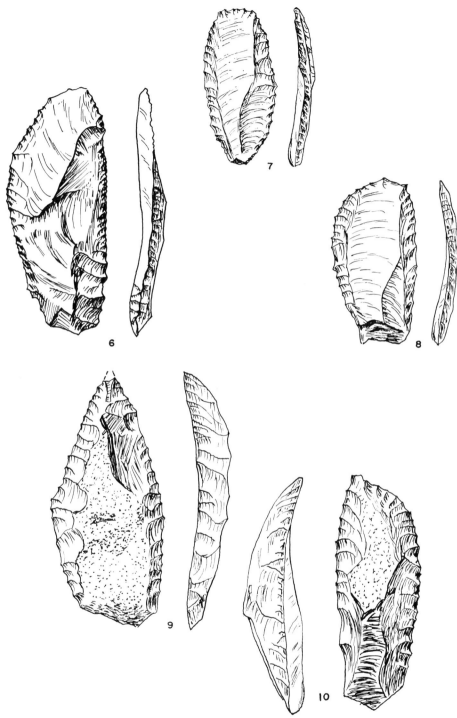

Flakeknives. (Actual size.)

that shown in Fig. 53, *5* and Pl. *69*, 12. Although the steep retouch about each of its edges has obscured the original form of this piece, fragments of similar pieces show this to have been a form of implement widely used in Flint complex times, and the presence of very similar specimens both in Norton culture deposits and at Ipiutak (Larsen and Rainey, 1948, Fig. 26, *D* and *E*) shows it to have been a persistent form forward through time. It is to be noted, however, that prepared blade cores do not occur either in the Norton culture or at Ipiutak. This suggests the possibility that irregular flakes might be chosen for lateral retouch, which would give them the final parallel-edged form without their having originated as parallel-edged raw blades. The presence of large parallel-edged blades at Choris Peninsula (Giddings, 1957*b*, Fig. 5, *2* and *3)* and the knowledge that fairly large microblade cores have existed at some past time in the Brooks Range (Solecki, 1950, p. 67) further indicate that prepared cores for large blades were in use at Cape Denbigh. Most of the flakeknives not obviously based on blades appear to have been hafted, exposing the forward part of two edges, sometimes with a rounded distal end as the carefully retouched part which would be most serviceable in a cutting process. Examples are shown in Fig. 53, *6–10,* and Pl. *69*, 1–4, 7, 9. Pl. *69*, 25 has been retouched on both faces only at the heavy end, suggesting that this end was thinned to fit into a handle while the sharp, thin edges were left to project as the cutting edges of some form of knife.

A few specimens, of which Pl. *69*, 18, 19 are examples, appear to have been "mitten-shaped" flakes suitable for burin manufacture but which, for some reason, were not used as burins but as flakeknives, especially for their concave edges. These and certain other pointed specimens, Pl. *69*, 15; Fig. 53, *9, 10,* would have been very serviceable in a boring or drilling process. A few examples, Pl. *69*, 5, 11,[1] 16, 17, 23; Fig. 53, *1,* would have been useful in a gouging process such as that manifested in historic times by the use of beaver teeth. Two steeply keeled scrapers, *70-a,* 5, 9; *72,* 16, might also be considered as gouges. The variety of flakeknife forms is further shown in *69,* 8, 10, 13, 14, 20–22, 24, and *70-a,* 2, 6–8. A "channeled" flakeknife or scraper (*70-b,* 5) resembles those of early man sites of the southwest, and another flakeknife (*70-b,* 16) is strongly channeled.

All of these forms of flakeknives were used, presumably at the same time, by people of the Denbigh Flint complex. We understand them to be mainly the hafted cutting and scraping edges which were useful in many of the processes of working wood, antler, skin, and other organic materials. Forms very similar to those of Cape Denbigh, perhaps excluding the blade forms, are to be found in the earliest St. Lawrence Island cultures and Ipiutak. The range of close agreement is greatest at Ipiutak among the uni-

---

[1] Also shown as a drill in Fig. *59, 1.*

faced forms described as side scrapers, end scrapers, and engravers. However, in view of the variety of more obviously specialized engraving tools at Iyatayet and of end scrapers more traditional in form, we shall not attempt a close comparison of possible functions between the two sites. It is suggested only that the earlier Flint complex flakeknives served a multiplicity of purposes, while the closest counterparts of individual specimens in Ipiutak had become specialized as to use (see flakeknives of Norton culture, pp. 166–67).

Flakeknives total 81, of which 47 are chert; 9, chalcedony; 9, jasper; 4, obsidian; 9, black chert; and 3, silicified slate.

Gravers

Four objects from the Denbigh level are closely similar to the "gravers" of early man sites in the western states. Each of the Denbigh gravers is pointed at one corner of a distinctive form of thin flake. Three of these specimens

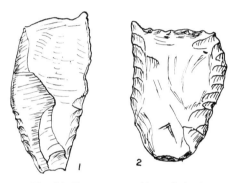

Fig. 54. Two gravers. (Actual size.)

rather resemble a human footprint, the point corresponding to the great toe (Fig. 54). In two specimens, one of chert and one of jasper, of very nearly the same proportions, the point is on the right-hand margin. The jasper specimen appears to have had a secondary point on the left distal corner as well. A chert specimen is pointed only at the left distal corner. A fourth graver, of chert (Pl. 70-a, 1), is shorter and squarish in outline and has its graving tip inset slightly from the right margin of the distal end. Each of these specimens has been trimmed on the dorsal face and lightly trimmed ventrally—possibly, but not obviously, for some form of hafting.

Core Scraper

A unique object of chert (Pl. 65, 1) looks at first glance like a miniature microblade core. In this view, the broadest face would be the striking platform, and the microblades represented by four scars about the top would angle almost precisely as do those of the true microblade cores, yet the length of this piece, if it were such a core, is suspiciously small. The whole object is only 25 mm. long and 11 mm. thick. It appears rather to have been created for use as a kind of end scraper or hafted scraper for heavy work. The forward part of the face, which corresponds to a striking platform of a microblade core, shows signs of hard usage, as though in pressing against resistant material in a process of grooving or scraping.

End Scrapers

Of 19 end scrapers found in place, nine conform to the same general form. This outline is somewhat pear-shaped: the scraping end widest, the two lateral edges slightly rounded, and the narrow end terminating in a remnant

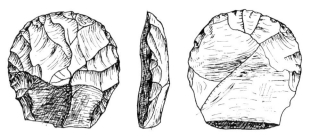

Fig. 55. An end scraper (from mixed levels), probably of Denbigh Flint complex. (Actual size.)

of the striking platform from which the original flake was struck (Pls. *70-b,* 2, 3, 8, 9–11; *72,* 12). Eight of these are of chert, one of chalcedony, and one of obsidian. All are thin and the scraping edge, though not high, is carefully executed in series of parallel scars. Four specimens—three of chert and one of obsidian—are stubby and slightly irregular in execution, as though accommodated to a shallow hafting notch (Pl. *70-b,* 4). Two thick specimens are considerably more rounded at the working edge, the scraper edge forming a semicircle (Pl. *70-b,* 1; Fig. 55 [displaced from the Denbigh Flint complex layer]).

Finally, two specimens, included as end scrapers with some reservation, are very thin flakes. One is of chert, rounded about one edge, end-scraper fashion, and left untreated elsewhere; the other is red jasper, trimmed narrowly at three edges of one face, the enclosed edge being the widest and resembling that of an end scraper more than the edge of any comparable implement (Pl. *70-b,* 7). Another, thicker specimen (Pl. *70-b,* 6) has the same outline.

228

Miscellaneous Knives and Scrapers

An obsidian flake has been retouched carefully over its convex face and the margins of its plane face in the form of a crescent. This appears to be neither flakeknife nor side blade of forms known at the site (Pl. *70-b,* 15). A curious object of black chert, *70-b,* 14, is trimmed on its convex face at three edges in such a way as to resemble superficially the Cody knives of the eastern slope of Nebraska (Wormington, 1957, p. 128, Figs. 41–43). Another black chert fragment appears to be part of a knife or scraper of the same type, and the obsidian specimen, *70-b,* 13, bears a superficial resemblance. A chert specimen (*70-a,* 3) is also very thin and retouched along two edges. The form, if one tip were not broken, is that of a crescent. The chert knife blade, *72,* 6, outwardly resembles certain Mousterian forms. A "saw" is formed by deep serrations in one edge of a flakeknife (*72,* 15).

Bifaced Forms

Side Blades

The delicately made thin flints here described as side blades (see also pp. 160–61) are thought to have been set in grooves along the sides of antler or ivory arrowheads, spear points, and harpoon heads. The manner of insetting can be surmised from the small side (inset) blades, many of which were found in place in their host artifacts at the Point Hope Ipiutak site (Larsen and Rainey, 1948, pp. 66–67, Pls. *1, 2, 32, 36*). Before the discovery of Ipiutak, the affixing of flint edges to arrow points and the like was known only from the Old World and from a limited number of Old Bering Sea and Birnirk toggle harpoon heads.

Among the hundreds of small side blades from Ipiutak appear only two distinct forms: a symmetrical one (Larsen and Rainey, 1948, Type 2, pp. 98–99) in which two long edges are of nearly the same degree of curvature, and an asymmetrical form (*Ibid.,* Type 1) in which one edge is straighter than the other, ranging to a lunate outline. It should be emphasized that while symmetrical forms similar in outline to those of the Ipiutak side blades occur in the Denbigh Flint complex, they are arrow points rather than side blades. The only form of side blade that appears to be shared by the Denbigh Flint complex and Ipiutak is the asymmetrical, lunate one—the form represented by the most specimens in each culture.[1] None of the large side blades of Ipiutak known to have been employed at that site as sword or knife blades appear in the Denbigh complex at Iyatayet. The resemblance in side blades between the two cultures, then, is based primarily on the outline and thinness of the lunate form. There are, however, generic differences. While many of the Ipiutak specimens were diagonally flaked, practi-

---

[1] Norton culture Type 1 (p. 160) embraces both of the Ipiutak types.

cally all of the Denbigh side blades are prepared by removing series of parallel flakes diagonally across one, and usually most of both, faces. The Denbigh side blades appear to have been in nearly all cases fashioned from microblades, while there is no evidence that microblades were used in any form at the Point Hope site (Larsen and Rainey, 1948, pp. 92–93).

The microblade evidence is to be seen in both complete and unfinished side blades on which one or both faces were not completely obscured by flaking. Thirty percent of all the side blades found in place thus show a bit of the concavity of the underside of a microblade which the Denbigh flint-workers did not find it practical to remove by diagonal flaking, and seven percent retain a bit of the ridge or ridges of the convex surface of the original microblade. One of the principal uses of microblades—the making of side blades—is thus indicated, although the production of obsidian micro-blades seems to have nothing to do with bifaced side blades. Only four side blades are made of obsidian (Table 15).

In addition to the crescentic side blade (Pl. *71-b,* 9, 13–16), there is a long, triangular form (Fig. 56, *a*; Pls. *71-b,* 10, 11; *72,* 4, 5), possibly designed to protrude at the wider end to form a barb. While this kind of side blade outwardly resembles some of the Ipiutak flints (Type 1-A, Larsen and Rainey, 1948, Pl. *35,* Figs. 21, 22, 24), the resemblance, as we previously observed, is superficial because the latter are much larger and occur in the tips of arrowheads rather than as side blades. The Denbigh specimens appear to be much too narrow for use as arrow points. Among the Denbigh side blades, only a very few are crude. These may have been the work of amateurs or, more likely, flakes discarded in the process of manufacture.

The Denbigh side blades range considerably in size. Of those that are whole, the length is between 25 and 44 mm. The mean length of 21 such specimens is 31.2 mm. However, some very small, broken specimens (Pl. *71-b,* 13, 14) appear to have been under 2 cm. in length. Many of the side blades are only 1 mm. thick at their thickest point, yet are diagonally flaked over the whole of both faces. The average maximum thickness of 84 specimens for which this measure could be made is only 2.2 mm. As to edge-to-edge width, the range is from 2 to 12 mm., with an average maximum breadth for 90 specimens of 8.4 mm.

In a total of 144 bifaced side blades and fragments found *in situ* in the Denbigh Flint complex level, only 13% are whole, while 65% retain one tip and 22% are center fragments. It is to be noted that 61% are carefully flaked diagonally on both faces while 22% are so treated on only one face. Others lack an edge-to-edge diagonal treatment, although most of them show parallel flaking at the edges.

A point of distinction in side blades is that in 76% of the specimens there is more meticulous retouching of one edge than of the other. This is most pronounced where serration is present. Presumably the serrations are

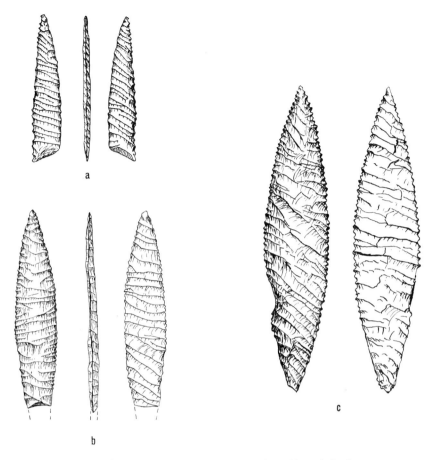

Fig. 56. Side blade and arrow points. (Actual size.)

intended to form cutting edges and would have little value on the edge to be inset. 25% of the side blades show a marked edge serration.

Three whole specimens have been repaired from pieces found separately in the old level. Determined efforts to match pieces, however, brought only this little success and indicate that the missing parts were lost away from camp and that, in the great majority of cases, only broken weapons were discarded at the site.

Evidence of handedness is seen in the direction of press of the small diagonals removed in side blade making. In 88% of the side blades and fragments on which diagonal flaking appears, the direction of the diagonals is downward to the right, while in 12% the direction is downward to the left. One might guess that the side blade was held by a right-handed person in his left hand and that the press was progressively about the edge away from the maker. It is to be noted that these proportions compare very

231

closely with those for supposed handedness in both burins and burin spalls (see pp. 219, 222).

In materials used, the side blades are remarkably like burins and burin spalls, as is shown in Table 15. A strong preference is indicated for light colored cherts in proportions comparable to those of the other implements. The proportion of chalcedony used is noticeably higher than that for burins and spalls, however, while the latter are more often made of black chert and jasper than are side blades. Both obsidian and silicified slate are included as side blade materials, though they were very rarely used. The indicated preference for chalcedony may have to do with the translucency of this material as well as its chert-like strength. Some of the side blades of chalcedony show exceptional care in flaking.

Table 15. COMPARISON OF MATERIALS USED IN SIDE BLADES,
BURINS, AND BURIN SPALLS

	% of Side blades	% of Burins	% of Burin spalls
Chert	69.0	72	72
Chalcedony	16.5	10	10
Black chert	5.5	8	7
Red jasper	5.0	6	7
Other	4.0	4	4

End Blades

Arrow points. A form of end-hafted biface is presumed to be an arrow point of a kind limited to the Denbigh Flint complex. 18 specimens of chert, jasper, and obsidian range in length from 22 to 55 mm. and appear to have been made from microblades (Fig. 56, *b* and *c*; Pls. *71-b, 1–8, 72, 3*). They invariably tend toward the plano-convex in form, and, in some, a good part of the plane or ventral flake scar is intact (Pl. *71-b, 7*), while on the same ones or others (Pl. *71-b, 4*) an original microblade ridge has not been entirely removed from the dorsal surface. A few specimens are flaked from either edge toward a ridge at center of the dorsal surface while the ventral surface is only partly retouched or given a complete face of nearly flat diagonal scars. The edges of these points are serrated, as a rule, sometimes with incredibly even and minute serrations (Fig. 56, *c*).

The identification of these pieces as end blades is based on the edge grinding of most specimens in such a way as to remove the serrations for one-fifth to one-third of one of their tips. These end blades were presumably fitted into a groove at the end of an arrow point of hard organic material. Arrow heads with open seatings of the kind proposed are known from Meldgaard's (1960, Pl. *2*) Parry Hill site, Igloolik Island, and from Ekseavik site, Kobuk River (Giddings, 1952, Pl. *27, 4, 5*).

232

In place of the more common double pointing, two specimens are lightly stemmed by retouching the edges. The stem of one, of black chert, is flaked only from the convex surface, while the stem of the other, of red jasper, has been formed by retouch from both edges of the ventral face. A type of probable arrow point to be compared with those of the Ipiutak Type 1 (Larsen and Rainey, 1948, Pl. *2*) is straight-based and parallel-edged for approximately two-thirds of its length (Pl. *72,* 8). Of eleven chert specimens, five have a more or less slanted base, as in the Ipiutak Type 1-A (*Ibid.*, Pl. *2,* esp. fig. 8). Both surfaces of these points tend to be diagonally flaked with skill. A single fragmentary, or broken, obsidian specimen of this type with a somewhat slanted base is lightly ground on both faces. This kind of arrow point is presumed to have been inserted in the bifurcated tip of a hard organic arrow head such as we know from Ipiutak (*Ibid.*, Pl. *1,* Type 2).

Points for toggle harpoons. A form of thin, straight- or concave-based, usually triangular, biface is regarded as the point for a toggle harpoon head. This classification is confidently based on the forms of Ipiutak harpoon points found hafted, as well as on the rather distinctive harpoon points of late Eskimo types executed in slate. Eight of these specimens are illustrated (Pls. *71-a, 72,* 9). These and others are executed in chert, jasper, black chert, and chalcedony. The edges are usually serrated and the bases thinned by the removal of a number of flat flakes from each face. The variety of sizes suggests their use as sealing harpoon heads meant for the taking of both small seals and the big walrus or bearded seal. It is recalled that the only remains of large mammals from the Denbigh Flint complex in place are a few charred fragments, two of the larger pieces of which can be identified as those of small seals.

Spear points or knife blades. Only a few specimens of large bifaces not identifiable as arrow points or harpoon blades occur in the Denbigh Flint complex in place. One might expect large spear points to be used more frequently at caribou crossings of the interior than on the seacoast, although, of course, arrows were probably used for procuring caribou here as they were later in the Ipiutak sites. Some of these points and fragments may be compared, on the basis of technology and form, with certain early American points.

A fluted point of chalcedony, Fig. 57, *a*; Pl. *72,* 13, is 42 mm. long, 23 mm. wide where the sides are parallel, and 5 mm. thick. A fluting extends along each face about two-thirds of the distance from base to tip. The ear-like projections were pronounced, to judge from the one which is intact and

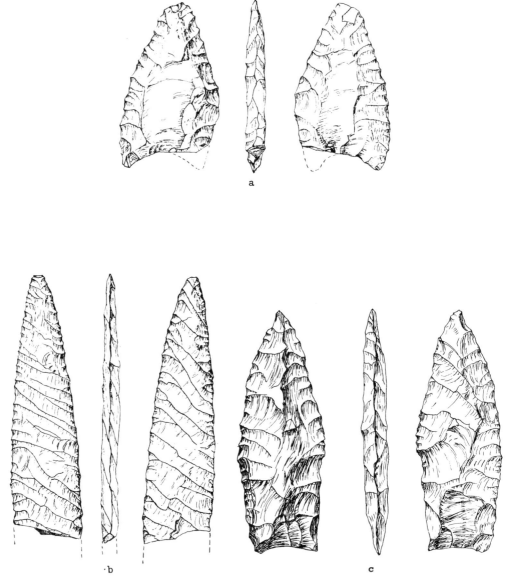

Fig. 57. Spear points. (Actual size.)

234

the prominent scar of the opposite ear which is broken away. Although the edges were parallel, this piece lacks the oblanceolate form of Folsom points and possesses a triangular, rather than a double-curved, outline towards the tip. Fluted points of the Folsom type are known from three other localities in Alaska and from none other, as far as I know, in the circumpolar region. One of these was described by R. M. Thompson (1948) from the Utukok River on the north slope of the Brooks Range.

The tip of a doubly fluted point was found in a site on Lake Natvakruak near Anaktuvuk Pass by members of the U. S. Geological Survey in the summer of 1950 (Solecki and Hackman, 1951). Associated with specimens most of which were excavated from beneath the surface covering of tundra at a depth of from five to ten inches, this specimen presumably belongs to a Denbigh-like complex now known by the site name of Natvakruak. Two other fragments of fluted points also collected by members of the U. S. Geological Survey during the summer of 1950 come from a hilltop site of the Brooks Range near where Thompson found his fluted point. The three artifacts found together at this site were the bases of two fluted points and a polyhedral microblade core (Solecki, 1951, p. 55). It thus becomes clear that fluted points are definitely associated with the Denbigh Flint complex in two widely separated localities and probably with microblades of Denbigh-like form in the third. Since no other fluted points have been found in this region, the type is not known to have existed in contexts other than that of the Denbigh Flint complex.

A diagonally flaked, straight-edge point or blade of chert is represented by a large part of the tip (Fig. 57, *b*; Pl. *72, 7*). This form is now sometimes designated "Angostura" (but was formerly called "oblique Yuma") and this particular specimen was one of the first of its kind found in direct association with a complex of other flint types in undisturbed stratigraphy. The type lasted in the Bering Strait region until at least 1000 B. C., as we now know especially from a beach ridge site at Cape Krusenstern (p. 256), from middle levels at Trail Creek (p. 255), and from sites of Choris culture (p. 255).

A rather small and relatively crude point of jasper, basally thinned and edge-ground (Fig. 57, *c*), resembles a specific Plainview form (Krieger, 1947, p. 952). A rather small point of black chert, Fig. 58, *7*, is slightly stemmed along the lower fifth of its edges, basally thinned, and parallel-flaked on one face. Several other large points are fragmentary and too small for positive classification. One of these, of chalcedony, Fig. 58, *5*, was apparently a wide, parallel-edged point with an edge-ground, slightly indented stem. Other specimens, probably knife blades of several forms, are indicated in Fig. 58, *1–4, 6*. The bifaced triangular object, Pl. *70-b, 12*, appears to be some form of knife blade.

The bifaced projectile points of the Flint complex at Iyatayet indicate, therefore, a strong emphasis on seal harpooning, a comparable one on hunting with bow and arrow, and little use of heavy spears. These emphases, we may note, are not unlike those of coastal sites of more recent times.

Drills

The identification of some flints as drills rests upon their drawing to a narrow tip at one end, together with signs of bifacing at that tip, such as might have been caused in part by the drilling process itself. A specimen of black chert (Fig. 59, *1*) is bifaced towards the constricted end. The tip is broken off but both edges show signs of the intensive wear of rotation. This appears to have been made on a parallel-edged blade, as were some flakeknives.

A smaller drill is very similar in that it is also of black chert and has been made from a microblade. The tip is bifaced and worn by drilling. This specimen could easily have been hafted in a bow drill of late Eskimo type, as could another specimen. Fig. 59, *2,* of chert, is a thin flake, perhaps a microblade, bifaced at its narrower end; the tip is broken off. Fig. 59, *3* is a thick chert drill, perhaps originally a flakeknife, the narrower end of which is bifaced and scarred at the edges as a result of burin process. This also could have been hafted.

A burin, Fig. 59, *4,* has been used as a drill at its narrow tip, apparently obscuring the scar of the last burin blow struck. Two other drills might perhaps be classed as bifaces, since the ventral faces, of a flakeknife in one case (Fig. 59, *5*) and a microblade in the other (Fig. 59, *6*), have been retouched almost their whole length. Both of these could easily have been hafted.

Drills are thus extremely rare in the Denbigh Flint complex, as they were at Ipiutak. With the exception that no Ipiutak drills were made on microblades, the drill typology of the two sites is remarkably alike (Larsen and

Fig. 58. Knife blades, projectile points, and fragments.

236

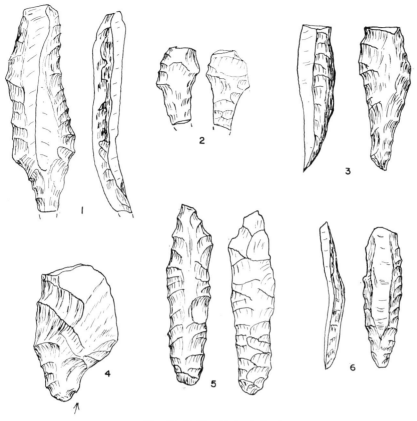

Fig. 59. Drills. (Actual size.)

Rainey, 1948, Pl. *20,* 8–16). Three delicate objects, all broken, (*71-b,* 12, 17 and one not illustrated) may be drills, lancets, or as the shape of one suggests, "double-pointed implements" (Giddings, 1956b).

Grinding, Polishing, etc.

Polished Burins

Twelve objects of basalt are burins, the broad faces of which have been more or less altered by polishing (Pl. *73,* 1–8, 13, 15, 16, 20). The burin facet in all cases is left unpolished as a cutting edge. In this respect these burins differ from the burin-like groovers of Norton culture (pp. 151–54) but closely resemble the partly polished burins of Sarqaq culture (Larsen and Meldgaard, 1958, pp. 50–51; Meldgaard, 1952, pp. 225–29). One of these burins has been rounded over by polishing to form a slightly concave distal margin. Others are thinned by polishing both faces near the distal end.

237

Polished Creasers

Seventeen objects, all of basalt except for three of dark silicified slate, are classed as creasers (Pls. *70-a,* 4; *73,* 9, 10, 14, 18). They are polished from one and usually from both faces to form a cutting edge (placed upward in the plate). These pieces, made on nondescript flakes, are sometimes polished elsewhere at various angles about either face. These are similar, in their working edge, at least, to boot sole creasers or feather setters, usually of ivory, recently in use by Eskimos.

Other Polished Objects

Polishing is noted on four other objects of basalt. A thick, small fragment, pointed at either end, has been rubbed to a polish on parts of three faces. Pl. *73,* 19 is a pointed object of basalt, probably used as a drill. The point is formed by polishing laterally at several angles as well as upon either face. The thick end may be the broken-off segment of a larger piece such as might have been held conveniently in the hands. *73,* 17 is a double-convex object, originally flaked on both faces, which has been polished near the center of part of each face and bevelled by polishing at the upper end, somewhat as is the bevel on an adz blade. Another polished piece is the fragment of a large object of basalt, possibly a bit of the surface of a large, polished implement.

Miscellaneous

A hand-sized granitic cobble has been hammered to a nearly flat surface at either end and partly shaped by pecking over the entire surface. While no hafting marks are to be discerned, this object might easily have served as a double-ended hammer head. It is the only hammer recognized in the Flint complex layer and is the largest worked object of any kind recovered from the old layer.

While some of the beach pebbles in the Flint complex layer could have served as grinding and whetting stones, only two were clearly used for such purposes. One is the fragment of a possible whetstone of shale, and the other is a pebble of flat, fine-grained sandstone, probably a whetstone.

A single triangular fragment of red, perhaps burnt, shale, 9 mm. thick, has been rubbed flat on four surfaces and slightly rubbed on two others. The limited number of polishing stones is in keeping with the small amount of stone polishing in the level. It seems probable that the objects of basalt and silicified slate were shaped on stones such as these.

The fragment of a sandstone shaft smoother, Pl. *73,* 11, shows that this instrument had parallel sides only 14 mm. apart and was meant for grooving a shaft of as little as 6 or 7 mm. diameter. One polished piece of red

238

ochre and many stains of red ochre in the Flint complex level attest to the coloring of objects.

Two fragments of birch bark are recognized as the parts of a container by marks of sewing on one, in which the stitches are 9 mm. from a straight cut edge and 17 mm. apart (Pl. *73*, 12). The stitching was done, apparently, by piercing the bark to make two holes 3 mm. apart, then drawing the thread tight between the two holes. A blackening of part of the surface of the other piece with a solid mass marked by one straight edge on one side and by blotches on the other is perhaps the part of a painted design (see p. 109).

Fragments of two small shafts of spruce wood are preserved as charcoal. One of these appears to be a shaft about 7 or 8 mm. in diameter; the other is considerably larger and perhaps not round in section. A curious biface of chert, Pl. *72*, 14, is four-pronged, or somewhat cruciform in shape, and slightly channeled longitudinally on both faces (Giddings, 1956b). The only bones identified from the old layer are eight burnt fragments of small animal bones.

The Denbigh Flint Culture

The people who first occupied Iyatayet site left behind an abundance of small flint implements and weapon edges but little else with which to reconstruct their culture. We learn almost as much from the things lacking in their site as from those collected and observed. The absence of house pits, or excavations of any kind, suggests that they did not spend the winter at Iyatayet. If they did, their winter dwellings were erected on the surface, or, at best, no deeper than sod. The absence of cache pits further removes the oldest Denbigh people from consideration with most of the later people who lived in the site or vicinity. The absence of notched stones, lamps, mortars, and pottery—all prevalent in later periods—suggests that they did not fish extensively with nets, illuminate their dwellings with seal oil, or cook meals in containers placed directly over a flame or on coals. The absence of large woodworking tools such as the heads of splitting adzes—or the blades of adzes of any kind, for that matter—makes it seem unlikely that they worked driftwood in quantity as did their successors at the site.

Their most prominent working tools were burins, burin spall artifacts, microblades, and flakeknives. The many burin spalls, evidently used as gravers, are most plausibly related to the engraving of hard organic material. The multiplicity of elements in the engraving art of recent Bering Strait people strongly suggests that the Denbigh Flint people widely employed decoration in the finishing of their antler or ivory artifacts. The continuity of burins to the present day, changed though they are from flint to slate to metal, implies a continuity also in the uses to which recent burins have been put—that is, grooving hard organic materials, especially ivory and antler, for making elongated objects such as arrow heads, harpoon heads, and awls. Evidence is incomplete as to whether or not walrus were hunted and ivory procured at Cape Denbigh, but broad end blades such as those illustrated (Pls. *71-a, 72,* 9) are of kinds recently used in the heads of thrusting harpoons for walrus and other large sea mammals. They are closely similar to those used in closed-socket, walrus-hunting harpoon heads of the Ipiutak culture.[1] Whether or not the old Denbigh people used ivory, they quite certainly fashioned caribou antler into a variety of handles, shafts, and fittings. Was Iyatayet a good caribou hunting site in Denbigh times? It could well have been. Caribou have seasonally visited the peninsula in recent times, and the House 6 excavation of the Early Nukleet period (p. 108) furnishes strong evidence that caribou were sought after locally about a thousand years ago.

Flakeknives, along with many used flakes, some of which may be assigned through evidence of frequent use to the category of side scraper, would have furnished a variety of whittling, piercing, and scraping tools useful in finishing the angular blanks of antler produced by burins and the wooden shafts of various kinds into which these antler and accompanying stone pieces were most likely fitted. The scarcity of drills makes it seem unlikely that extensive drilling of holes was done—either gauged or meeting from two surfaces, as is characteristic of recent Eskimo joining and fitting. We might guess, instead, that perforations in the harder materials were made more often by grooving with burins than by drilling. End scrapers are small, some remarkably so, and these seem scarcely adequate for the skin-scraping activities with which large end scrapers have been often associated in many recent Eskimo sites.

Women's activities, as we know them from Eskimo sites, are hardly recognizable in this Denbigh Flint layer. Neither *ulus* nor large scrapers of fixed form are recognized. A few of the larger flint bifaces may have been skinning knives, but, if so, they are both scarce and atypical by recent standards. Baskets of birch bark may have been fashioned by women, and the presence of fire-cracked pebbles about Denbigh hearths strongly indicates stone boiling in baskets.

None of the large bifaced side blades known from the Ipiutak site to have been inset as knives, hatchet-hafted choppers, swords, and the like were found in the Denbigh Flint layer at Iyatayet, though they begin to appear

---

[1] A recent analysis of the Ipiutak culture collection from Cape Krusenstern by Douglas Anderson (n. d., pp. 124–26), together with a close study of the uses to which were put the various styles of hunting equipment, brings out the probability that end-bladed harpoon heads were used by the Ipiutakers at Point Hope only for taking walrus.

in the very latest Denbigh hearths at Cape Krusenstern. Microblades are prominent in every section of the old layer, indicating that these implements were produced in quantity and used by all of the campers at the site in Denbigh times. We lack adequate ethnographic explanation for projection of microblades. Neither Eskimos nor other circumpolar people have used them regularly in modern times. While we know that in Asia they were inset as side blades in arrowheads, spear points, and daggers during the Siberian Neolithic period (for illustrations, see Michael, 1958, Figs. 17, 27, 56, 57; Okladnikov, 1959, Pl. 5; and other sources), we have only scant evidence of this practice at Cape Denbigh. On the other hand, most microblades of adequate size and regularity were put to use as cutting edges of one kind or another. These razor-like edges could have had many purposes, but one of the most obvious would have been for skin working and sewing. Some of the microblades bear small notches that suggest the cutting of sinew. Others are worn along one edge as though by the persistent cutting of a material not hard enough to spoil the edge, yet resistant enough to cause occasional small nicks. In the absence of other tools more suitable for the cutting of skin, it seems probable that microblades were a regular part of skin-working equipment.

Microblades may also have been associated with the making of excellent babiche-strung snowshoes of the recent northern Athapascan variety. It is generally assumed that life in the soft snow of the interior of Alaska and northern Canada would have been possible only after adequate snowshoes of this or an equivalent type were available. For those skilled individuals among the Athapascans who still shave babiche from deer hide, this is a meticulous undertaking. A razor-like steel edge is essential. Before steel, what could better have cut babiche than a microblade? This is not to suggest that all microblade cultures in the American Arctic had to do with the production of babiche, but that microblades would have furnished an ideal stimulus toward the invention or continuance of making babiche where this material served an important purpose, as in the fashioning of snowshoes.

In the absence of animal bones, excepting one or two fragments showing that seals were procured, we can only project forms of cutting-edge tools toward later forms in the same region or toward earlier or later ones at a considerable distance. The probable harpoon blades, as previously noted, closely resemble those of walrus-hunting harpoons of Ipiutak style and bring with them a strong implication of boating skill while hunting among masses of floating ice. Many of the side blades may have been fitted into harpoon heads of another kind well known from Ipiutak sites, but of this we have no direct evidence, as they could also have been inset in arrowheads.

Arrow points imply, first, the hunting of caribou or whatever other kind of herd animals may possibly have been on the Denbigh scene and, only secondarily, the hunting of small game. The abundance of side blades, and their disproportion to all other flints, strongly suggests that Iyatayet was primarily a caribou-hunting campsite during the time when it was customarily occupied.

All too few large spear points were recovered. Yet the resemblance of those few to bifaced points made by early hunters of the Great Plains and Rocky Mountain regions offers a striking contrast to the microblade and burin technology that is more easily associated with early developments of the Old World. The fluted point and gravers, in particular, form a combination most likely to be of American origin. While the dating of the Denbigh Flint complex is almost certainly later than that of any of the fluted point sites of the western states, we see here evidence of the persistence and diffusion of a combination much earlier conjoined.

The nature of the stone used by the makers of the Denbigh flints offers important evidence open to more than one interpretation. By far the greater number of the flints are of materials not known to be present in the vicinity of Cape Denbigh. As far as we now know, the nearest obsidian comes from the Koyukuk River, where it occurs in the form of pebbles washed from some unknown source in the neighboring mountains. The other materials, translucent chalcedony and chert, also occur in deposits of the Brooks Range. The only local materials used by the Flint complex people at Iyatayet were silicified slate and basalt, but in all cases these were treated by grinding and polishing, as was done later by Norton people. None of the other materials were ground (excepting the basal edges of some projectile points), nor have artifacts like these been found in any of the other Denbigh Flint complex sites of the coast north from Cape Prince of Wales around Kotzebue Sound. This suggests that the Denbigh people at Iyatayet resorted to the inferior materials only when the better ones were not available, making them into ground burins because they were not suitable for the making of regular burins shaped entirely by flaking.

The Denbigh Flint complex may be summarized speculatively, then, as representing people who visited Iyatayet only seasonally for sealing and caribou hunting, bringing with them the raw flints needed for temporary manufactures, foregoing the heavy work that one might expect around more permanent camps, and moving into the forest for the winter season. Skilled enough at boating to procure seal in quantity and to live along a very wide stretch of the seacoast of western Alaska, they may also have possessed the excellent snowshoes without which life in the dry, wind-free forests would be unthinkable, and they probably concentrated on caribou as a principal food source throughout most of the year. As to whether or not they were Eskimos, we can answer only by defining "Eskimo" more closely than we are accustomed to do. There is scarcely a Denbigh object in the same form used by Eskimos of Thule or later cultures, yet some continuites into the Ipiutak period of about 2000 years ago are quite direct. Regardless of how we designate them, these Denbigh people appear to be in a direct line of cultural continuity with Eskimos.

Technically, the Denbigh Flint complex is more closely related to the European Paleolithic (in burin techniques and variety, certain scrapers, and miscellaneous rare forms), the Mesolithic of Europe, and the early "Neolithic" of Siberia (in microblade industry and inset side-blading) than to early temperate America; yet fluted and diagonally flaked points and expert bifacing of small flints are old in America. The complex was unique in the world, however, in the meticulous skill employed in flint flaking, and probably in the origination of the burin spall artifact, the most minuscule of the widely used flint implements.

V. TIME AND CHANGE AT BERING STRAIT

The succession of dwellers at Cape Denbigh includes none who were foreign to the locality—no casual visitors from Asia or another part of America—for more recent excavations in neighboring parts of Alaska have revealed close relationships with the three basic kinds of culture at Cape Denbigh while at the same time furnishing some knowledge of the apparent gaps between. The work carried on under my direction for Brown University since 1956 will be dealt with fully in a later publication. Meanwhile, a brief treatment can be made of other sites in their relationship to Cape Denbigh.

Dating the Denbigh Sequence

The dating of the sites at Cape Denbigh rests upon several kinds of evidence. Cultural cross-dating based upon the comparison of styles between types of artifacts allows us to draw with confidence upon the tree-ring chronology of the Kobuk River sites (Giddings, 1952, pp. 105–10) for placing the Nukleet periods in time (p. 136). Nukleet, and perhaps Iyatayet (House 6), appear to have been occupied by direct ancestors of modern Eskimos a few decades, or a century or two, before 1250 A. D., and to have been finally abandoned between 1600 and 1700 A. D. Earlier than that, Iyatayet North site had been occupied by Norton people whose culture was closely like that of Near Ipiutak of Point Hope. Ipiutak culture is not indicated at Iyatayet; hence we may entertain the thought that the site was not attractive to Ipiutak people (possibly because it was isolated from the open sea where walrus could be taken) and that the second cultural hiatus at the site corresponds to the time of Ipiutak culture. Since Ipiutak culture has recently been shown to have flourished as early at least as 300 A. D. (Rainey and Ralph, 1959, p. 370), it seems likely that Norton culture had already merged with the new culture in the region of Seward Peninsula.

The radiocarbon dates for Norton culture at Iyatayet are as follows:

C–506[1] Charred wood from Cut PA. (The material   1460 ± 200 B. P.   492 A. D.
         submitted is from the upper Norton levels,
         but the date appears to be too late.)

---

[1] Radiocarbon dates beginning with "C" originate at the University of Chicago Laboratory and are reported by Johnson (1951) and Libby (1955); those beginning with "P" originate at the University of Pennsylvania Laboratory, as reported by Rainey and Ralph (1959); and the date preceded by "W" originates at the Washington, D. C. Laboratory of the U. S. Geological Survey, as reported by Rubin and Suess (1956).

244

C–562	Solid charcoal from a construction pole in House 7. (This also appears late as compared with identically preserved charcoal from the same location in:)	2016 ± 250 B. P.	16 B. C.
P–13	Three samples of charcoal from baseline timbers in House 7—same row as in C–562.	2420 ± 270 B. P.	463 B. C.
		2530 ± 330 B. P.	573 B. C.
		2130 ± 260 B. P.	173 B. C.
	Average:	2360 ± 170 B. P.	403 B. C.
	One CO_2 determination:	2213 ± 110 B. P.	255 B. C.

(This range of dates appears to accord best with the archeological sequence now developing in western Alaska.)

The Norton culture appears to have been differentiated from its parent Choris culture by 400 B. C. and to have continued until shortly after the beginning of the Christian era.

Dates for soil and peat forming at Iyatayet between the Denbigh Flint deposit and the first Norton deposit (see also p. 198) are the following:

P–104	Highest of the peat layer samples in Cut Z–5B. Three counting runs.	3240 ± 280 B. P.	1283 B. C.
		2730 ± 300 B. P.	773 B. C.
		3030 ± 280 B. P.	1073 B. C.
	Average:	3000 ± 170 B. P.	1043 B. C.
P–108	Lower in the peat layer of the preceding sample (P–104).	2880 ± 280 B. P.	923 B. C.
		3280 ± 300 B. P.	1323 B. C.
	Average:	3080 ± 210 B. P.	1123 B. C.
P–105	Detached peaty sample, lower than above, but well above Denbigh Flint level.	4040 ± 280 B. P.	2083 B. C.

The formation of the Denbigh Flint layer and its solifluction into folds must have taken place before the above dates; hence some of the following dates for the Denbigh Flint complex in place appear to be erroneous:

C–792	Charcoal flecks in mud, Cut Z–5B	3477 ± 310 B. P.	1525 B. C.
		3541 ± 315 B. P.	1589 B. C.
	Average:	3509 ± 230 B. P.	1557 B. C.
C–793	Charcoal, charred twigs, and mud, Cut R	4253 ± 290 B. P.	2301 B. C.
		5063 ± 340 B. P.	3111 B. C.

(As the second run was a test of the first after washing in acid, it would seem the more reliable date of the two, as I have pointed out before [Giddings, 1955]).

P–103	Charcoal, charred twigs, and mud, Cut Z–5D —same fireplace as in C–792.	3430 ± 280 B. P.	1473 B. C.
		3520 ± 290 B. P.	1563 B. C.
	Average:	3480 ± 200 B. P.	1523 B. C.

P–102 Another part of same sample as C–793.   3290 ± 290 B. P.   1333 B. C.
                                               3320 ± 200 B. P.   1363 B. C.

                          Average: 3310 ± 200 B. P.   1353 B. C.

W–298 Cut Z–5A; two small pillboxes of charcoal
      and earth from layer continuous with that
      from which came samples C–792 and P–103.
      A CO_2 determination: 3974 ± 600 B. P.   2019 B. C

The samples from the Denbigh Flint complex layer in place thus offer interesting contradictions both among themselves and with the overlying soils. The gas date for W-298 appears to cancel out samples C-792 and P-103, of the same kind of material only a few inches apart. Of the two Cut R runs by two laboratories of a single sample, I am inclined to accept the Chicago one as the more plausible, in view of all other radiocarbon samples, and to favor it as in better accord with the archeology. A radiocarbon date of 5993 ± 280 B. P., 4042 B. C., for a sample (C-560) of willows, possibly with charcoal, from deep in a cave at Trail Creek in levels where Denbigh-like microblades occurred, suggests another date for the Denbigh Flint complex. I look forward to reaching a more confining series of dates for the complex on the beach ridges of Kotzebue Sound and the stratified sites of the interior. Before this goal is reached, however, there seems to be unusual merit in presenting the views expressed by David M. Hopkins in 1958 after a careful consideration of the facts concerning the Denbigh Flint complex. The following excerpt is from a letter to me from Dr. Hopkins dated May 19, 1958:

I have reviewed all of our information bearing on the age of the Denbigh Flint Complex as objectively as possible in an effort to ascertain the degree of conflict, if any, between the geological evidence and the radiocarbon dating. The reappraisal leads me to the conclusion that the radiocarbon data indicates an age between 4,500 and 5,000 years. The geological and paleobotanical data now available indicate an age younger than 8,000 and older than 4,200 years; these data do not conflict with an assumed age of 4,500 to 5,000 years. I do not, of course, have an independent opinion concerning the archaeological evidence, but the fact that honest and well-informed people can disagree as to its significance seems to me to indicate that the question of age cannot be settled on the basis of the archaeological relationships alone.

During the five years that have elapsed since we wrote "Geological Background of the Iyatayet archaeological site" much new information has become available. My present understanding of the late Wisconsin and post-Wisconsin history of Seward Peninsula is summarized in the enclosed sheet, "Paleo-ecology of Seward Peninsula during the last 13,000 years".[1] I feel that the history developed for Seward Peninsula is applicable to coastal areas from the Yukon to Point Barrow, but this history differs in important respects from the climatic and vegetational history recorded in many other parts of the world.

---
[1] A detailed chart, not here reproduced.

Two factors appear to control the climates of coastal regions in northwestern Alaska: world-wide changes in the total heat received at the surface; and local changes in the position and duration of open water on Bering and Chukchi Sea. Major glaciations and refrigerations appear to be recorded on Seward Peninsula synchronously with those recorded in other parts of the world, and as far as one can tell, the major interglacial intervals on Seward Peninsula are also synchronized with those of other parts of the world. However, when world climates are fluctuating only within narrow limits due to extra-terrestrial factors, the local climate of the Bering-Chukchi area apparently can be profoundly affected by small changes in sea level. A world-wide lowering or raising of sea level by a few tens of feet can shift the strand line tens of miles across the flat, shallow bottom of Bering and Chukchi Sea and can cover or expose extremely large "coastal plain" areas. Expansion of the sea brings the strand line closer to present coast and with it brings more summer fog, low cloudiness, and drizzle; a lowering of sea level moves the strand line seaward and, given little change in the extra-terrestrial heat flux, can produce much warmer summers at points formerly on the shore. Effects of these sorts should be felt most strongly in places on the present coast, but they seem to be recorded in post-Wisconsin time as far inland as central Seward Peninsula.

As the "Paleoecology" chart shows, the climate of Seward Peninsula seems to have been extremely severe and governed by the world-wide refrigeration during late Wisconsin times 13,000 years ago. During the interval from 10,000 to 8,000 years ago, world climates though still cool had warmed enough to permit the presence of a broad expanse of land south of Seward Peninsula to play a dominant role; during this interval warm summers and deep thaw permitted an extension of forest west of its present limits and the development of soil profiles on well-drained sites. It was to this interval of warm summers that I originally ascribed the podsol beneath the Denbigh layer.

Unfortunately, the succeeding interval from 8,000 to 4,000 years was and still is a complete hiatus as far as my knowledge of the climate of the Bering Sea region is concerned—unless the Iyatayet site itself helps to fill this gap. We do know that in other parts of the world glaciers readvanced significantly about 7,000 or 8,000 years ago and then disappeared as world climates warmed to produce the thermal maximum during the period from about 6,000 to 4,000 years ago. Sea level probably stood at 50 or 60 feet below its present position during the Cochrane advance, and then rose rapidly to its present position throughout the last 5,000 years.

I would speculate that the Cochrane or Finiglacial readvance, 7,000 or 8,000 years ago, might be reflected by a brief period of cool summers on Seward Peninsula, that warm summers might resume until sea level lay within 10 or 20 feet of its present position, and that once sea level stood near its present position the climate of Seward Peninsula and the Bering Sea region would once again be controlled by extraterrestrial factors affecting the whole world. Presumably the sea-level fluctuations were so small that changes in the position of the strand line had no appreciable effect on summer climates.

With this preamble out of the way, I will now set down in 1–2–3 fashion the lines of non-archaeological evidence that bear on the age of the Denbigh Flint Complex:

I. RADIOCARBON DATES

(1) A specimen from the lower peat at Iyatayet gave a date of [4,040 ± 280] years. Other dates from higher in the sequence make it probable that this date is approximately correct. Using the statistical error, it is possible that the peat is

as young as 3,800 years. The Denbigh Flint culture therefore must be older than 3,800 years.

(2) Radiocarbon specimen C–792 gives ages of 3,541 and 3,477 for Denbigh Flint Complex. These dates are inconsistent with the age of the lower peat and also are reported to have been run during a period of abnormally high background. These dates must be disregarded.

(3) Radiocarbon specimen C–793 gives ages of 4,253 ± 290 and 5,063 ± 340 for the Denbigh Flint Complex. [William] Benninghoff estimates that about 5% of the specimen consisted of fresh rootlets, but it is entirely possible that this eye estimate is in error as much as 100% and that the true degree of contamination is as much as 10%. A minimum age for the sample can be obtained by subtracting the statistical error from the lower date and adding the error that would be introduced if 5% of the specimen were fresh roots: this procedure leads to a date of about 4,250 years. A maximum age for the sample can be obtained by adding the statistical error to the older date and adding the error that would be introduced if 10% of the specimen were fresh roots: this procedure leads to a date of 6,200 years.

(4) Radiocarbon specimen W–298, according to my understanding, consisted of bits of charcoal intimately mingled with the flints. I can't understand how there could be any significant contamination by material appreciably younger than the flints. However, the specimen was tiny, and perhaps the counting error was grossly underestimated. The reported age is 3,974 ± 600 years. If the counting error were actually 1,000 years, the true age might be as much as 5,000 years, but it could hardly be any greater.

Conclusions: Taken together, the results of the radiocarbon dating seem to indicate that the age of the Denbigh Flint Culture is more than 4,200 years and less than 5,000 years.

II. SEA LEVEL

(1) Various recently published studies indicate that sea level stood from 120 to 50 feet below its present position during the interval from 9,000 to 6,000 years ago; this means that the shoreline would have been several tens of miles away from Iyatayet during this period.

(2) Sea level stood within 10 feet above or below its present position during most of the intervals from 6,000 to 4,000 years ago; this means that the shoreline would have been practically in its present position at Iyatayet during this period.

(3) The valley fill underlying the Iyatayet site was undoubtedly deposited when sea level was lower and the shoreline further away than at present.

(4) The fill may or may not have been dissected to form a terrace when the Denbigh people occupied the site; however, additional erosion of the terrace edge has taken place since occupation began, for the Denbigh layer seems to end abruptly at the edge of the terrace (perhaps continued excavation along the edge of the terrace would modify this conclusion?).

(5) The Denbigh Flint Complex includes a few objects that seem to represent harpoon blades, suggesting that sea-mammal hunting played at least a minor role in the activities of the people of the Denbigh Flint Complex.

(6) Iyatayet is an attractive site for a group of people wishing to fish and hunt through the ice; however, if sea level were lower and Norton Sound were a flat tundra plain, Iyatayet would also be an attractive site for a group of people wishing a view out over an adjoining caribou range.

248

Conclusions: Evidence as to the position of sea level during occupation by the people of the Denbigh Flint Complex is conflicting and inconclusive. The observations available at present permit either the interpretation that sea level was low, the terrace undissected, and the Denbigh Flint Complex people there for caribou hunting or the interpretation that sea level was high, the terrace incompletely dissected, and the Denbigh Flint Complex people there for fishing and sealing.

III. CLIMATE AND VEGETATION

(1) The Denbigh Flint Complex is underlain by a thin but intensely developed podzol. The podzol could develop only if the surface were stable, not subject to much frost action, and not a site on which active deposition was taking place.

(2) The podzol undoubtedly required a long time to develop—perhaps 1,000 years.

(3) Podzols are common in well-drained, coarse soils in interior Alaska. Conspicuous ones are found along the Denali highway near altitude timberline, and I have also seen them at lower altitudes in the Copper River Basin.

(4) Podzols have not been reported from tundra regions; along the Denali highway, well-drained coarse soils well above timberline have a subarctic brown soil, and similar soils are reported from Point Barrow, Nome, and the hillslopes above Iyatayet. (The red-brown soils are also common within forested regions).

(5) Sparse pollen[1] from one of the hearths in the Denbigh layer suggests a treeless tundra vegetation. Lack of any spruce or alder pollen suggests that there were no spruce or alder within many miles.

(6) More abundant pollen from the overlying peat layers suggests a vegetation similar to the present vegetation near Iyatayet.

(7) The podzol may have been no longer forming when the Denbigh Flint Complex people camped at Iyatayet.

(8) After occupation of Iyatayet by the people of the Denbigh Flint Complex, silt was deposited on the surface of the terrace and then solifluction lobes developed, folding the culture layer.

Conclusions: The people of the Denbigh Flint Complex seem to have occupied Iyatayet at the moment of transition from a relatively mild, frost-free climate to a much more severe climate in which frost action was intense and frozen ground present at shallow depth. This moment could have occurred no longer ago than 8,000 years, and it could have been as recent as 4,500 years ago.

IV. TIME REQUIRED FOR GEOLOGIC PROCESSES

(1) The terrace at Iyatayet presumably supported some sort of vegetation cover during occupation. The wood in the hearth (Labrador tea, blueberry, crowberry) and the pollen (fireweed, lycopodium, sphagnum) suggest the possibility of a thin, dry, tough mat of heaths and weeds such as one finds today on gravel and rubble on Seward Peninsula.

(2) The vegetation mat has now disappeared, presumably shortly after burial by sterile silt. I have no absolute figures on rates of decay, but I would estimate that at least 100 years would be required to remove all traces of a thin, buried turf.

(3) The Denbigh Flint Complex is covered by a foot or two of sterile silt, evidently water transported. This mantle of silt could be added within a single year under favorable circumstances but is more likely to have been added slowly over a

---

[1] These and other botanical determinations were made by Dr. William Benninghoff.

period of several decades. Presumably the turf mat rotted out while and after the silt accumulated.

(4) After the silt was deposited, the Denbigh Flint layer was folded as a result of being involved in the movement of a group of solifluction lobes. Interruptions in the continuity of the flint layer upslope from the folds are at least 8 feet wide. Solifluction lobes probably don't move faster than an inch per year, and therefore a minimum of 96 years seems to be required for the formation of the folds and the interruptions. Several hundred years would seem a more reasonable figure.

(5) The lower peat layer appears to represent the confining cover at the top of the solifluction lobe; however, it contains a pollen suggestive of the present vegetation, and different from the vegetation that I would expect in a region where solifluction lobes were active. Assuming that several centuries are required to permit the vegetation to readjust to a minor climatic change, it seems likely that the radiocarbon date on the lower peat layer is several hundred years younger than the last movement of the solifluction lobe.

Conclusions: A span of 500 to 1,000 years seems to be required to provide sufficient time for the recorded events that separate the Denbigh Flint Complex from the lower peat layer. The interval between these two layers may be much greater than 1,000 years, but it doesn't have to be.

These lines of reasoning seem to add up as follows: the radiocarbon evidence indicates an age between 4,200 and 5,000 years; the paleoclimatic evidence permits an age no greater than 8,000 years; and consideration of the time required for geologic processes permits an age no younger that 4,500 years. It appears to me that the Denbigh Flint Complex at Iyatayet must be between 4,500 and 5,000 years old.

Relation to Other Areas

A chart, Table 16, has been drawn up, and a map provided (Fig. 60), to show the location of pertinent sites in Alaska and neighboring regions together with the cultural phases that they represent. The chronology is estimated from the available radiocarbon and dendrochronological dates and the relative dating afforded by obsidian hydration measures, stratigraphy, the weathering of flints, and other observations. Most of the recent progress has been made from Cape Prince of Wales around the shores of Kotzebue Sound to Cape Krusenstern. Still farther north are reported the excellent sequences of pre-Ipiutak to modern cultures at Point Hope, and Birnirk to modern at Point Barrow.

Cape Prince of Wales

Sites in and very near Cape Prince of Wales village carry the archeological record from modern times back to a well-defined Thule or Western Thule period and to late Birnirk or transitional levels (Collins, 1937a, 1940; Jenness, 1928) and to a small mound containing Birnirk burials (Collins, 1937a, Fig. 58). Little has been published on these excavations, however, and we shall draw mainly upon the earlier manifestations in the Wales vicinity.

First, however, it is my impression, from examining photographs and a series of drawings which Dr. Collins kindly showed to me and from a remark concerning the presence of pictographic art in the Thule levels at Wales (Collins, 1937, p. 366), that the form of culture called "Thule" here is closely paralleled in house remains of what we call "Western Thule," excavated between 1956 and 1961 at Cape Krusenstern. With respect to time and the resemblance of many basic artifacts between these areas, the Western Thule might be extended to encompass, as well, the Nukleet I cultural phase at Cape Denbigh. The later Nukleet phases do not as closely resemble those of their contemporary Chukchi Sea manifestations of Old Kotzebue, Ekseavik, Intermediate Kotzebue, and late Cape Krusenstern, however.

Between 12 and 20 miles north around the coast from Wales village we located and partly excavated several sites that fall culturally within the Norton category, although the time may overlap that of Choris to the east and some of Old Bering Sea to the west across Bering Strait. The latest manifestation lies on an old channel called Singauruk, between Lopp Lagoon and the sea. It appears to be the part of a single house floor, the profile of which was exposed in an eroding sand bank, and therefore representative of a single phase of culture. From it came an Old Bering Sea whaling harpoon head and a few other organic pieces suggesting Old Bering Sea culture and stone work mainly like that of Norton culture. Similar but older deposits also occur along Singauruk channel where earlier beaches are being washed out by tidal currents. The crossties in stone work are with Norton or Choris cultures rather than with Ipiutak or the St. Lawrence Island phases. On what appears to be the beach crest representing highest sea level in this region, we found one pure hearth area and another camping place of the Denbigh Flint complex, as well as a less localized, mixed site where Denbigh flints occurred with Choris-like stone and pottery inclusions. Elsewhere on the same beach, windblown areas disclosed the leavings of only Choris or Norton people.

Wales to Cape Espenberg

All of the beaches, old and recent, between Wales and Cape Espenberg are composed of sand. Dunes continue to form on the recent ones, while the older are firmly held, as a rule, by a carpet of thick, swampy sod. All are wider across the crest and farther apart than are the gravel beaches farther north. Subject as they are to erosion while still near the sea, these

Table 16. CHART SHOWING LOCATION OF SITES IN AL◢

	Asia		Cook Inlet	Aleutians	Cape Denbigh	Cape Prince of Wales	Cape Espenberg	Choris Peninsula	Trai
	Interior	Coast							
	Many tribes	Chukchi-Eskimo	Atha-pascan	Aleut	Eskimo Nukleet	Eskimo	Eskimo	Eskimo	Esk
1000		Punuk				Western Thule Birnirk			We Thı
			Kache-mak Bay III						
	Metal	Old Ber-ing Sea							Ipiı
A.D. B.C.	Ages	Okvik	Kache-mak Bay II			Singauruk II	Flint Stations		
						Singauruk I	Norton-Choris		
					Norton	Kugzruk		Choris	Laı dia nalı flaı poiı
1000			Kache-mak Bay I						
	Kitoi								
2000	Serovo								
3000	Isakovo			Microblades (?)	Denbigh Flint Complex	Denbigh Flint Complex	Denbigh Flint Complex	Denbigh Flint Complex	Deı Fliı Coı
4000									Miı blaı andı
Much older									

Paleo- to Neo-Aleutian physique and culture

252

CULTURAL PHASES OF THE ARCTIC.

pe astern	Battle Rock	Point Hope	Onion Portage	Other Kobuk	Central Brooks Range	Engigstciak	Dismal Lake	Igloolik	Greenland (Many sites)
							Canada		Greenland
imo	Eskimo	Eskimo	Eskimo	Eskimo	Eskimo (Indian?)	Eskimo (Indian?)	Eskimo (Indian?)	Eskimo	Eskimo
tern le irk	Western Thule	Western Thule						Thule	Thule
			Upper Middle		Undated sites and cultural phases	Long, undated sequence, not yet clearly isolated by stratigraphy			
tak r tak	Ipiutak Near Ipiutak	Ipiutak Near Ipiutak						Dorset	Dorset
ton	Battle Rock		Lower Middle						
ris									Sarqaq
l ek- ris			(Choris?)					(Sarqaq?) pre-Dorset	
aling			Old Hearth	Little Noatak			Dismal II		Inde-pendence I
bigh t nplex	Denbigh Flint Complex		Frozen In 1961		Several "small tool" sites				
ver ch sades				Kiana Bench	Undated sites and cultural phases		Dismal I?		
sades					Chemi-cally changed flints	Chemi-cally changed flints?			

253

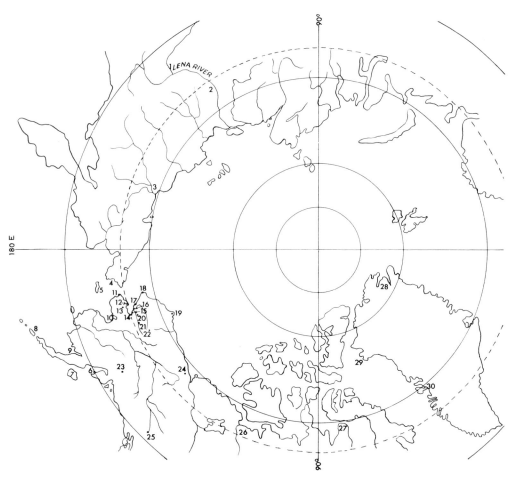

Fig. 60. Map showing site locations.

Asia

1. Lena River, Kullata site.
2. Lena River, Uolba site.
3. Kolyma River sites.
4. Coastal sites, East Cape to Indian Point.
5. Coastal sites, St. Lawrence Island.

Alaska

6. Cook Inlet sites.
7. Kodiak Island, Uyak site.
8. Aleutian Islands, Chaluka site.
9. Bristol Bay sites.
10. Cape Denbigh sites.
11. Cape Prince of Wales sites.
12. Cape Espenberg sites.
13. Trail Creek caves.
14. Choris sites.
15. Kotzebue and Little Noatak sites.
16. Cape Krusenstern sites.

17. Battle Rock site.
18. Point Hope sites.
19. Point Barrow sites.
20. Kobuk River, Kiana sites.
21. Kobuk River, Onion Portage site.
22. Brooks Range, Anaktuvuk Pass sites.
23. Susitna River sites.

Canada

24. Firth River, Engigstciak sites.
25. Southern Yukon Territory, Kluane Lake sites.
26. Coppermine River, Dismal Lake sites.
27. Melville Peninsula, Igloolik sites.

Greenland

28. Independence Fjord sites.
29. Thule sites.
30. Disko Bay sites.

sand beaches appear to have attracted fewer permanent residents than did those of gravel during nearly all of the earlier periods.

The sequence of beaches at Cape Espenberg is a mile and a half across and fifteen miles long. Because the deposits there were originally wind-driven, it is practically impossible to find signs of ancient dwellings where the sod cover is now intact. Our collecting was thus confined to the surface. We obtained enough information, nevertheless, to show that materials of the Denbigh Flint complex were present only on the oldest beaches while those of Choris or Norton culture were distributed along a prominent beach about two-thirds of the distance from the sea across the series of beaches. Our search at Cape Espenberg was nearly limited, however, to the older beaches, and it is presumed that the later ones will give equally good results when they are as thoroughly explored.

Trail Creek Caves

Several fissures and small caves in limestone hillside deposits, inland from Deering, were excavated by Helge Larsen (1951, 1953) in 1949 and 1950. Several phases of culture were indicated. In the lowest level was a microblade phase, presumably an aspect of Denbigh Flint complex. Near some microblades were examples of longitudinally grooved arrowheads, presumably for side-blading with microblades. In middle deposits were parallel-flaked spear points, burin facets on broken examples of these, and other objects probably of Choris and "pre-Choris beach" affinity. Ipiutak forms were near or at the top of deposits, and some quite recent objects were found on the top level of some caves. Larsen is preparing a full report on these important excavations.

Choris Peninsula

The old village for which Choris culture is named, and the intermediate archeology between that village and the present sea on Choris Peninsula, have been described in some detail (Giddings, 1957b). The oldest beaches remaining intact at Choris Peninsula seem to be those of Choris culture times, for microblades presumed to be those of the Denbigh Flint complex are found in the area only high above the present sea shore on the rim of a somewhat terraced hillside. Excavations at Choris brought to light house pits of the old Choris culture, tent and camp sites of a later phase of Choris culture two beaches forward of the old village, and, still farther toward the sea, chipping places and hearths probably of Norton culture, followed by a few house pits and caches of ages later than western Thule.

Kotzebue

Earlier excavations in and near the town of Kotzebue, on the second or third beach crest beyond the current one on the south shore of Hotham Inlet, exposed the remains of houses and villages dating, by dendro-chronological means, from before 1400 to 1550 A. D. and culturally typed as Old Kotzebue and Intermediate Kotzebue.

Shesualek

On the north side of Hotham Inlet at the white-whaling camp of Shesualek, several houses of Western Thule culture were identified on one of the earliest beaches to form at that peninsula of sand and gravel. Two house excavations at this site crosstie very closely with Western Thule excavations at Cape Krusenstern.

Cape Krusenstern

A succession of more than 100 gravel beaches at Cape Krusenstern offers a remarkable sequence of cultural features extending from the present day back through the full time span of Denbigh Flint complex and, on a neigh-boring hillside, to even earlier cultural manifestations. This site has been described or referred to in preliminary articles (Giddings, 1960a, b, c, 1961, 1962; Moore, 1960). The beach crests vary no more than 1½ meters in height above sea level, and the highest crest is about 3 meters above present sea level. Taking into consideration several unconformities representing probable changes in ocean current direction, we recognized 114 beach crests in this series. The cultural sequence is roughly as follows:

The current ocean front beach is the location of recent camps, burials, and pit houses. Beyond this beach on the successively older ones are found signs of human habitation or casual camping back to the lagoon which represents, presumably, the first beaches to form after sea level reached its greatest post glacial height, perhaps 6000 or 7000 years ago. Sites of Western Thule culture dating from, perhaps, 800 to 1200 A. D. are found on beaches 9 to 19, while the Ipiutak culture appears in its developed form on beaches 29 to 35, in a range of dating probably from 100 B. C. to 600 A. D. Small campsites of the Norton, Choris, and a pre-Choris phase of culture are found between beaches 35 and 50. This particular pre-Choris phase is known only at Cape Krusenstern at this time of writing. It seems to represent occasional hunters of whales who carried on some of the techniques of Denbigh Flint complex, although they made no microblades and few burins.

On beach 53 is found a village of five deep, large, half-underground house foundations in a compact village and, near them, the remains of five summer lodges built on the surface of the ground. Whale bones and large flints that seem to be whaling harpoon blades indicate that the hunters of sea mammals who lived in this combination village were accomplished whalers after the manner of much later Eskimos. The dating of the Old Whaling village appears to be about 1800 B. C. on the basis of an incomplete series of radiocarbon dates.

Behind the Old Whaling beach, only a few hearths and chipping places have been located as far back as beach 78, which is the terminal one for the Denbigh Flint complex. Between beaches 78 and 102 were located many campsites of the Denbigh Flint complex, presumably existing for the hundreds of years indicated by the beach successions.

Even older sites are found at Cape Krusenstern, however. Across a wide lagoon from the inner edge of the beach ridge series lies an earlier shoreline, presumably the shoreline available to the people who were present while the ocean was still rising to its greatest height after the last glaciation. Behind it is the steep slope of a hill, or small mountain. On a lower bench of this limestone slope are found microblades and certain other artifacts of Denbigh-like form that suggest a continuity with sites of the beach ridge series. On a higher bench, or terrace, called Palisades, about 500 feet above sea level, we located two kinds of stone tools: one set (Palisades I) distinguished from the other by a much greater weathering—indeed, by a chemical change throughout the flinty stone. The objects so weathered are of cruder, percussion-flaked forms unlike others at the site. They include ax-like or chopper tools like those of early sites in Asia. The remaining flints are chemically unchanged, though somewhat patinated, and they include notched points of a kind not known as an important element of culture in Alaska until they were found here and at two or three other points in the far interior. This Palisades II material appears to date from a time slightly before sea level had reached its greatest height and preceding the appearance of the Denbigh Flint complex on the coast. The Palisades I flints, on the other hand, promise to be of great antiquity, although we have as yet no means by which they may be dated.

Battle Rock

The Battle Rock site a few miles north of Cape Krusenstern on the coast is a weathered limestone outcrop rounded over and bearing a thin sod on top, where several culture phases are represented, mainly in the form of burials. Stone-lined graves of Western Thule or related cultural affinity were preceded by surface or above-surface burials of Ipiutak culture, only the ivory, antler, and stone burial goods of which remain. A few artifacts of stone discovered on the surface or just under sod represent the Norton or Choris periods, though positive identification is not possible. Preceding

Ipiutak and presumably as early as Norton or Choris, on the strength of linear-stamped or cord-marked pottery, there was a culture which left the remains of a large, stone-lined, multiple burial. Though widely scattered by ground squirrels, this burial presented parts of more than one human skeleton—but no bones of a head—together with more than 300 antler projectile points and other artifacts and a few stone objects. This burial indicated for us a Battle Rock phase of culture not yet identified elsewhere. The styles of projectile points show a close relationship to Norton culture, but the large size of all the Battle Rock pieces and a new engraving style (Giddings, 1961, Fig. 12) indicate that the dating will prove to be earlier than Near Ipiutak at Point Hope. Microblades and cores of some phase of the Denbigh Flint complex were found scattered about the site and, in one or two places, well under the surface. This suggests that the Denbigh people visited Battle Rock for purposes other than those of burial. No earlier artifacts were identified.

Point Hope and Point Barrow

It is hard to explain why no remains earlier than Near Ipiutak have been identified from Battle Rock all the way around the north coast of Alaska to the Yukon Territory of Canada. Point Hope, the site of the original Ipiutak village, encompasses also a series of house and burial sites from those of the present day back through a Western Thule phase, a Birnirk phase, an Ipiutak, and a Near Ipiutak phase (Larsen and Rainey, 1948, pp. 162–68), now known to be earlier than that of Ipiutak proper. These are arranged in what appears to be a progressive time order from the earliest beaches forward to the present beaches. Point Barrow has failed to reveal cultures earlier than Birnirk, though the Birnirk, Western Thule, and recent periods are exceptionally well represented (Ford, 1959; Mason, 1930; Mathiassen, 1930, pp. 31–53).

Firth River

On the Firth River, which heads in Alaska and flows northward through the Yukon Territory to the Arctic Sea, R. S. MacNeish in 1954 first visited Engigstciak a few miles from the Arctic Sea. Returning three subsequent summers, he recovered a wide range of artifacts, most of which could be identified with objects of the coastal cultural phases of western Alaska. Some were felt to be distinctive, however, and of these, some were classed as early enough to be associated with extinct mammals. The British Mountain complex, first defined as containing crude, plano-convex scrapers and large "scraping planes" among other objects of unsophisticated workmanship, was said to be associated with extinct bison (MacNeish, 1956, p. 95) and possibly horse (MacNeish, 1959, p. 44).

Following the British Mountain phase, MacNeish saw a Flint Creek phase associated with buffalo (possibly extinct), caribou, hare, and Arctic birds, indicating that the climate had turned colder and wetter than at present. Still later came a New Mountain phase containing burins and microblades like those of the Denbigh Flint complex together with numbers of artifacts unassociated with known Denbigh sites of the west. MacNeish reported several cultural phases later than New Mountain in which were cord-marked and, later, stamped pottery of varieties known in the Kotzebue Sound region. Unfortunately, however, the earlier interpretations of geology and stratigraphy did not bear this out, and there now seems to be serious question about whether the stratigraphy can be trusted in any but possibly one part of the vast Engigstciak site (Mackay, Mathews, and MacNeish, 1961).

Field work was projected for 1962 under the direction of Gordon Lowther to check the stratigraphy of the one exceptional locality within the site and to find additional reliable stratigraphy if it existed. In this writer's opinion, the several cultural phases proposed for Engigstciak are very dubious as associations. It appears to me, for example, that the New Mountain phase contains some Denbigh artifacts and others definitely not Denbigh, though familiar in other well-known contexts in Alaska. Changes in the labelling of illustrated artifacts between the 1956 publication and that of 1959 further confound attempts to find order in published reports of the proposed Engigstciak phases. In view of the doubtful nature of the Engig- stciak stratigraphy and of the mixture of materials in the proposed cultural phases, I shall assume for the present only that the artifacts of Engig- stciak indicate a long time span through which people hunted at this locality. It is hoped that further excavations will establish firm associations and dating for the site.

Coppermine River

Somewhat farther inland from the Arctic Sea are described associations of artifacts at Dismal Lake and Kamut Lake, along the Coppermine River of central Canada. Unstratified though they are, they give the impression of marking two distinct periods of time (Harp, 1958). The presumably older association is that of relatively crude, large flake tools, end and side scrapers, and bifaced projectile points, including one notched point, of a cast suggesting most closely the work of far inland people such as those of central Alaska and the Mackenzie River drainage area. Another association resembles the Denbigh Flint complex in that it contains mainly small arti- facts including burins, burin spalls, microblades, and small bifaced projectile points. Harp sees this second combination as continuous with the Denbigh Flint complex to the west and the microlithic continuity eastward to Greenland and the Dorset area of Canada (*Ibid.,* pp. 246–47). As the Dismal II site containing the microlithic element was located 60 miles from the sea, Harp attributes to it a dual economy based upon inland as well as coastal hunting, and sees in this a part of a continuum stretching across Canada and Alaska.

Igloolik and Southampton Island

Still farther around the coast of continental Canada, Jørgen Meldgaard in 1954 and 1957 investigated a remarkable series of raised beaches in the Igloolik area of the Northwest Territories. Here, Thule culture sites were found on beaches only 3 to 8 meters above present sea level, while sites of the Dorset and pre-Dorset (Sarqaq?) cultures continued on up from 8 to 54 meters, the top of the plateau. Besides showing various differences within Dorset culture, this series of house floors disclosed that the pre-Dorset people existed here from about 2000 B. C. until considerably later and were replaced by people of Dorset culture by at least 700 B. C. (Meldgaard, 1960).

Many Thule sites are known throughout the central region and Greenland (Collins, 1950, 1951, 1956*b;* Holtved, 1944; Larsen, 1934, 1938; Lethbridge, 1939; Manning, 1956; Mathiassen, 1927), and the more easterly part of this range, at least, is shared with the earlier Dorset culture. Dorset culture sites, most of them undated, cover a large region overlapping in eastern Canada as far south as Newfoundland and in Greenland (Collins, 1950, 1956*a,* 1956*b,* 1958; Harp, 1951, 1953; Holtved, 1944; Knuth, 1954; Larsen and Meldgaard, 1958; Leechman, 1943; Lethbridge, 1939; Mathiassen, 1958; Rowley, 1940; Taylor, 1959; Wintemberg, 1939).

A Dorset culture site at Native Point, Southampton Island, in part at least 2000 years old, yielded a large number of backed blades and triangular microliths in addition to microblades. It seems not only to furnish a link between Dorset and Denbigh cultures but to anticipate Mesolithic-like stone industries not yet found elsewhere in America (Collins, 1956*b*).

Greenland and Atlantic

While some uncertainty exists about the spatial position of Sarqaq culture with respect to Dorset and other pre-Dorset phases in the east, there can be no doubt of Sarqaq as a distinct aspect of culture in West Greenland (Larsen and Meldgaard, 1958; Mathiassen, 1958; Meldgaard, 1952). Here it is known to date between at least 1000 B. C. and 500 B. C. A Sarqaq-like assemblage is known from North Knife River, Manitoba (Giddings,

1956*a*), but Sarqaq may not exist in northernmost Greenland, where Knuth has discovered an Independence I, a microblade and burin culture perhaps closer to the Denbigh Flint complex than to any other phase in the east, and an Independence II culture containing notched points, among other objects, that may prove to fit into the early Dorset classification. Independence I apparently dates from around 2000 B. C., and Independence II, from 1000 B. C. (Knuth, 1952, 1954, 1958). If the pre-Dorset people at Igloolik Peninsula are to be classed as Sarqaq, as Meldgaard has suggested (1960, pp. 72–75), this brings up the question of whether or not Independence I represents an earlier migration or drift to Greenland than that represented by the contemporary site at Igloolik.

Thus, moving from the Bering Strait region around the coast of Alaska and Canada to Greenland, one finds clear-cut evidence of a continuity of the Denbigh Flint complex—in a "small tool" horizon—the entire distance, though with a time lag of 1000 or 2000 years between sites of Denbigh Flint complex of western Alaska and Independence I in Greenland. Whether or not there proves to be a still earlier Greenland manifestation, the derivation of Independence I from a Denbigh-like base is clear. As I interpret the data, a Sarqaq-like cast of culture in the east resembles the Choris and pre-Choris casts in the west enough to suggest a second and following continuity across the Arctic. This shows up in the forms of several artifacts (especially in the resemblance of some organic artifacts in both Choris and Sarqaq cultures to artifacts of recent Eskimos) and in a few other respects. On the other hand, it would be difficult for the Dorset phases proper to be derived directly out of the west, and I prefer to see all of Dorset culture as an eastern amalgam tracing its line of descent directly back to the Independence I associations and changing forward through time by the selective addition of elements from various culture phases while the people of Dorset culture occupy essentially one area.

Bristol Bay

The lines of continuity southward from Cape Denbigh are more difficult to follow at this stage of our knowledge than are those just considered. Wendell Oswalt (1952), at Hooper Bay, found only a limited number of recent centuries represented in a mound that he tested, and James VanStone (1957) located no early sites on Nunivak Island.

The next cultural sequence of importance south of Cape Denbigh is the one in Bristol Bay where Larsen (1950) discovered a Platinum phase of culture related to Ipiutak in some respects, including an absence of pottery, and what now appear to be earlier phases of culture—those of Chagvan Bay and Nanvak Bay, which are related to the Norton culture of Cape Denbigh.

Brooks River

Quite recent excavations along the Brooks River of the north shore of the Alaska Peninsula, not yet reported in detail by University of Oregon archeologists, show that Denbigh-like small weapon points and a few microblades occur at the bottom of a stratigraphic column above which are pottery and other artifacts reminiscent of Norton culture. The Norton-like culture apparently lasts longer here, at the base of the Alaska Peninsula, that it does farther north.

Cook Inlet and Kodiak Island

Across the Alaska Peninsula on Cook Inlet (de Laguna, 1934) and on Kodiak Island (Heizer, 1956), a continuous sequence of cultural phases is indicated, the earliest aspect of which is Kachemak Bay I, of about 700 B. C. No particular relationship to the Denbigh Flint complex is seen in these sites, but individual traits and combinations recall both Norton and Nukleet cultural phases, though not necessarily in time correspondence.

Aleutian Islands

The oldest site on the Pacific coast of Alaska appears to be the deep mound at Chaluka on Umnak Island, where William Laughlin and his colleagues (Laughlin, 1958; Laughlin and Marsh, 1951) have postulated a paleo-Aleut physical type and culture at bottom, with a change later to a neo-Aleut physical type but with little sharp change in culture from the earliest to the latest stages. Radiocarbon dates just announced by Laughlin for the bottom of Chaluka site indicate that the mound began nearly four millenniums ago.

Some products of a blade and core technology appear at the bottom of Chaluka, and true microblades and cores are found on neighboring Anangula Island in a blowout representing, presumably, an earlier aspect of culture than anything found in Chaluka site (Laughlin and Marsh, 1956). If the microblade site is later found to represent an earlier aspect of an Aleutian culture, we may expect to learn that the Aleutian Islands, as Laughlin suggests, were occupied by an Eskimo people at the time of Denbigh Flint complex farther north.

Kobuk River

The sequence at Cape Denbigh, related as it is to coastal archeology in both directions, also merits close comparison with the interior. Until quite recently no firm dating was available for the sites of the interior. In the summer of 1961, however, we located on the Kobuk River a stratified site of remarkably clear-cut separations of culture as well as other sites that aid us in giving time and space dimension to the Denbigh sequence (Giddings, 1962). In brief, the Onion Portage site about 175 miles up the river from Kotzebue Sound contains in its most recent deposit, of the past three or four centuries, many Indian-like traits and an advanced jade industry in which jade has replaced slate. Earlier, a Western Thule influence was manifest in the site, where houses were deeply excavated, as they were on the coast, and where sea-hunting artifacts lay buried with objects designed for local caribou hunting and fishing. An earlier deposit contained opaque obsidian and an array of artifacts unlike any seen before. Since these materials bear no relation to those of the coast, they can be assumed to come from the Indian country of the interior—perhaps the Koyukuk, where the only known local deposit of obsidian is to be found.

Beneath these levels, which date, perhaps, to Ipiutak times on the coast, are found earlier deposits showing strong crossties with the coast—specifically, with Norton culture. Still deeper, in a yellow sand, are traces of Choris culture, and, below the sand, a cultural layer called, at the moment, simply "Old Hearth," which appears, again, to be Indian-like and to bear little, if any, relationship to cultures of the coast. Although our excavations at Onion Portage were limited by frost, a few displaced finds of burins and micro-blades indicate that some of the lower levels will contain, when sufficiently excavated, materials of the Denbigh Flint complex. Since several layers are deeper than the Old Hearth, there is hope of finding even earlier deposits than those with a Denbigh affinity.

On a series of beach or moraine remnants near Kiana on the lower Kobuk River we also found, in 1961, a site of blades and microblades, notched and stemmed obsidian points, and other objects reminiscent of Palisades II of the coast and, especially, the Tuktu site in Anaktuvuk Pass (Campbell, 1961b). The presence at Onion Portage of two or three cultural horizons more referable to sites of the far interior—presumably Indian— than to sites of the coast suggests an explanation for some of the cultural phases recently uncovered at Anaktuvuk Pass.

Brooks Range

In the central Brooks Range of Alaska, William Irving (1951, 1953, n. d.) and Ralph Solecki (1950, 1951, 1951a; Solecki and Hackman, 1951) found sites of Denbigh-like materials at Imaigenik and Natvakruak Lake and elsewhere in the Anaktuvuk Pass and Howard Pass regions. More recently, John M. Campbell has excavated a series of shallow sites in and near Anaktuvuk Pass revealing new cultural combinations. Where Campbell at first identified his Kayuk culture as falling in time between the Denbigh Flint complex and Ipiutak culture (Campbell, 1959), he more recently has proclaimed it to be older than the Denbigh Flint complex, and he would now have his Tuktu culture containing notched points like those of Palisades II later than the Denbigh Flint complex (Campbell, 1961a, 1961b). I shall not here go into my detailed reasons[1] for questioning Campbell's cultural order. I shall only say that I favor his first placement of Kayuk and regard Tuktu culture as falling between Palisades II and Denbigh Flint complex in time.

No pottery earlier than Western Thule appears to have been found in the Anaktuvuk Pass sites. This correlates with the absence of pottery at Onion Portage on the Kobuk River until Western Thule times (Giddings, 1962).

In these two areas, obsidian appears to have lasted late, in contrast to its early disappearance from the coast along with the Denbigh Flint complex. This recalls also the boundary between the area of recent Eskimo pottery and the Athapascan cultural area in which pottery is absent. In the far interior near Fairbanks, the Campus site (Nelson, 1937; Rainey, 1939, pp. 381–89) contains microblades and cores as a principal ingredient, with a burin or two (Irving, 1955), and thus seems to crosstie in some fashion with the microblade continuum of the coast.

Susitna River Valley

To the south of the Alaska Range, in the Susitna River valley, finds of microblades have been made and also finds in which occurred notched points like those of the Palisades II and Tuktu cultures (Irving, 1957; Skarland and Keim, 1958). As stratigraphy is lacking, we can only assume some relationship with sites of the coast and await the appearance of stratified or dateable sites.

Southern Yukon Territory

MacNeish's several excavations in the southern Yukon Territory have produced both notched points and microblades either together or in separate associations. According to MacNeish (1960), the side-notched and large corner-notched points appear in the middle of his time columns, but a large series of measures of obsidian hydration layers indicates that these horizons containing notched points are older than those having few or none.[2] It is to be hoped that radiocarbon dates for these sites will resolve a puzzling problem.

---

[1] These are based upon what I take to be crossties in typology, together with the time order indicated at Cape Krusenstern and Onion Portage, as already partly reported (in Giddings, 1961 and 1962) and further projected in an article that I have committed to a symposium volume on early Alaskan archeology now being compiled for *The Anthropological Publications of the University of Alaska.*

[2] The hydration measures are recorded partly in a published account (Friedman and Smith, 1960), but mainly in mimeographed progress reports issued from time to time between 1960 and 1962 by Dr. Donavan Clark, who has measured some 200 specimens of obsidian from the Arctic and sub-Arctic sites.

Great Slave Lake Region

In his 1949 reconnaissance of the Mackenzie River drainage system of Northwestern Canada, R. S. MacNeish (1951) identified a Lockhart River complex and named an Artillery Lake and a Taltheilei complex. The last two contained lanceolate points somewhat resembling those of "early man" sites farther south. The Lockhart complex, on the other hand, contained notched points of forms now closely replicated by those recently turning up in Palisades II and Tuktu and other sites to the west.

Thelon River

Farther to the east, the Thelon River district west of Baker Lake in the Northwest Territories of Canada has recently yielded a series of sites, lucidly reported by Elmer Harp (1961), some of which include notched points and Indian-like artifacts resembling early Alaskan manifestations. The crossties with the west are thin, however, and those most easily seen between Alaska and this area are again with the Palisades II, Tuktu, and related sites, rather than with sites of the Denbigh Flint complex and later periods.

Siberia

Finally, a survey of sites bearing upon the problems of Cape Denbigh requires a treatment of Siberia. On the Asian side of Bering Strait are found a Thule-like, Punuk aspect of culture contemporary with the Western Thule of the Alaskan mainland and, preceding this, a Birnirk phase which has grown out of an Old Bering Sea phase of culture (Collins, 1937; Geist and Rainey, 1936; Rudenko, 1961). The Okvik phase (Rainey, 1941), preceding that of Old Bering Sea proper, probably dates from a century or two before Christ. As far as the shores adjacent to Bering Strait are concerned, this completes the known phases of culture. Inland, on the Chukchi Peninsula, however, are beginning to appear flint and pottery sites of promise for relating the Baikal-Lena sequences of inland culture to those of Bering Strait and inland North America (Chard, 1955*b*, 1960; Krader, 1952; Okladnikov, 1959, 1960; Okladnikov and Nekrasov, 1959; Tolstoy, 1958).

At this stage of our knowledge of the Siberian archeology, however, I see little reason to make close comparisons of any of the Alaskan phases from Ipiutak back through Old Whaling with the far-inland sequences of Siberia. This is because the Neolithic appears to continue late on the Siberian side, in the sense that microblades are strongly present there long after they have disappeared (with the Denbigh Flint complex) from coastal Alaska. Since the named phases of Siberian culture are dated at this writing mainly by extensions of artifact typology out of Asia to the south or out of Europe itself, and such terms as "Neolithic," "Bronze Age," and "Iron Age" are assigned, it is difficult to place the range of Denbigh Flint complex in precise juxtaposition to phases of post-Paleolithic in Siberia. I suspect, however, that the burins—the very few of them—in the phases of Lena River culture at Kullata are derived from the direction of Bering Strait rather than from the west and thus owe little directly to burins of other parts of the Old World. The presence of pottery, ground stone, ground burin-like instruments, and several other classes of artifacts in the Siberian Neolithic suggests to me that the earliest Denbigh Flint complex and the earliest (Isakovo?), rather than the middle, Siberian Neolithic may be roughly contemporary. I doubt strongly that the Denbigh Flint complex is to be derived from any well-known aspect of the Siberian Neolithic, including the phases defined from stratigraphy at Lake Baikal, although some surge of Mesolithic diffusion out of the Old World appears to have sent Denbigh-like waves along the coasts and northern interior of America. Recent reports that Soviet scientists are anticipating radiocarbon dates for their archeology are most encouraging in our search for directions of diffusion.

Several thoughtful analyses of Siberian materials are stimulating to those of us who work in the Arctic. Paul Tolstoy (1958), working critically with Russian sources, has provided a widening range of facts from which to judge such circumpolar and circumboreal views of archeology as those of Gjessing (1944) and Spaulding (1946). James B. Griffin (1960) and Marie Wormington (1962) have added valuable first-hand descriptions of Siberian artifacts in attempts to appraise the Old World origins of American Indians, and Henry Michael (1958) and Chester Chard (1955a, 1955b, 1956, 1958a, 1958b, 1959) continue to provide English translations and appraisals of the Asian literature of a kind that we shall all need in as great a quantity as possible before the archeology of northern North America and northern Asia can become one.

Japan

The newly emerging early Japanese archeology, with its elaborate micro-blade technology and its phenomenally early pottery, promises to shed ultimate light on the archeology of Siberia and, through it, on the Bering Strait region. The Japanese literature has proliferated in recent years, and one looks hopefully toward intermediate areas for the clues that must be excavated before the relationship of Japan's archeology to that of the Arctic region can be properly assessed.

Conclusions

The archeology of north coastal Alaska has come a long way since the middle 1930's. The facts unearthed before then admirably traced the changes in a single economy for two thousand years on our Asian island of St. Lawrence. The Okvik and Old Bering Sea people had hunted whales, seals and walruses by methods that continued through the Punuk phase to the time of modern Eskimos. On the North American side of Bering Strait, things seemed to begin later than Old Bering Sea, with the Birnirk phase, changing to Thule, of a culture based on caribou hunting, whaling, and sealing. Basic changes in this pattern were slight almost to the present day, though stylistic changes in artifact form and engraving art were frequent enough to allow the precise typing of implement forms. The Dorset culture of Greenland and coastal eastern Canada, now known to have long preceded Thule, had hardly entered the picture, for it had not yet been fully exposed through excavation. Theorists could admire the high standards of field work and scientific writing set by Arctic investigators while yet finding no great help toward determining how man had first come to America. A few flints recovered from questionable associations with the glacial age silt deposits in the interior of Alaska more readily stirred the imagination of those interested in transferring early populations from temperate Asia to temperate America than did the detailed account of how for two millenniums people had continuously prospered, without migrating southward, in the crucial area between the continents. Eskimo archeology appeared to be one thing and that of early Indians another. Now, we are not so sure.

A turning point came in 1939, with the discovery of the immense Ipiutak site of houses and burials at Point Hope. The excavations up to that time had exposed a logical path of transfers. The Old Bering Sea in Asia had seeded the Birnirk in Alaska, it seemed, and this culture had changed into the streamlined Thule which rapidly spread as far as the sea mammal lanes of Greenland and Labrador. The unexpected content of Ipiutak raised a vital question. Thousands of thin and delicate bifaced side and end blades of flinty material, an elaborate, often grotesque, style of carving walrus ivory, and a complex death cult were among the striking differences from other known cultures. The absences were equally remarkable. If Ipiutak paralleled or exceeded Old Bering Sea in age, as its lack of lamps, polished slate, pottery, and signs of whaling suggested it did, might this not point to an even greater time depth for Eskimos in America than that demonstrated for Asia? Some years earlier, Kaj Birket-Smith and his friend and co-worker, Therkel Mathiassen, had reluctantly disagreed on this same question. Mathiassen's direct evidence from the ground *(Archaeology of the Central Eskimos)* had led him to postulate a rapid spread of the Thule people as the first eastern Eskimos, while Birket-Smith's inferential evidence, based on detailed ethnographic studies *(The Caribou Eskimos)* had forced him to conclude that Eskimo culture had been long established in America.

Ipiutak now seemed to form a western outpost, as Dorset did the eastern, of Birket-Smith's "palae-Eskimo." Its art work and burial practices were clearly related, however, to the early Iron Age of Siberia. Helge Larsen and Froelich Rainey, in *Ipiutak, and the Arctic Whale Hunting Culture,* designated the Ipiutak culture "palae-Eskimo" while at the same time they rejected a central Canadian origin in favor of one in Asia.

It was during the year of publication of the Ipiutak monograph, 1948, that the Denbigh Flint complex came upon the scene. It lay at the bottom of a stratified site separated from the Norton—another "palae-Eskimo" form of culture—and, above that, the Nukleet culture with its close resemblances to both Punuk and Thule. The presence of diagonally flaked spear points, a fluted point, and gravers and scrapers like those of early southwestern sites, together with a basic microblade technology, and burins until then unrecognized in America, seemed at first glance to mark a stopping place along the hypothetical trail from Asia to America. The assumption was a reasonable one in those days when radiocarbon dating was just becoming known and hardly any New World archeologist estimated his continuous sequences to date much beyond two thousand years and anything else tended to vanish into the hazy category of "early man."

Assumptions of great antiquity did not intentionally originate with the excavators of the site, however. I first suggested a specific dating for the Denbigh layer four years after its discovery when I wrote, in 1952, that it was probably laid down as much as 6000 years ago (Giddings, 1952b, p. 91). Later appraisal of geological and archeological evidence and newly issued radiocarbon dates for frozen silt deposits in Alaska led David M. Hopkins and me (1953) to offer two possible correlations, the earlier of which we soon ruled out (Giddings, 1955) and the later of which we now wish to modify as explained on pages 244–50.

As the range of Denbigh-like disclosures widened to the Brooks Range, and then to distant parts of Canada and Greenland, and traces of intermediate phases began to turn up across the American Arctic, I became increasingly impressed with the evidence that Arctic peoples, wherever we found their traces, had been well prepared to live comfortably in their environment. In 1954, I wrote:

> The clues that we have so far are only bits and patches, but two possible alternate patterns are beginning to take form. We may reason, on one hand, that the sterile layers between the deposits of artifacts represent periods when the population had moved away from the whole region, and that the successive occupations were by new migrations. An extreme proponent of the migration theory might say that the Denbigh flint people came from Asia and then journeyed south, that much later the

paleo-Eskimos came out of Asia and settled for a time in Alaska before moving to the eastern Arctic, and that finally the Eskimos of today arrived and remained.

In the opposite view, we can assume that the village sites that have been unearthed were merely abandoned for other habitations nearby. A hunting people move about in search of game but seldom venture far from the familiar hills, streams and meeting places that they know as home. We may suppose that our discoveries of flint collections are rare glimpses of a hunting people at rest. I am inclined to this second view. The movement of a northern hunting family in the course of a year from its spring hunting grounds to its summer fishing banks to its autumn caribou crossings does not lessen its feelings of attachment to any of these places. "Home" for such people is often the area within which customary social and economic contacts are made, rather than any fixed village.

I am most skeptical of the idea that people from Asia picked up and deliberately undertook a long migration. Rather, I favor the theory that a very sparse Arctic population slowly spread over the belt of northern climate, neither pursuing nor evading pursuit, but simply existing and adjusting at random to the environment, the sons sometimes hunting beyond the range of their fathers but never really leaving home. Once established in the Bering Strait region, a population can hardly ever have drifted away completely, for the area had the resources of the predictable sea plus those of the rivers and nearby forests.

The flint work of the Denbigh complex, the oldest cultural horizon yet identified in the Bering Strait region, is not only unique but possibly the world's most sophisticated. It shows no signs of having been brought there *in toto* from elsewhere. The Bering Strait region was already a "culture center" at the time of deposit of the Denbigh flint layer. Its emanations were being felt both to the east and to the west. Since the culture at Bering Strait was more complicated than that nearby, there cannot have been a strictly one-way diffusion of ideas to either continent. People at Bering Strait could have passed along ideas received from either direction, but they would also have originated and disseminated ideas of their own.

One is struck by the fact that most of the early flint techniques were distributed primarily in a broad band centering at the Arctic Circle; they seldom strayed south. Proponents of a "circumpolar" culture have shown repeatedly that a high degree of identity exists in specific forms of objects across all of the Arctic—including hair combs, knife blades, skin boats, side blades and many other examples. To these may be added, for very early times and with emphasis, microblades and burins.

Shall we, then, regard the Arctic as a broad region where thin populations long ago spread themselves into all of the parts where meat was available—enjoying slowly changing cultures that have surmounted and actually taken advantage of the environment? Such a view leaves little room for migrating hordes. It suggests instead that America was first settled by people slowly filtering down from the Arctic population, reassorting their genes variously in the New World down through the millennia and drawing at first for their changing culture on circumpolar ideas.

—Giddings, 1954, pp. 86–88.

Partly, it was the desire to resolve the dating of the Denbigh flints that led to a search for series of beach ridges and the working out of "beach ridge dating" over the period 1956–1961. There could have been no prediction, however, of the diversity of cultures that we were to find along the shores of Kotzebue Sound and at Cape Prince of Wales.

Different though the flints of one period may be from those of the next, the changes still promise to be explained within the general region of Bering Strait, rather than from some distant points of origin. But a great deal of time has yet to be filled by information from sites not yet discovered before we are prepared to reach out and tie together the cultural manifestations far to the east and west.

Meanwhile, the materials from Cape Denbigh, when placed in the perspective thus far indicated, suggest the following order of cultural change for northern Alaska: The microblade and burin technology, as it was practiced in the Denbigh Flint culture, spread into Alaska from Asia about 4000 B. C., pushing aside, or overriding, the more Indian-like (possibly Athapascan) cast of culture represented by Palisades II. By 2500 B. C., the Denbigh culture had lost its main ingredients—microblades and specialized burins—in the west, though these persisted and became more important in both eastern North America and the forests of Siberia. During the time gap at Cape Denbigh between Denbigh Flint and Norton cultures, the side-blading aspects of the Denbigh Flint culture continued somewhere near, becoming prominent again in Ipiutak and Norton times, and the parallel-flaking of spear points continued elsewhere into "pre-Choris" and Choris culture periods. The Indian-like aspects of culture remained inland during post-Denbigh Flint times, though they now and then pressed near or to the coasts of the Chukchi and Bering Seas. A heavy population of Okvik-Old Bering Sea culture bearers on the Asian side of Bering Strait, and a counterbalancing Ipiutak population on the American side, overwhelmed local forms of culture, including Norton, for a while in the early centuries of the Christian era, establishing the practice of living in large and permanent villages; but slowly, culminating about 1000 A. D., an earlier whaling pattern of life (modified in such non-whaling areas as Nukleet) prevailed, and the people of the entire American Arctic coast became the Eskimos we have known in recent centuries.

APPENDIX I

The Ceramic Complexes at Iyatayet

James B. Griffin and Roscoe H. Wilmeth, Jr.

Foreword

This paper had its beginning in 1952 when J. L. Giddings asked J. B. Griffin if he would prepare a report on the pottery from the midden at Cape Denbigh. The pottery was shipped to Ann Arbor and with the help of Eugene Koslovich a summary paper (Griffin, 1953) was read at the 1952 New York meeting of the American Association for the Advancement of Science and a special session of the Society for American Archaeology. In 1953–54, Griffin was able to study northern Eurasian prehistoric material in western European museums through a grant from the Wenner-Gren Foundation for Anthropological Research. This support was most valuable for the presentation of this paper. Subsequently the Horace H. Rackham School of Graduate Studies at the University of Michigan supported a series of translations of Russian archaeological literature by Mrs. Percival Price which has been very helpful. In 1959–60, Miss Phyllis Anderson studied the Iyatayet pottery and left valuable notes. From October 1961 to January 1962, Griffin was able to study Siberian collections in Moscow, Leningrad and Irkutsk with support from the American Council of Learned Societies and the Wenner-Gren Foundation. Most of the detailed analysis has been done by Roscoe H. Wilmeth, Jr. The comparisons are a joint effort. The measurements, observations and location within the site of the sherds grouped as Norton Check Stamped, Norton Linear Stamped, Norton Plain, Barrow Curvilinear Paddled, Barrow Plain and Yukon Line-Dot are given in Chart A. The data on this chart was used for the statistical validation of the types which is presented following the type descriptions.

Iyatayet Pottery

Norton Check Stamped (Plates I and II; IV, Fig. 1)

Name: Griffin, 1953.
Material: 652 sherds, including 72 rims.
Temper: fiber impressions observable in about 53%, generally plant fiber, though a few resemble feather or down impressions. Sand grains present in about 16%, scanty, ranging from below .5 to 5 mm., majority from .5 to 4 mm. Rare occurrence of dark non-reflective particles, some

perhaps iron ore, others suggesting basalt. Rare angular fragments, probably pyrites or something of similar structure. Bluish stain (copper?) on one sherd. Reddish inclusion noted in another, nearly leached out, leaving a pit (this may account for the pits noted in many sherds). Almost 90% contain minute sparkling particles, usually common and often abundant; these may have been present in the clay.

Texture: coarse, flaky and laminated, often pitted; irregular flaking fracture, frequently with splitting. Only a very few show a relatively clean fracture, and are only moderately coarse. Lumps in the paste occur rarely.

Thickness: range from 3–18 mm., mean about 7 mm. Rims range from 4–13 mm., mean about 8 mm. Bases range from 7–32 mm., mean 13.5 mm. Variability of several millimeters is possible on a single sherd, especially bases.

Color: exterior black through gray to tan or brown, rarely slightly reddish. Black and tan predominate. Core and interior same, but gray predominates in former and black in latter.

Surface Treatment: check stamped paddle impressions over entire surface, up to outer margin of lip and across the base. Subsequently smoothed, so that checks are not everywhere distinct. Impressions are rectangular or square, in about equal number. Rectangular impressions range from 2–5 mm. in length (mean about 3.5 mm.) and in width from 1–4 mm. (mean about 2 mm.). Square checks range in size from 1–4 mm. (mean about 2 mm.). Variation in size and shape of the checks may be produced by overlapping of impressions and by the direction and force of application of the paddle. Rows of checks nearly always parallel to the rim. Where observable, which is not often, continuous bands of checks vary from 20–25 mm. in width, indicating the approximate width of the paddle. Overlapping application may reduce this width to 10 mm. The greatest length of a band observed was 40 mm. The paddle apparently was applied with a rocking motion rather than being simply slapped against the side of the vessel.

Rim and Lip Form: rim generally convex and bowl-like, though some are straight and a few slightly flared. Occasionally thickened in lip area, where thickening may be confined to interior and extend for a distance of 7–10 mm. below the lip. Lip is generally flat (in 47 pieces) but may be rounded (in 22). Flat lips may be straight (7), beveled or tilted to a greater or lesser degree toward the exterior (26) or interior (6), or "keeled," i. e., a central ridge running along the lip separates it into two sloping sections, yielding an inverted "V" (7). Several lips were slightly extruded, and one was both intruded and extruded yielding a modified "T" shape. A number of rounded lips were noticeably everted. Several rims had a ridge or carina on the exterior, placed from about 25 to 40 mm. below the lip (Plate I, Figure 2, right).

272

Bases: flat on the exterior and usually on the interior, though the latter may be rounded (Plate II, Fig. 1). The wall rises from the base at an angle of from 35–80 degrees from the horizontal.

Special Features: a number of sherds have been ground along one or more edges. One of these has bluish copper-like stains which may be associated with the grinding rather than being inclusions. Lacing holes, drilled from one or both sides, are occasionally present. Many sherds have a carbonized cake on the exterior, interior, or both.

Norton Linear Stamped (Plate III; IV, Fig. 1; VI, Fig. 2)

Name: Griffin, 1953.

Material: 221 sherds, including 21 rims.

Temper: fiber impressions visible in about 76%. Sand grains occur rarely (16%) and are scanty, usually 1 mm. in size, but up to 4 mm. Nearly all sherds contain minute sparkling particles, normally common, occasionally abundant.

Texture: coarse, flaky, and laminated, often pitted. Irregular flaking fracture usually accompanied by splitting.

Thickness: 4–12 mm., mean 7.2 mm. Rims range from 6–8 mm., mean 7 mm. Bases range from 4–17 mm.

Color: exterior black to gray, and tan through red and reddish brown to brown, black and tan predominating. Core black and gray to tan and reddish brown, usually gray. Interior black and gray or tan through reddish brown to brown, black predominating.

Surface Finish: linear stamp, overall application, up to edge of lip and over base. Lines are vertical or oblique from the rim. Smoothed over stamp, so impressions often indistinct (Plate VI, Fig. 2). Many overlapping impressions, and when these are crisscrossed, the impression of a check stamp may be given. The lands range in width from .5–2 mm., mean 1 mm. Troughs range from .5–3 mm., mean about 1.5 mm. Not more than 10 mm. width of parallel lines was observed. Overlapping produces a band narrower than the width of the paddle. Greatest length of rows is about 20 mm. The paddle was apparently applied with less care than the check stamped paddle.

Rim and Lip Form: generally convex, rarely almost straight. Lip usually flat, only 5 being rounded; usually unthickened. Flat lips may be straight (5), tilted toward the exterior (8) or interior (2), or "keeled" (1). One of the out-tilted lips is both intruded and extruded, yielding a modified "T" shape.

Bases: exterior flat, interior flat or rounded. Line between base and body wall may be rather indistinct. Body wall flares from base at an angle of about 25–65 degrees from the horizontal.

Special Features: worked sherds present, with grinding along broken edges.

Norton Plain

Name: New type (plain sherds separated on basis of distinctions between Norton and Barrow ware).

Material: 99 sherds, including 31 rims.

Temper: fiber impressions noted in 50%. Sand grains in 31%, scanty to common, usually below .5 mm. to 1 mm., may go up to 4 mm. 1 angular quartz fragment. Nearly all have minute sparkling particles, usually common, probably originally included in the clay.

Texture: coarse, flaky, and laminated, occasionally pitted; irregular flaking and splitting fracture.

Thickness: 4.5–10 mm., mean about 7 mm. Rims range from 5–10 mm., mean about 8 mm.

Bases: 6–16 mm.

Color: Black and gray to tan, black and gray predominating on exterior, gray in core, and black on interior.

Surface Finish: smoothed, but often poorly. Usually uneven, sometimes rough. Rarely well-smoothed, almost polished.

Rim and Lip Form: rim usually convex or bowl-like but may be straight. Lip flat (24) or rounded (7). Flat lips may be straight (11), beveled towards the exterior (11), or beveled towards the interior (2). They may be extruded or extruded and intruded ("T" shape). Rounded lips may be extruded or everted.

Bases: the single example is flattened with slightly convex sides and a distinct separation between the base and the wall. The interior is more rounded.

Barrow Curvilinear Paddled (Plate IV, Fig. 2; V, Fig. 1)

Name: Mason, 1930; Oswalt, 1955.

Material: 52 sherds, including 9 rims.

Temper: About 81% are tempered with sand grains and pebbles, generally common or abundant, ranging from below .5 to 6 mm., usually from .5 to 2 mm. 22% have limestone inclusions, usually scanty, but occasionally abundant, ranging from 1–10 mm. in size, usually 3–4 mm. Fiber impressions noted in about 31%, including one down impression 20 mm. long. All have common or abundant minute sparkling particles, perhaps included in the clay.

Texture: coarse, granular, and/or laminated and flaky, the two types occurring in about equal numbers, but occasionally mixed, *i. e.,* granular sherds may be laminated. Usually pitted, rarely lumpy. Irregular fracture, usually crumbling (rarely with splitting) but occasionally flaking fracture.

Thickness: range 5–16 mm., mean about 9.6 mm. Rims range from 6–14 mm., mean about 10 mm.

Surface Finish: curvilinear stamp, in patterns of concentric circles around a central dot. Patterns much obscured by smoothing and overlapping, but where observable, consist of from 4 to 8 rings, with over-all diameters ranging from 22 to 44 mm. The central dots range from 3.5–9 mm. in diameter, centering at about 6 mm. Lands range from 1–4 mm. in width (mean 2 mm.), the troughs from .5–1.5 mm. (mean 1 mm.).

Rim and Lip Form: rim usually convex, may be straight. All become thicker as lip is approached. Lips are flat, either straight (2), tilted toward the exterior (6), or tilted toward the interior (1); they are occasionally intruded or extruded. One is thickened or expanded on the interior for a distance of 11 mm. below the lip margin, and is grooved at the base of the expanded area. Flat plates or lamps occur in this type, the single example having a broad flat lip expanded on the interior.

Barrow Plain (Plate VI, Fig. 1; VII, Fig. 2)

Name: New type (plain sherds separated on the basis of the distinction between Norton and Barrow ware).

Material: 146 sherds, including 87 rims.

Temper: Sand grains and pebbles present in about 80%, usually common to abundant, from below .5 mm. to 7 mm., with one pebble 12 mm. long. Usually 1–3 mm. One instance of dull white pebbles, not quartz sand or limestone, abundant, up to 4 mm. Rare occurrence of limestone inclusions, rare to common, 2.5–5 mm. Fiber impressions in about 57%. Minute sparkling particles in about 92%, usually common, probably included in clay originally.

Texture: coarse, either flaky and laminated or granular, occasionally both. Rarely pitted. Fracture irregular, splitting and flaking or crumbling, occasionally both.

Thickness: ranges from 6–22 mm., mean about 11 mm. Rims same, bases fall within range.

Color: black and gray to tan and red to brown. Black predominates on surfaces, gray in core.

Surface Finish: smoothed, but usually rough and uneven, often pitted.

Rim and Lip Form: rim generally convex or bowl-like, occasionally straight. Usually thickened in lip area; this may be confined to the interior for distance of about 15 mm. below the lip margin. One is exteriorly thickened for 18 mm. below lip, with a distinct demarcation at the lower edge. One rim has a ridge or carina on the exterior about 15 mm. below the lip. Lips are flat (65) or rounded (15). Flat lips may be straight (30), tilted toward the exterior (22) or interior (7), or "keeled" (6). They may also be intruded (6) or extruded (10), or both, yielding a modified "T" (4); the last occurs only on straight lips. A few flat lips, including 2 keeled examples, are sharply everted. Rounded lips are usually simple, but one example is intruded.

Bases: flat, distinct juncture between base and wall. Interior rounded. Flat plates also occur in this type, with rounded lips (Plate VI, Fig. 1).

Special Features: rare occurrence of decorated lip, in all cases on "keeled" lip form. Incised lines extend from keel to edge, forming a chevron-like pattern. Lacing holes are present, either conical or biconical (Plate VI, Fig. 1).

Yukon Line-Dot (Plate V, Fig. 2; VII, Fig. 1)

Name: Oswalt, 1955 (Oswalt also defines a lined type which lacks the dots below the rows of horizontal lines. Since the presence or absence of dots is indeterminable on many sherds, I am placing all of the Denbigh material in the Yukon Line-Dot category).

Material: 130 sherds, including 8 rims (probably represents only a small number of vessels).

Temper: Abundant sand grains or pebbles, dark-colored fire-blackened, .5–6 mm. in diameter. Occasional limestone inclusions. Minute sparkling particles common.

Texture: coarse and lumpy, rarely flaky and laminated; irregular crumbling fracture.

Thickness: 6–15 mm. (mean about 9 mm.).

Color: Exterior black or tan, or even red. Core gray to black. Interior black.

Surface Finish: plain, poorly smoothed, usually rather rough and pitted. Pebbly appearance of the surface is characteristic, and serves to identify body sherds lacking decoration.

Decoration: incised horizontal lines, 1–4 in number, parallel, from 12–32 mm. below the lip. Troughs 1–2 mm. broad, lands 2–7 mm. broad. Rectangular tool-impressions occur above or below the series of lines, or even between lines.

Rim and Lip Form: usually slightly concave or flaring, but may be slightly convex or bowl-like. Usually unthickened. Lip usually flat, only 1 being rounded. Flat lips are straight (4) or tilted toward the interior (3); one of the latter is extruded.

276

Dentate Stamp: one sherd, from IYEB 6–10, in the Norton ware category, has dentate stamp impressions rather than check stamp. Three rows, parallel to the rim and apparently made individually, are fairly clear and distinct. Lands between these rows are much broader than those of the check stamped sherds. The impressions are rectangular, 4×2 mm. This is a rim sherd, slightly convex, with unthickened lip, flat, and steeply tilted toward the exterior.

Another Norton ware sherd from IYEB may also be dentate stamp, though the rows of impressions are obscured by overlapping. Lands are broad and distinct from the "check." On this specimen impressions are rectangular, 5×3 mm.

Miniatures: two plain surfaced miniature vessel fragments. One, from IYC, was tempered with rare sand grains under .5 mm., and contained abundant minute sparkling particles. In texture, it was coarse and laminated, with irregular splitting fracture. Thickness: 6 mm. The base was slightly rounded and slightly projecting, *i. e.,* the wall of the vessel is concave just above the base. The interior was rounded. Diameter of the base is 20 mm. The other specimen, from IYEM Upper, was tempered with sand grains, 1–4 mm. in size, occasional limestone inclusions, 2.5–5 mm., and contained common minute sparkling particles. It is relatively coarse, pitted and laminated, with irregular flaking fracture, and from 5–6 mm. in thickness. The shape of the vessel is that of a cup, with rounded unthickened lip, and at the base, a button-like protrusion 13–14 mm. in diameter, projecting about 4 mm. from the bottom of the vessel. The total height is about 57 mm., the rim diameter about 75 mm.

Statistical Validation of Types

The types described were originally separated on the basis of surface finish. Comparison indicated that on the basis of temper and thickness, the check stamp and linear stamp fell into one group, while the curvilinear stamp and the incised and punctated fell into another. In these characteristics, the plain ware fell between the two groups, suggesting there were two plain wares, one allied to the former grouping, the other to the latter.

To determine whether the similarities and differences were real or were due to chance factors, various statistical tests were employed. The first series of tests was to determine the relationship of thickness to surface finish. The mean thickness for the check stamped, linear stamped and curvilinear stamped varieties had already been determined. Standard deviations from the means were determined using the formula:

$$s = c \sqrt{\frac{\Sigma ft^2}{\Sigma f} - \left(\frac{\Sigma ft}{\Sigma f}\right)^2}$$

where c is the cell interval (in this case, 1) between the values (measurements of thickness), f is the frequency with which the values occur, and t is the deviation of each class from the assumed mean.

Surface Finish Type	Mean Thickness	Standard Deviation
Check Stamp	7 mm.	1.50
Linear Stamp	7.2 mm.	2.31
Curvilinear Stamp	9.6 mm.	2.44

To determine the significance of the differences in mean thickness, the variance for the distribution of the difference of these means can be determined by the formula

$$\text{Var } (\bar{x}_1 - \bar{x}_2) = \frac{\sigma_1^2}{n_1} + \frac{\sigma_2^2}{n_2}$$

where $\bar{x}$ is the mean, σ is the standard deviation, and n is the number of cases. The standard error of the difference is the square root of the variance of this difference. A difference between the means of more than two of these standard errors is regarded as significant (Moroney 1956, pp. 220–21).

The standard error of difference between the mean thickness of the check stamp and the linear stamp pottery, determined by this formula, was .238, while the actual difference in mean thickness was only .2 mm. Since the difference in mean thickness is less than the standard error, the difference is not significant, and the two varieties can be lumped in terms of thickness. However, the difference between these two and the curvilinear stamped ware is significant. The difference in mean thickness between curvilinear and check stamp is 2.5 mm., which is about three times the standard error of difference .782. The difference in mean thickness between curvilinear and linear stamped is 2.3 mm., which is 2.8 times the standard error of difference .809. The difference is too great to be due to chance, and in terms of thickness, two types are present.

To determine the significance of differences in the presence of sand temper, a different formula was used. Here instead of dealing with measureable quantities, we are concerned only with presence and absence of a characteristic. If we adopt a Null Hypothesis and assume that sand temper is not related to surface finish, then the probability that any sherd in the two series will contain sand temper is expressed by the formula

$$p = \frac{x_1 + x_2}{n_1 + n_2}$$

278

where p is the probability, x the number of sherds with sand temper, and n the total number of sherds in the sample.

If p is the probability that a sherd will contain sand temper, then the probability that a sherd will *not* contain sand temper (q) is 1-p. The standard error of the difference between the two samples can be represented by

$$\sigma_w = \sqrt{\frac{pq}{n_1} + \frac{pq}{n_2}}$$

With these two formulas, the difference in proportion of sand temper in the two samples can be judged in terms of the standard error of difference (Moroney, *op. cit.*, p. 222).

When the check stamped pottery was compared with the linear stamped, it was found that the difference in proportion of sand temper was .063, which is less than 1 standard error (.067); the difference in proportions is therefore not significant, and the check stamp and linear stamp can be lumped in regard to sand temper.

But when the check stamped pottery was compared with the curvilinear, the difference in proportion was found to be .659 or more than 6 standard errors (.097). Therefore the difference in sand temper here is significant, and two types are represented.

Therefore, we have the check stamped and the linear stamped material forming one category, as opposed to the curvilinear stamped material which forms another. It was on the basis of these distinctions in thickness and temper that the plain ware types, Norton Plain and Barrow Plain, were separated. The Yukon Line-Dot type falls with the Barrow ware in terms of thickness and temper, but a statistical check was not carried out due to the small size of the Yukon sample (although the total sherd count is fairly high, it is clear that the large number of sherds from locations IYH-2 and IYK-2 Under Sod represent a single vessel for each location).

Tests were also conducted to determine the significance of the proportions of lip forms. The difference in the proportion of flat (versus round) lips in Norton Check Stamped and Norton Linear Stamped was .08, less than one standard error of the difference (.109). The difference in proportion of flat lips tilted outwards was .072, also less that one standard error (.214). Therefore, lip form in these two types does not appear to be significantly different.

The same lip forms occur on Barrow ware, but in slightly different proportions. When the relative proportion of flat lips in Norton Check Stamped and Barrow Plain was considered, the difference was .131, not quite two standard errors (.07) and therefore still below the threshold of significance. However, the difference in proportion of flat lips tilted outward was .215, a little over two standard errors (.0943) and therefore probably significant.

To summarize the results of these tests, Norton Check Stamped, Norton Linear Stamped and Norton Plain can be considered varieties of one ware in terms of temper, thickness, and rim form. These two can be separated from Barrow Ware (Barrow Curvilinear Paddled and Barrow Plain) in terms of thickness and temper; two wares are represented. However, there is continuity between the two wares in lip form, since the same forms are represented in both, and the proportion of flat lips to round lips does not change significantly. Within the flat lips, the proportion of those tilted outward does change significantly, so that changes in style were taking place while the basic forms remained the same. In addition, there are distinctions that can't be checked statistically due to lack of data: *e. g.,* flat plates or lamps apparently are found only in the Barrow ware.

Comparisons

In this discussion, the sites compared to Iyatayet are arranged from north to south along the coastal area of Alaska, with Iyatayet itself falling about midway in this distribution.

Norton Ware

At sites in the Mackenzie Delta–Yukon Arctic Coast area, MacNeish found two sherds of what appears to be Norton Linear Stamped or a close relative. MacNeish (1957) calls this Firth River ware.

A number of components are present at the Engigstciak Site in the Firth River area (MacNeish 1956), though their stratigraphic placement is not always clear. The Firth River Grooved Pottery horizon yielded Norton Linear Stamped together with smoothed sherds of the same ware, which is called Norton Plain at Iyatayet. MacNeish has this period following a Firth River Dentate horizon. At Iyatayet only a few sherds of dentate were found. A small amount of Norton Check Stamped occurred with the linear at Engigstciak. The latter type becomes dominant in the succeeding Cliff complex according to MacNeish.

The stratigraphy at Engigstciak gives no evidence for placing the dentate stamped material at an earlier date than linear or check stamped pottery. Only one location showed the Firth River Grooved horizon to be earlier than the Cliff (Norton complex). As there appears to be no gap between the two levels and as some check stamp was associated with the linear, the distinction between these two levels does not seem justifiable. A small part of the collection has been examined by J. B. Griffin, who finds no significant difference in ware characteristics between the check, dentate, and linear stamped pottery. The early Engigstciak pottery is Norton ware. There seems no reason for not regarding them as essentially contemporary, coinciding with the evidence at Iyatayet.

None of the material from sites around Point Barrow is related to Norton ware (Ford, 1959), although the type St. Lawrence Corrugated has a type of surface treatment similar to Norton Linear Stamped (ibid. p. 199; Oswalt 1955, p. 32). In addition to the notable differences in ware characteristics, the northern type has grooves which are much broader than those of Norton and should be a later expression of the linear stamped technique.

At Ipiutak, Larsen and Rainey (1948) found both check and linear stamped pottery in "Near Ipiutak" burials, and also in Ipiutak burials; they were regarded as intrusive in the latter. When Griffin examined these "Near Ipiutak" sherds in the American Museum collections in 1952, it was quite clear that they were Norton ware and as such must represent an early occupation of the Ipiutak site. Oswalt (1955) types this material as Norton ware, although there are minor differences from the Iyatayet material. The description is not adequate for real comparisons, and the relative proportions of the two types of surface finish are not given. But at least "Near Ipiutak" must be roughly contemporary with the Norton component at Iyatayet.

One type of ware from Ahteut on the Kobuk River resembles Norton ware, or rather, falls between it and Barrow (Giddings 1952). The decoration, however, is that of Barrow Curvilinear Paddled. Conceivably this material would fall in time between the Norton and Barrow occupations at Iyatayet, and Giddings's date of 1250 A. D. for Ahteut would fit this interpretation.

Norton Linear Stamped was found by Giddings at Choris (Giddings, 1957), not in association with check stamped. Judging from the limited description, this material is closer to Norton ware from Iyatayet than any of the other linear and check stamped pottery. The absence of check stamping at Choris[1] might suggest that linear stamping is slightly earlier than check stamping, in view of the radiocarbon dates from the two sites (Rainey and Ralph 1959, p. 370).

At Cape Nome on the Seward Peninsula, Oswalt (1953) reports several pottery types resembling Barrow rather than Norton ware. One of these is said to be check stamped, with relatively small squares shaped like inverted pyramids extending in a single line (ibid. p. 10). From the description and the photography of one of the two sherds recovered, this appears to be dentate rather than check stamping. Oswalt later refers to this type as

---

[1] Examples of check stamped as well as linear stamped pottery were found in a series of hearths and small middens located two beach ridges forward of the Choris houses and presumed to date some decades or centuries later.—J.L.G.

Deering Pyramid Paddled (Oswalt 1955, p. 35). Here the illustration is very definitely of a dentate stamped sherd. Oswalt assigns to this type a vessel reported by Gordon (1906, Pl. *24*, 2). The latter, however, does not fit the description of Deering Pyramid Paddled, and seems to be neither dentate nor check stamped. Oswalt's derivation of this type from Norton and Nunivak Check Stamped is suggestive rather than definitive.

Linear stamp was reported at one site, and both linear and check stamp at another in the Chukchi Peninsula (Rudenko 1947), opposite Seward Peninsula. The ware, however, is more like Barrow than Norton, being thicker and tempered with sand and gravel, suggesting a later date than the Norton component at Iyatayet. Rudenko (*op. cit.* p. 41) assigns this material to the Old Bering Sea culture (this section translated by Mark Papworth), and Old Bering Sea does seem to run somewhat later than the Norton complex (Rainey and Ralph 1959, p. 373). Linear and check stamped pottery was recovered from Kukulik, Hillside, and Miyowagh on St. Lawrence Island (Geist and Rainey 1936; Collins 1937; Oswalt 1953). The collections represent a time-span from Old Bering Sea to the historic period. In ware characteristics the linear and check stamp seem to fall between Norton and Barrow ware, and there are differences in the proportions of rim and lip forms. The flat base of Norton ware is absent.

Here the width of the grooves on the linear stamp is greater than that of Norton, while the checks also average larger and tend to be square, rather than both square and rectangular. Oswalt (1955, pp. 32 and 35) classifies these types respectively as St. Lawrence Corrugated and Nunivak Check Stamped. The former is common in Old Bering Sea but becomes rarer in Punuk and later times, while the latter may date as early as Old Bering Sea, but is generally recent. The chronological relationship of the two on St. Lawrence Island is uncertain, but both post-date the Norton component at Iyatayet. The similarity of this material to Rudenko's Chukchi Peninsula pottery should be noted.

Pottery resembling Norton ware is reported from Nunivak Island (Van Stone 1954). The two types present are identified as Norton Check Stamped and Nunivak Check Stamped. The former averages slightly thinner than at Iyatayet, and differs in relative proportions of lip forms. VanStone regards the two types as contemporary here, which seems unwarranted in the light of other data. Nunivak Check Stamped first appears, and is rare, in Old Bering Sea times (Oswalt 1955, p. 35), while there is no evidence that Norton Check Stamped survived this late. There has been no association of the two types at any other site. VanStone also regards the two as contemporary with Yukon Line-Dot, which is even less likely. In view of this ceramic assemblage it is impossible to accept his statement that "testing determined the fact that all the sites belonged to the contact or immediately

282

precontact period." Unquestionably the sites yielding these three types were multicomponent.

Norton Check Stamped with an associated plain ware (Norton Plain) was found at Chagvan Bay in the Kuskokwim area (Larsen 1950). With this was a thick plain ware unlike anything from Iyatayet. In view of the radiocarbon date for the Norton complex. Larsen's estimated date of 1000 A. D. seems too late for the check stamped material. Larsen also reported the same check stamped pottery at Nanvak Bay, in association with pottery bearing horizontal impressions probably from a cord-wrapped paddle, like pottery from Ipiutak middens (*ibid.,* p. 183). It seems far more likely that the latter is linear stamped rather than cord-marked. Larsen and Rainey's (1948) description of the Ipiutak material indicates linear stamping and the only other alleged occurrence of cord-marking, that from the Firth River area (MacNeish 1956), is also doubtful on the basis of Griffin's examination of some of the sherds.

At a 19th century site on the east side of Bristol Bay, Larsen (1950) found pottery which in form and ware characteristics resembles Norton. In view of the date, the resemblance is either fortuitous or the Bristol Bay site has more than one occupation. No linear or check stamping is reported.

Pottery of the Norton variety is thus found to be distributed along the Alaskan coast from the Firth River area to Kuskokwim Bay. Similarities are close enough to indicate that all this material is roughly contemporary. On the basis of the radiocarbon dates from Iyatayet (Rainey and Ralph 1959, p. 370), we suggest a time span of about 500–100 B. C. for the Norton complex. The Choris material may be somewhat earlier. We may note here the implication that "Near Ipiutak," directly associated with Norton ware, is earlier than the Ipiutak culture itself, given a C14 date of about 300 A. D. Linear and check stamped pottery were introduced into this area from a source in the Lena Valley, where similar ceramics were established between 1500–1000 B. C. (Griffin 1960, pp. 810–11; Griffin, n. d.). The logical area in Alaska for this complex to have been first established is the region immediately adjacent to the Bering Strait, where a group of sites yielding Norton ware have been reported (Iyatayet, Choris, Near Ipiutak). The spread along the north coast of Alaska would be subsequent to its initial appearance, so that the Norton ware of the Firth River area must be later, rather than earlier, as would be indicated by MacNeish's estimates.

With the passage of time, changes took place in the ware characteristics of this pottery, with an increase in thickness, coarseness, and the addition of heavy pebble temper, yielding a ware more like Barrow than Norton. At the same time, there was an increase in the size of the check patterns and an increasing tendency for these to be square rather than rectangular.

The width of the grooves on the linear stamped pottery also became greater. These new types, St. Lawrence Corrugated and Nunivak Check Stamped, have a somewhat different and more limited distribution than Norton Linear Stamped and Norton Check Stamped, being found at Point Barrow (former type only), the Chukchi Peninsula, St. Lawrence Island, and Nunivak Island (check stamped only, at the last). Where the stratigraphy is clear, both types are associated with Old Bering Sea material, though the check stamped is very rare. In the sources cited by Oswalt (1955, pp. 32 and 35) we are unable to find substantiation for his statement that St. Lawrence Corrugated is found occasionally in Early Punuk and rarely as late as historic contact; and that Nunivak Check Stamped is relatively recent. Rainey found both types at the Okvik Site on Punuk Island, falling somewhat later than Old Bering Sea (Rainey and Ralph 1959, p. 373), but elsewhere the stratigraphic sequence is confused.

Barrow Ware

The late period pottery from the Mackenzie Delta and Yukon Coast of Alaska has limited similarities to the Barrow ware of Iyatayet (MacNeish 1957). Specific resemblances are between Thule Grit Tempered and Barrow Plain in ware characteristics and between Mackenzie Complicated Stamped and Barrow Curvilinear Paddled in decoration. The similarities are not, however, very great. MacNeish assigns this material to proto-Thule and later cultural levels. One sherd of Barrow Curvilinear Paddled, together with St. Lawrence Plain, was found by MacNeish on the surface at the Engigstciak Site.

Pottery from some of the sites in the Point Barrow area shows greater or lesser resemblance to the Barrow ware from Iyatayet (Ford 1959, pp. 201–4). Closest of all is Barrow Curvilinear Paddled from the Birnirk Site. The same type at Iyatayet averages somewhat thinner. The ware from Nungiak is somewhat like our Barrow Plain, but is softer and more crumbly, with a greater average thickness. The same ware is found at Utkiavik, but with a decoration unlike anything at Iyatayet.

Barrow Curvilinear Paddled, seemingly identical to that from Iyatayet, was found in historic period burials at Tigara (Larsen and Rainey 1948), in association with a plain ware identical to Barrow Plain. One grooved sherd possibly represents Yukon Line-Dot, while a check stamped and a linear stamped sherd are presumably of earlier date. It seems very questionable that all this material should be in actual association with historic period burials.

The same curvilinear paddled type was found in house structures at the nearby Jabbertown Site (Larsen and Rainey 1948, p. 173). The writers refer to the Birnirk associations of this ware, but note that its presence at Jabbertown indicates survival to a later date.

This type is again reported by Giddings (1952) in the Kotzebue–Kobuk River area, specifically at Old Kotzebue and Ekseavik (*ibid.* p. 95). Spirals occur in addition to concentric circles. The Ekseavik material is somewhat thicker than that from Iyatayet and there are differences in the proportions of the lip types. But at this site there are also fabric-impressed and brushed or combed sherds, which are not present at Iyatayet. Giddings dates both these sites at 1400 A. D., on the basis of tree-ring studies (*ibid.* pp. 107–108). This is considerably later than Birnirk, with which the curvilinear paddled pottery is also associated.

A closely related type was reported from Ahteut (Giddings 1952, p. 95), and has been called Ahteut Curvilinear Paddled by Oswalt (1955, p. 36), who regards it as a finer variety of Barrow. Textile or basket impressed pottery was found at the same site, and is labeled Ahteut Textile Impressed by Oswalt (1955, p. 35). This is the only type from the Arctic, either in America or Asia, that resembles the much earlier "fabric" impressed types of the Ohio and Tennessee valleys. There is no reason to suggest any kind of direct connection between these two groups of pottery. Giddings' tree-ring date for Ahteut is 1250 A. D. (*ibid.* p. 108).

Some of the ceramics described by Oswalt (1953) from the Seward Peninsula resemble Barrow in ware characteristics and lip form, but are often thicker than that from Iyatayet, and the curvilinear paddle technique is absent. Further south along the coast, there is no mention of this decorative style, although ware characteristics and rim form are superficially like those of Barrow Plain.

The distribution of Barrow ware, or specifically of the Barrow Curvilinear Paddled type, ranges from the Firth River area along the coast as far south as the Kobuk River. Temporally, it is associated on the one hand with Birnirk at about 800 A. D. (Rainey and Ralph 1959, p. 373) and on the other with Old Kotzebue and Ekseavik at about 1400 A. D. The related type, Ahteut Curvilinear Paddled, is found in the intervening period, while the Mackenzie Complicated Stamp may be late. In this distribution there is no correlation between observed differences in ware characteristics and design and the time periods suggested. The Iyatayet material does not show more specific resemblance to one variety than to another, where the data presented are sufficient to make real comparisons possible.

Yukon Ware

The most northern occurrence of pottery definitely similar to the Yukon Line-Dot at Iyatayet is at sites on the Seward Peninsula (Oswalt 1953). These are Igloo Point, Chamisso Island, and Cape Nome. There are variations in thickness, relative proportions of lip forms, and decorative elements, but all fall within the limits of the criteria for this type (Oswalt 1955, p. 37).

Some of the pottery from Kukulik on St. Lawrence Island has the same general type of decoration, but with elements not present at Iyatayet. Again there are differences in thickness and relative proportions of lip forms. Further, lugs were attached to rims at Kukulik, but did not appear on any of the few rims found at Iyatayet.

There is a very close similarity between the latter and the historic Tena and Eskimo pottery from the Yukon (de Laguna 1947), both in ware characteristics and decorative elements. There are rim modifications at the Yukon sites missing at Iyatayet, but this could be a factor of the small size of the sample. The same ware and decorative techniques are reported from Nunivak Island (VanStone 1954), though there is a difference in the predominant lip form.

Similar but not so closely related pottery was found at Platinum South Spit in the Kuskokwim Bay area (Larsen 1950, p. 180). Here, decoration extends farther down the sides of vessels than at Iyatayet, and interior grooves are absent. The rim modifications of the Yukon area do not appear here. In addition, the Kuskokwim vessels bear fine vertical or oblique striations, contrasting with the pebbly surface finish at Iyatayet.

This is a fairly limited distribution, from Seward Peninsula to Kuskokwim Bay. There is nothing to indicate that any of it is much earlier than 1600 A. D., as Oswalt (1955, p. 37) points out. Rare sherds with lines or grooves from Tigara (Larsen and Rainey 1948) and Intermediate Kotzebue (Giddings 1952), possibly related to Yukon Line-Dot, are also relatively late.

The comparative data indicates that three time periods are represented by the Iyatayet ceramics. Earliest is the Norton component, represented by Norton Check Stamped, Norton Linear Stamped, and Norton Plain, probably falling between 500–100 B. C. The second can be called the Barrow component, represented by Barrow Curvilinear Paddled, and Barrow Plain. It is uncertain whether this comes from a Birnirk time level at 800 A. D. or from the time period represented by Old Kotzebue and Ekseavik at 1400 A. D., or from the intervening period. Finally, there is a Yukon component, probably dating no earlier than about 1600 A. D.

In view of the relative closeness of these last dates, and the similarity in temper, texture, and thickness between Barrow ware and Yukon Line-Dot, it may be questioned whether or not these two are contemporary at Iyatayet, and therefore only two components are represented. However, at none of the sites mentioned were Barrow Curvilinear Paddled and Yukon Line-Dot found in clear association, even though the sites are in the same geographic area. Therefore, it seems unlikely that the two types are contemporary.

286

From the time of manufacture of Norton ware to the historic period, there is a trend toward increasing vessel wall thickness, increasing coarseness of paste, and increasing size and abundance of sand and pebble temper. At the same time, there is continuity in lip form, with flat lips nearly always predominant, but with variations in the relative proportions of straight, out-tilted, in-tilted, and keeled lips.

In contrast to this stability and gradual change, techniques of surface treatment change qualitatively and apparently fairly suddenly, and may therefore serve as time markers. There is a shift from linear and check stamping to curvilinear stamping between 500 A. D. (Okvik) and 800 A. D. (Birnirk). A change from the latter to decoration by incising and punctating takes place somewhere between 1400 A. D. (Old Kotzebue and Ekseavik) and about 1600 A. D. There is strong continuity in the Arctic ceramic tradition and the latest types in that area are the modified derivatives of the earliest introduction of pottery.

Museum of Anthropology
University of Michigan
Ann Arbor.

REFERENCES

Collins, H. B., Jr.
1928. Check-Stamped Pottery from Alaska. *Journal of the Washington Academy of Sciences,* Vol. 18, No. 9, pp. 254–56. Washington.
1937. Archaeology of St. Lawrence Island, Alaska. *Smithsonian Miscellaneous Collections,* Vol. 96, No. 1. Washington.
Ford, J. A.
1959. Eskimo Prehistory in the Vicinity of Point Barrow, Alaska. *American Museum of Natural History, Anthropological Papers,* Vol. 47, Part 1. New York.
Geist, O. W., and F. G. Rainey
1936. Archaeological Excavations at Kukulik, St. Lawrence Island, Alaska. *University of Alaska, Miscellaneous Publications,* Vol. 2. Washington, D. C.
Giddings, J. L., Jr.
1952. The Arctic Woodland Culture of the Kobuk River. *Museum Monographs, University Museum, University of Pennsylvania.* Philadelphia.
1957. Round Houses in the Western Arctic. *American Antiquity,* Vol. 23, No. 2, Pt. 1, pp. 121–35. Salt Lake City.
Gordon, G. B.
1906. Notes on the Western Eskimo. *Transactions of the Free Museum of Science and Art, University of Pennsylvania,* Vol. 1, pp. 69–101. Philadelphia.
Griffin, J. B.
1953. A Preliminary Statement on the Pottery from Cape Denbigh, Alaska. In "Asia and North America: Transpacific Contacts," assembled by M. W. Smith. *Memoirs of the Society for American Archaeology,* No. 9, pp. 40–42. Salt Lake City.

1960. Some Prehistoric Connections between Siberia and America. *Science,* Vol. 131, No. 3403, pp. 801–12.

n. d. A Discussion of Prehistoric Similarities and Connections between the Arctic and Temperate Zones of North America. In *A.I.N.A. Technical Series,* John Campbell, ed.

Hopkins, D. M., and J. L. Giddings, Jr.

1953. Geological Background of the Iyatayet Archaeological Site, Cape Denbigh, Alaska. *Smithsonian Miscellaneous Collections,* Vol. 121, No. 11. Washington. D. C.

de Laguna, Frederica

1939. A Pottery Vessel from Kodiak Island, Alaska. *American Antiquity,* Vol. 4, No. 4, pp. 334–43. Menasha.

1947. The Prehistory of Northern North America as Seen from the Yukon. *Memoirs of the Society for American Archaeology,* No. 3. Menasha.

Larsen, Helge

1950. Archaeological Investigations in Southwestern Alaska. *American Antiquity,* Vol. 15, No. 3, pp. 177–86. Menasha.

Larsen, Helge, and Froelich Rainey

1948. Ipiutak and the Arctic Whale Hunting Culture. *American Museum of Natural History, Anthropological Papers,* Vol. 42. New York.

MacNeish, R. S.

1956. The Engigstciak Site on the Yukon Arctic Coast. *University of Alaska, Anthropological Papers,* Vol. 4, No. 2, pp. 91–112. College, Alaska.

1957. Archaeological Reconnaissance of the Delta of the Mackenzie River and the Yukon Coast. Canada, Department of Northern Affairs and National Resources, National Museum, *Bulletin,* No. 142, pp. 46–81. Ottawa.

Mason, J. A.

1930. Excavations of Eskimo Thule Culture Sites at Point Barrow, Alaska. *Proceedings of the 23rd International Congress of Americanists, held at New York, Sept. 17–22, 1928,* pp. 389–94. New York.

Moroney, M. J.

1956. *Facts from Figures.* 3rd edition. Penguin Books. Harmondsworth, Middlesex.

Oswalt, Wendell

1952. Pottery from Hooper Bay Village, Alaska. *American Antiquity,* Vol. 18, No. 1, pp. 18–29. Salt Lake City.

1953. Recent Pottery from the Bering Strait Region. University of Alaska, *Anthropological Papers,* Vol. 2, No. 1, pp. 5–18. College, Alaska.

1955. Alaskan Pottery: a Classification and Historical Reconstruction. *American Antiquity,* Vol. 21, No. 1, pp. 32–43. Salt Lake City.

Rainey, F. G.

1941. Eskimo Prehistory: the Okvik Site on the Punuk Islands. American Museum of Natural History, *Anthropological Papers,* Vol. 37, Pt. 4, pp. 451–569. New York.

Rainey, Froelich, and Elizabeth Ralph

1959. Radiocarbon Dating in the Arctic. *American Antiquity,* Vol. 24, No. 4, pp. 365–74. Salt Lake City.

Rudenko, S. I.

1947. Dvernaya kul'tura Beringova Mora i Eskimosskaya Problema. *Izdatel'stvo Glavsev-mor-puti.* Moskva-Leningrad.

VanStone, J. W.

1954. Pottery from Nunivak Island, Alaska. University of Alaska, *Anthropological Papers,* Vol. 2, No. 2, pp. 181–94. College, Alaska.

ATTRIBUTE DISTRIBUTION
RIM SHERDS

NORTON CHECK STAMPED

Location	Cat. No.	Thickness					Sand temper		Rim form			Lip form		Flat lips			
		1–5 mm	6–10 mm	11–15 mm	16–20 mm	21 mm +	Present	Absent	Convex	Straight	Concave	Round	Flat	Straight	Out-tilted	In-tilted	Keeled
IYA–1 4–6	74	Split					·	x	x	·	·	Split		·	·	·	·
IYA–2 1–3	81	·	x	·	·	·	·	x	x	·	·	·	x	·	x	·	·
IYA–2 LL........	2	·	x	·	·	·	x	·	·	x	·	·	x	x	·	·	·
IYA–3 1–4	3	·	x	·	·	·	x	·	·	x	·	·	x	·	x	·	·
IYA–3 4 clay	8	·	x	·	·	·	·	x	x	·	·	x	·	·	·	·	·
IYA–3₆	9	·	·	x	·	·	·	x	x	·	·	·	x	·	x	·	·
—	11	·	x	·	·	·	·	x	x	·	·	·	x	·	x	·	·
—	93	x	·	·	·	·	·	x	Too short			x	·	·	·	·	·
—	94	·	x	·	·	·	·	x	x	·	·	·	x	·	·	x	·
IYB	99	x	·	·	·	·	·	x	x	·	·	·	x	·	·	x	·
—	100	·	x	·	·	·	x	·	x	·	·	·	x	·	·	x	·
IYB bottom	27	·	x	·	·	·	·	x	x	·	·	·	x	x	·	·	·
—	106	x	·	·	·	·	·	x	x	·	·	·	x	·	·	x	·
—	107	x	·	·	·	·	·	x	Too short			·	x	·	·	x	·
IYE Mid.	43	·	x	·	·	·	·	x	x	·	·	·	x	·	x	·	·
—	132	·	x	·	·	·	·	x	·	x	·	x	·	x	·	·	·
IYEA............	46	·	x	·	·	·	·	x	Too short			·	x	·	·	·	x
—	47	·	x	·	·	·	·	x	x	·	·	·	x	·	x	·	·
—	48	·	x	·	·	·	·	x	·	·	x	·	x	·	x	·	·
—	138	·	x	·	·	·	·	x	x	·	·	x	·	·	·	·	·
IYEB............	58	·	x	·	·	·	x	·	·	x	·	·	x	·	x	·	·
—	151	·	·	·	·	·	·	·	x	·	·	x	·	x	·	·	·
IYEB 6–10	62	·	x	·	·	·	·	x	x	·	·	·	x	·	x	·	·
IYH............	293	·	x	·	·	·	·	x	·	·	x	·	x	·	x	·	·
—	297	·	x	·	·	·	·	x	x	·	·	·	·	·	x	·	·
IYH(?)	295	·	x	·	·	·	·	x	x	·	·	·	x	·	·	x	·
IYH–1 uf 1.......	300	·	x	·	·	·	·	x	x	·	·	x	·	·	·	·	·
—	301	·	x	·	·	·	·	x	·	·	x	·	x	·	x	·	·
IYH–1 uf 2.......	303	·	x	·	·	·	·	x	·	x	·	·	x	x	·	·	·
IYH–1 t	307	·	x	·	·	·	·	x	·	x	·	·	x	·	x	·	·
IYH–1 c uf/2	320	·	x	·	·	·	·	x	·	·	x	·	x	·	x	·	·
IYH–1 D uf 1–3 ..	323	·	x	·	·	·	·	x	·	·	x	·	x	·	x	·	·
IYH–3...........	334	·	x	·	·	·	·	x	x	·	·	·	x	·	x	·	·
—	335	x	·	·	·	·	·	x	x	·	·	·	x	·	x	·	·
IYH–7 f.r.	354	·	x	·	·	·	·	x	x	·	·	·	x	x	·	·	·
—	355	Split					·	x	Too short			·	x	·	x	·	·

Location	Cat. No.	Thickness					Sand temper		Rim form			Lip form		Flat lips			
		1–5 mm	6–10 mm	11–15 mm	16–20 mm	21 mm +	Present	Absent	Convex	Straight	Concave	Round	Flat	Straight	Out-tilted	In-tilted	Keeled
IYH–7 btm.	356	·	x	·	·	·	·	x	x	·	·	·	x	x	·	·	·
–	357	x	·	·	·	·	·	x	·	x	·	x	·	·	·	·	·
–	358	·	x	·	·	·	·	x	Too short			·	x	·	·	·	x
–	359	·	x	·	·	·	·	x	x	·	·	·	x	·	x	·	·
IYK–5₄	369	·	x	·	·	·	·	x	Too short			·	x	·	x	·	·
IYK–5₅	371	·	x	·	·	·	·	x	Too short			·	x	·	x	·	·
IYM	373	·	x	·	·	·	·	x	·	x	·	·	x	·	x	·	·
–	374	·	x	·	·	·	·	x	x	·	·	·	x	·	·	x	·
–	375	x	·	·	·	·	·	x	x	·	·	Broken		Broken			
–	376	·	x	·	·	·	·	x	·	x	·	x	·	·	·	·	·
IYO	379	·	x	·	·	·	·	x	·	·	x	·	x	·	x	·	·
IYP	380	·	x	·	·	·	·	x	·	x	·	·	x	·	·	x	·
IYP	381	·	x	·	·	·	·	x	x	·	·	x	·	·	·	·	·
IYP–A(?)	382	·	x	·	·	·	·	x	·	·	x	·	x	·	x	·	·
IYP–A–H	383	x	·	·	·	·	·	x	x	·	·	x	·	·	·	·	·
IYP B	384	·	x	·	·	·	x	·	x	·	·	·	x	·	·	x	·
IYPB mid.	393	·	x	·	·	·	·	x	·	·	x	·	x	·	·	·	x
–	394	·	x	·	·	·	·	x	x	·	·	·	x	·	x	·	·
–	395	·	x	·	·	·	·	x	·	x	·	·	x	·	·	·	x
–	396	·	x	·	·	·	·	x	·	x	·	·	x	·	·	·	x
IYPC mid	400	·	x	·	·	·	·	x	x	·	·	x	·	·	·	·	·
–	401	·	x	·	·	·	·	x	·	·	x	x	·	·	·	·	·
–	402	x	·	·	·	·	·	x	·	·	x	·	x	·	x	·	·
IYPD	409	x	·	·	·	·	·	x	x	·	·	x	·	·	·	·	·
–	410	·	x	·	·	·	·	x	·	·	x	x	·	·	·	·	·
–	411	·	x	·	·	·	·	x	·	·	x	x	·	·	·	·	·
–	412	·	x	·	·	·	·	x	x	·	·	·	x	·	x	·	·
–	413	·	x	·	·	·	·	x	x	·	·	·	x	·	x	·	·
IYPD upper	414	·	x	·	·	·	·	x	·	x	·	x	·	·	·	·	·
IYPE–5	435	·	x	·	·	·	·	x	Too short			·	x	·	x	·	·
IYPE–7 upp. & mi.	439	·	x	·	·	·	·	x	·	·	x	·	x	·	x	·	·
–	440	·	x	·	·	·	·	x	x	·	·	·	x	·	x	·	·
–	441	·	x	·	·	·	·	x	·	·	x	x	·	·	·	·	·
IYPF–1 lower mid.	447	·	x	·	·	·	·	x	·	·	x	·	x	·	x	·	·
IYPH mid.	454	·	x	·	·	·	·	x	x	·	·	x	·	·	·	·	·
–	455	·	x	·	·	·	·	x	x	·	·	·	x	·	x	·	·
–	456	·	x	·	·	·	x	·	x	·	·	·	x	·	x	·	·
IYZ–1 middle	465	·	x	·	·	·	·	x	x	·	·	·	x	·	x	·	·
IYZ–4 middle	476	·	x	·	·	·	·	x	·	·	x	·	x	·	x	·	·

290

Location	Cat. No.	Thickness					Sand temper		Rim form			Lip form		Flat lips			
		1–5 mm	6–10 mm	11–15 mm	16–20 mm	21 mm +	Present	Absent	Convex	Straight	Concave	Round	Flat	Straight	Out-tilted	In-tilted	Keeled
IYAA	173	·	·	·	·	·	·	·	X	·	·	·	X	X	·	·	·
IYE misc.	180	·	X	·	·	·	·	X	X	·	·	X	·	·	·	·	·
–	181	·	X	·	·	·	·	X	X	·	·	·	X	·	X	·	·
IYEB	192	·	X	·	·	·	·	X	X	·	·	·	X	·	·	·	X
IYH	294	·	X	·	·	·	·	X	Too short			X	·	·	·	·	·
–	296	·	X	·	·	·	·	X	X	·	·	X	·	·	·	·	·
IYH	298	·	X	·	·	·	·	X	X	·	·	·	X	X	·	·	·
IYH–1 uf 1	302	·	X	·	·	·	·	X	·	·	X	·	X	·	·	X	·
IYH–1 uf 2	304	·	X	·	·	·	·	X	X	·	·	·	X	·	·	X	·
IYH–1 uf 3	305	·	X	·	·	·	·	X	X	·	·	X	·	·	·	·	·
IYH–1 t	308	·	X	·	·	·	·	X	X	·	·	·	X	X	·	·	·
–	309	·	X	·	·	·	·	X	X	·	·	·	X	·	·	X	·
IYH–1 c uf/2	321	·	X	·	·	·	X	·	X	·	·	·	X	X	·	·	·
IYH–1 D uf 1–3	324	·	X	·	·	·	·	X	·	X	·	·	X	·	X	·	·
–	325	·	X	·	·	·	·	X	X	·	·	X	·	·	·	·	·
IYH–3	336	·	X	·	·	·	·	X	X	·	·	·	X	X	·	·	·
–	337	·	X	·	·	·	·	X	X	·	·	·	X	X	·	·	·
IYH–7	338	·	X	·	·	·	·	X	X	·	·	·	X	X	·	·	·
IYH–7 mid.	344	·	X	·	·	·	·	X	X	·	·	·	X	X	·	·	·
IYK	362	·	X	·	·	·	·	X	X	·	·	·	X	·	X	·	·
IYM	377	·	X	·	·	·	·	X	X	·	·	·	X	·	X	·	·
IYPB	385	·	X	·	·	·	X	·	X	·	·	·	X	·	X	·	·
IYPB tunnel floor	398	·	X	·	·	·	·	X	X	·	·	·	X	·	·	X	·
IYPC mid.	403	·	X	·	·	·	·	X	X	·	·	·	X	·	·	X	·
IYPF–1 lower mid.	448	·	X	·	·	·	·	X	·	X	·	·	X	X	·	·	·
–	449	·	X	·	·	·	·	X	X	·	·	·	X	·	X	·	·

Location Cat. No.	1-5 mm	6-10 mm	11-15 mm	16-20 mm	21 mm +	Present	Absent	Convex	Straight	Concave	Round	Flat	Straight	Out-tilted	In-tilted	Keeled
			Thickness			Sand temper		Rim form			Lip form		Flat lips			
IYA-3 LL4....... 234	·	x	·	·	·	·	x	x	·	·	·	x	·	x	·	·
IYE misc......... 253	·	x	·	·	·	x	·	x	·	·	·	x	x	·	·	·
IYE rt. side 261	·	x	·	·	·	·	x	·	x	·	x	·	·	·	·	·
IYEA............ 264	·	x	·	·	·	x	·	·	x	·	·	x	·	x	·	·
IYEM lower...... 279	·	x	·	·	·	x	·	x	·	·	·	x	·	x	·	·
— 282	·	x	·	·	·	x	·	x	·	·	x	·	·	·	·	·
IYH............. 299	·	x	·	·	·	·	x	Too short			·	x	·	x	·	·
IYH-1 uf 3....... 306	·	x	·	·	·	·	x	Too short			x	·	·	·	·	·
IYH-1 t 310	·	x	·	·	·	·	x	·	x	·	·	x	x	·	·	·
— 311	·	x	·	·	·	·	x	·	x	·	·	x	x	·	·	·
IYH-1 D 322	·	x	·	·	·	·	x	x	·	·	·	x	·	x	·	·
IYH-7........... 339	·	x	·	·	·	·	x	x	·	·	·	x	·	x	·	·
IYH-7 mid. 345	·	x	·	·	·	·	x	·	x	·	·	x	·	x	·	·
IYH-7 up. tunnel . 349	·	x	·	·	·	·	x	x	·	·	·	x	x	·	·	·
IYH-7 btm. 360	·	x	·	·	·	·	x	x	·	·	·	x	·	x	·	·
IYK-2 4 364	·	x	·	·	·	·	x	x	·	·	x	·	·	·	·	·
IYM 378	·	x	·	·	·	·	x	x	·	·	x	·	·	·	·	·
IYPC mid. 404	·	x	·	·	·	·	x	x	·	·	·	x	x	·	·	·
— 405	·	x	·	·	·	·	x	x	·	·	x	·	·	·	·	·
— 406	·	x	·	·	·	·	x	·	·	x	x	·	·	·	·	·
— 407	·	x	·	·	·	x	·	Too short			·	x	·	x	·	·
IYPE-2 lower mid. 429	·	x	·	·	·	·	x	x	·	·	·	x	·	·	x	·
IYPE-5 lower mid. 436	·	x	·	·	·	·	x	x	·	·	·	x	x	·	·	·
— 437	·	x	·	·	·	·	x	x	·	·	x	·	·	·	·	·
IYPF-1 lower mid. 450	·	x	·	·	·	x	·	·	·	x	·	x	·	x	·	·
IYPH mid........ 457	·	x	·	·	·	·	x	Too short			·	x	·	x	·	·
IYT-3 458	x	·	·	·	·	·	x	·	x	·	·	x	x	·	·	·
IYZ-1 middle..... 466	·	x	·	·	·	·	x	Too short			·	x	·	x	·	·
IYZ-4 middle..... 477	·	x	·	·	·	·	x	·	x	·	·	x	·	x	·	·

292

BARROW CURVILINEAR PADDLED

Location	Cat. No.	Thickness					Sand temper		Rim form			Lip form		Flat lips			
		1–5 mm	6–10 mm	11–15 mm	16–20 mm	21 mm +	Present	Absent	Convex	Straight	Concave	Round	Flat	Straight	Out-tilted	In-tilted	Keeled
IYA–2 4–6	209	·	x	·	·	·	x	·	x	·	·	·	x	x	·	·	·
IYC gen'l	212	·	x	·	·	·	·	x	Too short			·	x	·	x	·	·
IYE rt. side	214	·	·	x	·	·	x	·	x	·	·	·	x	·	x	·	·
IYEM upper	229	·	·	x	·	·	x	·	x	·	·	·	x	·	x	·	·
IYEM led	230	·	x	·	·	·	x	·	x	·	·	·	x	·	x	·	·
–	231	·	x	·	·	·	·	x	·	x	·	·	x	·	·	x	·
IYH–1 t	313	·	x	·	·	·	·	x	x	·	·	·	x	·	·	x	·
IYK–2 4	365	·	·	x	·	·	·	x	x	plate		·	x	x	·	·	·
–	366	·	·	·	x	·	x	·	x	·	·	·	x	·	·	x	·
IYK–5₄	370	·	x	·	·	·	x	·	x	·	·	·	x	·	x	·	·
IYPB mid.	397	·	·	x	·	·	x	·	Too short			·	x	x	·	·	·
IYPE7 upper & mi.	442	·	·	x	·	·	x	·	x	·	·	·	x	·	x	·	·
–	443	·	·	x	·	·	x	·	x	plate		x	·	·	·	·	·
IYZ–1 upper	459	·	x	·	·	·	·	x	·	x	·	·	x	x	·	·	·

Location	Cat. No.	1–5 mm	6–10 mm	11–15 mm	16–20 mm	21 mm +	Present	Absent	Convex	Straight	Concave	Round	Flat	Straight	Out-tilted	In-tilted	Keeled
							Sand temper		Rim form			Lip form		Flat lips			
IYAA	235	·	·	x	·	·	·	x	x	·	·	·	x	·	x	·	·
–	236	·	x	·	·	·	x	·	x	·	·	·	x	·	x	·	·
IYE misc.	246	·	·	x	·	·	·	x	x	·	·	Split					
–	247	·	x	·	·	·	x	·	x	·	·	·	x	·	x	·	·
–	250	·	x	·	·	·	x	·	·	x	·	·	x	·	x	·	·
–	251	·	x	·	·	·	x	·	x	·	·	x	·	·	·	·	·
–	252	·	x	·	·	·	x	·	x	·	·	·	x	·	x	·	·
IYE mid.	254	·	·	x	·	·	·	x	x	·	·	·	x	·	·	·	x
–	255	·	·	x	·	·	x	·	x	·	·	·	x	x	·	·	·
–	256	·	·	x	·	·	x	·	x	·	·	·	x	·	·	x	·
IYE rt. side	257	·	·	x	·	·	x	·	x	·	·	·	x	·	x	·	·
–	258	·	·	x	·	·	x	·	x	·	·	·	x	x	·	·	·
–	259	·	·	x	·	·	x	·	·	x	·	·	x	x	·	·	·
–	262	·	·	x	·	·	x	·	·	x	·	·	x	·	·	x	·
–	263	·	x	·	·	·	x	·	x	·	·	·	x	x	·	·	·
IYEB 6–10	268	·	x	·	·	·	·	x	·	x	·	·	x	x	·	·	·
–	290	·	·	x	·	·	x	·	x	·	·	·	x	·	·	x	·
IYEM upper	276	·	·	x	·	·	x	·	x	·	·	·	x	·	·	·	x
–	277	·	x	·	·	·	x	·	x	·	·	·	x	x	·	·	·
IYEM led	284	·	·	x	·	·	x	·	x	·	·	·	x	·	x	·	·
IYH–1 t	312	·	x	·	·	·	·	x	·	x	·	·	x	x	·	·	·
–	314	·	x	·	·	·	x	·	·	x	·	·	x	x	·	·	·
–	315	·	x	·	·	·	x	·	·	·	x	·	x	·	x	·	·
–	316	·	·	·	·	·	x	·	·	·	x	·	x	·	x	·	·
–	317	·	·	x	·	·	x	·	x	plate		x	·	·	·	·	·
–	318	·	·	x	·	·	x	·	x	plate		x	·	·	·	·	·
IYH–1 t uf/gen'l	319	·	·	x	·	·	x	·	x	plate		·	x	·	·	x	·
IYH–2	326	·	·	x	·	·	x	·	x	plate		x	·	·	·	·	·
–	327	·	x	·	·	·	·	x	x	plate		x	·	·	·	·	·
–	328	·	x	·	·	·	x	·	x	plate		x	·	·	·	·	·
–	329	·	·	x	·	·	x	·	·	x	pl.	·	x	·	x	·	·
–	330	·	x	·	·	·	x	·	x	·	·	·	x	x	·	·	·
IYH–7 mid. up.	340	·	x	·	·	·	·	x	·	x	·	·	x	x	·	·	·
–	341	·	x	·	·	·	x	·	x	·	·	·	x	x	·	·	·
–	342	·	x	·	·	·	x	·	x	·	·	·	x	x	·	·	·
–	343	·	·	x	·	·	x	·	x	plate		x	·	·	·	·	·
IYH–7 mid.	346	·	x	·	·	·	·	x	·	x	·	·	x	x	·	·	·
–	347	·	x	·	·	·	x	·	·	x	·	·	x	·	x	·	·
–	348	·	x	·	·	·	x	·	·	x	·	·	x	x	·	·	·
IYH–7 up. tunnel	350	·	x	·	·	·	x	·	·	x	·	·	x	·	x	·	·
–	350	·	·	x	·	·	x	·	Too short			x	·	·	·	·	·
–	352	·	x	·	·	·	x	·	x	·	·	·	x	·	x	·	·

Location	Cat. No.	1–5 mm	6–10 mm	11–15 mm	16–20 mm	21 mm +	Present	Absent	Convex	Straight	Concave	Round	Flat	Straight	Out-tilted	In-tilted	Keeled
				Thickness			Sand temper		Rim form			Lip form		Flat lips			
IYH–7 up. tunnel	353	·	·	x	·	·	x	·	x	·	·	x	·	·	·	·	·
IYH–Z	361	·	·	x	·	·	x	·	x	·	·	·	x	x	·	·	·
IYK–2 4	367	·	x	·	·	·	x	·	x	·	·	x	·	·	·	·	·
−	368	·	x	·	·	·	x	·	x	·	·	·	x	x	·	·	·
IYK–6	372	·	·	x	·	·	x	·	x	·	·	·	x	·	x	·	·
IYPB upper	386	·	·	x	·	·	x	·	x	·	·	·	x	·	·	·	x
−	387	·	x	·	·	·	x	·	·	x	·	·	x	x	·	·	·
−	388	·	x	·	·	·	x	·	·	x	·	·	x	x	·	·	·
−	389	·	·	x	·	·	x	·	x	·	·	·	x	·	x	·	·
−	390	·	x	·	·	·	x	·	x plate		·	·	x	·	x	·	·
−	391	·	·	·	x	·	x	·	x plate		·	·	x	·	·	x	·
−	392	·	x	·	·	·	x	·	·	·	x	·	x	·	x	·	·
IYPB tunnel floor	399	·	·	x	·	·	x	·	x plate		·	x	·	·	·	·	·
IYPC mid.	408	·	·	x	·	·	x	·	x	·	·	·	x	·	x	·	·
IYPD upper	415	·	x	·	·	·	·	x	·	x	·	·	x	·	x	·	·
−	416	·	x	·	·	·	x	·	Too short			·	x	x	·	·	·
−	417	·	x	·	·	·	x	·	x	·	·	·	x	x	·	·	·
−	418	·	x	·	·	·	x	·	Too short			·	x	·	x	·	·
−	419	·	x	·	·	·	x	·	Too short			·	x	x	·	·	·
−	420	·	·	x	·	·	x	·	x	·	·	·	x	·	x	·	·
−	421	·	·	x	·	·	·	x	·	x	·	·	x	·	x	·	·
−	422	·	·	x	·	·	x	·	x	·	·	·	x	x	·	·	·
−	423	·	·	x	·	·	·	x	x	·	·	·	x	x	·	·	·
IYPE–2	424	·	·	x	·	·	x	·	·	x	·	·	x	·	x	·	·
−	425	·	·	x	·	·	x	·	x	·	·	·	x	x	·	·	·
IYPE–2 upper	426	·	x	·	·	·	x	·	·	x	·	·	x	x	·	·	·
−	427	·	x	·	·	·	·	x	Too short			·	x	x	·	·	·
−	428	·	·	x	·	·	·	x	Too short			x	·	·	·	·	·
IYPE–4 upper mid.	430	·	·	x	·	·	x	·	·	·	x	·	x	x	·	·	·
−	431	·	·	x	·	·	x	·	·	x	·	·	x	x	·	·	·
−	432	·	x	·	·	·	·	x	·	x	·	·	x	x	·	·	·
−	433	·	x	·	·	·	·	x	·	x	·	x	·	·	·	·	·
−	434	·	x	·	·	·	x	·	·	x	·	·	x	x	·	·	·
IYPE–5 lower mid.	438	·	x	·	·	·	·	x	·	x	·	·	x	x	·	·	·
IYPE7 upper & mid.	444	·	x	·	·	·	x	·	x plate		·	·	x	x	·	·	·
−	445	·	·	x	·	·	x	·	x plate		·	x	·	·	·	·	·
IYPH upper	451	·	x	·	·	·	x	·	·	x	·	·	x	·	x	·	·
−	452	·	x	·	·	·	x	·	x	·	·	·	x	·	x	·	·
−	453	·	x	·	·	·	x	·	x	·	·	·	x	·	x	·	·
IYZ–1 upper	460	·	x	·	·	·	x	·	·	x	·	·	x	x	·	·	·
−	461	·	·	x	·	·	x	·	x	·	·	·	x	·	·	x	·
−	462	·	·	x	·	·	x	·	Too short			·	x	·	x	·	·

BARROW PLAIN (cont.)

Location	Cat. No.	Thickness					Sand temper		Rim form			Lip form		Flat lips			
		1-5 mm	6-10 mm	11-15 mm	16-20 mm	21 mm +	Present	Absent	Convex	Straight	Concave	Round	Flat	Straight	Out-tilted	In-tilted	Keeled
IYZ–1 upper	463	·	x	·	·	·	x	·	·	x	·	·	x	·	·	·	x
–	464	·	x	·	·	·	x	·	·	x	·	·	x	·	·	·	x
IYZ–3 upper	467	·	·	x	·	·	x	·	x plate			x	·	·	·	·	·
–	468	·	x	·	·	·	x	·	·	x	·	·	x	·	x	·	·
–	469	·	x	·	·	·	x	·	·	x	·	·	x	x	·	·	·
–	470	·	·	x	·	·	·	x	Too short			·	x	x	·	·	·
–	471	·	x	·	·	·	x	·	·	x	·	·	x	·	x	·	·
–	472	·	x	·	·	·	·	x	Too short			x	·	·	·	·	·
–	473	·	·	x	·	·	x	·	·	x	·	·	x	·	x	·	·
–	474	·	·	x	·	·	x	·	x	·	·	·	x	x	·	·	·
–	475	·	x	·	·	·	x	·	·	x	·	·	x	·	·	x	·
IYZ–4 middle.....	478	·	x	·	·	·	x	·	Too short			·	x	x	·	·	·

YUKON LINE-DOT

Location	Cat. No	Thickness					Sand temper		Rim form			Lip form		Flat lips			
		1-5 mm	6-10 mm	11-15 mm	16-20 mm	21 mm +	Present	Absent	Convex	Straight	Concave	Round	Flat	Straight	Out-tilted	In-tilted	Keeled
IYE misc.........	206	·	·	x	·	·	x	·	x	·	·	·	x	·	·	x	·
IYEA............	207	·	x	·	·	·	x	·	·	·	x	·	x	·	·	x	·
IYH–2...........	331	·	x	·	·	·	x	·	·	·	x	·	x	·	·	x	·
–	332	·	x	·	·	·	x	·	·	x	·	·	x	x	·	·	·
–	333	·	·	x	·	·	x	·	·	·	x	·	x	·	·	x	·
IYK–2 undersod ..	363	·	x	·	·	·	x	·	·	·	x	·	x	·	·	·	x
IYPE7 upper & mid.	446	·	x	·	·	·	x	·	·	·	x	·	x	x	·	·	·

PLATE I

Figure 1. U.M.M.A. Neg. # 14071. Norton Check Stamped rim and body sherd from location IYA-3₆.

Figure 2. U.M.M.A. Neg. # 14073. Norton Check Stamped rim sherds from location IYA-3₆. Height of sherd on left is about 3 inches.

PLATE II

Figure 1. U.M.M.A. Neg. #14077. Two basal fragments of Norton Check Stamped vessels. Upper sherd is about 3¼ inches high. Upper sherd from location IYE (Misc.); lower sherd from IYE Middle.

Figure 2. U.M.M.A. Neg. #14082. Norton Check Stamped rim and body sherds from location IYM. Height of sherd on upper left is about 2½ inches.

PLATE III

Figure 1. U.M.M.A. Neg. #14081. Norton Linear Stamped rim sherd from location IYH-IUF₃. Height about 6 inches.

Figure 2. U.M.M.A. Neg. #14089. Norton Linear Stamped with wide grooves. Sherd on the left is from location IYO; on the right from IYK-5₆.

PLATE IV

Figure 1. U.M.M.A. Neg. #14088. 1a. Norton Linear Stamped identified as from IYPA. 1b. Norton Check Stamped identified as from IYPA.

Figure 2. U.M.M.A. Neg. #14078. Barrow Curvilinear Paddled sherds from location IYEA (218) on the left and IYEA (219) on the right.

PLATE V

Figure 1. U.M.M.A. Neg. # 14090. Body sherd of Barrow Curvilinear Paddled from location IYO.

Figure 2. U.M.M.A. Neg. #14080. Yukon Line-Dot sherds from location IYH2. Height of A is 5½ inches.

PLATE VI

Figure 1. U.M.M.A. Neg. #14079. Barrow Plain sherds from IYEA. Note cracked lacing hole on sherd on right. Height of sherd on left is about 5 inches.

Figure 2. U.M.M.A. Neg. #14087. Large section of rim and upper body of faintly marked Norton Linear Stamped. It is listed as IYPB Tunnel Floor. Height is about 6½ inches.

PLATE VII

Figure 1. U.M.M.A. Neg. # 14⸹76. Barrow Plain and Yukon Line-Dot rim sherds from location IYE (Misc.). The sherd on the left is 3 inches high.

Figure 2. U.M.M.A. Neg. #14075. Large rim sherd of Barrow Plain from location IYE. Right side, about 5 inches high.

APPENDIX II

Skull Fragments from Norton Levels at Iyatayet

Daris R. Swindler

(The fragments of a skull here treated were found crushed among fragments of rotten wood in the upper middle levels of Cut Z-5 at Iyatayet. The associated materials were those of Norton culture, and we found no evidence of intrusion from above. No other human bones were recovered. These fragments may, therefore, be among the earliest human remains known in the Bering Strait region.—J. L. G.—*See* Pl. A.)

Material Present

The present material was excavated in a fragmentary condition (some fifteen pieces of skull bones found) and lay within the paleo-Eskimo horizon. An extensive search in the area failed to uncover additional skeletal material. There are three animal bones (perhaps a dog?) and four human pieces too fragmentary for accurate identification. The human material consisted of a well-preserved fragment of the right temporal bone with the glenoid fossa intact. The frontal, parietal, and occipital bones are present, although somewhat distorted from the effects of ground pressure. These bones are practically in toto and had been separated along their respective sutures, thus permitting a reasonable reconstruction of the cranial vault. This chore was performed by Mr. Albert Jehle of the University Museum, Philadelphia.

Age of Skull

The three sutures of the vault are patent. Since it is generally accepted that the sagittal suture commences closing at about 22 years, the individual was probably less than 22 years old. Another indication of age is the slight development of the frontal air sinuses. The pneumatic cavities are about the size of garden peas in the present frontal bone, and, according to Weinmann and Sicher (1947), the air sinuses enlarge at an age when normal growth has ceased. In fact, they state (p. 110) that, "In later years . . . the sinus extends more and more and may then hollow out the orbital roof to a variable extent." By considering this evidence in conjunction with the patent cranial sutures, it is impossible to ascribe an age greater than about 22 years to the bones.

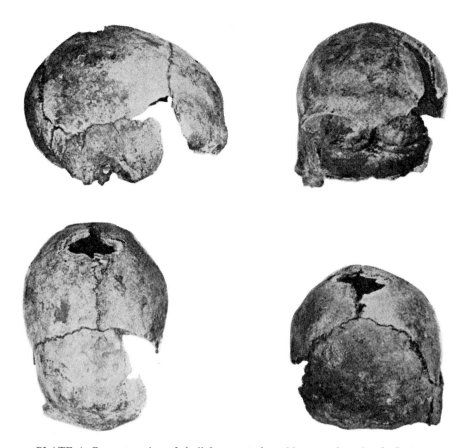

PLATE A. Reconstruction of skull fragments from Norton culture levels, Iyatayet.

Sex of Skull

Sexing cranial material is always a risky business and this becomes especially true when dealing with an isolated skull belonging to an unknown human group. In determining the sex, we utilized the three criteria listed by Keen (1950) as the most valuable when confronted with crania of doubtful or unknown relationships. These are: supra-orbital ridges, occipital crest and nuchal lines, and ridge at upper rim of auditory meatus (suprameatal ridge). The skull, according to these criteria, is female.

Discussion

The skull is long and narrow, with a cranial index of 70.2. As is well known, a low cranial index is usually found among the eastern Eskimos. It has also been recorded for crania from certain prehistoric sites in the west—namely, the Old Igloo burials at Pt. Barrow (Hrdlička, 1930) and the interments of Old Bering Sea times from St. Lawrence Island (Collins, 1937). Hrdlička lists the Old Igloo cranial index for 27 males as 69.1 and for 25 females as 70.2. Unfortunately, Collins presents neither measurements nor indices, but states that the two skulls are extremely dolichocranic. If the bones under study are those of an Eskimo, we have further substantiation for Collins's (1951) theory that the long, narrow, high-headed variety antedates other Eskimo types in Alaska.

The slope of the forehead is moderate and the supra-orbital ridge is of medium development. The skull is oblong from above and the parietal bosses, not pronounced, are located about midway between the coronal and lambdoid sutures. The occipital bone has a rather marked backward and downward bend from lambda, which places the position of inion higher and farther back than is normally encountered. This is demonstrable when one measures the glabella-inion (176 mm.) and glabella-lambda (173 mm.) distances. This condition was described by Fischer-Møller in his study of the Central Eskimo crania unearthed by the Fifth Thule Expedition, and he believes the "occipital bone in the Eskimo is undoubtedly the most characteristic of the bones of theca in a racial sense" (1937, p. 35). It is unfortunate that we do not know the frequency of this morphologic feature in other groups, for such a criterion has little diagnostic value until we know more concerning its functional and genetic makeup. Since it is impossible to articulate the temporal fragment with any accuracy, auricular height cannot be taken. However, the skull appears to be moderately high-headed. (*See* Plate A.)

Another morphologic characteristic which bears mentioning is the presence of a slight sagittal crest. When viewed from the front, the crest is discernible running posteriorly along the frontal and parietal bones. The keel has been the object of many discussions whenever Eskimo racial characteristics are considered and is usually listed as having a high incidence among the long- and narrow-headed Eskimos.

The last bone to be described is the right temporal fragment. The glenoid cavity is well preserved, as is the tympanic bone, while the mastoid process is broken off at the level of the inferior border of the tympanic bone. The articular eminence (the bony structure which forms the anterior boundary of the mandibular fossa) appears to be slightly worn in an anterior-posterior direction, giving the impression of a somewhat shallow glenoid cavity. It is difficult to assess the degree of functional attrition at this joint since there are no standards, and, furthermore, the articular disc (a piece of fibro-cartilage between the mandibular condyle and the glenoid fossa) undoubtedly limits the amount of wear of the articular eminence unless the disc wears through, permitting bone-to-bone contact.

The wearing down of the articular eminence has been offered as evidence for the shallow glenoid fossa which is rather common among the Eskimos (Knowles, 1915), but until more is known concerning the efficacy of the mandibular condyle on the articular eminence, one can only view this hypothesis as one of perhaps several explanations for a shallow glenoid cavity. Indeed, we would view the condition of a shallow glenoid cavity as being indicative of Eskimo affinity rather skeptically until more is learned of its frequency in man and whether the definitive configuration of the cavity is primarily controlled by heredity or by function. Some light has been shed on this problem by Ashton and Zuckerman (1954) in their study of the articular fossa in men and apes. They found that the main difference between the fossa in adults and apes is essentially due to the fact that in the ape (shallow, broad) growth appears to take place in all directions, whereas in man (deep, narrow) relatively less growth occurs in the antero-posterior axis of the fossa than in other directions. Perhaps we have a similar developmental process among the Eskimos, if, indeed, the shallow fossa can be shown to be characteristic of these people. The writer has examined some 65 crania from Point Barrow, which repose in the Wistar Institute of Anatomy and Biology in Philadelphia. These specimens are from the W. B. van Valin collection, a primary group in Hrdlička's studies. Among these crania, somewhat less than half exhibited a shallow glenoid fossa. However, our observations were entirely subjective, since no attempt was made to verify them.

The tympanic bone lies just posterior to the glenoid fossa and its anterior surface forms the posterior wall of the glenoid cavity. The morphology of the tympanic region has been offered as evidence for Eskimo relationships by several authorities. Some years ago, Stewart presented a detailed study of the tympanic region in several different skeletal populations. He showed that a thickened tympanic plate is characteristic of the Eskimo and stated, "The above facts lead invariably to the conclusion that the thickened tympanic plate of the Eskimos and related groups is an hereditary character" (1933, p. 496). He utilized several measurements which we have taken on our material for comparison. Although not giving ranges for the measurements, he did present means and standard deviations. He also presented dimensions for the right and left sides and according to sex. Since our fragment is from the right side and, we believe, female, comparisons are made accordingly in Table 1. Appreciating the limitations involved when comparing only a single specimen, it would appear that the Cape Denbigh cranium was more similar to those of the Eskimos, especially with respect to length below the porus, breadth of the tympanic plate, and breadth anterior to the porus.

The form of the external auditory meatus was also described by Stewart. He found that a "tube-like" meatus was common in the Eskimo, in contradistinction to a funnel-shaped canal exhibited by other groups. In this feature, the Cape Denbigh temporal fragment appears more funnel-shaped than tube-

Table 1. MEASUREMENTS

Measurements	Cape Denbigh	Eskimo						
		Alaska			Greenland			
		No.	Mean	S D.	No.	Mean	S.D.	
Length of								
Tympanic Plate	17.0 mm	50	17.31 ± 0.14	1.52	48	17.27 ± 0.13	1.35	
Length below Porus	7.0 mm	50	7.63 ± 0.18	1.85	48	6.99 ± 0.14	1.44	
Length of Porus........	10.0 mm	50	9.68 ± 0.13	1.39	48	10.28 ± 0.15	1.53	
Breadth of								
Tympanic Plate	11.5 mm	50	10.66 ± 0.14	1.52	48	11.46 ± 0.12	1.21	
Breadth anterior to Porus	3.0 mm	50	3.56 ± 0.12	1.22	48	3.56 ± 0.10	1.04	
Breadth of Porus.......	8.5 mm	50	7.10 ± 0.11	1.17	48	7.90 ± 0.10	0.98	

like. However, as Stewart (1933) mentioned, too much significance should not be attributed to this feature because of the difficulty in classification. Collins (1951), in his discussion of the characteristics of the Eskimo skull, suggests that pinched-up nasal bones, thickened tympanic plate, and mandibular, maxillary, and palatine tori may be of equal, if not greater, significance genetically than are metrical features. This statement may be correct, especially in view of the findings of Woo (1950). His investigations seem to indicate that the torus palatinus is a hominid character, determined by heredity, in contradistinction to the pressure theory proposed by Hooton (1918). Of the 65 Point Barrow skulls examined for tympanic thickness, it is estimated that about three-quarters of them had an unusually thickened tympanic plate.

Little can be said concerning the mastoid process except that it appears to be of normal proportions—perhaps on the smaller side of the range for mastoid processes. This small size would also indicate a female skull.

Conclusion

We have described in some detail certain morphologic features of the present material which have been considered from time to time as being characteristic of Eskimo crania. It was shown that the Cape Denbigh calvarium presents a majority of "Eskimo" features, while other characteristics, though less pronounced, are probably of equal morphologic value for ascertaining Eskimo affinity. Such a combination of traits is usually seen in a single skull whatever its temporal or spatial relationship. About all one can do is present a morphologic description of the remains and hope there will be more material forthcoming. If, however, the anthropologist is feeling particularly temerarious, he may suggest a tentative relationship for the remains. We shall follow the

| | Aleuts | | | Indians | | | | | |
| | | | | Alaska | | | California | | |
No.	Mean	S.D.	No.	Mean	S.D.	No.	Mean	S.D.
40	16.12 ± 0.18	1.71	36	16.71 ± 0.18	1.58	50	17.17 ± 0.14	1.42
40	6.11 ± 0.18	1.70	36	6.71 ± 0.17	1.53	50	5.66 ± 0.12	1.31
40	10.01 ± 0.14	1.29	36	10.00 ± 0.15	1.34	50	11.51 ± 0.09	0.99
40	10.33 ± 0.13	1.23	36	9.79 ± 0.12	1.08	50	8.83 ± 0.12	1.21
40	2.81 ± 0.10	0.91	36	2.71 ± 0.09	0.82	50	2.00 ± 0.06	0.66
40	7.52 ± 0.11	1.06	36	7.08 ± 0.10	0.88	50	6.83 ± 0.10	1.01

ll measurements are of the right side.

latter course and suggest that the Cape Denbigh remains are those of a young (less than 22 years old) female, possibly Eskimo.

Department of Anatomy
Medical College of South Carolina
Charleston.

REFERENCES

Ashton, E. H., and S. Zuckerman
1954. The Anatomy of the Articular Fossa (Fossa Mandibularis) in Man and Apes. *American Journal of Physical Anthropology,* n. s., vol. 12, pp. 29–62.

Collins, H. B.
1937. Archeology of St. Lawrence Island, Alaska. *Smithsonian Miscellaneous Collections,* vol. 96, no. 1. Washington, D. C.
1951. The Origin and Antiquity of the Eskimo. *Smithsonian Report for 1950,* pp. 423–467. Washington, D. C.

Fischer-Møller, K.
1937. Skeletal Remains of the Central Eskimo. *Report of the Fifth Thule Expedition,* vol. 3, no. 1, pp. 21–24.

Hooton, E.
1918. On Certain Eskimoid Characters in Icelandic Skulls. *American Journal of Physical Anthropology,* vol. 1, pp. 58–62.

Hrdlička, A.
1930. Anthropological Survey in Alaska. *46th Annual Report of the Bureau of American Ethnology.* Smithsonian Institution, Washington, D. C.

Keen, J. A.
1950. A Study of the Differences Between Male and Female Skulls. *American Journal of Physical Anthropology,* n. s., vol. 8, pp. 65–80.

Knowles, F. H. S.
1915. The Glenoid Fossa in the Skull of the Eskimo. *Canada Geological Survey Museum Bulletin,* no. 9, pp. 1–25 (Anthropological series).

Stewart, T. D.

1933. The Tympanic Plate and External Auditory Meatus in the Eskimo. *American Journal of Physical Anthropology,* vol. 17, pp. 481–96.

Weinmann, J. P., and H. Sicher

1947. *Bone and Bones. Fundamentals of Bone Biology.* The C. V. Mosby Company, St. Louis.

Woo, Ju-Kang

1950. Torus Palatinus. *American Journal of Physical Anthropology,* n s., vol. 8, pp. 81–111.

BIBLIOGRAPHY

Anderson, Douglas D.
n. d.   *Cape Krusenstern Ipiutak Economic and Settlement Patterns.* 1962. M. A. Thesis,
        Brown University. Providence.

Bandi, Hans-Georg, and Jørgen Meldgaard
1952.   Archaeological Investigations on Clavering Ø., Northeast Greenland. *Meddelelser
        om Grønland,* bd. 126, no. 4. Copenhagen.

Bank, Theodore P. II
1953.   Cultural Succession in the Aleutians. *American Antiquity,* vol. 19, no. 1, pp. 40–
        49. Salt Lake City.

Birket-Smith, Kaj
1929.   The Caribou Eskimos. Material and Social Life and their Cultural Position.
        Report of the 5th Thule Expedition, 1921–1924, vol. 5, parts I and II. Copen-
        hagen.

Bourlon, Lt.
1911.   Essai de Classification des Burins. *Revue Anthropologique,* vol. 21, pp. 267–68.
        Paris.

Bryan, Kirk
1946.   Cryopedology—the Study of Frozen Ground and Intensive Frost Action, with
        Suggestions on Nomenclature. *American Journal of Science,* vol. 244, pp. 622–42.
        New Haven.

Burkitt, Miles C.
1920.   Classification of Burins or Gravers. *Proceedings of the Prehistoric Society of
        East Anglia for 1919–20,* vol. 3, pt. 2, pp. 306–10. London.
1925.   *Prehistory, A Study of Early Culture in Europe and the Mediterranean Basin.*
        Cambridge.
1948.   *The Old Stone Age.* Cambridge.

Campbell, John M.
1959.   The Kayuk Complex of Arctic Alaska. *American Antiquity,* vol. 25, no. 1, pp.
        94–105. Salt Lake City.
1961a. The Kogruk Complex of Anaktuvuk Pass, Alaska. *Anthropologica,* n. s., vol. 3,
        no. 1, pp. 3–20. Ottawa.
1961b. The Tuktu Complex of Anaktuvuk Pass. *Anthropological Papers of the Univer-
        sity of Alaska,* vol. 9, no. 2, pp. 61–80. College.

Chard, Chester S.
1955a. Eskimo Archaeology in Siberia. *Southwestern Journal of Anthropology,* vol. 11,
        no. 2, pp. 150–77. Albuquerque.
1955b. An Early Pottery Site in the Chukchi Peninsula. *American Antiquity,* vol. 20,
        no. 3, pp. 283–84. Salt Lake City.
1956.   The Oldest Sites of Northeast Siberia. *American Antiquity,* vol. 21, no. 4, pp.
        405–9. Salt Lake City.
1958a. An Outline of the Prehistory of Siberia. Part 1. The Pre-Metal Periods. *South-
        western Journal of Anthropology,* vol. 14, no. 1, pp. 1–33. Albuquerque.
1958b. Regional Reports: Northeast Asia. *Asian Perspectives,* vol. 2, no. 1, pp. 13–21.
        Tucson.

1959. New World Origins: A Reappraisal. *Antiquity*, vol. 33, no. 129, pp. 44–49. Newbury.

1960. Recent Archaeological Work in the Chukchi Peninsula. *Anthropological Papers of the University of Alaska*, vol. 8, no. 2, pp. 119–30. College.

Clark, J. G. D.

1932. *Mesolithic Age in Britain*. Cambridge.

Collins, Henry B., Jr.

1930. Prehistoric Eskimo Culture in Alaska. *Smithsonian Institution; Explorations and Field-Work, 1929*, pp. 147–56. Washington, D. C.

1932. Archeological Investigations in Northern Alaska. *Explorations and Field-Work of the Smithsonian Institution in 1931*, pp. 103–12. Washington, D. C.

1934. Archaeology of the Bering Sea Region. *Proceedings of the Fifth Pacific Science Congress, Canada, 1933*, vol. 4, pp. 2825–39. Toronto.

1937. Archeology of St. Lawrence Island, Alaska. *Smithsonian Miscellaneous Collections*, vol. 96, no. 1. Washington, D. C.

1937a. Archeological Excavations at Bering Strait. *Explorations and Field-Work of the Smithsonian Institution in 1936*, pp. 63–68. Washington, D. C.

1940. Outline of Eskimo Prehistory. *Smithsonian Miscellaneous Collections*, vol. 100, pp. 533–92. Washington, D. C.

1950. Excavations at Frobisher Bay, Baffin Island, Northwest Territories. *Canada National Museum, Bulletin 118*, pp. 18–43. Ottawa.

1951. The Origin and Antiquity of the Eskimo. *Smithsonian Institution, Annual Report for 1950*, pp. 423–67. Washington, D. C.

1953. Recent Developments in the Dorset Culture Area. *Memoirs of the Society for American Archaeology*, no. 9, pp. 32–39. Salt Lake City.

1956a. The T1 Site at Native Point, Southampton Island, N. W. T. *Anthropological Papers of the University of Alaska*, vol. 4, no. 2, pp. 63–89. College.

1956b. Archaeological Investigations on Southampton and Coats Islands, N. W. T. *Annual Report of the National Museum of Canada*, bull. 142, pp. 82–113. Ottawa.

1958. Present Status of the Dorset Problem. *Proceedings of the 32nd International Congress of Americanists, Copenhagen, 1956*, pp. 557–60.

Cook, James, and James King

1784. *A Voyage to the Pacific Ocean*, etc. Vol. 2 by Cook. London.

Flint, Richard Foster (ed.)

1946. A Program of Desirable Scientific Investigations in Arctic North America. *Arctic Institute of North America*, bull. 1, pp. 1–65. Montreal.

Ford, James A.

1959. Eskimo Prehistory in the Vicinity of Point Barrow, Alaska. *Anthropological Papers of the American Museum of Natural History*, vol. 47, pt. 1. New York.

Friedman, Irving, and Robert L. Smith

1960. A New Dating Method Using Obsidian: Part I, The Development of the Method. *American Antiquity*, vol. 25, no. 4, pp. 476–93. Salt Lake City.

Geist, Otto William, and Froelich G. Rainey

1936. Archaeological Excavations at Kukulik, St. Lawrence Island, Alaska. *Miscellaneous Publications of the University of Alaska*, vol. 2. Washington, D. C.

Giddings, James L.

1941. Dendrochronology in Northern Alaska. *University of Arizona Bulletin*, vol. 12, no. 4, and *University of Alaska Publications*, vol. 4. Tucson.

1948. Chronology of the Kobuk-Kotzebue Sites. *Tree-Ring Bulletin*, vol. 14, no. 4, pp. 26–32. Tucson.

1949. Early Flint Horizons on the North Bering Sea Coast. *Journal of the Washington Academy of Sciences,* vol. 39, no. 3, pp. 85–90. Washington, D C.

1951. The Denbigh Flint Complex. *American Antiquity,* vol. 16, no. 3, pp. 193–203. Salt Lake City.

1952. *The Arctic Woodland Culture of the Kobuk River.* Museum Monographs, University Museum. Philadelphia.

1952*a.* Driftwood and Problems of Arctic Sea Currents. *Proceedings of the American Philosophical Society,* vol. 96, no. 2, pp. 129–42. Philadelphia.

1952*b.* Ancient Bering Strait and Population Spread. In *Science in Alaska,* Arctic Institute of North America Special Publication No. 1 (Henry B. Collins, ed.), pp. 85–102. Washington, D. C.

1954. Early Man in the Arctic. *Scientific American,* vol. 190, no. 6, pp. 82–88. New York.

1955. The Denbigh Flint Complex Is Not Yet Dated. *American Antiquity,* vol. 20, no. 4, pt. 1, pp. 375–76. Salt Lake City.

1956. The Burin Spall Artifact. *Arctic,* vol. 9, no. 4, pp. 229–37. Montreal.

1956*a.* A Flint Site in Northernmost Manitoba. *American Antiquity,* vol. 21, no. 3, pp. 255–68. Salt Lake City.

1956*b.* "Pillows" and Other Rare Flints. *Anthropological Papers of the University of Alaska,* vol. 4, no. 2, pp. 117–20. College.

1957*a.* The Tenuous Beaufort Sea Archeology. *Science in Alaska, 1954.* Proceedings of the Fifth Alaskan Science Conference. Fairbanks.

1957*b.* Round Houses in the Western Arctic. *American Antiquity,* vol. 23, no. 2, pp. 121–35. Salt Lake City.

1960*a.* A View of Archeology about Bering Strait. *Acta Arctica,* fasc. 12, pp. 27–33. Copenhagen.

1960*b.* The Archeology of Bering Strait. *Current Anthropology,* vol. 1, no. 2, pp. 121–38. Chicago.

1960*c.* First Traces of Man in the Arctic. *Natural History,* vol. 69, no. 9, pp. 10–19. New York.

1961. Cultural Continuities of Eskimos. *American Antiquity,* vol. 27, no. 2, pp. 155–73. Salt Lake City.

1962. Onion Portage and Other Flint Sites of the Kobuk River. *Arctic Anthropologist,* vol. 1, no. 1, pp. 6–27. Madison.

Gjessing, Gutorm
1944. Circumpolar Stone Age. *Acta Arctica,* fasc. 2. Copenhagen.

Griffin, James B.
1953. A Preliminary Statement on the Pottery from Cape Denbigh, Alaska. In *Asia and North America—Transpacific Contacts,* assembled by Marian W. Smith, *American Antiquity,* vol. 18, no. 3, pt. 2, pp. 40–42. Salt Lake City.

1960. Some Prehistoric Connections between Siberia and America. *Science,* vol. 131, no. 3403, pp. 801–12. Washington, D. C.

Harp, Elmer, Jr.
1951. An Archaeological Survey in the Strait of Belle Isle Area. *American Antiquity,* vol. 16, no. 3, pp. 203–20. Salt Lake City.

1953. New World Affinities of Cape Dorset Eskimo Culture. *Anthropological Papers of the University of Alaska,* vol. 1, no. 2, pp. 37–52. College.

1958. Prehistory in the Dismal Lake Area, N. W. T., Canada. *Arctic,* vol. 11, no. 4, pp. 219–49. Montreal.

1961. The Archaeology of the Lower and Middle Thelon, Northwest Territories. *Arctic Institute of North America Technical Paper,* no. 8. Montreal.

313

Heizer, Robert F.
1956. Archaeology of the Uyak Site, Kodiak Island, Alaska. *Anthropological Records,* vol. 17, no. 1. Berkeley.

Henderson, Gerald M.
1952. A Neo-Eskimo House Excavation at the Iyatayet Site on Cape Denbigh. Master's thesis, University of Pennsylvania. Philadelphia.

Hoffman, W. J.
1897. The Graphic Art of the Eskimo. *Annual Report of the United States National Museum, 1895,* pp. 739–968. Washington, D. C.

Holtved, Erik
1944. Archaeological Investigations in the Thule District. *Meddelelser om Grønland,* vol. 141, nos. 1 and 2. Copenhagen.
1954. Archaeological Investigations in the Thule District. III Nûgdlît, and Comer's Midden. *Meddelelser om Grønland,* vol. 146, no. 3. Copenhagen.

Hopkins, David M., and J. L. Giddings
1953. Geological Background of the Iyatayet Archeological Site, Cape Denbigh, Alaska. *Smithsonian Miscellaneous Collections,* vol. 121, no. 11. Washington, D. C.

Hrdlička, Aleš
1930. Anthropological Survey of Alaska. *46th Annual Report of the Bureau of American Ethnology, Smithsonian Institution.* Washington, D. C.

Irving, William N.
1951. Archaeology in the Brooks Range of Alaska. *American Antiquity,* vol. 17, no. 1, p. 52. Salt Lake City.
1953. Evidence of Early Tundra Cultures in Northern Alaska. *Anthropological Papers of the University of Alaska,* vol. 1, no. 2, pp. 55–85. College.
1955. Burins from Central Alaska. *American Antiquity,* vol. 20, no. 4, pp. 380–83. Salt Lake City.
n. d. Preliminary Report on an Archaeological Reconnaissance in the Western part of the Brooks Range of Alaska. Manuscript.

Jenness, Diamond
1928. Archaeological Investigation in Bering Strait. *Annual Report of the National Museum of Canada, 1926,* bull. 50, pp. 71–80. Ottawa.

Jochelson, Waldemar
1925. Archaeological Investigations in the Aleutian Islands. *Carnegie Institution of Washington,* pub. 367. Washington, D. C.
1928. Archaeological Investigations in Kamchatka. *Carnegie Institution of Washington,* pub. 388. Washington, D. C.

Johnson, Frederick
1946. An Archaeological Survey along the Alaska Highway, 1944. *American Antiquity,* vol. 11, no. 3, pp. 183–86. Menasha.
1951. Radiocarbon Dating. *Memoirs of the Society for American Archaeology.* Supplement to *American Antiquity,* vol. 17, no. 1, pt. 2. Salt Lake City.

Knuth, Eigil
1952. An Outline of the Archaeology of Pearyland. *Arctic,* vol. 5, no. 1, pp. 17–33. Ottawa.
1954. The Paleo-Eskimo Culture of Northeast Greenland Elucidated by Three New Sites. *American Antiquity,* vol. 19, no. 4, pp. 367–81. Salt Lake City.
1958. Archaeology of the Farthest North. *Proceedings of the 32nd International Congress of Americanists, Copenhagen, 1956,* pp. 562–73. Copenhagen.

Krader, Lawrence
1952. Neolithic Find in the Chukchi Peninsula. *American Antiquity,* vol. 17, no. 3, pp. 261–62. Salt Lake City.

Krieger, Alex D.
1947. Artifacts from the Plainview Bison Bed. In Sellards, Evans and Meade, *Bulletin of the Geological Society of America,* vol. 58, pp. 938–52. New York.

de Laguna, Frederica
1934. *The Archaeology of Cook Inlet, Alaska.* University of Pennsylvania Press. Philadelphia.
1947. The Prehistory of Northern North America as Seen from the Yukon. *Memoirs of the Society for American Archaelogy, No. 3.* Supplement to *American Antiquity,* vol. 12, no. 3, pt. 2. Menasha.

Larsen, Helge
1934. Dødemandsbugten, an Eskimo Settlement on Clavering Island. *Meddelelser om Grønland,* bd. 102, no. 1. Copenhagen.
1938. Archaeological Investigations in Knud Rasmussen's Land. *Meddelelser om Grønland,* bd. 119, no. 8. Copenhagen.
1950. Archaeological Investigations in Southwestern Alaska. *American Antiquity,* vol. 15, no. 3, pp. 177–86. Menasha.
1951. De Dansk-Amerikanske Alaska-ekspeditioner, 1949–50. *Geografisk Tidsskrift,* 51 bind, pp. 63–93. Copenhagen.
1953. Archaeological Investigations in Alaska Since 1939. *Polar Record,* vol. 6, no. 45, pp. 593–607. Cambridge, England.

Larsen, Helge, and Jørgen Meldgaard
1958. Paleo-Eskimo Cultures in Disko Bugt, West Greenland, *Meddelelser om Grønland,* bd. 161, no. 2. Copenhagen.

Larsen, Helge, and Froelich Rainey
1948. *Ipiutak and the Arctic Whale Hunting Culture.* Anthropological Papers of the American Museum of Natural History, vol. 42. New York.

Laughlin, William S.
1958. Neo-Aleut and Paleo-Aleut Prehistory. *Proceedings of the 32nd International Congress of Americanists, Copenhagen, 1956,* pp. 516–30. Copenhagen.

Laughlin, William S., and Gordon H. Marsh
1951. A New View of the History of the Aleutians. *Arctic,* vol. 4, no. 2, pp. 75–88. Montreal.
1954. The Lamellar Flake Manufacturing Site on Anangula Island. *American Antiquity,* vol. 20, no. 1, pp. 27–39. Salt Lake City.
1956. Trends in Aleutian Chipped Stone Artifacts. *Anthropological Papers of the University of Alaska,* vol. 5, no. 1, pp. 5–21. College.

Leechman, Douglas
1943. Two New Cape Dorset Sites. *American Antiquity,* vol. 8, no. 4, pp. 363–75. Menasha.

Lethbridge, T. C.
1939. Archaeological Data from the Canadian Arctic. *Journal of the Royal Anthropological Institute of Great Britain and Ireland,* vol. 69, pt. 2, pp. 187–233. London.

Libby, W. F.
1955. *Radiocarbon Dating.* Second edition, University of Chicago Press. Chicago.

Mackay, J. R., W. H. Mathews, and R. S. MacNeish
1961. Geology of the Engigstciak Archaeological Site, Yukon Territory. *Arctic,* vol. 14, no. 1, pp. 25–52. Montreal.

MacNeish, Richard S.

1951. An Archaeological Reconnaissance in the Northwest Territories. *Annual Report of the National Museum of Canada, 1949–50,* bull. 123, pp. 24–41. Ottawa.

1954. The Pointed Mountain Site near Fort Liard, Northwest Territories, Canada. *American Antiquity,* vol. 19, no. 3, pp. 234–53. Salt Lake City.

1956. The Engigstciak Site on the Yukon Arctic Coast. *Anthropological Papers of the University of Alaska,* vol. 4, no. 2, pp. 91–111. College.

1959. Men Out of Asia; As Seen from the Northwest Yukon. *Anthropological Papers of the University of Alaska,* vol. 7, no. 2, pp. 41–70. College.

1960. Archaeological Projects in Canada, 1959. *Archaeology,* vol. 13, no. 3, pp. 194–201. New York.

Manning, T. H.

1956. Narrative of a Second Defence Research Board Expedition to Banks Island, with Notes on the Country and Its History. *Arctic,* vol. 9, nos. 1 and 2, pp. 3–77. Montreal.

Maringer, John

1950. Contributions to the Prehistory of Mongolia. *The Sino-Swedish Expedition,* pub. 34. Stockholm.

Mason, J. Alden

1930. Excavations of Eskimo Thule Culture Sites at Point Barrow, Alaska. *Proceedings of the 23rd International Congress of Americanists,* pp. 383–94. New York.

Mathiassen, Therkel

1927. Archaeology of the Central Eskimos, the Thule Culture and Its Position Within the Eskimo Culture. *Report of the Fifth Thule Expedition, 1921–24,* vol. 4, pts. 1 and 2. Copenhagen.

1930. Archaeological Collections from the Western Eskimos. *Report of the Fifth Thule Expedition, 1921–24,* vol. 10, no. 1. Copenhagen.

1948. Ældre stenalder. *Danske Oldsager,* I. Copenhagen.

1958. The Sermermiut Excavations, 1955. *Meddelelser om Grønland,* vol. 161, no. 3. Copenhagen.

Meldgaard, Jørgen

1952. A Paleo-Eskimo Culture in West Greenland. *American Antiquity,* vol. 17, no. 3, pp. 222–30. Salt Lake City.

1960. Origin and Evolution of Eskimo Cultures in the Eastern Arctic. *Canadian Geographic Journal,* vol. 60, no. 2, pp. 64–75. Montreal.

Michael, Henry N.

1958. The Neolithic Age in Eastern Siberia. *Transactions of the American Philosophical Society,* n. s., vol. 48, pt. 2. Philadelphia.

Moore, George W.

1960. Recent Eustatic Sea-level Fluctuations Recorded by Arctic Beach Ridges. Geological Survey Professional Paper 400-B. *Geological Survey Research, 1960,* pp. B335–37. Washington, D. C.

Nelson, E. W.

1899. The Eskimo about Bering Strait. *Bureau of American Ethnology, 18th Annual Report.* Washington, D. C.

Nelson, N. C.

1935. Early Migrations of Man to North America. *Natural History,* vol. 35, p. 356. New York.

1937. Notes on Cultural Relations between Asia and America. *American Antiquity,* vol. 2, no. 4, pp. 267–72. Menasha.

316

Niederlender, A., R. Lacam and D. de Sonneville-Bordes

1956. L'Abri Pagès a Rocamadour et la Question de l'Azilien dans le Lot (Avec une note paléontologique par J. Bouchud). *L'Anthropologie,* vol. 60, nos. 5–6, pp. 417–46. Paris.

Noone, H. V. V.

1934. A Classification of Flint Burins or Gravers. *Journal of the Royal Anthropological Institute of Great Britain and Ireland,* vol. 64, pp. 81–92. London.

Okladnikov, A. P.

1959. Ancient Cultures in the Continental Part of North-East Asia. *Proceedings of the 33rd International Congress of Americanists, 1958,* vol. 2, pp. 72–80. San Jose.

1960. A Note on the Lake El'gytkhyn Finds. *American Antiquity,* vol. 26, no. 1, pp. 97–98. Salt Lake City.

Okladnikov, A. P., and I. A. Nekrasov

1959. New Traces of an Inland Neolithic Culture in the Chukstsk (Chukchi) Peninsula. *American Antiquity,* vol. 25, no. 2, pp. 247–56. Salt Lake City.

Osgood, Cornelius

1940. Ingalik Material Culture. *Yale University Publications in Anthropology,* No. 22. New Haven.

Oswalt, Wendell

1952. The Archaeology of Hooper Bay Village, Alaska. *Anthropological Papers of the University of Alaska,* vol. 1, no. 1, pp. 47–91. College.

1953. Northeast Asian and Alaskan Pottery Relationships. *Southwestern Journal of Anthropology,* vol. 9, no. 4, pp. 394–407. Albuquerque.

1955. Alaskan Pottery: A Classification and Historical Reconstruction. *American Antiquity,* vol. 21, no. 1, pp. 32–43. Salt Lake City.

Rainey, Froelich G.

1939. Archaeology in Central Alaska. *Anthropological Papers of the American Museum of Natural History,* vol. 36, pt. 4. New York.

1940. Archaeological Investigations in Central Alaska. *American Antiquity,* vol. 5, no. 4, pp. 299–308. Menasha.

1941. Eskimo Prehistory: The Okvik Site on the Punuk Islands. *Anthropological Papers of the American Museum of Natural History,* vol. 37, pt. 4. New York.

Rainey, Froelich G., and Elizabeth Ralph

1959. Radiocarbon Dating in the Arctic. *American Antiquity,* vol. 24, no. 4, pp. 365–74. Salt Lake City.

Ralph, Elizabeth, and Robert Ackerman

1961. University of Pennsylvania Radiocarbon Dates, IV. *Radiocarbon,* vol. 3, pp. 4–14. New Haven.

Rowley, Graham

1940. The Dorset Culture of the Eastern Arctic. *American Anthropologist,* vol. 42, no. 3, pp. 490–99. Menasha.

Rubin, Meyer, and H. E. Suess

1956. U. S. Geological Survey Radiocarbon Dates I. *Science,* vol. 121, no. 3136, pp. 149–51. Washington, D. C.

Rudenko, S. I.

1961. The Ancient Culture of the Bering Sea and the Eskimo Problem. *Arctic Institute of North America, Anthropology of the North; Translations from Russian Sources,* no. 1. Toronto.

317

Sellards, E. H., Glen L. Evans, and Grayson E. Meade
1947. Fossil Bison and Associated Artifacts from Plainview, Texas. *Bulletin of the Geological Society of America,* vol. 58, pp. 927–54. New York.

Skarland, Ivar, and C. J. Keim
1958. Archaeological Discoveries on the Denali Highway, Alaska. *Anthropological Papers of the University of Alaska,* vol. 6, no. 2, pp. 79–88. College.

Solberg, O.
1907. Beiträge zur Vorgeschichte der Osteskimo. *Videnskabsselskabets Skrifter,* II. Hist.-Fil. klasse, no. 2. Oslo.

Solecki, Ralph S.
1950. A Preliminary Report of an Archaeological Reconnaissance of the Kukpowruk and Kokolik Rivers in Northwest Alaska. *American Antiquity,* vol. 16, no. 1, pp. 66–69. Menasha.

1951. Notes on Two Archaeological Discoveries in Alaska, 1950. *American Antiquity,* vol. 17, no. 1, pp. 55–57. Salt Lake City.

1951a. Archaeology and Ecology of the Arctic Slope. *Annual Report of the Smithsonian Institution, 1950,* pp. 469–95. Washington.

Solecki, Ralph S., and R. J. Hackman
1951. Additional Data on the Denbigh Flint Complex in Northern Alaska. *Journal of the Washington Academy of Sciences,* vol. 41, no. 3, pp. 85–88. Washington, D. C.

Spaulding, Albert C.
1946. Northeastern Archaeology and General Trends in the Northern Forest Zone. In *Man in Northeastern North America,* Frederick Johnson, ed. Papers of the Robert S. Peabody Foundation for Anthropology, vol. 3, pp. 143–67. Andover.

Speck, Frank G.
1941. Art Processes in Birchbark of the River Desert Algonquin, a Circumboreal Trait. *Bureau of American Ethnology,* bull. 128, pp. 231–74. Washington Anthropological Papers, no. 17. Washington, D. C.

Taylor, William E.
1959. Review and Assessment of the Dorset Problem. *Anthropologica,* n. s., vol. 1, nos. 1 and 2, pp. 24–46. Ottawa.

Thompson, Raymond M.
1948. Notes on the Archaeology of the Utukok River, Northwestern Alaska. *American Antiquity,* vol. 14, no. 1, pp. 62–65. Menasha.

Tolstoy, Paul
1958. The Archaeology of the Lena Basin and Its New World Relationships. *American Antiquity,* part 1, vol. 23, no. 4, pp. 397–418; part 2, vol. 24, no. 1, pp. 63–81. Salt Lake City.

VanStone, James W.
1957. An Archaeological Reconnaissance of Nunivak Island, Alaska. *Anthropological Papers of the University of Alaska,* vol. 5, no. 2, pp. 97–117. College.

Wintemberg, W. J.
1939. Eskimo Sites of the Dorset Culture in Newfoundland. *American Antiquity,* vol. 5, no. 2, pp. 83–102; no. 4, pp. 309–33. Menasha.

Wormington, H. Marie
1957. *Ancient Man in North America.* Denver Museum of Natural History, Popular Series No. 4 (4th ed. revised). Denver.

1962. A Survey of Early American Prehistory. *American Scientist,* vol. 50, no. 1, pp. 230–42. Easton, Pa.

318

INDEX

320

hammer head, 144; Pl. 36
harpoon dart head, 41; Pl. 8
harpoon finger rest, 43; Pl. 8
harpoon foreshaft, 41; Pl. 8
harpoon head, 38–40; Pl. 6
harpoon ice pick, 43, 143–44; Pls. 7, 38
knife, 145; Pl. 36
labret, 73–74; Pl. 30
line guide, 78; Pl. 31
marble, Pl. 31
needle case, 73; Pl. 29
objects, 37, 65, 144, 147; Pls. 36–38
peg, 34, 80; Pls. 5, 31
pendant, 77; Pls. 31, 33
pick, 64; Pl. 21
prong, 162–63; Pl. 36
ring, Pl. 31
sinker, 50; Pl. 11
socket piece, 42; Pl. 7
swivel part, 78, 82; Pl. 31
throwing board peg, 34; Pl. 5
toggle, 78; Pl. 31
tube, 77–78; Pl. 31
wedge, 80; Pls. 31, 33
Iyatayet
artifacts found at, 6–7, 139–76
excavating of, 4, 6–9, 119–37
legend of, 4
site, 1, 2, 4, 120–22

Jabbertown, 40, 47
Jade
adz head, 61, 124; Pl. 19
blade, 55, 85; Pls. 29, 33
drill bit, 63; Pl. 33
lancet, 85; Pl. 29
pendant, 76–77; Pl. 29
Japan, 266
Jasper
blade, 160, 165, 181; Pls. 46, 52, 62
burin, 218; Pls. 66-a, 72
flakeknife, 167, 181; Pls. 54, 62
knife, 181; Pls. 62, 70-b
point, 162–63, 165, 234, 235; Pls. 47–49
scraper, 168, 228; Pls. 55–56, 62, 70-b
Jehle, Albert, 304
Jehol Province, 206
Jenness, Diamond, 251
Jet labret, 148; Pl. 39

Jochelson, Waldemar, 100–1, 158, 160, 172, 174
Johnson, Frederick, 202, 245

Kachemak Bay, 42, 149, 158, 178, 262
Kamchatka, 103, 160, 172
Kamut Lake, 259
Kayak, 45–46, 75
harpoon rest, 43; Pl. 8
model, 89; Pl. 32
parts, 70, 83–84; Pl. 28
Kayuk, 263–64
Keen, J. A., 305
Keim, C. J., 264
Kiana, 263
King, James, 11, 179–80
Kitneapalok, 175
Knife
beaver tooth, 5, 58, 59, 66–67
blade, 55–58, 150–51, 165–68, 177, 181–83, 222–23, 226, 229, 233, 235, 236, 269; Pls. 41-a, 52, 62, 64, 70-b, 72
composite, 145; Pl. 36
draw, 58
flake-, 166–67, 181–82, 216, 218–29, 223–26; Pls. 54, 62, 69,
handle, 56–58; Pls. 14, 15, 27
men's, 54–58; Pl. 16
microblade, 207, 208
slate, 54–58, 151, 183; Pls. 16, 41-a, 62
women's, 57–58, 166; Pl. 16
Knife sharpener, 59–60; Pls. 15, 17
Knowles, F. H. S., 307
Knuth, Eigil, 203, 210, 260–61
Kobuk River, 1, 3, 19, 28–29, 33, 41, 43, 47, 49–51, 53–54, 59–61, 63, 66–67, 69–71, 75–78, 80–82, 85, 101, 107, 114–16, 124, 139, 146, 158, 174, 187, 203, 244, 262–63
Kodiak Island, 262
Koslovich, Eugene, 271
Kotzebue culture
Intermediate, 28, 30, 33–34, 37–38, 41–42, 47, 49–50, 56–57, 59, 62–63, 69–70, 73, 76–77, 80, 82, 85, 90, 94, 101, 107, 116, 124, 251, 256
Old, 28, 41, 47, 50, 54–55, 58–59, 61–62, 64, 73–74, 77, 85, 104, 107, 116, 251, 256

329

Western Thule culture, 29, 40, 43, 83, 251, 256
Whale bone, 38
Whetstone, 59–60, 67, 155–58, 182–83, 188, 238; Pls. 17, 42, 43, 62, 64
Whittling, beaver tooth, 43, 52, 54, 59, 66, 67, 146, 189
Wintemberg, W. J., 202, 260
Wistar Institute of Anatomy and Biology, 307
Women's activities, 240
Women's knives, 57–58; Pl. 16
Woo, Ju-Kang, 308
Wood
  air plug, 44; Pl. 8
  arrow, 30–32; Pl. 2
  awl, 61; Pl. 23
  block, 83; Pl. 28
  bow sinew twister, 33; Pl. 3
  buzz, 85; Pl. 34
  comb, 74, 86; Pl. 32
  cutting board, 73; Pl. 29
  dart shaft, 43; Pls. 8, 10
  decorated, 99; Pl. 29
  deposits at Nukleet, 19, 21–23, 26
  dolls, 86–87; Pl. 32
  drill bow, 63; Pl. 4
  engraving tool, 72, 75–76; Pl. 30
  fish arrow shaft, 49; Pl. 9
  fish hook shank, 49; Pl. 11
  flaker handle, 64; Pl. 15
  float mending disc, 44; Pl. 8
  float mouthpiece, 44; Pl. 8
  float toggle, 43–44; Pl. 8
  goggles, 44–45; Pl. 34
  guard, 83; Pl. 28
  handle, 55–56, 58, 68; Pls. 14, 15, 26, 27
  harpoon shaft, 43; Pls. 8, 10
  kayak harpoon rest, 43; Pl. 8
  kayak parts, 83; Pl. 28
  labret, 73–74; Pl. 30
  lance foreshaft, 43, 47; Pl. 7
  miscellaneous objects, 65, 147; Pl. 38
  net float, 52, 54; Pl. 13
  net gauge, 52; Pl. 11
  reel, 50, 73; Pls. 12, 29
  salmon spear prong, 49; Pl. 9
  shaft, 31, 33, 36–37, 43, 63, 95, 97, 141; Pls. 10, 36
  shuttle, net, 53; Pl. 13
  sinew twister, 33; Pl. 3
  snare peg, 65, 97; Pl. 23
  snowshoe parts, 82; Pl. 27
  throwing board, 34; Pl. 5
  tray, 23, 26
Wormington, H. Marie, 229, 266
Wound plug, 43–44; Pl. 8
Wrist guard, 33; Pl. 3

Ymyyakhtakh, 209
Yukon Island culture, 38, 41, 51, 56, 58, 62, 88, 145–46, 158, 169, 172
Yukon River, 1, 3
Yukon Territory, 264

Zuckerman, S., 307

Plates

to

THE ARCHEOLOGY OF
CAPE DENBIGH

PLATE 1

	Identity		Reference page	Location
1	Arrowhead, antler, Type	3	30	NB–1
2	Arrowhead, antler, Type	2	30	NA
3	Arrowhead, antler, Type	3	30	NB–5$_{3-5}$
4	Arrowhead, antler, Type	3	30	NA–7$_6$
5	Arrowhead, antler, Type	7A	30	NR
6	Arrowhead, antler, Type	4	30	NA–2$_4$
7	Arrowhead, antler, Type	1	30	NH–1
8	Arrowhead, ivory, Type	2	30	IYH–1
9	Arrowhead, antler, Type	7	30	NA
10	Arrowhead, antler, Type	2	30	NH–1
11	Arrowhead, antler, Type	7A	30	NB–5$_6$
12	Arrowhead, antler, Type	10	30–31	NA–7$_6$
13	Arrowhead, antler, Type	6	30	NA–2$_2$
14	Arrowhead, antler, Type	6	30	NC–1$_4$
15	Arrowhead, antler, Type	5	30	NA–1$_3$
16	Arrowhead, antler, Type	5	30	NA
17	Arrowhead, antler, Type	8	30–31	NC–1$_4$
18	Arrowhead, ivory, Type	9	30–31	NB–4$_{10}$
19	Arrowhead, ivory, Type	9	30–31	NA–10$_3$
20	Arrowhead, antler, Type	7	30	NA–3$_2$
21	Arrowhead, ivory, Type	9	30–31	NA–3$_2$

Nukleet—Arrowheads

0 1 2 3 4 5 6 7 8 9 10 cm.

PLATE 2

	Identity	Reference page	Location
1	Arrowhead, ivory, Type 11	30–31	NB
2	Arrowhead, antler, Type 12	30–31	NB–3
3	Arrowhead, antler, Type 14	30–31	NB–3$_8$
4	Arrowhead, antler, Type 16	30–31	NB–3$_{11}$
5	Blunt arrowhead (?), antler	30–31, 33	NA–6$_5$
6	Blunt arrow fragment, wood	30–32	NB–3$_9$
7	Blunt arrow fragment, wood	30–32	NC–1$_9$
8	Blunt arrow fragment, wood	30–32	NB–4$_{10}$
9	Arrowhead, antler, Type 16	30–31	NB–3$_{11}$
10	Arrowhead, antler, Type 15	30–31	NB–3$_8$
11	Arrowhead, antler, Type 15	30–31	NB–4$_9$
12	Arrowhead, antler, Type 12	30–31	NB–4$_8$
13	Arrowhead, antler, Type 12	30–31	NA–4$_{11}$
14	Arrowhead, antler, Type 14	30–31	NB–4$_8$
15	Arrowhead, antler, Type 16	30–31	NB–3$_8$
16	Arrowhead, antler, Type 13	30–31	IYH–1
17	Arrowhead, antler, Type 14	30–31	NB–2$_6$

Nukleet—Arrowheads

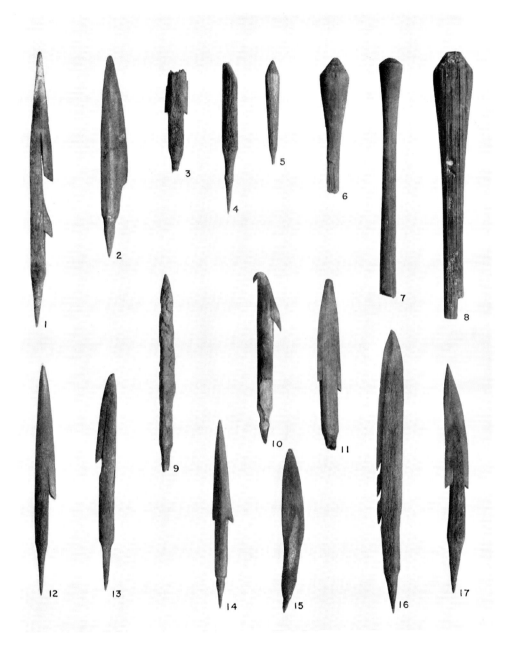

0 1 2 3 4 5 6 7 8 9 10 cm.

PLATE 3

	Identity	Reference page	Location
1	Arrow shaft (probably toy), Type 4	31, 90	NA–4$_{11}$
2	Arrow shaft, Type 1	31	NA–3$_{5}$
3	Arrow shaft, Type 5	31	NA–2$_{5}$
4	Arrow shaft, Type 4	31	NA–1$_{7}$
5	Arrow shaft, Type 3	31	NA–2
6	Arrow shaft, Type 3	31	NB–4$_{8}$
7	Arrow shaft, Type 2	31	IYB
8	Arrow shaft, Type 3	31	NB–4$_{14}$
9	Arrow shaft, Type 1	31	NB–4$_{9}$
10	Arrow point, chert	30–31	NH–1$_{5}$
11	Arrow point, chert	30–31	NR
12	Arrow point, chert	30–31	NA–9$_{3}$
13	Wrist guard, antler	30, 33	NH–1
14	Wrist guard, antler	30, 33	IYH–1
15	Bow marline spike	30, 33	NA–1$_{3}$
16	Bow sinew twister, wood	30, 33	NB
17	Bow sinew twister, bone	30, 33	NB–4$_{7}$
18	Bow sinew twister, bone	30, 33	NB–3$_{11}$
19	Shaft straightener, antler	31, 33	NB–1$_{4}$

Nukleet—Arrow Shafts, Points, etc.

1   2   3   4   5   6   7   8   9

10   11   12

13   14   15   16   17   18   19

0 1 2 3 4 5 6 7 8 9 10 cm.

PLATE 4

	Identity	Reference page	Location
1	Bow fragment, Type A	30–31	NB–1_3
2	Bow fragment, Type C	30, 32	NH–1uf
3	Bow fragment, drill or toy	30, 57, 63	NB–4_{14}
4	Bow fragment, Type B	30, 32	NR
5	Bow fragment, Type B	30, 32	NR
6	Bow fragment, Type C	30, 32	NB–3_{13}
7	Bow fragment, Type C	30, 32	NB–3_{13}
8	Bow fragment, Type C	30, 32	NB–3_8
9	Bow fragment, Type B	30, 32	NB–1_6
10	Bow fragment, composite	30, 32	NB–4_{11}
11	Bow fragment, drill or toy	30, 57, 63	NA–7_{11}
12	Bow fragment, drill or toy	30, 57, 63	NB–3_{5-6}
13	Bow fragment, Type D	30, 32	NB–3_{13}
14	Bow fragment, Type D	30, 32	NB–4_{11}
15	Bow fragment	30, 32	NB–3_{5-6}
16	Bow fragment, Type D	30, 32	NB–3_{13}
17	Bow fragment, composite	30, 32	NB–3_8

Nukleet—Bow Fragments

1	2	3	4	5	6	7	8	9	10	11	12	13	14	15	16	17

0 1 2 3 4 5 6 7 8 9 10 cm.

PLATE 5

	Identity	Reference page	Location
1	Throwing board fragment, wood	31, 34	NB–2₇
2	Blunt arrowhead, bone	31–33, 35	NA–1₃
3	Blunt arrowhead, bone	31–33	NA–4₂
4	Blunt arrowhead, antler	31–33	NA–5₂
5	Blunt arrowhead, antler	31–33	NA–7₂
6	Blunt arrowhead, antler (toy)	31–33	NH–1
7	Bird spear end prong (?), antler	31, 34	NH–1uf
8	Bird spear end prong, antler	31, 34	NB–4₁₁
9	Throwing board peg, ivory	31, 34	NA–8₃
10	Bird spear side prong, antler	31, 33	NB–2₃
11	Bird spear side prong, antler	31, 34	NH–1₅
12	Bird spear end prong (?), antler	31, 34	ND–1₁₋₂
13	Bird spear side prong, antler	31, 33	NA–7₂
14	Bird spear side prong, antler	31, 34	NB–4₁₂
15	Bird spear side prong, ivory	31, 34	NB–4₁₄
16	Throwing board fragment, wood	31, 34	NB–4₁₁
17	Bola weight (?), antler	31, 33	NA–5₂
18	Bola weight, ivory	31, 33	NB–2₆
19	Bola weight, ivory	31, 33	IYE
20	Bird spear side prong, ivory	31, 34	NB–4₁₀
21	Bird spear side prong, antler	31, 34	NB–4₁₀
22	Bird spear end prong (?), ivory	31, 34	IYD

Nukleet—Arrowheads, Bird Spear Prongs, Bola Weights, etc.

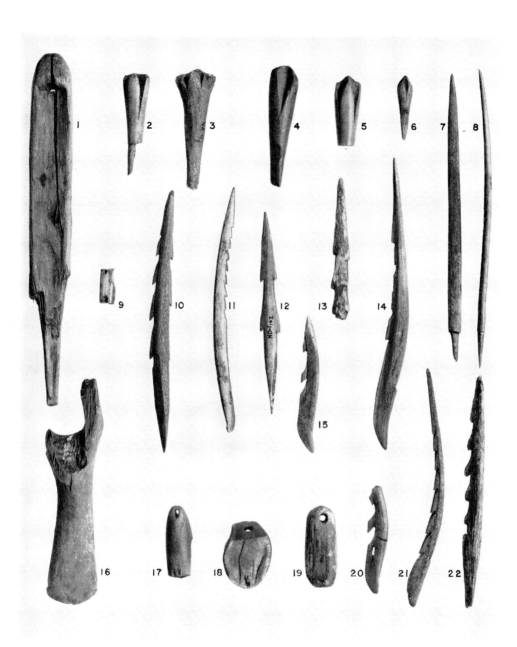

0 1 2 3 4 5 6 7 8 9 10 cm.

PLATE 6

	Identity	Reference page	Location
1	Harpoon head, Type 1, antler	36, 38	NA–2_{12}
2	Harpoon head, Type 1, antler	36, 38	NB–5_5
3	Harpoon head, Type 1, antler	36, 38	NB–4_9
4	Harpoon head, Type 6, antler	36, 39	NA–4_4
5	Harpoon head, Type 1, antler	36, 38	NH–1
6	Harpoon head, Type 1, antler	36, 38	NA–6_5
7	Harpoon head, Type 1, antler	36, 38	NB–2_5
8	Harpoon head, Type 2, antler	36, 38	NA–1_4
9	Harpoon head, Type 2, antler	36, 38	NA–2_4
10	Harpoon head, Type 1, antler	36, 38	NB–3_7
11	Harpoon head, Type 1, ivory	36, 38	NB–3_{11}
12	Harpoon head, Type 1, antler	36, 38	NB–3_7
13	Harpoon head, Type 4, antler	36, 39	NA–3_2
14	Harpoon head, Type 3, antler	36, 38	NA–sod
15	Harpoon head, Type 7, antler	36, 39	NB–5_{3-5}
16	Harpoon head, Type 1, ivory	36, 38	NB–3_{5-6}
17	Harpoon head, Type 1, antler	36, 38	NB–3_7
18	Harpoon head, Type 1, antler	36, 38	NA–8_{11}
19	Harpoon head, Type 1, ivory	36, 38	NB–3_9
20	Harpoon head, Type 4, antler	36, 39	NA–1_{10}
21	Harpoon head, Type 4, antler	36, 39	NA–5_5
22	Harpoon head, Type 2, antler	36, 38	NA–8_{11}
23	Harpoon head, Type 7, antler	36, 39	NB–5_8
24	Harpoon head, Type 7, ivory	36, 39	IYE-upper
25	Harpoon head, Type 1, bone	36, 38	NB–3_{5-6}
26	Harpoon head, Type 10, bone (toy?)	36, 40, 90	NB–3_{13}
27	Harpoon head, Type 9, antler	36, 40	NB–5_7
28	Harpoon head, Type 5, ivory	36, 39	NA–3_8
29	Harpoon head, Type 5, ivory	36, 39	NB–4_8
30	Harpoon head, Type 8, ivory	36, 40	NB–3_9
31	Harpoon head, Type 9, antler	36, 40	NB–4_{13}
32	Harpoon head, Type 8, ivory	36, 40	NB–4_9
33	Harpoon head, Type 7, antler	36, 40	NB–3_8
34	Harpoon head, Type 9, ivory	36, 40	NB–3_{11}
35	Harpoon head, Type 7, ivory	36, 40	NB–3_9
36	Harpoon head, Type 7, ivory	36, 40	NB–4_9
37	Harpoon head, Type 7, ivory	36, 40	NB–3_{11}

Nukleet—Harpoon Heads

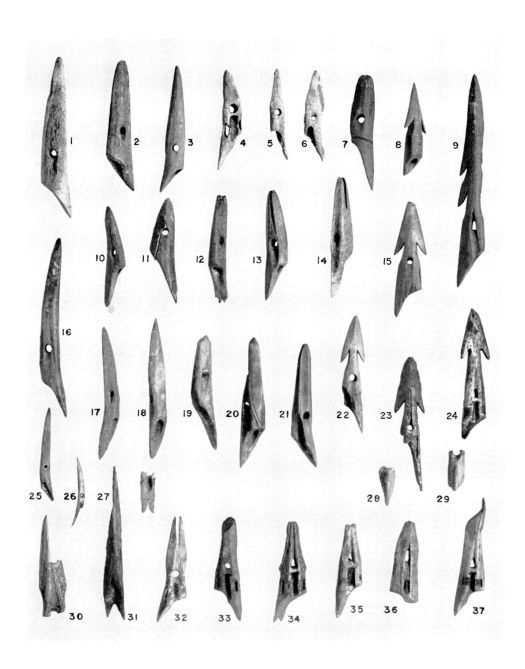

0 1 2 3 4 5 6 7 8 9 10 cm.

PLATE 7

	Identity	Reference page	Location
1	Socket piece, composite, ivory	36, 42	NB–3_9
2	Socket piece, tubular, antler	36, 42	NA–2_{10}
3	Socket piece, socket each end, antler	36, 42	NA–7_2
4	Dart socket piece, bone	36, 42	NA–sod
5	Dart socket piece, bone	36, 42	NA–1_3
6	Lance foreshaft (?), wood	37, 43, 47, 59	NA–2_7
7	Socket piece, tubular, antler	36, 42	NC–1_4
8	Dart socket piece, antler	36, 42	NB–3_8
9	Composite socket piece, ivory	36, 42	NB–4_{14}
10	Dart socket piece, ivory	36, 42	NB–3_{13}
11	Harpoon ice pick, ivory	37, 43	IYE
12	Harpoon ice pick, ivory	37, 43	IYD
13	Harpoon ice pick, antler	37, 43	NH–1
14	Harpoon ice pick, bone	37, 43	NB–1_6

Nukleet—Socket Pieces, Ice Picks, etc.

PLATE 8

	Identity	Reference page	Location
1	Harpoon shaft fragment, wood	37, 42	NB–4$_7$
2	Harpoon shaft fragment, wood	37, 42	NB–4$_{12}$
3	Dart shaft fragment, wood	37, 43	NB–4$_{11}$
4	Harpoon shaft fragment, wood	37, 42	NB–3$_{10}$
5	Float mouthpiece, wood	37, 44	NC–1$_9$
6	Float mouthpiece, wood	37, 44	NB–4$_{12}$
7	Float mouthpiece, wood	37, 44, 59	NA–10$_6$
8	Float mending disc, wood	37, 44	NH–1
9	Harpoon foreshaft, antler	36, 40	NH–1
10	Harpoon foreshaft, antler	36, 40, 42	NB–5$_7$
11	Harpoon foreshaft, ivory	36, 41	NB–3$_9$
12	Harpoon finger rest, ivory	37, 43	NA–2$_7$
13	Harpoon finger rest, ivory	37, 43	NA–1$_3$
14	Finger rest or throwing board peg, antler	34, 37, 43	NA–4$_8$
15	Float toggle, antler	37, 44	NH–1$_5$
16	Float toggle, wood	37, 44	NB–5$_{3-5}$
17	Wound plug or "air plug," wood	37, 44	NB–3$_{5-6}$
18	Wound plug or "air plug," wood	37, 44	NH–1uf
19	Kayak harpoon rest, wood	37, 43, 59	NA–5$_3$
20	Harpoon dart head, ivory	37, 41	NA–8$_8$
21	Harpoon dart head, ivory	37, 41	NA–4$_{11}$
22	Harpoon dart head, ivory	37, 41	NH–1
23	Harpoon dart head, ivory	37, 41	NA–9$_3$
24	Harpoon dart head, antler	37, 41	NB–4$_7$
25	Harpoon dart head, antler	37, 41	IYF
26	Harpoon dart head, ivory	37, 41	NA–4$_{11}$
27	Harpoon dart head, ivory	37, 41	NB–4$_{13}$
28	Harpoon dart head, antler	37, 41	NB–1$_2$
29	Harpoon dart head, ivory	37, 41	NB–3$_9$
30	Harpoon dart head, ivory	37, 41	NA–4$_3$
21	Harpoon dart head, ivory	37, 41	NA–1$_3$
32	Harpoon dart head, ivory	37, 41	NB–lower

Nukleet—Fishing Equipment, etc.

PLATE 9

	Identity	Reference page	Location
1	Salmon spear side prong, toy (?), wood	48–49	NB–4_{14}
2	Fish arrow shaft, wood	48–49	NB–3,4_{10-14}
3	Fish arrow shaft, wood	48–49	NH–1uf
4	Fish arrow shaft, wood	48–49	NB–3_8
5	Fish arrow shaft, wood	48–49	NB–3_{11}
6	Fish spear center prong (?), antler	48–49	NH–1uf
7	Leister prong, antler	48–49	NB–3_{13}
8	Leister prong, antler	48–49	NA–3_{11}
9	Salmon harpoon head, antler	48–49	NB–5_{1-4}
10	Fish arrow barb, antler	47–48	NA–sod
11	Fish arrow barb, antler	47–48	NB–lower
12	Fish arrow barb, antler	47–48	NH–1
13	Fish arrow barb, antler	47–48	NA–7_{11}
14	Fish arrow barb, antler	47–48	NA–1_4
15	Fish arrow barb, antler	47–48	NA–3_{11}
16	Leister prong, antler	48–49	NB–5_{3-5}
17	Fish arrow barb, antler	47–48	ND–1_{1-2}
18	Fish arrow barb, antler	47–48	NA–1_3
19	Fish arrow barb, antler	47–48	NB–2_3
20	Fish hook barb (?), antler	48–49	NA–3_2
21	Salmon spear barb (?), antler	48–49	NA–7_{11}
22	Salmon spear side prong, wood	48–49	NB–4_{12}
23	Salmon spear barb, ivory	48–49, 54	NB–4_{13}
24	Fish spear center prong, antler	48–49	NB–5_{1-4}
25	Fish spear center prong, ivory	48–49	NB
26	Fish spear center prong, ivory	48–49	NB–3_7
27	Fish spear center prong, ivory	48–49	NB–3_8
28	Fish spear center prong, ivory	48–49	NB–4_3

Nukleet—Fish Spears, etc.

	Identity	Reference page	Location
1	Shaft, square socket, wood	63, 95, 97	NB
2	Harpoon dart shaft, wood	37, 43	NB–2_4
3	Harpoon dart shaft, wood	37, 43	NB–4_{10}
4	Harpoon dart shaft, wood	37, 43	NB–3_8
5	Harpoon dart shaft, wood	37, 43	NB–3_9
6	Harpoon dart shaft, wood	37, 43	NB–3_8
7	Harpoon dart socket piece, antler (?)	37, 43	IYD
8	Blunt arrow (?) shaft, wood	31, 33, 36	NB–4_{12}
9	Blunt arrow shaft, wood	31, 33, 36	NB–4_{11}
10	Blunt arrow shaft, wood	31, 33, 36	NB–3_{5-6}
11	Blunt arrow shaft, wood	31, 33, 36	NB–4_{12}
12	Blunt arrow shaft, wood	31, 33, 36	NA–9_7

Nukleet—Harpoon and Arrow Shafts

0 1 2 3 4 5 6 7 8 9 10 cm.

PLATE 11

	Identity	Reference page	Location
1	Net gauge, large mesh, wood	48, 52	NA–1$_7$
2	Net gauge, large mesh, wood	48, 52, 100	NA–7$_6$
3	Net gauge handle, wood	48, 52	NB–2$_5$
4	Net gauge, small mesh, antler	48, 52	NB–5$_5$
5	Net gauge, small mesh, antler	48, 52, 82	NH–1
6	Net gauge, medium mesh, antler	48, 52	NA
7	Gorge, ivory	48–49	NH–1
8	Gorge, ivory	48–49	NA–1$_3$
9	Fish line guide tip (?), antler	48, 50	NH–1
10	Fish hook shank, bone	48–49	NA–7$_5$
11	Fish hook shank, wood	48–49	NB–4$_{11}$
12	Fish line sinker, ivory	48, 50	ND–1$_3$
13	Fish line sinker, bone	48, 50	NB–3$_{5-6}$
14	Fish line sinker, bone	48, 50	NA–3$_4$
15	Shee hook shank, bone	48–49	IYH–1
16	Fish line sinker, walrus tooth	48, 50	IYH–1
17	Fish line sinker, bone	48, 50	NH–1uf

Nukleet—Gauges, Sinkers, etc.

1   2   3   4   5   6

7   8   9   10   11   12   13   14   15   16   17

0 1 2 3 4 5 6 7 8 9 10 cm.

PLATE 12

	Identity	Reference page	Location
1	Ice strainer, antler	48, 50	NH–1
2	Ice strainer, antler	48, 50	NA–1$_3$
3	Ice strainer, antler	48, 50	NH–1
4	Ice strainer, antler	48, 50	NB–3$_8$
5	Ice strainer, antler	48, 50	NA–4$_3$
6	Fish line reel (?), wood	48, 50	NB–4$_{12}$
7	Net sinker, stone	48, 51, 174	NA–1$_3$
8	Net sinker, stone	48, 51, 174	NA–1$_4$
9	Net sinker, stone	48, 51, 174	NA–6$_5$
10	Net sinker, stone	48, 51, 174	NB–5$_{1-4}$
11	Ice strainer, antler	48, 50	NA–7$_6$

Nukleet—Ice Strainers, Net Sinkers, Reel

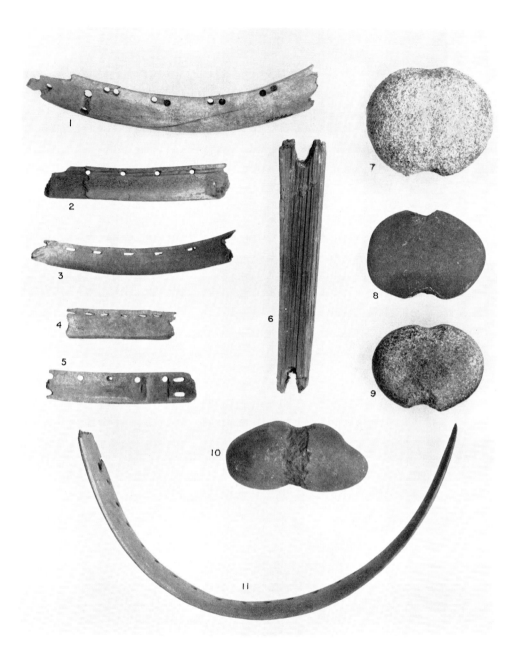

PLATE 13

	Identity	Reference page	Location
1	Net float, wood	48, 52, 54, 59	NA–6$_5$
2	Net float, wood	48, 52, 54, 59	NA–10$_3$
3	Net sinker, antler	48, 51	NA–10$_6$
4	Net float, bark	48, 52	NA–8$_8$
5	Net sinker, bone	48, 51	NH–1
6	Net shuttle fragment, wood	48, 53	NA–3$_4$
7	Net shuttle fragment, antler	48, 53	NA–4$_2$
8	Net sinker, bone	48, 51	IYD

Nukleet—Floats, Sinkers, Shuttles

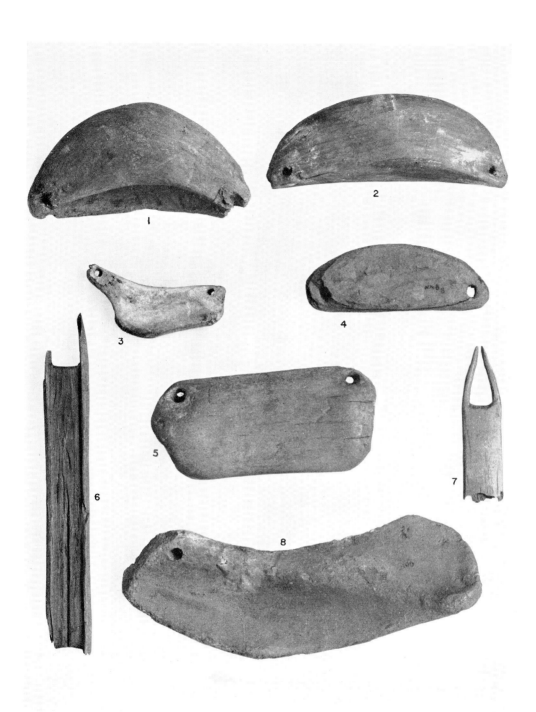

1   2

3   4

5   6   7

8

0 1 2 3 4 5 6 7 8 9 10 cm.

PLATE 14

	Identity	Reference page	Location
1	Beaver tooth knife handle and spoon, antler	55, 58	NA
2	Beaver tooth knife handle, bone	55, 58	NA–2
3	Beaver tooth knife handle, bone	55, 58	NA–2
4	Beaver tooth knife handle, wood	55, 58	NB–2_6
5	Beaver tooth knife handle, wood	55, 58	NB–3
6	Beaver tooth knife handle, wood	55, 58	NA–6_5
7	Beaver tooth	55, 59	NA–4_6
8	Beaver tooth	55, 59	NA–4_6
9	Beaver tooth	55, 59	NB–3_8
10	Beaver tooth knife handle, antler	55, 58	NB–3_{11}
11	Beaver tooth knife handle, wood	55, 58	NB
12	Beaver tooth knife handle, wood	55, 58	NB–4_{10}
13	Beaver tooth knife handle, wood	55, 58	NB–$3_{5\text{-}6}$
14	Beaver tooth knife handle, antler	55, 58	NR–3
15	Beaver tooth knife handle, side haft, wood	54, 58	NB–2_7
16	Beaver tooth knife handle, side haft, wood	54, 58	NB–2_7

Nukleet—Beaver Tooth Knife Handles

0 1 2 3 4 5 6 7 8 9 10 cm.

PLATE 15

	Identity	Reference page	Location
1	Knife handle for side blade, antler	54, 57	NH–1
2	Knife handle for side blade, antler	54, 57	NB–1_2
3	Knife handle, composite, antler	54, 57	NA–1_3
4	Knife handle, composite, antler	54, 57	IYE
5	Knife handle, composite, antler	54, 57	NB–5_{3-5}
6	Knife handle, composite, antler	54, 57	NH–1
7	Knife handle, composite, wood	54, 56	NA–1_7
8	Knife handle fragment for side blade, antler	54, 57	NA–4_8
9	Knife handle fragment for side blade, antler	54, 57	NB–4_{14}
10	Knife handle, composite, antler	54, 57	NB–2_5
11	Knife handle, composite, antler	54, 57	NB–2_6
12	Knife sharpener or ornament, sea lion (?) tooth	55, 60	NA–7_5
13	Knife sharpener or ornament, bear (?) tooth	55, 60	NA–2_2
14	Knife handle, composite, antler	54, 57	NB–5_{1-4}
15	Knife handle, composite, antler	54, 57	NA–7_8
16	Gauged drill, ivory	56, 62, 145	NB–4_{11}
17	Gauged drill, antler	56, 62, 145	NA
18	Gauged drill, bone	56, 62, 145	NB–4_8
19	Drill bit, chert	57, 63	NA–7_2
20	Drill bit, chert	57, 63	NB–4_3
21	Drill bit, chert	57, 63	NA–2_2
22	Side scraper, chert	57, 64	NH–1uf
23	End scraper, chert	57, 64	NH–1_5
24	End scraper, chert	57, 64	NB–5_{3-5}
25	Gauged drill, bone	56, 62, 145	NA–4_6
26	Gauged drill, antler	56, 62, 145	NA–1_2
27	Flaker point, bone	57, 64	NB–3_8
28	Flaker handle, wood	57, 64	NA–4_8
29	Side scraper, chert	57, 64	NH–1uf

Nukleet—Knife Handles, Sharpeners, Scrapers

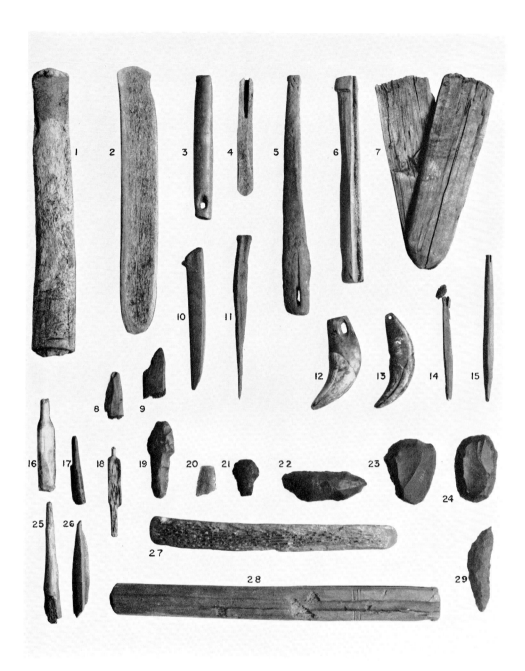

PLATE 16

	Identity	Reference page	Location
1	Knife blade, single-edged, slate	54–55	NB–4$_{10}$
2	Knife blade, single-edged, slate	54–55	NB–5$_{1-4}$
3	Knife blade, single-edged, slate	54–55	NB–5$_{1-4}$
4	Knife blade, double-edged, slate	54–55	NH–1
5	Knife blade, double-edged, slate	54–55	IYD
6	Knife blade, double-edged, slate	54–55	NA–7$_{8}$
7	Ulu blade, stemless, slate	54, 57	NA–1$_{3}$
8	Ulu blade, stemmed, slate	54, 57	IYB
9	Ulu blade, stemless, slate	54, 57–58	NA–sod
10	Blade, Cook Inlet type, slate	54, 56	NB–5$_{1-4}$
11	Ulu blade, stemless, slate	54, 57–58	NA–6$_{6}$
12	Ulu blade, stemmed, slate	54, 57–58	NB–4$_{7}$
13	Ulu blade, stemless, slate	54, 57–58	NA–8$_{4}$
14	Ulu blade, stemless, slate	54, 58	NA–1$_{3}$
15	Ulu blank, slate	54, 58	NH–1uf

Nukleet—Knife and Ulu Blades

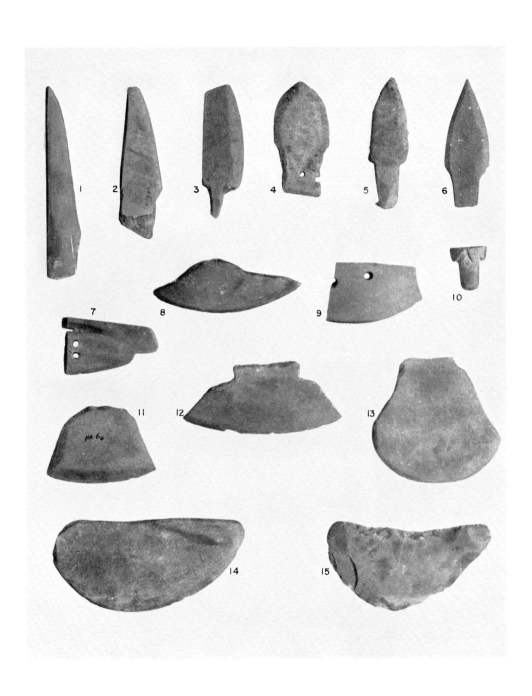

0 1 2 3 4 5 6 7 8 9 10 cm.

PLATE 17

	Identity	Reference page	Location
1	Whetstone, irregular sandstone	55, 59	NA–3$_{3-4}$
2	Whetstone, beveled edge	55, 59	NA–1$_6$
3	Whetstone, flat beach stone	55, 59	NA–3$_{11}$
4	Whetstone, irregular slate	55, 59	NH–1$_5$
5	Whetstone, irregular shale	55, 59	NA–3$_5$
6	Whetstone, long rectangular, slate	55, 59	IYC
7	Whetstone, long rectangular, 4-sided	55, 59	IYC
8	Whetstone, irregular sandstone	55, 59	NB–3$_{11}$
9	Whetstone, long, thin pebble	55, 59	NA–7$_5$
10	Whetstone, long, rectangular shale	55, 59	NB–3$_{5-6}$
11	Whetstone, long, rectangular, 4-sided	55, 59	NH–1
12	Whetstone, long, thin pebble	55, 59	NH–1uf
13	Whetstone, long, rectangular, 4-sided	55, 59	NA–1$_4$
14	Whetstone, long, rectangular, slate	55, 59	NB–3$_8$
15	Whetstone, beveled edge	55, 59	NA
16	Grooved round stone	65, 95	NA–4$_{11}$
17	Polishing stone (?)	55, 60	IYB
18	Grindstone fragment, sandstone	55, 60	NH–1
19	Sawed fragment, schist	59	NA–11$_4$
20	Graphite	72, 76	IYE
21	Drilled stone fragment	57, 64	NA–3$_3$
22	Drilled stone fragment	57, 64	NB–1$_3$

Nukleet—Whetstones, etc.

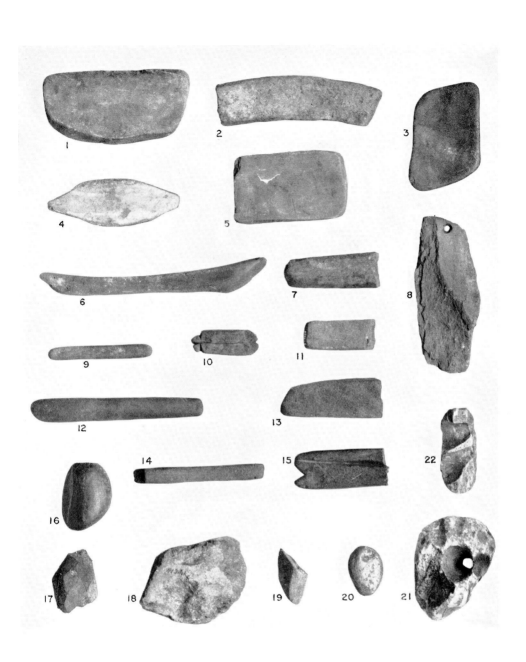

PLATE 18

	Identity	Reference page	Location
1	Adz head, antler	56, 61	NH–1
2	Adz head, antler, with blade	56, 61	NA–?$_3$
3	Adz head, antler	56, 61	IYH–1
4	Adz handle, antler	56, 61	NH–1$_5$
5	Adz handle, antler	56, 61	IYD
6	Wedge, antler	56, 62	IYD
7	Wedge, antler	56, 62	NH–1
8	Wedge, antler	56, 62	ND–1$_{1-2}$
9	Wedge, bone	56, 62	NA–5$_2$

Nukleet—Wedges, Adz Heads and Handles

PLATE 19

	Identity	Reference page	Location
1	Adz head, jade	56, 61, 124	IYH–1
2	Adz head, stone	55, 60	IYF
3	Adz head, silicified slate	56, 61	NA–10$_6$
4	Adz head, stone	55, 60	NC–1$_2$
5	Adz head, silicified slate	56, 61	NH–1uf
6	Adz head, blade, stone	55, 60	IYH–1
7	Adz head, blade, stone	55, 60	NH–1uf
8	Adz head, blade, stone	55, 60	NC–1$_4$

Nukleet—Adz Heads and Blades

0 1 2 3 4 5 6 7 8 9 10 cm.

PLATE 20

	Identity	Reference page	Location
1	Splitting-adz head, silicified slate	55, 60	NA–3$_{11}$
2	Splitting-adz head fragment, silicified slate	55, 60	NA–11$_4$
3	Splitting-adz head fragment, silicified slate	55, 60	IYH–1
4	Splitting-adz head fragment, silicified slate	55, 60	IYD
5	Pick fragment, silicified slate	55, 60	NB–4$_{14}$
6	Splitting-adz head fragment, silicified slate	55, 60	NA–5$_3$
7	Hammerstone	55, 60	NA–2$_7$
8	Hammerstone	55, 60	NA–3$_4$
9	Splitting-adz head fragment, silicified slate	55, 60	NA–1$_3$

Nukleet—Adz Heads, Hammerstones

PLATE 21

	Identity	Reference page	Location
1	Maul, whale bone	57, 64	NA–7_6
2	Rake, antler	68–69	NA–2_5
3	Pick, antler	57, 64	IYD
4	Pick, bone	57, 64	NA–4_4
5	Pick, ivory	57, 64	IYH–1

Nukleet—Picks, Maul, Rake

PLATE 22

	Identity	Reference page	Location
1	Two-hand scraper, bone	56, 62	NA–1_2
2	Two-hand scraper, bone	56, 62	NA–4_6
3	Two-hand scraper, bone	56, 62	NA–4_4
4	Two-hand scraper, bone	56, 62	NA–3_{3-4}
5	Bark peeler, bone	57, 63	IYH–1
6	Awl, bone	56, 61	NA–1_7
7	Awl, bone	56, 61	NH–1
8	Awl, bone	56, 61	NB–3_8
9	Bark peeler, bone	57, 63	NB–5_{3-5}

Nukleet—Scrapers, Peelers, Awls

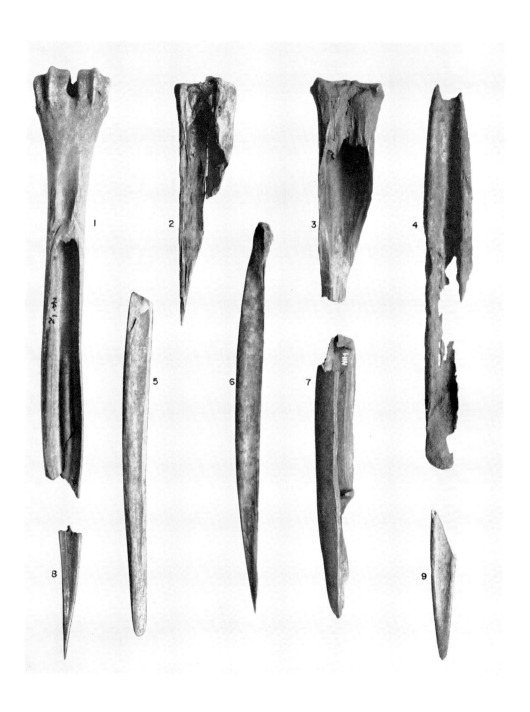

0 1 2 3 4 5 6 7 8 9 10 cm.

PLATE 23

	Identity	Reference page	Location
1	Pointed wooden implement (snare peg?)	65, 95, 97	$NC1_9$
2	Pointed wooden implement (snare peg?)	65, 95, 97	$NB-4_{11}$
3	Pointed wooden implement (snare peg?)	65, 95, 97	$NB-3,4_{10-14}$
4	Awl, antler	56, 61	$NA-4_3$
5	Awl, wood	56, 61	$NB-3_{11}$
6	Awl, antler	56, 61	$NA-3_8$
7	Awl, antler	56, 61	$NB-4_{11}$
8	Awl, antler	56, 61	$NB-5_{3-5}$
9	Awl, antler	56, 61	$NB-3_2$
10	Awl, antler	56, 61	$NA-1_3$
11	Awl, antler	56, 61	$NA-1_4$
12	Awl, bone splinter	56, 61	$NB-3_9$
13	Awl, antler	56, 61	$IYH-1$
14	Awl, bone	56, 61	$NB-4_{10}$
15	Awl, ivory	56, 61–62	$NA-4_8$
16	Awl, bone	56, 61–62	$NA-4_8$
17	Awl, bone	56, 61–62	NB–lower

Nukleet—Awls

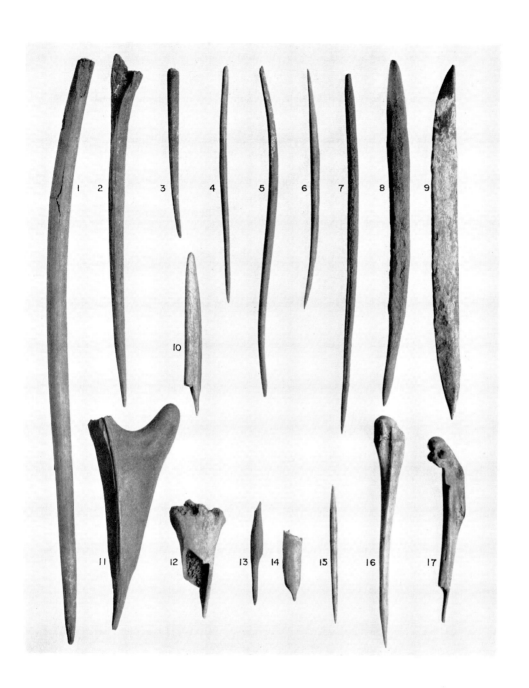

PLATE 24

	Identity	Reference page	Location
1	Baleen, worked fragment	64, 95	NA–1$_7$
2	Baleen, lashing strips	64, 95	NA–2$_7$
3	Baleen, perforated strip	64, 95	NB–4$_{14}$
4	Scraper, scapula (scaler?)	68–69	NB–lower
5	Scraper, scapula (scaler?)	68–69	NH–1uf
6	Birch bark, sewn	68, 70	IYH–1
7	Birch bark, worked	68, 70	NA–7$_6$
8	Birch bark, worked	68, 70	NB–4$_{12}$
9	Drill bearing, astragalus	57, 63	NA–3$_{3-4}$
10	Drill bearing, astragalus	57, 63	NA–2$_3$

Nukleet—Baleen, Birch Bark, etc.

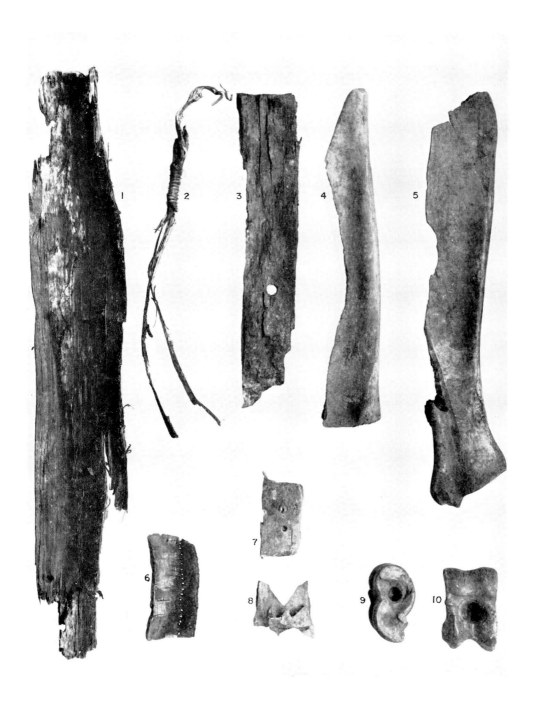

0 1 2 3 4 5 6 7 8 9 10 cm.

4

PLATE 25

	Identity	Reference page	Location
1	Twined grass matting	68, 70	NR–3
2	Birch bark basket fragment	68, 70	NA–1$_6$
3	Root fiber line	65, 95	NA–4$_8$
4	Pebble wrapped in birch bark	65, 95	NB–3$_{11}$
5	Stick with lashing	65, 95	NB–3$_8$
6	Birch bark basket fragment	68, 70	IYH–1
7	Birch bark basket fragment	68, 70	IYH–1
8	Stick bound with grass	65, 95	NA–4$_8$
9	Insole of grass	72–73	NA–9$_7$

Nukleet—Matting, Birch Bark, etc.

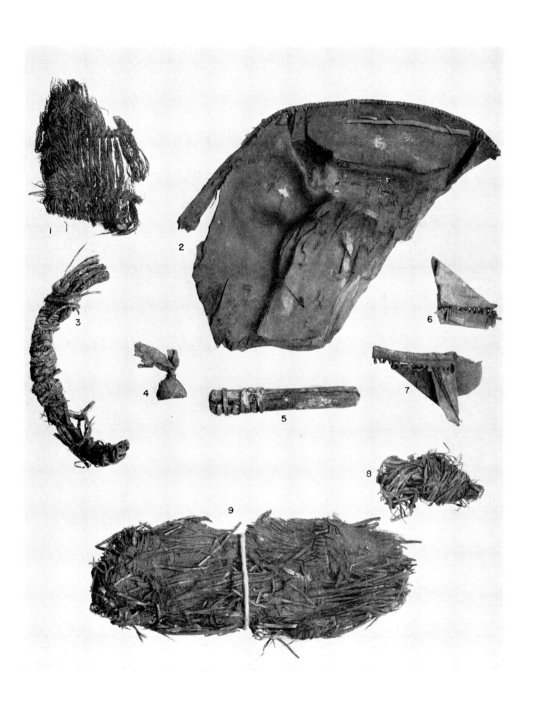

PLATE 26

	Identity	Reference page	Location
1	Bucket or bag handle, wood	68	NA–10$_3$
2	Bucket or bag handle, wood	68	NB–4$_{14}$
3	Bucket or bag handle, wood	68	NB–4$_{11}$
4	Bucket or bag handle, antler	68	IYH–1
5	Bucket or bag handle, wood	68	NB–3$_{10-14}$
6	Shovel blade, antler	68–69	NB–4$_{12}$
7	Shovel blade, scapula	68–69	IYE
8	Hook (for pots?), antler	68	NA–3$_2$
9	Hook (for pots?), antler	68	NC–1$_4$

Nukleet—Handles, Hooks, Shovel Blades

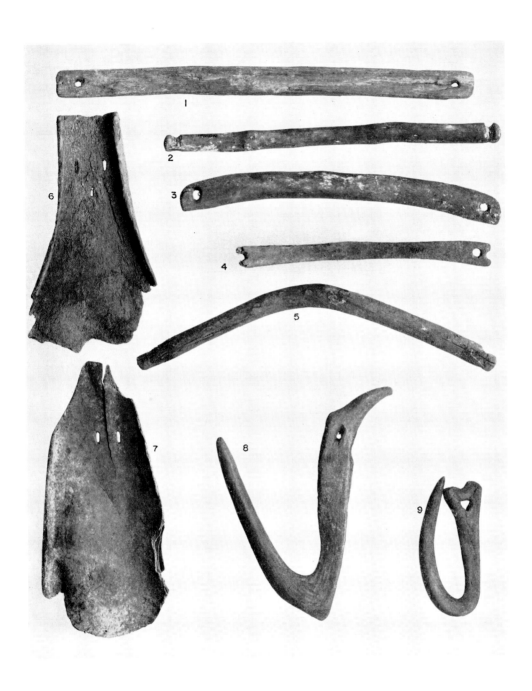

1

2

3

4

5

6

7

8

9

0 1 2 3 4 5 6 7 8 9 10 cm.

PLATE 27

	Identity	Reference page	Location
1	Sledge shoe, antler	81–82	NA–1$_2$
2	Sledge shoe, antler	81–82	NH–1
3	Snowshoe crosspiece, wood	81–82	NB–4$_7$
4	Snowshoe crosspiece, wood	81–82	NB–3$_8$
5	Snowshoe frame fragment, wood	81–82	NB–1$_{12}$
6	Snowshoe frame fragment, wood	81–82	NB–4$_{12}$
7	Snowshoe frame fragment, wood	81–82	NA–1$_7$
8	Snowshoe frame fragment, wood	81–82	NA–3$_{3-4}$
9	Snowshoe needle, wood	81–82	NB–3$_9$
10	Snowshoe needle, wood	81–82	NB–3$_8$
11	Snowshoe needle, wood	81–82	NB–3$_8$
12	Snowshoe needle, antler	81, 83	NA–4$_4$
13	Ulu handle, wood	55, 58	NB–3
14	Ulu handle, wood	55, 58	NB–3
15	Ulu handle, wood	55, 58	NC–1$_4$

Nukleet—Sledge Shoes, Snowshoe Crosspieces, Ulu Handles, etc.

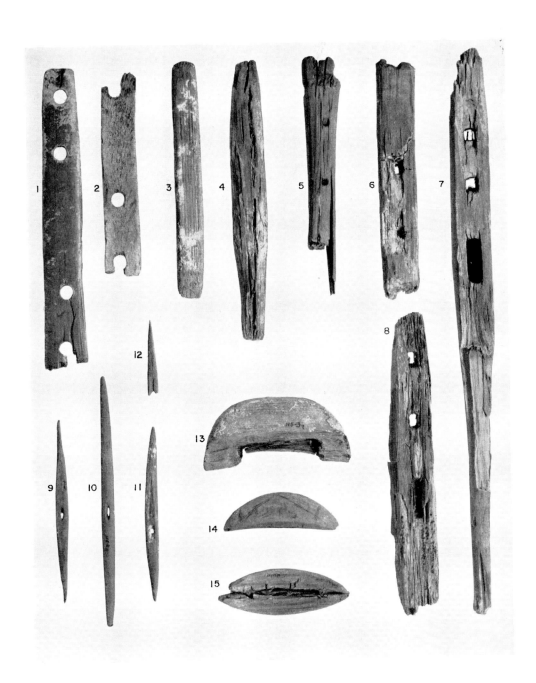

PLATE 28

	Identity	Reference page	Location
1	Kayak bow piece, wood	81, 83	NA–1
2	Pierced block, wood (boat part?)	81, 83	NA–1
3	Kayak deck crosspiece	81, 83	NA–1
4	Kayak deck crosspiece	81, 83	NA–1
5	Kayak spear or paddle guard	81, 83	NA–1
6	Kayak spear or paddle guard	81, 83	NA–1

Nukleet—Kayak Pieces

PLATE 29

	Identity	Reference page	Location
1	Decorated wooden fragment	79, 100	NB–4_{10}
2	Needle case, ivory	72–73	NA–2_{10}
3	Needle, bone	72–73	NB–3_7
4	Needle, bone	72–73	NB–3_{13}
5	Sinew reel, wood	72–73	NB–3_8
6	Cutting board, wood	72–73	NA–7_5
7	Lancet (?), slate	84–85	IYH–1
8	Lancet (?), jade	84–85	NA–7_2
9	Tube of antler	73	NB–4_{12}
10	Unidentified antler	79	NB–4_{11}
11	Grooved seal tooth	72, 76	NB–1_3
12	Jade pendant	72, 76	NA–7_8

Nukleet—Needles, Lancets, etc.

0 1 2 3 4 5 6 7 8 9 10 cm.

PLATE 30

	Identity	Reference page	Location
1	Engraving tool, wood	72, 75, 146	NB–3$_{5-6}$
2	Engraving tool, wood and ivory	72, 75, 100	NA–2$_5$
3	Engraving tool, wood	72, 75, 146	NA–8$_6$
4	Engraving tool, antler	72, 75, 146	NA–2$_{12}$
5	Engraving tool (?), ivory	72, 75, 76	NA–10$_5$
6	Engraving tool, ivory	72, 75	NB–3$_9$
7	Engraving tool (?), ivory	72, 75	NB–3$_9$
8	Compass or threader, bone	43, 72, 75	NB–4$_{10}$
9	Labret, tooth	72–73	IYH–1
10	Labret, ivory	72–73	NA–1$_3$
11	Labret, tooth	72–74	NA–4$_8$
12	Labret, tooth	72–74	NA–1$_6$
13	Labret, tooth	72–74	NA–1$_3$
14	Labret, ivory	72–74	NA–3$_3$
15	Labret, tooth	72–74	NA–4$_3$
16	Labret, tooth	72–73	NA–1$_2$
17	Labret, ivory	72–73	NB–4$_{13}$
18	Labret, ivory	72–73	IYH–1
19	Labret, ivory	72–73	NA–1$_3$
20	Labret, ivory	72–74	NB–4$_{10}$
21	Labret, tooth	72–74	NB–4$_{14}$
22	Labret, tooth	72–74	NB–3$_8$
23	Labret, ivory	72–73	NA–5$_3$
24	Labret, wood	72–74	NA–1$_3$
25	Labret, ivory	72–73	NA–1$_4$
26	Labret, ivory	72–73	NA
27	Labret, medial, stone	72–73	NH–1
28	Labret, oval, ivory	72–74	NB–4$_{12}$
29	Labret, ivory	72–74	NA–2

Nukleet—Labrets, Engraving Tools, Compass

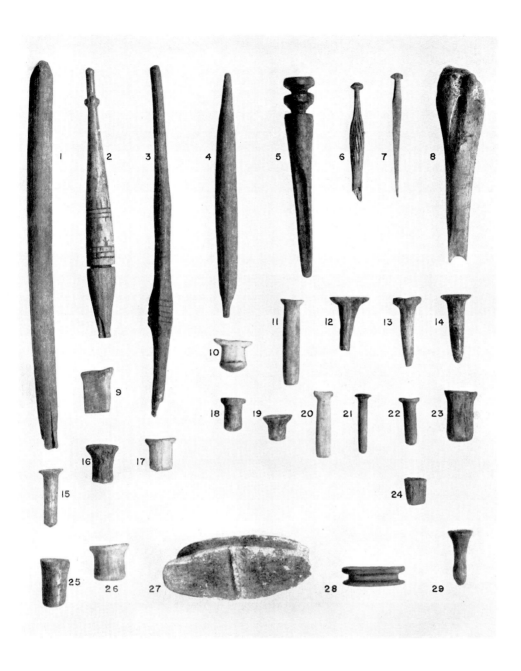

0   1   2   3   4   5   6   7   8   9   10 cm.

PLATE 31

	Identity	Reference page	Location
1	Bear head carving, walrus tooth	79	NA–4₃
2	Pendant, tooth	72, 76	NC–1₃
3	Pendant, ivory	72, 77	NA–1₃
4	Chain pendant, ivory	72, 77	NB–3₇
5	Tube, ivory	77	NA–5₅
6	Ornamental carving, ivory	79, 100	NH–1
7	Unidentified ivory object, animal head carved	77	NA–5₁₀
8	Tube, soapstone	77, 78	IYD–2
9	Tube, ivory	77, 78	IYF
10	Whale carving, ivory	79	NB–3₁₁
11	Walrus head carving on creaser (?), ivory	79	NC–3
12	Peg or wedge, ivory	80	NB–3₁₃
13	Ring with inset dots, ivory	78	NA–1₃
14	Decorated marble, concave ends, ivory	77	NB–4₁₀
15	Decorated marble, concave ends, ivory	77	NB–4₁₀
16	Necklace tooth	72, 76	NB–4₁₂
17	Necklace tooth	72, 76	NB–4₁₄
18	Joined claws	78	NB–3₆
19	Ball pendant, ivory	72, 77	NB–3₁₁
20	Ball pendant, ivory	72, 77	NB–3₁₁
21	Ball pendant, ivory	72, 77	NB–3₁₁
22	Pendant, ivory	72, 77	NB–3₄
23	Oval ring, ivory	78	NB–4₁₀
24	Square button, ivory	78	NB–4₈
25	Square button, ivory	78	NB–4₈
26	Line guide (?), ivory	78	NB–4₁₂
27	Line guide (?), ivory	78	NB–3₁₁
28	Line guide (?), ivory	78	NB–3₁₂
29	Toggle, ivory	78	NB–5₃₋₅
30	Rectangular plate, antler	78	NC–1₄
31	Pendant, tooth	72, 76	NC–1₃
32	Pendant, bark	72, 77	NB–4₁₄
33	Swivel part, ivory	78, 81, 82	NB–5₃₋₅
34	Bird carving, tooth	78	NA–2₁₀

Nukleet—Ivory and Tooth Objects

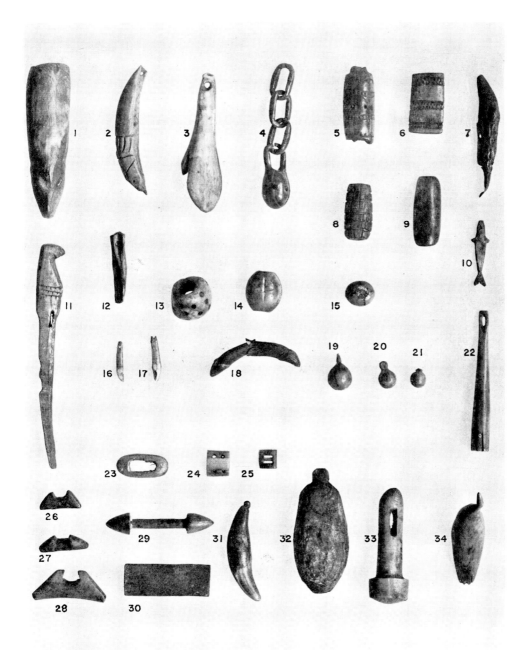

0 1 2 3 4 5 6 7 8 9 10 cm.

PLATE 32

	Identity	Reference page	Location
1	Doll, wood	84, 86, 88	NB lower
2	Doll, wood	84, 86, 88	NA–4_9
3	Doll, wood	84, 86	NB–3_{12}
4	Doll, wood	84, 86	NB–4_9
5	Doll, wood	84, 86	NA–8_8
6	Doll, wood	84, 86	NH–1uf
7	Comb, wood	59, 72, 74, 84, 86	NH–1uf
8	Doll, wood	84, 86, 88	NH–1uf
9	Doll, wood	84, 88	NA–4_9
10	Doll, wood	84, 88	NB lower
11	Doll, wood	84, 88	NB–3_{11}
12	Doll, wood	84, 88	NB–3_{12}
13	Doll, wood	84, 88	NB–4_{12}
14	Doll, wood	84, 88	NB–3_{11}
15	Dish or model, bark	84, 89	NH–1uf
16	Kayak model, bark	84, 89	NC–1_9
17	Kayak model, bark	84, 89	NC–1_9
18	Dish or model, bark	84, 89	NH–1uf

Nukleet—Dolls, Comb, Dishes, etc.

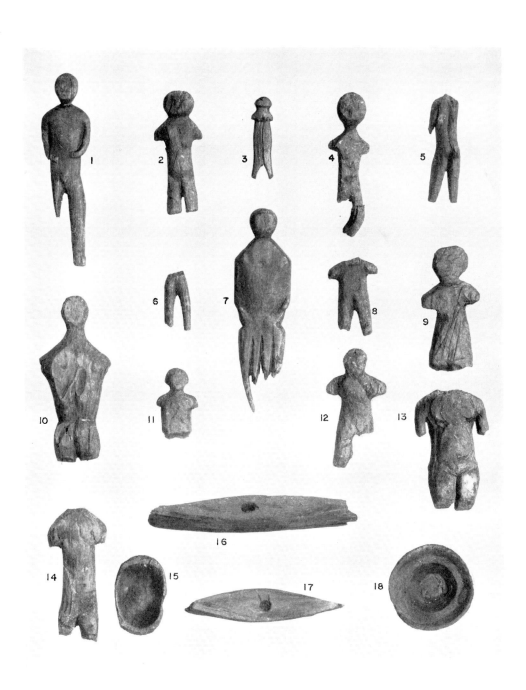

0 1 2 3 4 5 6 7 8 9 10 cm.

PLATE 33

	Identity	Reference page	Location
1	Cord attacher, ivory	37, 43, 47, 97, 99–100	IYB–2$_3$
2	Cord attacher, ivory	37, 43, 47, 97, 99–100	NA–9$_2$
3	Cord attacher, ivory	37, 43, 47, 97	NA–sod
4	Walrus-head button, ivory	79	NB–3$_{11}$
5	Curved ornamental piece, antler	80, 99–100	NC–1$_3$
6	Bear head fastener	79, 99–100	NB–3$_7$
7	Fish hook barb (?), ivory	48–49	NB–3$_9$
8	Necklace tooth	72, 76	NH–1
9	Necklace tooth	72, 76	NB–4$_{12}$
10	Pendant, ivory	72, 77	NA–8$_3$
11	Engraved wedge fragment, ivory	80	NB–4$_{14}$
12	Jade blade	55	IYH–1
13	Drill bit, jade	57, 63	NH–1
14	Drill bit, silicified slate	57, 63	NA–sod
15	Antler rectangle	78	NB–4$_{11}$

Nukleet—Miscellaneous

0 1 2 3 4 5 6 7 8 9 10 cm.

PLATE 34

	Identity	Reference page	Location
1	Comb, antler	72, 74	NB–3
2	Comb. antler	72, 74	NB–4$_{11}$
3	Snow goggles, wood	37, 44, 59	NB–5$_9$
4	Snow goggles fragment, wood	37, 44, 59	NA–4$_8$
5	Snow goggles fragment, wood	37, 44, 59	NB–4$_9$
6	Spoon, antler	59, 68–69	NA–8$_4$
7	Spoon, antler	68–69	NA–10$_6$
8	Spoon, antler	59, 68–69	NA–4$_8$
9	Handle fragment, antler	79	IYH–1
10	Armor plate, antler	84–85	NA–5$_3$
11	Armor plate, antler	84–85	NB–2$_2$
12	Armor plate, antler	84–85	NA–1$_5$
13	Buzz, wood	84–85	NA–10$_6$

Nukleet—Combs, Goggles, Spoons, etc.

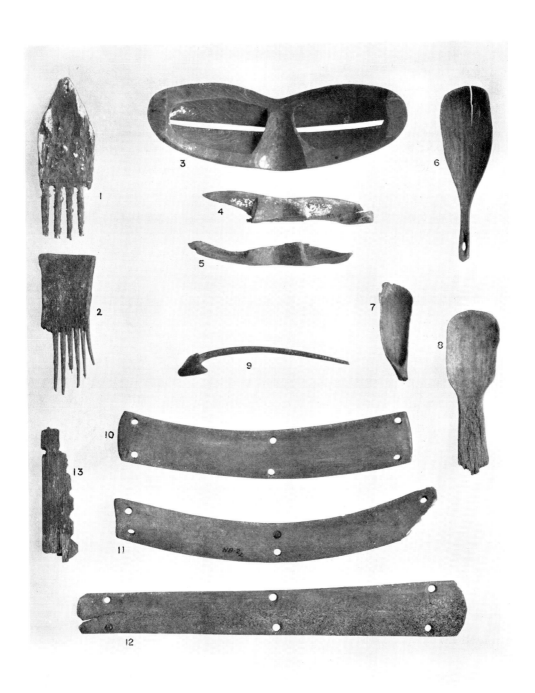

0 1 2 3 4 5 6 7 8 9 10 cm.

PLATE 35

	Identity	Reference page	Location
1	Potsherd	104	NR
2	Potsherd	104	NR
3	Potsherd	104	NR
4	Potsherd	104	NR
5	Potsherd	104	$NA-3_3$
6	Potsherd	105	NR
7	Potsherd	105	NR
8	Potsherd	104	NR
9	Potsherd	105	NR
10	Potsherd	104	$NA-4_3$
11	Potsherd	104	NR
12	Potsherd	104	$NC-1_3$

Nukleet—Potsherds

0 1 2 3 4 5 6 7 8 9 10 cm.

PLATE 36

	Identity	Reference page	Location
1	Center prong fragment, ivory	139, 140	H1
2	Leister prong (?) fragment, antler	139, 140	PA
3	Center prong, ivory	139, 140	PA
4	Leister or fish arrow prong fragment, ivory	139, 140	PA
5	Leister or fish arrow prong fragment, ivory	139, 140	H1
6	Flattened shaft fragment, wood; red-painted	139, 141	PA
7	Leister prong, antler	139, 140	PA
8	Object, ivory	139, 147	PA
9	Socket piece fragment, bone	139, 144	H1
10	Arrowhead fragment, antler	139, 141, 161	PA
11	Arrowhead fragment, antler	139, 141	PA
12	Fragment, antler	139, 147	PA
13	Flaking hammer head, ivory	139, 144	PA
14	Composite knife half, ivory	139, 145	PA
15	Gorge, reworked at upper end, ivory	139, 141	A1
16	Blunt arrowhead, antler	139, 141	PA
17	Harpoon head, antler	139, 142, 161	PA
18	Harpoon head, antler	139, 142	PA
19	Harpoon head fragment, antler	139, 142	PA
20	Harpoon head, antler	139, 142	PA
21	Harpoon head fragment, antler	139, 142	PA
22	Harpoon foreshaft, antler	139, 142	PA
23	Flaking hammer	139, 144	PA

Norton: Iyatayet—Prongs, Harpoon Heads, etc.

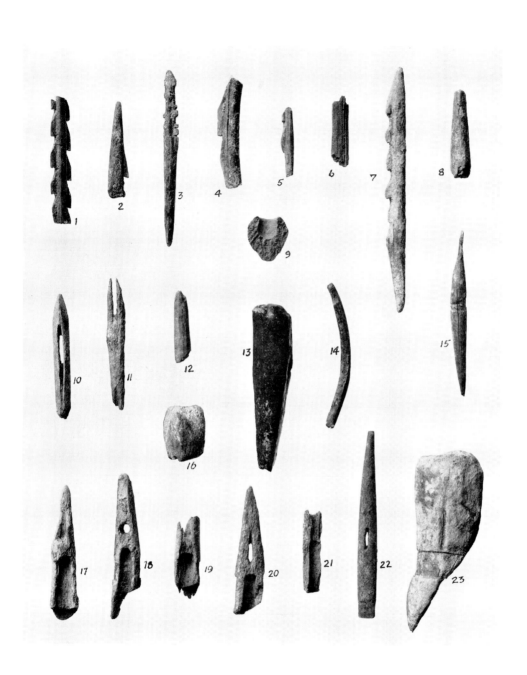

0 1 2 3 4 5 6 7 8 9 10 cm.

PLATE 37

	Identity	Reference page	Location
1	Object, ivory	139, 145	PA
2	Object, ivory	139, 147	PA
3	Tube, bone	139, 146	PA
4	Beaver tooth	139, 146	PA
5	Object, antler	139, 145	PA
6	Object, antler	139, 145	PA
7	Object, antler	139, 145	PA
8	Object, antler	139, 145	PA
9	Gauged drill, bone	139, 145	PA
10	Pointed object, ivory	139, 145	PA
11	Engraving tool, ivory	139, 146	H1
12	Engraving tool for rodent tooth, ivory	139, 145	PA
13	Engraving tool for rodent tooth (?), ivory	139, 146	E
14	Doll, ivory	139, 146	PA
15	Bluntly pointed object, bone	139, 147	PA
16	Bluntly pointed object, ivory	139, 144	PA
17	Bird bone with guide lines for needle-cutting (?)	139, 145	PA
18	Fragment, antler	139, 147	PA
19	Object, antler	139, 147	PA
20	Object, antler	139, 147	PA
21	Barb for fish spear prong, antler	139, 140	PA
22	Fragment, bone	139, 147	PA

Norton: Iyatayet—Ivory, Bone, and Antler Objects

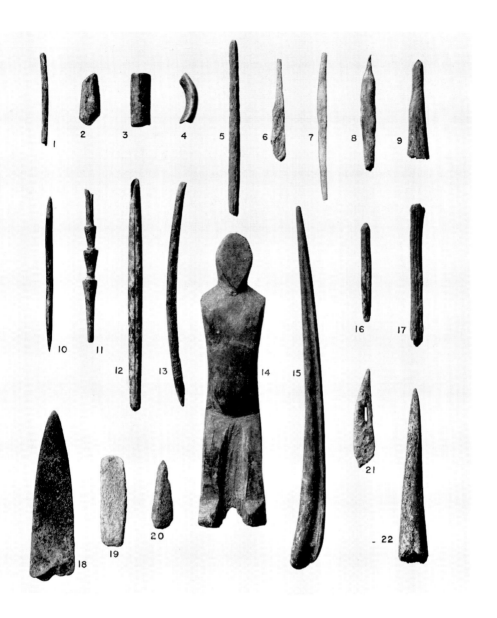

PLATE 38

	Identity	Reference page	Location
1	Fragment, birch wood object	139, 147	PA
2	Engraved fragment, mammoth ivory	139, 147	PA
3	Plank fragment, spruce wood	139, 147	PA
4	Fragment, split seal rib	139, 147	PA
5	Grooved fragment, spruce wood	139, 147	PA
6	Meat fork (?), split rib	139, 147	PA
7	Scaler (?) fragment, caribou scapula	139, 146	PA
8	Toy adz head (?), cottonwood bark	139, 146–147	PA
9	Fragment, worked caribou scapula	139, 146	PA
10	Scaler (?) fragment, caribou scapula	139, 146	PA
11	Flaker, split seal rib	139, 144	PA
12	Harpoon (?) ice pick, ivory	139, 143	PA

Norton: Iyatayet—Miscellaneous Fragments, etc.

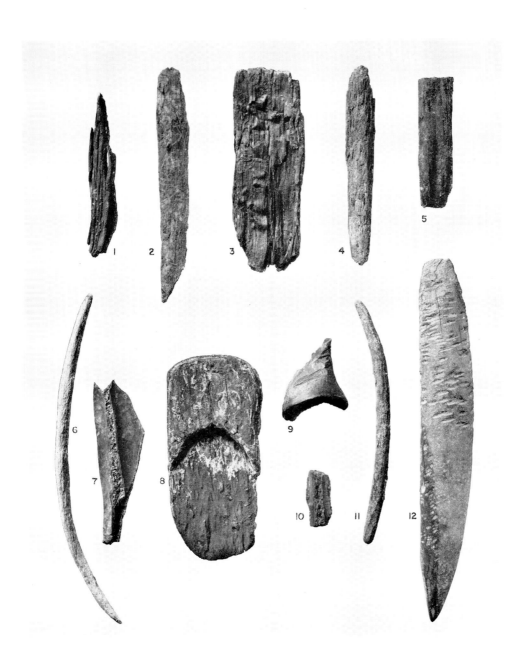

PLATE 39

	Identity	Reference page	Location
1	Labret, slate	148	E
2	Labret fragment, shale	148	K–5/6
3	Labret fragment, shale	148	A
4	Labret, bitumen	148	H7

Norton: Iyatayet—Labrets

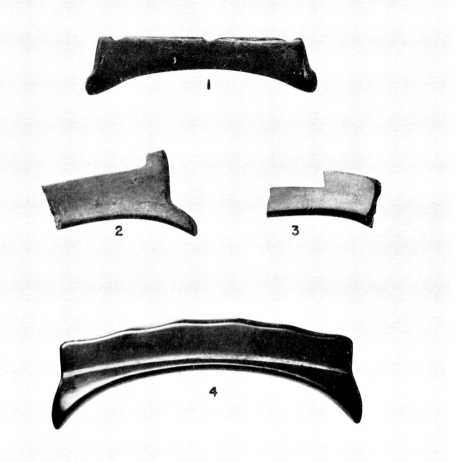

1

2   3

4

0   1   2   3   4   5   6   7   8   9   10 cm.

PLATE 40

	Identity	Reference page	Location
1	Object, baked shale	149	H4
2	Object, baked shale	150	E
3	Object, baked shale	150	H7
4	Object, baked shale	150	PB
5	Object, baked shale	150	EB
6	Object, baked shale	149	EB
7	Object, baked shale	150	H
8	Object, baked shale	150	ED
9	Object, baked shale	149	H4–F
10	Object, baked shale	150	K–4/6

Norton: Iyatayet—Baked Shale Objects

PLATE 41-a

	Identity	Reference page	Location
1	Slate knife fragment	151	H
2	Slate knife fragment	151	H1–T
3	Slate knife fragment	151	E
4	Slate knife fragment	151	Z–1
5	Slate knife fragment	151	E
6	Slate knife fragment	151	H7
7	Slate knife fragment	151	E

Norton: Iyatayet—Slate Knife Fragments

PLATE 41-b

	Identity	Reference page	Location
1	Burin-like groover fragment	154	PE–7
2	Burin-like groover fragment	153	E
3	Burin-like groover fragment	153	E
4	Burin-like groover fragment	154	PB
5	Burin-like groover fragment	153	PE–5
6	Burin-like groover fragment	154	Z–1
7	Burin-like groover fragment	154	H7
8	Burin-like groover fragment	154	E
9	Burin-like groover fragment	153	E
10	Burin-like groover fragment	154	M
11	Burin-like groover fragment	153	E
12	Burin-like groover fragment	154	PE–4

Norton: Iyatayet—Burin-like Groover Fragments

PLATE 42

	Identity	Reference page	Location
1	Whetstone fragment, sandstone; 5-sided	157	H7
2	Whetstone, sandstone; 4-sided	156	PE–7
3	Whetstone and pointer, shale; 2-sided	157	H1
4	Whetstone, sandstone	156	PA
5	Whetstone, sandstone; 5-sided	156	H7
6	Whetstone or shaft smoother; 4-sided	156	PE–5
7	Whetstone or shaft smoother; 4-sided	156	EM
8	Whetstone fragment, scoria; 4-sided	156	PD
9	Whetstone, sandstone; 3 flat, 1 convex surface	156	M
10	Whetstone, sandstone	156	PE–5
11	Whetstone fragment, sandstone; 6-sided	156	H7
12	Grindstone, sandstone; 2 ground faces	156	PE–2
13	Whetstone, sandstone; one surface scratched	156	H7

Norton: Iyatayet—Whetstones, Grindstone

TYPE 2
1 rдd.

0 1 2 3 4 5 6 7 8 9 10 cm.

PLATE 43

	Identity	Reference page	Location
1	Whetstone, schist	155	H
2	Whetstone, shale; 2 pieces	155	PA and PE–2
3	Whetstone, shale	155	E
4	Whetstone, schist	155	PA
5	Whetstone (?), igneous pebble	156	H7
6	Whetstone, igneous pebble	156	PA
7	Whetstone, schist	155	PE–3
8	Whetstone, shale	155	PD

Norton: Iyatayet—Whetstones

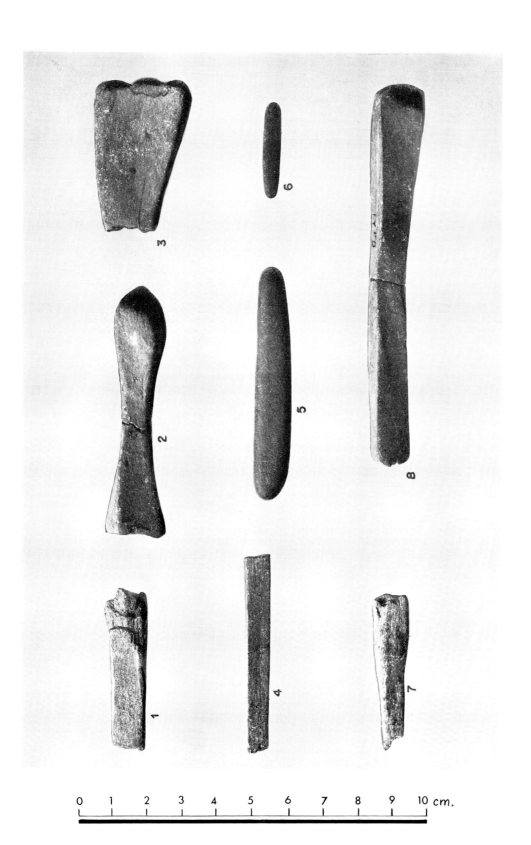

0 1 2 3 4 5 6 7 8 9 10 cm.

PLATE 44

	Identity	Reference page	Location
1	Adz blade, silicified slate	157	M
2	Adz blade, basalt	158	O
3	Adz blade, silicified slate	157, 178	M
4	Chisel-like adz blade or head, silicified slate	158	H7
5	Adz blade, silicified slate	158	M
6	Adz blade, silicified slate	157	H1
7	Adz blade, silicified slate	157	PA
8	Adz blade, silicified slate	157, 178	E
9	Adz blade, silicified slate	157	H4
10	Adz blade, silicified slate	158, 178	Z–4
11	Adz blade, basalt	158	H7

Norton: Iyatayet—Adz Blades

0 1 2 3 4 5 6 7 8 9 10 cm.

PLATE 45

	Identity	Reference page	Location
1	Shaft smoother, porous quartzite	158	E
2	Shaft smoother, sandstone	158	H
3	Grooved abrader, sandstone	160	PA
4	Shaft smoother, sandstone	159	H
5	Shaft smoother, sandstone	159	PE–3
6	Grooved abrader, sandstone	159	H1
7	Shaft smoother, sandstone	159	H7
8	Shaft smoother, sandstone	158	PC
9	Shaft smoother, sandstone	158	PC
10	Shaft smoother, sandstone	158	H7
11	Grooved abrader, sandstone	159	H
12	Shaft smoother, pumice	158	K–3/6
13	Shaft smoother, sandstone	158	A
14	Grooved abrader, sandstone	160	E
15	Abrader, sandstone	159	PE–3
16	Grooved abrader, sandstone	160	PB
17	Abrader, sandstone	160	H3
18	Grooved abrader, sandstone	159	E

Norton: Iyatayet—Smoothers, Abraders

0 1 2 3 4 5 6 7 8 9 10 cm.

PLATE 46

	Identity	Reference page	Location
1	Side blade, chert	160	PE–7
2	Side blade fragment, chert	160	M
3	Side blade, black chert	160	P
4	Side blade, black chert	141, 160	E
5	Side blade, chert	141, 160	E
6	Side blade, silicified slate	160, 161	PE–1
7	Side blade, jasper	160	E
8	Side blade, basalt	160	M
9	Side blade, jasper	160	A
10	Side blade, chert	142, 161	PE–5
11	Side blade, chalcedony	142, 161	M
12	Side blade, chert	142, 161	E
13	Side blade, black chert	142, 161	M
14	Side blade, chert	142, 161	M
15	Side blade, chalcedony	142, 161	E
16	Side blade, chert	142, 161	E
17	Side blade, chert	161	E
18	Side blade, silicified slate	161	B
19	Side blade, chert	161	E
20	Side blade, basalt	161	K–5/6
21	Side blade, chalcedony	161	M
22	Side blade, black chert	161	PA
23	Side blade, basalt	161	PA
24	Side blade, black chert	161	E
25	Side blade, silicified slate	161	A
26	Side blade, black chert	161	E
27	Side blade, chalcedony	161	H1
28	Side blade, black chert	161	H1
29	Side blade, silicified slate	161	H1
30	Side blade, chert	161	H1
31	Side blade, basalt	161	EM

Norton: Iyatayet—Side Blades

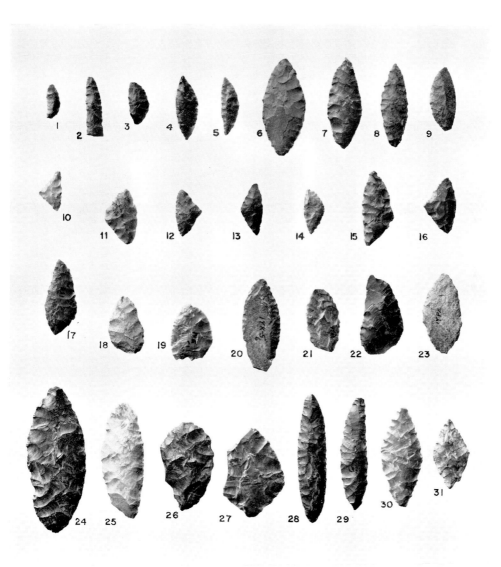

0 1 2 3 4 5 6 7 8 9 10 cm.

PLATE 47

	Identity	Reference page	Location
1	Projectile point, chert	162	E
2	Projectile point, basalt	162	B
3	Projectile point, chert	162	E
4	Projectile point, chert	162	PA
5	Projectile point, basalt	162	H
6	Projectile point, black chert	162	PA
7	Projectile point, black chert	162	E
8	Projectile point, black chert	162	EB
9	Projectile point, basalt	163	M
10	Projectile point, basalt	162	H1
11	Projectile point, jasper	162	PL
12	Projectile point, basalt	162	PE–5
13	Projectile point, basalt	162	E
14	Projectile point, basalt	163	PE
15	Projectile point, basalt	162	H7
16	Projectile point, silicified slate	163	O
17	Projectile point, silicified slate	163	K–5/6
18	Projectile point, chert	162	PB
19	Projectile point, chert	162	H7
20	Projectile point, basalt	163	E
21	Projectile point, basalt	163	PD
22	Projectile point, silicified slate	163	PE–1
23	Projectile point, chalcedony	162	AA
24	Projectile point, basalt	162	H
25	Projectile point, black chert	162–163	H3
26	Projectile point, chalcedony	162	H7
27	Projectile point, black chert	162	EM
28	Projectile point, jasper	162	E
29	Projectile point, basalt	162	E
30	Projectile point, silicified slate	162–163	PE–7
31	Projectile point, basalt	163	PD
32	Projectile point, black chert	162	PC
33	Projectile point, silicified slate	163	H7
34	Projectile point, chalcedony	162	P
35	Projectile point, basalt	163	E
36	Projectile point, chert	162–163	E

Norton: Iyatayet—Projectile Points

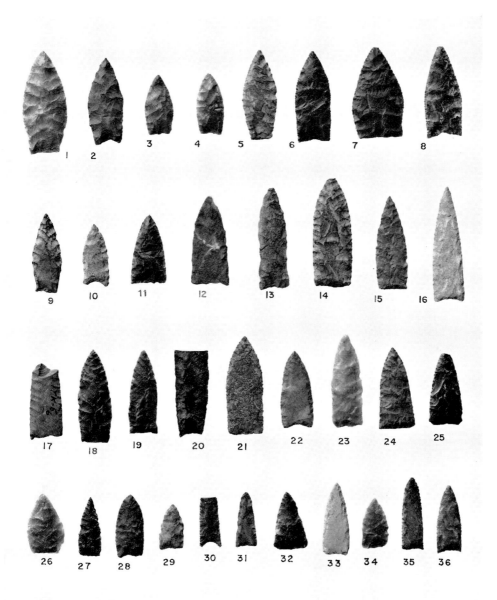

1   2   3   4   5   6   7   8

9   10   11   12   13   14   15   16

17   18   19   20   21   22   23   24   25

26   27   28   29   30   31   32   33   34   35   36

0   1   2   3   4   5   6   7   8   9   10 cm.

PLATE 48

	Identity	Reference page	Location
1	Projectile point, silicified slate	163	P
2	Projectile point, black chert	163	M
3	Projectile point, black chert	163	H
4	Projectile point, silicified slate	163	H1
5	Projectile point, basalt	163	PE–5
6	Projectile point, chert	163	PE–2
7	Projectile point, black chert	163	P
8	Projectile point, basalt	163	PD
9	Projectile point, silicified slate	163	E
10	Projectile point, chalcedony	163	M
11	Projectile point, basalt	163	E
12	Projectile point, black chert	163	M
13	Projectile point, chalcedony	163	E
14	Projectile point, black chert	163	P
15	Projectile point, basalt	163	PE–1
16	Projectile point, chert	163	PE–8
17	Projectile point, basalt	163	PD
18	Projectile point, chalcedony	163	E
19	Projectile point, jasper	163, 177	E
20	Projectile point, silicified slate	163	M
21	Projectile point, silicified slate	163, 177	–
22	Projectile point, black chert	163	E
23	Projectile point, black chert	163	E
24	Projectile point, chalcedony	163	M
25	Projectile point, black chert	163, 177	PE–2
26	Projectile point, black chert	163, 177	E
27	Projectile point, chalcedony	163	E

Norton: Iyatayet—Projectile Points

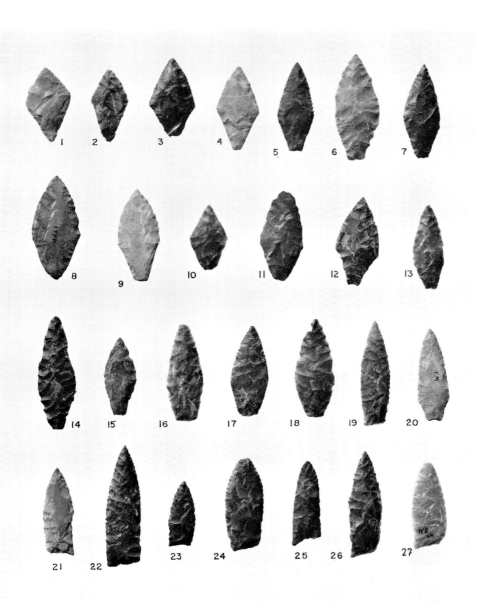

PLATE 49

	Identity	Reference page	Location
1	Projectile point, black chert	164	PE–5
2	Projectile point, chert	164	PE–5
3	Projectile point, basalt	164	H7
4	Projectile point, chert	164	A
5	Projectile point, silicified slate	163–164	E
6	Projectile point, basalt	164	E
7	Projectile point, basalt	164	K–5/6
8	Projectile point, basalt	164	PA
9	Projectile point, basalt	164	H7
10	Projectile point, basalt	164	Z–4
11	Projectile point, quartz crystal	164	E
12	Projectile point, basalt	164	E
13	Projectile point, black chert	163–164	E
14	Projectile point, basalt	164	PE–1
15	Projectile point, basalt	164	H
16	Projectile point, basalt	164	H1
17	Projectile point, basalt	164	E
18	Projectile point, basalt	164	Z–1
19	Projectile point, basalt	164	H7
20	Projectile point, basalt	164	M
21	Projectile point, black chert	164	E
22	Projectile point, black chert	164	–
23	Projectile point, basalt	164	H3
24	Projectile point, basalt	164	E
25	Projectile point, basalt	164	E
26	Projectile point, jasper	163–164	H7
27	Projectile point, basalt	164	H1
28	Projectile point, chalcedony	163	E
29	Projectile point, basalt	164	PD
30	Projectile point, silicified slate	163–164	PE–2
31	Projectile point, basalt	164	E
32	Projectile point, basalt	164	E

Norton: Iyatayet—Projectile Points

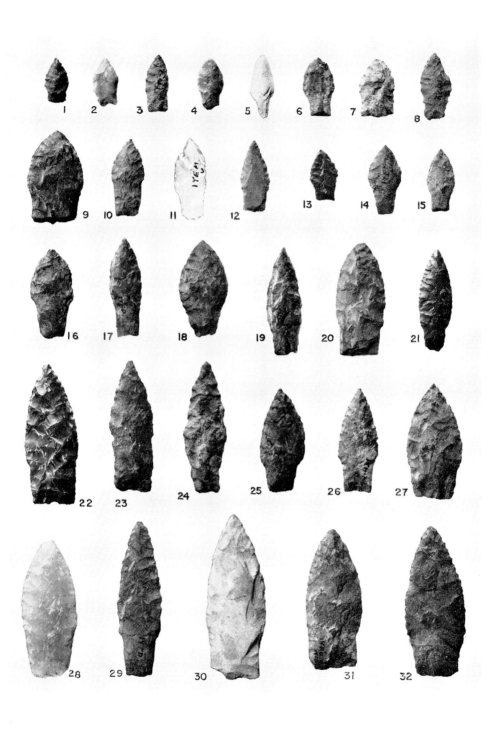

PLATE 50

	Identity	Reference page	Location
1	Projectile point, chalcedony	164	H1
2	Projectile point, black chert	164	PE–5
3	Projectile point, jasper	164	PE–6
4	Projectile point, basalt	164, 181	E
5	Projectile point, basalt	164	A
6	Projectile point, black chert	164	E
7	Projectile point, black chert	164	E
8	Projectile point, chalcedony	164	F
9	Projectile point, obsidian	164	H1
10	Projectile point, basalt	164	E
11	Projectile point, black chert	164	H7
12	Projectile point, black chert	164	E
13	Projectile point, chalcedony	164	H4
14	Projectile point, obsidian	164	–
15	Projectile point, basalt	164	H2
16	Projectile point, chert	164	PC
17	Projectile point, silicified slate	164	PE–6

Norton: Iyatayet—Projectile Points

PLATE 51

	Identity	Reference page	Location
1	Bifaced blade, silicified slate	165	H1
2	Lance (?) point, basalt	165	E
3	Blade blank (?), basalt	165	E
4	Lance (?) point, basalt	165	PC
5	Lance (?) point, basalt	165	E
6	Lance (?) point fragment, basalt	165	H1
7	Lance (?) point, basalt	165	Z–4
8	Lance (?) point, basalt	165	PE–1
9	Blade blank (?), basalt	165	E
10	Blade blank (?), basalt	165	E
11	Blade blank (?), basalt	165	K–5/5
12	Blade blank (?), basalt	165	PE
13	Blade blank (?), basalt	165	PE

Norton: Iyatayet—Lance Points, Blade Blanks

1   2   3

4   5   6   7   8

9   10   11   12   13

0 1 2 3 4 5 6 7 8 9 10 cm.

PLATE 52

	Identity	Reference page	Location
1	Bifaced blade, chert	165	PA
2	Bifaced blade, basalt	165	H7
3	Bifaced blade, basalt	165	P
4	Bifaced blade, obsidian	165	E
5	Bifaced blade, chalcedony	165	E
6	Bifaced blade, basalt	165	PC
7	Bifaced blade, basalt	165	P
8	Bifaced blade, jasper	165	PC
9	Bifaced blade, basalt	165	PC
10	Bifaced blade, basalt	165	B
11	Bifaced blade, basalt	165–166	PA
12	Bifaced blade, basalt	165–166	H3
13	Bifaced blade, basalt	165–166	E
14	Bifaced blade, basalt	165–166	PA
15	Bifaced blade, basalt	165–166	H
16	Bifaced blade, black chert	165–166, 182	E
17	Bifaced blade, basalt	165–166	PE–2
18	Bifaced blade, silicified slate	165–166	E
19	Bifaced blade, basalt	165–166	PE–1

Norton: Iyatayet—Bifaced Blades

0 1 2 3 4 5 6 7 8 9 10 cm.

PLATE 53

	Identity	Reference page	Location
1	Drill bit, basalt	173	E
2	Drill bit, basalt	173	E
3	Drill bit, basalt	173	E
4	Drill bit, basalt	173	PB
5	Drill bit, silicified slate	173	E
6	Drill bit, basalt	173	PD
7	Drill bit, basalt	174	PD
8	Drill bit, basalt	173	E
9	Drill bit, basalt	173	E
10	Drill bit, basalt	173	H
11	Drill bit, basalt	173	H1
12	Drill bit, chert	173	H4
13	Hand drill, black chert	173	E
14	Drill bit, black chert	173–174	PA
15	Drill bit, black chert	173	PE–5
16	Hand drill, black chert	173	PA
17	Drill bit, basalt	173	E
18	Hand drill, basalt	173	K–6/4
19	Drill bit, basalt	173	H7
20	Hand drill, black chert	173	H1
21	Hand drill, basalt	173	H1
22	Drill bit, basalt	173	H7
23	Hand drill, chert	173	E
24	Hand drill, basalt	173	E
25	Hand drill, basalt	173	H7
26	Drill bit, basalt	173–174	E
27	Drill bit, basalt	173–174	H7

Norton: Iyatayet—Drills and Drill Bits

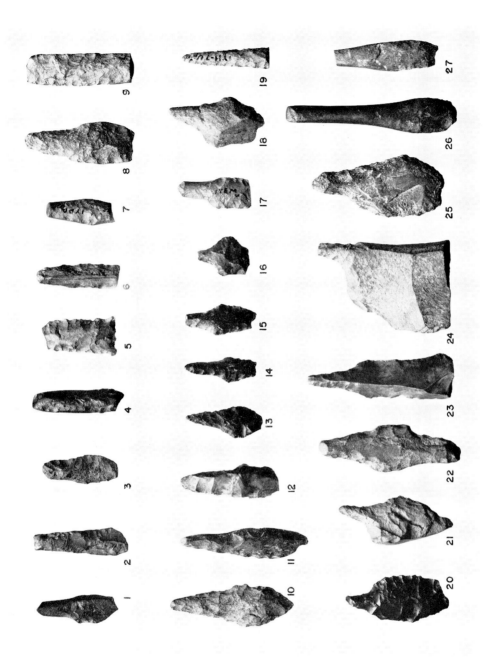

0 1 2 3 4 5 6 7 8 9 10 cm.

PLATE 54

	Identity	Reference page	Location
1	Flakeknife, black chert	167	PA
2	Flakeknife, chert	167	PE–2
3	Flakeknife, black chert	167	H7
4	Flakeknife, chert	167	H7
5	Flakeknife, black chert	167	E
6	Flakeknife, jasper	167	PA
7	Fiakeknife, obsidian	167	M
8	Flakeknife, black chert	167	PC
9	Flakeknife, black chert	167	E
10	Flakeknife, black chert	167	H3
11	Flakeknife, chert	167	H7
12	Flakeknife, chalcedony	166, 167	E
13	Flakeknife, chert	167	PE–7
14	Flakeknife, jasper	167	PA
15	Flakeknife, black chert	167	–
16	Flakeknife, black chert	167	E
17	Flakeknife, chert	167	H7
18	Flakeknife, jasper	167	E
19	Fiakeknife, black chert	167	PB
20	Flakeknife, chert	167	M
21	Flakeknife, jasper	167	H7
22	Flakeknife, chert	167	E

Norton: Iyatayet—Flakeknives

1 2 3 4 5 6 7

8 9 10 11 12 13 14 15

16 17 18 19 20 21 22

0 1 2 3 4 5 6 7 8 9 10 cm.

PLATE 55

	Identity	Reference page	Location
1	Plano-convex scraper, black chert	168	H3
2	Plano-convex scraper, black chert	168	H
3	Plano-convex scraper, jasper	168	PB
4	Plano-convex scraper, chert	168	E
5	Plano-convex scraper, obsidian	168	E
6	Plano-convex scraper, basalt	168	A
7	Plano-convex scraper, basalt	168	H1
8	Plano-convex scraper, basalt	168	H1
9	Plano-convex scraper, basalt	168	PB
10	Plano-convex scraper, silicified slate	168	A
11	Plano-convex scraper, basalt	168	PE–2
12	Plano-convex scraper, basalt	168	A3
13	Scraper, basalt	168	PC
14	Chopper, metamorphic pebble	168	H1
15	Plano-convex scraper, basalt	168	T3
16	Chopper (?), metamorphic pebble	168	E
14	Chopper, metamorphic pebble	168	PD
18	Chopper, basalt pebble	168	H4
19	Plano-convex scraper, chert	168	PE–5
20	Chopper, silicified slate	168	H2

Norton: Iyatayet—Scrapers, Choppers

PLATE 56

	Identity	Reference page	Location
1	Discoidal scraper, jasper	168	E
2	Discoidal scraper, brown chert	168	E
3	Discoidal scraper, chert	168	E
4	Discoidal scraper, chert	168	E
5	Discoidal scraper, chalcedony	168	E
6	Discoidal scraper, chert	168	E
7	Discoidal scraper, black chert	168	E
8	Discoidal scraper, black chert	168	–
9	Discoidal scraper, black chert	168	E
10	Discoidal scraper, chert	168	H7
11	Discoidal scraper, black chert	168	E
12	Discoidal scraper, chert	168	E

Norton: Iyatayet—Discoidal Scrapers

PLATE 57

	Identity	Reference page	Location
1	Bifaced end scraper, quartz	169	E
2	Bifaced end scraper, quartz	169	A
3	Bifaced end scraper, quartz	169	H
4	Bifaced end scraper, basalt	169	H7
5	Bifaced end scraper, basalt	169	PD
6	Bifaced end scraper, basalt	169	H1
7	Bifaced end scraper, basalt	169	PE–3
8	Bifaced end scraper, basalt	169	H7
9	Bifaced end scraper, basalt	169	E
10	Bifaced end scraper, basalt	169	P
11	Bifaced end scraper, basalt	169	PE–5
12	Bifaced end scraper, basalt	169	E
13	Bifaced end scraper, basalt	169	PC
14	Bifaced end scraper, basalt	169	H
15	Bifaced end scraper, basalt	169	PE–8
16	Bifaced end scraper, basalt	169	E
17	Bifaced end scraper, basalt	169	H
18	Bifaced end scraper, basalt	169	H7

Norton: Iyatayet—End Scrapers

0 1 2 3 4 5 6 7 8 9 10 cm.

PLATE 58

	Identity	Reference page	Location
1	Lamp, igneous rock	170	PE–8
2	Lamp, schistose sandstone	170	PE–8
3	Lamp fragment, sandstone	170	H7
4	Lamp, igneous rock	170–172	H
5	Lamp fragment, igneous rock	170	E and M
6	Lamp, igneous rock	170	M

Norton: Iyatayet—Lamps

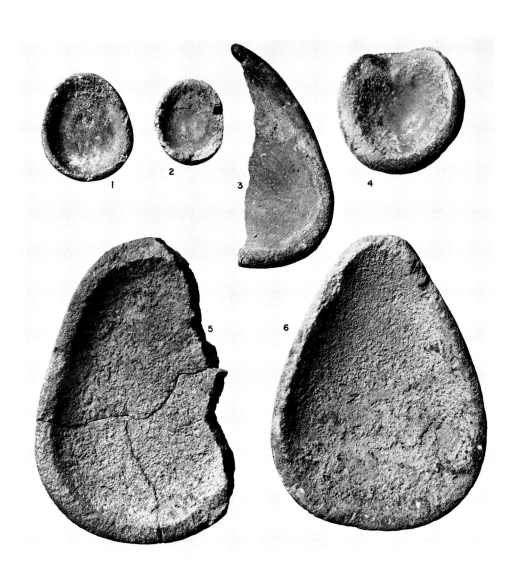

PLATE 59

	Identity	Reference page	Location
1	Lamp fragment, shaly schist	170	H7
2	Lamp, sandstone	170	E
3	Lamp, igneous rock	171	H1
4	Lamp, pottery	170, 176	K–2/4
5	Lamp, vesicular basalt	170	E
6	Lamp, sandstone	170	E

Norton: Iyatayet—Lamps

0 1 2 3 4 5 6 7 8 9 10 cm.

PLATE 60

	Identity	Reference page	Location
1	Lamp fragment, limestone	171	K–4/5
2	Lamp or dish fragment, igneous rock	171	E
3	Vessel fragment, metamorphic rock	171, 172	M
4	Vessel fragment, metamorphic rock	171	PA
5	Vessel fragment, shale	171	H1
6	Vessel fragment, metamorphic rock	171	B
7	Lamp, metamorphic pebble	171, 172	PB
8	Vessel fragment, metamorphic pebble	171, 172	M
9	Lamp (?), sandstone pebble	171	E
10	Lamp or mortar, igneous pebble	171	Z–3
11	Lamp or mortar, igneous pebble	171	H4
12	Lamp or mortar, igneous pebble	171, 172	H2
13	Lamp or mortar, igneous pebble	171, 172	PF
14	Lamp or mortar, igneous pebble	171	PE–2
15	Lamp or mortar, igneous pebble	171	Z–1
16	Lamp or mortar, igneous pebble	171	PE

Norton: Iyatayet—Lamps, Vessels

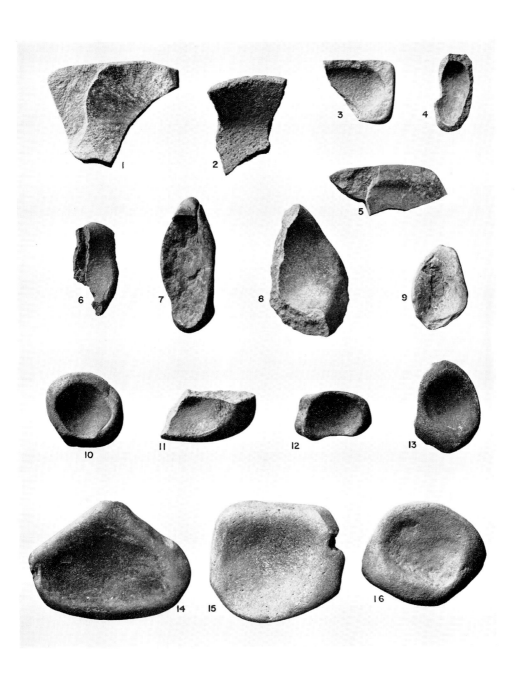

PLATE 61

	Identity	Reference page
1	Saw fragment, sandstone	174
2	Saw fragment, sandstone	174
3	Net sinker, stone	174
4	Net sinker, stone	174
5	Net sinker, stone	174
6	Net sinker, stone	174
7	Net sinker, stone	174

Norton: Iyatayet—Stone Saws and Net Sinkers

1

2

3

4

5

6

7

PLATE 62

	Identity	Reference page	Location
1	Flakeknife, jasper	181	Gungnuk house
2	Whetstone fragment, shale	182	Gungnuk house
3	Flakeknife, chert	181	Gungnuk house
4	Flakeknife, basalt	181	Gungnuk house
5	Side scraper, jasper	181	Gungnuk house
6	Side scraper, black chert	181	Gungnuk house
7	Side blade, silicified slate	181	Gungnuk house
8	Bifaced blade fragment, black chert	181	Gungnuk house
9	Side blade, jasper	181	Gungnuk house
10	Hammer head (?), igneous pebble	183	Gungnuk house
11	Side scraper, chert	182	Gungnuk house
12	Burin-like groover, silicified slate	182	Gungnuk house
13	Whetstone fragment, shale	182	Gungnuk house
14	Whetstone, shale	182	Gungnuk house
15	Bifaced blade fragment, black chert	181	Gungnuk house
16	Shaft smoother, sandstone, fragment	182	Gungnuk house
17	Adz blade fragment, silicified slate	182	Gungnuk house
18	Side scraper, black chert	182	Gungnuk house
19	Chopper (?), slate	183	Gungnuk house
20	Lamp or mortar, metamorphic rock	183	Gungnuk house
21	Net sinker, metamorphic pebble	183	Gungnuk house
22	Net sinker, metamorphic pebble	183	Gungnuk house

Norton: Gungnuk—Miscellaneous

0 1 2 3 4 5 6 7 8 9 10 cm.

PLATE 63

	Identity	Reference page	Location
1	Lamp, sandy schist	183	Gungnuk house
2	Shovel (?), metamorphic rock	183	Gungnuk house
3	Hammer, metamorphic rock	183	Gungnuk house

Norton: Gungnuk—Lamp, Shovel, Hammer

PLATE 64

	Identity	Reference page	Location
1	Bifaced blade fragment	177	Madjujuinuk
2	End blade, chalcedony	177	Madjujuinuk
3	Side blade, basalt	177	Madjujuinuk
4	Side blade, obsidian	177	Madjujuinuk
5	Bifaced blade fragment, basalt	177	Madjujuinuk
6	Side blade fragment, basalt	177	Madjujuinuk
7	Bifaced blade (?), basalt	177	Madjujuinuk
8	Side or end blade, basalt	177	Madjujuinuk
9	Bifaced blade, basalt	177	Madjujuinuk
10	Bifaced blade, basalt	177	Madjujuinuk
11	Drill, basalt	177	Madjujuinuk
12	Scraper, black chert	177	Madjujuinuk
13	Scraper fragment, basalt	177	Madjujuinuk
14	Whetstone fragment, shale	178	Madjujuinuk
15	Side blade fragment, chalcedony	177	Madjujuinuk
16	Side blade, basalt	177	Madjujuinuk
17	Side blade, basalt	177	Madjujuinuk
18	Scraper, silicified slate	177	Madjujuinuk
19	Adz blade blank (?), silicified slate	177	Madjujuinuk
20	Check stamped potsherd	178	Madjujuinuk
21	Grooved stone, sandstone	178	Madjujuinuk
22	Net sinker, basalt pebble	178	Madjujuinuk
23	Whetstone or grindstone, sandstone	178	Madjujuinuk
24	Maul fragment, vesicular basalt	178	Madjujuinuk

Norton: Madjujuinuk—Blades, Scrapers, etc.

0 1 2 3 4 5 6 7 8 9 10 cm.

PLATE 65

	Identity	Reference page
1	"Core scraper," chert	227–228
2	Microblade core, obsidian	203
3	Burin on a microblade, chert	203, 206, 218
4	Microblade, obsidian	203
5	Retouched microblade, obsidian	203, 206
6	Retouched microblade, obsidian	203, 206
7	Retouched microblade, chert	203, 206
8	Retouched microblade, obsidian	203, 206
9	Retouched microblade, chert	203, 206
10	Retouched microblade, obsidian	203
11	Microblade, chalcedony	203
12	Microblade, obsidian	203, 206
13	Microblade, obsidian	203
14	Microblade, obsidian	203
15	Microblade, chert	203
16	Microblade, obsidian	203
17	Microblade, chert	203
18	Microblade, chert	203
19	Microblade, chert	203
20	Microblade, chert	203

Denbigh Flint complex, *in situ*—Microcores and Microblades

0 1 2 3 4 5 6 7 8 9 10 cm.

PLATE 66-a

	Identity	Reference page
1	Single-faceted angle burin, chert	210, 214, 217
2	Double-faceted burin, chert	210, 214, 219
3	Burin spall, chert	210, 214, 220
4	Burin spall, chert	210, 214, 220
5	Single-faceted angle burin, black chert	210, 214, 217
6	Single-faceted angle burin, chert	210, 214, 217
7	Single-faceted transverse burin, jasper (same as Pl. *72, 11*)	210, 214, 217
8	Double-faceted shaved burin, chert (obverse of Pl. *66-b, 3*)	210, 214, 219
9	Beaked burin, chert (obverse of Pl. *66-b, 2*; same as Pl. *72, 10*)	210, 214, 217

Denbigh Flint complex, *in situ*—Burins and Burin Spalls

PLATE 66-b

	Identity	Reference page
1	Single-faceted burin, chert	210, 214, 217
2	Beaked burin, chert (reverse of Pl. *66-a,* 9)	210, 214, 217
3	Double-faceted burin, chert (reverse of Pl. *66-a,* 8)	210, 214, 219
4	Double-faceted burin, chert	210, 214, 219
5	Single-faceted angle burin, chert	210, 214, 217
6	Single-faceted transverse burin fragment, chert	210, 214, 217
7	Single-faceted angle burin, chert	210, 214, 217
8	Single-faceted angle burin, chert	210, 214, 217
9	Double-faceted burin, chert	210, 214, 219
10	Double-ended burin	210, 214, 219

Denbigh Flint complex, *in situ*—Burins

PLATE 67

Reference pages 220–222 and Plate *68*.

Denbigh Flint complex, *in situ*—Burin Spall Artifacts
of Chert and Chalcedony. Double actual size.

PLATE 68

Reference Pl. *67* and pages 220–222.

Top: 1 Burin spall artifact shown in Pl. *67, 3,* tilted at 45° angle to show retouch. Double actual size.

2 Burin spall artifact shown in Pl. *67,* 11, tilted at 45° angle to show retouch. Double actual size.

3 Burin spall artifact shown in Pl. *67,* 1, tilted at 45° angle to show retouch. Double actual size.

4 Burin spall artifact shown in Pl. *67,* 8, tilted at 45° angle to show retouch. Double actual size.

Bottom: The tip of Pl. *68,* 4, above, enlarged 20 times to show cutting edge.

Denbigh Flint complex, *in situ*—Burin Spall Artifacts

PLATE 69

	Identity	Reference page
1	Flakeknife	226
2	Flakeknife	226
3	Flakeknife	226
4	Flakeknife	226
5	Flakeknife	226
6	Flakeknife	223
7	Flakeknife	226
8	Flakeknife	226
9	Flakeknife	226
10	Flakeknife	226
11	Flakeknife	226
12	Flakeknife	226
13	Flakeknife	226
14	Flakeknife	226
15	Flakeknife	226
16	Flakeknife	226
17	Flakeknife	226
18	Flakeknife	226
19	Flakeknife	226
20	Flakeknife	226
21	Flakeknife	226
22	Flakeknife	226
23	Flakeknife	226
24	Flakeknife	226
25	Flakeknife	226

Denbigh Flint complex, *in situ*—Flakeknives of Chert and Obsidian

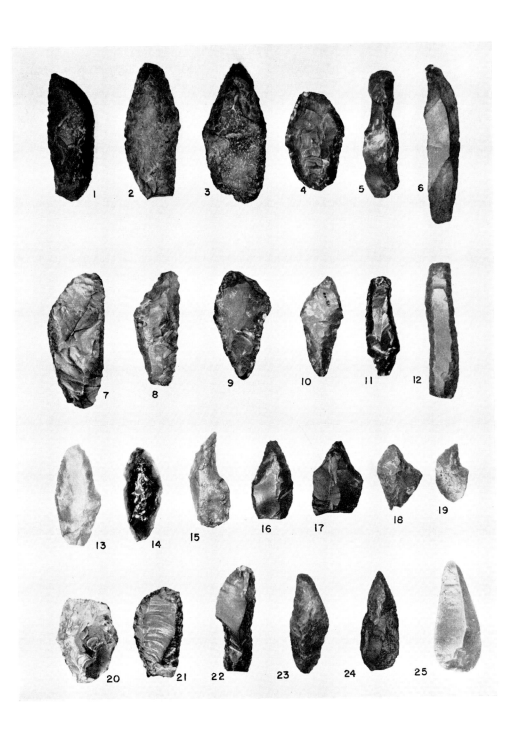

PLATE 70-a

	Identity	Reference page
1	Graver, chert	227
2	Flakeknife, chert	226
3	Flakeknife, chert	229
4	Polished creaser, basalt	238
5	Keeled scraper, chert	226
6	Flakeknife, chert	226
7	Flakeknife, chert	226
8	Flakeknife, chert	226
9	Keeled scraper, chert (same as Pl. *72*, 16)	226

Denbigh Flint complex, *in situ*—Graver, Creaser, Flakeknives,
and Keeled Scrapers

0   1   2   3   4   5   6   7   8   9   10 cm.

PLATE 70-b

	Identity	Reference page
1	End scraper, jasper	228
2	End scraper, chert	228
3	End scraper, chert	228
4	End scraper, chert	228
5	Channeled knife or scraper, chert	226
6	End scraper, chert	228
7	End scraper, jasper	228
8	End scraper, chert	228
9	End scraper, chert	228
10	End scraper, chert (same as Pl. *72*, 12)	228
11	End scraper, chert	228
12	Bifaced, 3-edged knife or scraper, jasper	235
13	Unifaced knife, or scraper, obsidian	229
14	Unifaced knife, black chert	229
15	Lunate knife blade, obsidian	229
16	Channeled knife blade, black chert	226

Denbigh Flint complex, *in situ*—End Scrapers, Side Scrapers, and Knife Blades

0 1 2 3 4 5 6 7 8 9 10 cm.

PLATE 71-a

Reference pages 233, 240.

Denbigh Flint complex, *in situ*—Harpoon Blades of Chert

1   2   3

4   5   6   7

0   1   2   3   4   5   6   7   8   9   10 cm.

PLATE 71-b

	Identity	Reference page
1	End blade fragment, chert	232
2	End blade, chert	232
3	End blade fragment, chert	232
4	Unfinished (?) end blade, silicified slate	232
5	End blade, black chert	232
6	End blade, chert	232
7	End blade fragment, black chert	232
8	End blade fragment, black chert	232
9	Side blade, chert	230
10	Side blade, chert	230
11	Side blade, chert	230
12	Drill, or lancet, chert	237
13	Side blade, chert	230
14	Side blade fragment, chert	230
15	Side blade fragment, chert	230
16	Side blade fragment, chert	230
17	Drill, or lancet, fragment, black chert	237

Denbigh Flint complex, *in situ*—Bifaced End and Side Blades

PLATE 72

	Identity	Reference page
1	Microblade core, obsidian	203
2	Microblade, chert	203
3	End blade, obsidian	232
4	Side blade, chert	230
5	Side blade, chert	230
6	Unifaced knife blade, chert	229
7	Spear point fragment, chert	235
8	Arrow point, chert	233
9	Harpoon blade, chert	233
10	Burin (same as Pl. *66-a,* 9)	217
11	Burin (same as Pl. *66-a,* 7)	217
12	End Scraper (same as Pl. *70-b,* 10)	228
13	Fluted point, chalcedony	233
14	Cruciform object, chert	239
15	"Saw," chert	229
16	Keeled scraper, chert (same as Pl. *70-a,* 9)	226

Denbigh Flint complex, *in situ*—Miscellaneous Specimens

PLATE 73

	Identity	Reference page
1	Polished burin, basalt	237
2	Polished burin, basalt	237
3	Polished burin, basalt	237
4	Polished burin, basalt	237
5	Polished burin, basalt	237
6	Polished burin, basalt	237
7	Polished burin, basalt	237
8	Polished burin, basalt	237
9	Polished creaser, basalt	238
10	Polished creaser, basalt	238
11	Shaft smoother, sandstone	238
12	Sewn birch bark fragment	239
13	Polished burin, basalt	237
14	Polished creaser, basalt	238
15	Polished burin, basalt	237
16	Polished burin, basalt	237
17	Polished object, basalt	238
18	Polished creaser, basalt	238
19	Polished object, basalt	238
20	Polished burin, basalt	237

Denbigh Flint complex, *in situ*—Miscellaneous Specimens

0   1   2   3   4   5   6   7   8   9   10 cm.